Untoured Sydney

by Jacqueline Huié

*An insider's guide
to the best places to stay,
things to see, do, eat and buy*

UNTOURIST SYDNEY

Published by
UnTourist Co Pty Ltd
(A.C.N. 064 272 966)
PO Box 209
Balmain NSW 2041 Australia

Editorial director
Suzanne Baker

Editorial consultant
Karen Hammial

Editorial assistance
Constance Ganong

Interior layout and typesetting:
Martin Taylor Design.

Cover & additional photography:
Benjamin Huie

Printed by
David J. File Printers

Although the author and publisher have tried to make the information as accurate as possible, they accept no responsibility for any loss, injury or inconvenience sustained by any person using this book.

First published
December 1995
Revised reprint September 1996

© Copyright The UnTourist
Company Pty Ltd, 1995
ISBN 0 646 24529 5

MV Reliance *sets out from Circular Quay to Lane Cove River and the Lane Cove National Park.*

JACQUELINE HUIÉ

After a prominent career in the communications industry where she won many international and national awards, in 1982 Jacqueline formed Product Development International. In 1983 she decided to focus her new product development skills on tourism and leisure, establishing the Joseph Banks Group which enabled her to research, analyse and forecast the impact of tourism in Australia. In this role she has been an adviser to governments and the private sector, and her work has long been used as benchmark indicators for the industry and the basis for her university lectures. The Banks' research data is now being kept up-to-date in association with the University of Queensland.

Jacqueline has often been an outspoken critic of big development trends of Australian tourism. Well before eco, green and cultural tourism became fashionable labels, she predicted the rise of independent travellers and their need for an appropriate information system – hence the formation of the UnTourist Co.

Jacqueline has three sons and four grand-daughters. While writing this book, she discovered that she is a direct descendant of Owen Cavenough, a First Fleeter reputed to be the first white man ashore on Sydney Cove.

WITH THANKS TO THE SAVVY LOCALS

UnTourist guidebooks are only made possible with the contribution of valuable insider knowledge from the savvy locals. For UnTourist Sydney we heartily thank the following: Bryce Courtney, Leo Schofield, Gwen Chater, Stephanie King, Margaret Pearce, Harold Wells, Barbara Cail, Linda Browne, Megan Hall, Karen Hammial, Jessica Anderson, Patricia Lovell, Burnum Burnum, Angela Finnigan, Ruth Fischer, Pauline Sheldrake, Sarah and Jean-Luc Clavel, Susan Talbot, Annette Taylor, Ken Done, Don and Vicki Fish, Philip Salmon, Graeme Murphy, Janet Vernon, Hamish Campbell, Jytte Beauman, Andrew Kidman, Sioned Faye, Anne Deveson, Joyce Belfrage, Ian Kiernan, Valerie Tring, Katherine Knight, Carolynne Skinner, Jennifer McGregor, Russell Morgan, Isabelle Fogarty, Department of Ethnic Affairs, and also the helpful people at the Mitchell Library and to Charles Little, Colin Whitfield and savvy visitor, Jane von Sponeck-Krumnow.

COVER KEY

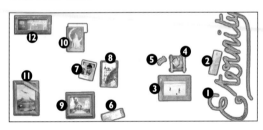

1 The omnipresent "Eternity" by Arthur Stace, Chapter 2

2 Ticket to the Sydney Theatre Company, Chapter 11

3 Bondi in Winter, by Benjamin Huie, Chapter 3

4 Cuisine as an art form, Chapter 9

5 Art deco brooch as a memento, Chapter 8

6 The Australian Opera, Chapter 11

7 Ritz-Carlton, Chapter 7

8 Russell Hotel Chapter 7

9 Opening of the Sydney Harbour Bridge, Chapter 6

10 Belvoir Theatre, Chapter 11

11 Bridge under construction, Chapter 6

12 Chinatown, Chapter 2

Untourist Sydney

by Jacqueline Huié

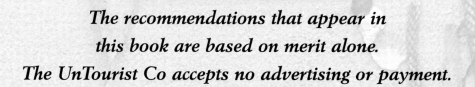

*The recommendations that appear in
this book are based on merit alone.
The UnTourist Co accepts no advertising or payment.*

An introduction to UnTourism

"SO WHAT IS AN UNTOURIST, AND AM I ONE?"

UnTourists are tourists who don't want to be tourists.

They are the kind of people who would drive past four, perfectly reasonable, convenient motels complete with pool, air con, en suite and TV in search of some quaint off-road "mum and dad" guesthouse with dubious plumbing – just because if offers home-baked bread.

The UnTourist would trek through the wilderness carrying biscuits, cheese and wine-soaked maps rather than relax in the comfort of an air-conditioned tour bus.

It would be easy to come to the conclusion that UnTourists would relish exerting enormous effort to ensure that they are uncomfortable, or that they disapprove of tourism generally. But this is untrue. They are extremely partial to, and spend freely on, travel comforts, both gastronomic and spiritual.

Generally speaking, UnTourists consider tourism to be a pollution industry; however, they will grant grudgingly that it is not without some redeeming qualities. Given the choice, better a wilderness lodge than a logging camp, a grand hotel than an open-cut mine, a luxury resort than a chemical plant – any day.

In an effort to understand them, tourism industry analysts have given the UnTourist many labels – eco-tourists, green tourists, cultural tourists, alternative tourists and educational tourists. All are correct, and each UnTourist would identify, to a greater or lesser degree, with all those labels. The thing that fuses these fellow-travellers together into a resolute band, however, is their shared dislike of touristy places. Some may prefer opera to bird-watching, or camping to silk pillows, but they will all seek out the "authentic" environments, both man-made and natural, avoiding those either spoiled by, or developed for, the tourist trade.

INFORMATION AND THE UNTOURIST

For a regular tourist, it is relatively easy to find out about suitable places to eat and sleep, and sights to see. Glossy brochures can be picked up at any travel agent; TV advertisements extol the virtues of destinations. Their illustrations imply that tourists with money want to spend their time in 5-star places while "poor" tourists camp out because they can't afford anything else.

Our research also tells us that most people, particularly UnTourists, prefer simplicity and personal style rather than overt luxury, regardless of cost; that they camp out because they want to; that the same person books into a grand hotel or restaurant for the same reason.

So if, after reading this piece, you have decided that you are indeed of an UnTourist persuasion, then you will be pleased to know that in researching this book we sought out all the most discerning UnTourist people we knew – the insiders, the writers, the foodies, fishermen, sailors and farmers, culture buffs and historians, and the savvy locals – they helped us determine the best of everything Sydney could offer in things to do, see, eat and buy, and in places to stay.

We hope you profit from the results.

After enjoying a rewarding career as a film and television producer, and receiving an Academy Award in 1977 for the film *Leisure*, it would seem a natural follow-on to "produce" a series of guide books on another aspect of the subject. As co-founder of the UnTourist Co, Suzanne wrote the first guide book in the series, *Tasmania for the UnTourist*. Coming from a family of journalists, Suzanne started her professional career as one too, moving from the *Sydney Morning Herald* (where she was considered, at the time, a somewhat controversial women's editor), into the world of television and film where she produced many films, including the internationally released television series *The Human Face of China*, the book of which was also written by her.

Suzanne Baker, Editorial Director

"So what is an UnTourist, and am I one?"

Al & Joan Maloney, third generation Dairy Farmers since 1862, wearing
Blundstone Boots $49.95, Gowings Flanelette Shirt (Joan) $16.95
& Akubra Pastoralist Hat (Al) $79.95. All available at Gowings, Chapter 8.
NOTE: Prices may vary

Contents

"What is an UnTourist and am
I one?" It would be easy to
come to the conclusion that
UnTourists would relish
exerting enormous effort to
ensure that they are
uncomfortable, or that they
disapprove of tourism
generally. But this is untrue.
They are extremely partial to,
and spend freely on, travel comforts,
both gastronomic and spiritual.

How to use this guide to find places
which are not the regular tourist
haunts. *UnTourist Sydney* is a
selective guide – what not to expect,
the criteria for selection, the duck
award system explained.

Burnum Burnum describes how the first
Australians felt about Sydney; how the Green
Bans and Jack Mundey helped preserve some
of Sydney's best historic sites and introducing
the Joseph Banks Institute and its plans for
the future.

The Lifestyle Capital of the World
Sydneysiders have an almost compulsive
concern with elevating leisure time to artform
status.

We choose the six best things about Sydney:
The New Food; The Ferries; The Beaches;
The Wild Things; The Opera House
Experience; The Lifestyle

Sydney's Showplace

The best ways to use and enjoy the
harbour – on it , in it and beside it.
The harbour as a highway,
with all its special
destinations – the ferry
wharf parks, harbourside
restaurants, the islands,
the secret places. Up the
Lane Cove River on a vintage
boat; to Parramatta on "The Cat";
and to Manly on the grand old ferries. The
good things and the bad things about "the
finest harbour in the world".

As is the case with all large city centres,
environments and experiences can change
immensely within a few blocks. Because of
this we have divided Central Sydney into four
neighbourhoods, each of them offering
something different.

The environs surrounding the Opera House,
Circular Quay and The Rocks form the
showcase of Sydney.

Posh old Macquarie Street, starting at the
Conservatorium of Music; in and around
The Domain and the Royal Botanic Gardens;
Museum of Sydney; Martin Place, shopping.

The Australian Museum; "Mr Eternity"; the
Queen Victoria Building; and the cinemas.

The Chinese Gardens; Chinatown; Darling
Harbour; The Aquarium; Maritime Museum;
Powerhouse Museum.

The High and the
Low Life of Sydney
Kings Cross;
Darlinghurst; The Gay
and Lesbian Mardi Gras;
Centennial Park; The
Paddington Markets; Bondi
Beach; Antiques in
Woollahra; Double Bay;
Watson's Bay; and some of
the best places to stay and eat.

West of the Bridge, South of the River
The avant-garde Inner West to the Outer
West where an innovative grassroots culture is
brewing – the West is the melting pot where
most of Sydney lives, where there is a
smorgasbord of things to see, eat and do:
Italian Leichhardt, Lebanese Dulwich Hill,
Greek Marrickville, Portuguese Petersham,
Asian Cabramatta, the Aussie "island" of
Balmain and, the place where it all started,
the old English capital city of Parramatta.

The Secret South
Captain Cook's historic stop in Botany Bay.
Two of the many great ways to see the Royal
National Park – up the Hacking River on the
little *MV Tom Thumb III* or a short excursion
by Parklink tram. Surprising Cronulla,
larger-than-life Sylvania
Waters and the secret

upper reaches of the Georges River. Oyster farmers' tips on where to get the best – and zany King Street, Newtown.

A Guide to this Guide
•The easiest way to find what you are looking for
•How to get additional information when a guidebook isn't enough
•Criteria for inclusion: how we make our selections

UnTourist Sydney is a selective guide-book. To be more explicit, we've selected and recommended certain things, items, places or experiences, and left the rest of the information to be covered in more general, across-the-board travel guides.

This means that if you happen to share our philosophy about what makes a great place to stay, or what constitutes a terrific meal, then you will get a great deal of useful information out of this guidebook.

On the other hand, if you are of a different persuasion, you could end up crossly writing a letter to the editor, complaining that our recom-mended hotel didn't have air-conditioning, or that you were forced to bring your own wine to the little brasserie we so highly rated, or that we left out a lot of perfectly good motels or tours – and we are probably guilty as charged, because we cater for particular travellers who have particular likes and dislikes when they travel.

While we don't presume to cover everything, we go to great lengths to uncover all the best UnTourist things to do, things and places that haven't sold out to the mass-tourist industry, but remain a real and a genuine part of the experience of visiting Sydney.

GENERAL INFORMATION

- Chapters 13 and 14 give general information on things for overseas visitors (eg visa information) and bread-and-butter local information like public transport, currency, postage, public communications, what to do in an emergency etc – all the things you didn't know you needed to know until the moment arrives.

- For easy sourcing of our recommendations throughout the guide, use our handy **Directory** of telephone numbers and addresses at the start of the yellow pages at the back. In the chapters where we think it will be convenient to have the telephone number as you are reading, addresses and telephone numbers are given at the time.

THE DISABLED

Facilities for the disabled are extensive in Sydney – eg most key footpaths are curbed for easy wheelchair access and the vast majority of accommodation places have appropriate facilities. You will find information on disabled services in Chapter 14.

DOLLAR SYMBOLS – WHAT THEY MEAN

When it comes to cost we believe all our recommendations to be good value for money - regardless of their prices. We have divided all entries into several categories.

ACCOMMODATION
(Per standard double, per night)

$	(Cheap and good)	$15 - $40
$$	(Budget)	$40-$75
$$$	(Moderate)	$75-$150
$$$$	(Premium)	$150-$250
$$$$$	(Top)	$250+

EAT AND DRINK
(Per person – drinks extra)

$	(Inexpensive)	Under $15
$$	(Moderate)	$15–$35
$$$	(High)	$35–$50
$$$$	(Expensive)	$50+

THINGS TO BUY

Here we will give you a general guideline on the shop or the item using the same symbols:

$	Budget
$$	Moderate
$$$	Expensive
$$$$	Be warned

ADDITIONAL UNTOURIST SERVICES

It takes slightly more than a year to research, write and publish a good guidebook. This means that information becomes out-of-date, new places emerge, and conditions need to be amended and added to regularly. To handle this, we have set up an **Events Update** service and an **Insider's Consultancy.** The Events Update provides additional information which has come in since the book was published, plus a detailed program of cultural and special events taking places while you are visiting Sydney. Information on how to access these services is in the yellow pages at the back.

The Insider's Consultancy puts you in touch with one of our staff who will give you all that extra detail you'd get from a knowledgable friend – if you had access to one. If someone has nicked the pages from the back of this book, call or fax us at the UnTourist Co and we'll answer your query direct. We'd like to hear from you anyway – even if it is just to tell us we got it right or wrong.

PS: At the UnTourist Co we are not enthusiastic about list-brokers, so, in the interest of your privacy, we guarantee not to pass on your name and address to anyone.

ALL ABOUT DUCKS

Our symbol of  excellence derives from that previously common trilogy of glossy coloured pottery ducks that invariably adorned the wall-papered lounge-room of every suburban bungalow in Sydney in the '50s. Long may they fly – as a reminder that architecture, design, the arts, food and wine have, indeed, taken a giant flight forward.

 A duck beside an entry signifies a special recommendation

 Two ducks mean a very special recommendation

Three ducks denotes the ultimate – close to heaven

CRITERIA FOR SELECTION

The final recommendations in this book on UnTourism are based on the following criteria:

- 1 They added to the value of the man-made or natural environment of their region
- 2 They are not predominantly patronised by mass-market tourists or, if they are, it is because they are in a class by themselves and even the presence of the hoards doesn't effect

them. Some examples are the Sydney Opera House, Buckingham Palace, or MOMA in New York

- 3 They appeared on the "favourite" lists given to us by our appointed experts
- 4 They are patronised by discerning locals
- 5 They meet the UnTourist Co's standards of excellence
- 6 A decade of market research conducted by the Joseph Banks Group (our founding company) into the likes and dislikes of the independent traveller, judged them to be what our particular market is seeking

METHOD OF SELECTION

- First, we conducted research into the experience preferences of discerning Sydney locals and experts in the respective fields
- In selecting the best accommodation, more than 1000 letters were sent to establishments listed in the greater Sydney area that looked as if they might meet our criteria. We invited their managers to submit particulars to the UnTourist Co for possible inclusion in this guide. These lists and establishments were checked by our researchers and cross-checked with our previous research
- Final recommendations in all categories were made only after a researcher had personally and anonymously checked them out

YOU CAN'T BUY YOUR WAY INTO AN UNTOURIST GUIDE BOOK

We take no advertising or payment of any kind. Recommendations which make it into UnTourist guide books are earned by merit only. It's nice to know that there are some things money can't buy.

Acknowledgements

THIS MAGNIFICENTLY BEAUTIFUL PLACE CALLED SYDNEY

My ancestors relished the plentiful supply of land and water foods in the harbour setting. Our Picassos and their apprentices etched upon the sandstone tens of thousands of rock art about events which took place so long ago. The backdrop setting of the Blue Mountains, embracing the majestic Jenolan Caves contrasted with rivers, bays and estuaries with strong ocean tides breaking unrelentingly upon golden sandy beaches.

This is my part of the earth and it is part of me - I love it with a deep, deep respect and when I travel east from west over the mountains I can smell the saltwater air beckoning like a man to his beloved.

Thank you, oh thou Great Spirit, for allowing me the honour to repose in this magnificently beautiful place called Sydney.

Burnum Burnum

THE GREEN BANS WHICH HELPED SAVE HISTORIC SYDNEY

"It is amazing to now have such respectability," says Jack who, at the height of the fight for The Rocks in the 1970s, was carried away from the scene by policemen.

In June, 1971, a group of middle-class women from Hunters Hill, one of Sydney's smartest suburbs, asked the communist-led Builders Labourers Federation of NSW to help them save Kelly's Bush, one of the last pieces of bushland on the Parramatta River.

"A left-wing union and some middle-class people with a social conscience found they were natural allies," said the union's leader and secretary, Jack Mundey.

"At the time there was no state legislation in place to give the National Trust any authority to protect heritage buildings and areas. So when developers bought the properties, we refused to demolish them. We simply refused to pull down any building the people of Sydney wanted to keep.

"And we kept up the bans as they were required, until a new Labor government enacted a whole heap of heritage and environmental legislation between 1977 and 1979."

Just before this book was published, Jack was belatedly thanked by the government of New South Wales when asked to chair its flagship heritage institution, the Historic Houses Trust of New South Wales.

The Sydney we present to you in this book would not be the same but for feisty Mundey and his mates. Thank you, Jack.

The Joseph Banks Institute

A percentage of the UnTourist Co's profits go to the funding of the Joseph Banks Institute, a non-profit research organisation with a charter to research and develop environmentally sensitive tourism.

This charter is based on the belief that it is possible for a region, city, state or country to profit from tourism without destroying its intrinsic culture or natural environment, and that there are enough people around the world who want to spend their leisure time in destinations unspoiled by tourism to make such a concept both viable and profitable.

The role of the Joseph Banks Institute is to provide research and information to further this concept and to balance other voices promoting fast-track mass-market-driven tourism development.

But wait on – isn't the UnTourist Co itself at odds with this charter? If UnTourist guide books bring hordes of tourists to these special places, won't this be degrading the very quality originally sought?

We will be surprised if our guide books could have such a marked effect on the biggest industry in the world; however, should they be the cause of people patronising these places in large numbers, it means that there are many more fellow-travellers out there than we thought. Maybe this means that more "small tourism" products catering for this market will be taken more seriously.

Given time, people have a way of finding special places, with or without the UnTourist guide books. The real question is, when tourist numbers get to the point where the local environment is threatened, should their numbers be limited or should they be catered for? We say the most effective way to keep the mass-marketers out is to restrict numbers. If we have to book ahead to get into the best restaurant, why can't we apply the same concept to a country or region?

JOSEPH BANKS THE UNTOURIST

Sir Joseph Banks was Australia's first eco or environmentally sensitive tourist. He paid his passage to Australia on Cook's Endeavour *– a Cook's tour, you might say. As a prominent ethnologist and botanist of his day, his trip to Australia was taken solely with the purpose of studying flora, fauna and local indigenes. He did this with much skill, energy and respect for his subjects.*

Enough of the soap-box philosophy – if you would like more information, contact the UnTourist Co at PO Box 209, Balmain NSW 2041, Australia. Tel 61 2 9974 1326; Fax 61 2 9974 1396; e-mail untouris@acay.com.au

13

Sydney, Lifestyle Capital of the World

Sydney is one of the world's great resort cities. This is the natural consequence of being the leader of the pack in a country that's largely and frankly dedicated to having a good time. The responses, "No worries" and the more yuppified version "Not a problem", set the mood.

"Aveagoodweegend?" is not an idle inquiry in Sydney – it seeks a genuine revelation of the enquirer's ability to create quality leisure time. Just as the Chinese greet each other with "Chi fan ne?", "Have you eaten?" – thus reflecting the risk factor in getting a square meal under your belt – so the Australian, and particularly the Sydney-sider's, greeting reflects an almost compulsive concern with elevating leisure time to artform status.

This may not be such good news for the Australian Gross National Product but it is certainly very fortunate for those people who either live in or spend time in this fabulous city.

SUBURBAN SPRAWL

Sydney is feisty, sophisticated, up-front, warm, comparatively clean, green, youthful. It is big – very big. Greater Sydney occupies more than 12.5 thousand square kilometres: Its built-up area is twice the size of Beijing and six times as big as Rome. Its residents, for the most part, are sprawled (not literally, of course) across the city, many on quarter-acre blocks, in single-storey houses complete with nature strip (that bit of grass needing mowing at the front of the house between the fence and road), a front-yard for

The official flag for the City of Sydney

flowers and a backyard for the barbie (barbecue) and, today more than ever, the swimming pool. You see these little leisure centres like "blue beads of brightener" spread out all over the vast terracotta landscape as you peer down from the air.

This is the awesome Sydney suburban spread– and all in only 200 years. Somehow she looks older. Probably too much partying.

It is difficult to speak of Sydney without speaking of Australia, because Australia started in Sydney and the city has led the way since the beginning – the white man's beginning, that is.

BEGINNINGS

The indigenous people came via what is now Indonesia around 40,000 years ago when Australia was one continuous land mass loosely joined to its northern neighbours. When Captain Cook landed in Botany Bay in 1770, Aborigines from the Iora tribe were fearful and suspicious – appropriate forebodings for *their* future.

When the British were in charge they began building the buildings and naming the streets of the settlement which was to be called Albion, the ancient and poetic name for Britain.

This, fortunately, was changed in order to honour Lord Sydney, the then British Home Secretary who gets the credit for having the idea of starting a penal colony in *Terra Australis*, given that the British had just carelessly lost their preferred option – America!

The British maintained the Protestant ethic and the status quo in the "squalid little settlement". During the next few decades, the Irish, increasingly as political prisoners, were despatched here in their thousands. With their inherent disrespect for authority and love of life, they were to leave a significant imprint on the Australian character. Although life was extremely harsh for most of the first 100 years of settlement, the fact that Australia offered a better option for many is reflected in the fact that when the end of transportation was called, some prisoners awaiting dispatch to the colonies rioted in protest.

For nearly a century after transportation, Australia remained mainly Anglo-Celtic, with its people, in the most part, behaving like happy little Albions. They adopted a British legal and political system; the BBC lived again through the Australian Broadcasting Commission; going "home" to Britain was the accepted travel pattern.

CHANGES

It wasn't until after World War II that things began to change. The Americans had come on to the scene, and new waves of immigration from southern Europe flowed into the country during the next two decades, breaking the Anglo-ice and giving Australia, and particularly Sydney, a lifestyle lesson that its residents grasped with both hands (and a grateful palate).

Which was just in time because Sydney, in the 1950s, was hardly a place to write home about – its bio-rhythms were at a low ebb; its cuisine, seemed to be mediocre "imitation everything". Sydney was neither a good copy of a British city nor was it yet an individual statement of the new world. English actor Robert Morley,

Robert Morley asked: "Why didn't they call it Bert?" *In fact Governor Phillip nearly called it Albion.*

looking at Sydney around that time, queried "Why didn't they call it Bert?"

"When I first wrote about Sydney in 1958," wrote celebrated travel writer Jan Morris in her 1983 essay on Sydney, *"I disliked the city so much that it was five full years before the last furious response reached me from Australia."* Ten years on, she wrote a more flattering book on Sydney, *Sydney* by Jan Morris Viking, 1992).

When the Greeks and the Italians began to arrive in the 1950s, they brought huge social, cultural and gastronomic influences which enhanced *la dolce vita* in Australia no end. In fact, as this book illustrates, it is hard to imagine the culinary lifestyle of Sydney without them – not just because of the omni-present cappuccino and Greek salad, but also because what is now referred to as "Modern Australian Cuisine" probably owes its origins as much to Italians as it does to Asian cooking. As Sydney in the late 1990s is very much a "food city", without a celebration of its culinary style this UnTourist guide would have been a much slimmer volume.

It was also in the 1950s that the Australian love affair with the United States blossomed, despite the occasional remembrance of the war years ("Over-paid, over-sexed and over-here: Yanks go home!").

The Clark Gable/Lana Turner smart-world of plenty was looking much more attractive than Bombay-bloomered, duty-bound Britannia. The Americans were riding high on our commercial radio, television and movie-waves, and because of this strong influence, seemed to be winning another battle – for the social and cultural identity of Australia's population.

SYDNEY STEPS OUT

But gradually we were beginning to develop and find our real selves and, by the mid-'80s, we had well and truly stopped calling England "home", the American love affair had broken up, and we were starting to talk of Australia one day becoming a republic.

This confidence has been propelled by the international success of our entertainers, musicians, writers, entrepreneurs, film directors, chefs, scientists and sportsmen and women. It's a confidence which has been well-maintained and shines brightest in Sydney in particular.

Given the strong European and American influences, it took a long time for Australians to accept that we are, in fact part of an Asian neighbourhood. The first Chinese arrived in the early 1800s, then later in large numbers during the goldrushes and, in the past few decades, they, and other Asian nationals, have come in their thousands, for many reasons – social, financial and political. Australia, with Sydney attracting the largest intake, has consistently been able to assimilate its immigrants peacefully and with a certain good humour. Our Asian connection is continuing to grow, and by the beginning of the second millennium, when Sydney hosts the 42nd Olympiad, the Asian population of the city will have increased to the point where talk will be of Sydney evolving into an Eurasian city.

THE CUTTING-EDGE CITY

Sydney is now the social, financial, cultural and energy centre of Australia. It's a "cutting-edge" city – where it is all happening – whatever "it" may be. As such, other cities have a tendency to measure against it.

"It's too big for its boots," Monash University, Victoria, lecturer and Capital Cities Report author Kevin O'Connor.

"… they believe they are the centre of the universe. Sydney's hot, smoggy and miserable - with the world's worst taxi drivers." South Australian Arts bureaucrat, Malcolm Moore.

"They're divorced from the real world and don't know what's happening out in country Australia." Tasmanian anti-Green, logging industry spokesman, Barry Chipman.

Compared with the rest of Australia, Sydney people gamble more, go to more concerts, theatre, opera and ballet; they consume more, and travel more, to more places. They will be the first to adopt a new product idea or service; the first to catch a trend – and the first to discard it.

THE ENTHUSIASTS

They are not as physical as they think they are or as myth would have it, but they might just be the most competitive people on earth. Those who are born here are typical products of a well-fed, unthreatened upbringing and are, therefore, confident that most desires are attainable – whether social, cultural or financial. To own a home, to buy a new car, or to dress-up and attend a first night at the Opera House – all are within their rights and reach, regardless of their parents' incomes or where they went to school.

Sydney people love displays, exhibitions, parades, spectacles, demonstrations and celebrations. As the majestic QE II glides secretly" out of Sydney Harbour at midnight, there will be a fleet of hundreds of small craft on the water to savour the experience.

If Sydney people decide that the Gay and Lesbian Mardi Gras looks like fun, they will gather up their families and line the streets for hours in the pouring rain rather than miss an opportunity to party.

And, of course, Sydney people, whether their forebears came from Ireland, Italy or China, are convinced they live in the best place on earth – and they just might.

Because of all these influences on its natural assets, Sydney can now lay claim to being the lifestyle capital of the world – a great place to live, for a lifetime, or a month, a week, or a few days.

The insider who best expressed this joy of belonging to Sydney is journalist/author Gavin Souter in Sydney by Gavin Souter and Quinton Davis (Angus and Robertson Ltd, 1965): "The one pleasure Sydney has denied me is that of seeing it for the first time. This is the price of being born here."

The very best things about Sydney

The criteria were clear: "best" had to be indigenous; it had to be a Sydney product, service, place or experience that was a world-beater. Here are our conclusions:

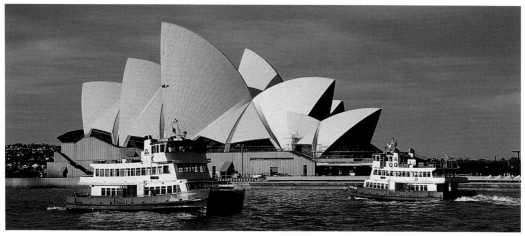

THE OPERA HOUSE EXPERIENCE

To stroll toward this icon at sunset, as the city lights up, to sip a Sunday coffee while the sails parade by and the buskers play, to step out at interval into the northern foyer where the brilliant blue John Olsen mural presents itself to the harbour at night. You take a sip of your champagne and feel privileged to be there, within the whole experience of the Sydney Opera House.

THE NEW FOOD

Fresh ingredients, the lush fruit and vegies, the fish markets brimful of snapper, sand whiting, Balmain bugs and plump creamy Sydney rock oysters. The Asian, Italian, Greek, French, Middle Eastern, Japanese influences. The many restaurants that bring it together with respect for the ingredients, a good dollop of creativity, and unpretentious Aussie service.

THE WILD THINGS

Within cooee of the centre of the city, you can be assailed by rainbow lorikeets, button-eyed possums and giant pelicans, or find kookaburras or cockatoos on your clothesline. Because Sydney is girded by so much protected, natural bushland, the wild things live close to the people – and there's a bit of the wild thing in Sydney people too.

THE FERRIES

The ferry service in Sydney has to be the most enjoyable public transport system in the world. True, not many cities have a "highway" of such beauty, size and diversity as Sydney Harbour on which to run. Sydney ferries give you access to more than half the areas of Sydney, so live a little, jump a ferry.

The Beaches

Sydney has 70 beaches. Close to half of them are gentle, secluded harbour beaches where the eucalypts hang low; the other half are beaches with classic golden sand and rolling surf. All these magic places are within the greater Sydney area. By anyone's standards, this is a rare blessing; what a cruel joke it would have been had Sydney not been also given plenty of sunny weather to take advantage of them.

THE LIFESTYLE

City life is often crowded, unsafe, polluted and stressful, and Sydney certainly has its share of these problems. But in a larger measure, it has sun, beauty, water access, fresh produce, stimulating arts and entertainment, a generous welfare system, a stable government and reasonable working hours (some would say too reasonable). Sydney people have enough natural effervescence and nous to take advantage of all of it.

In 1988, the yacht Blackmore's First Lady, *with Kay Cottee at the helm, arrived in the harbour after 189 days at sea – the first woman in history to sail the world, unassisted, non-stop and alone. She sailed up the harbour, in tears, with what seemed like half of Sydney, there, on the water, cheering her home.*

1 SYDNEY HARBOUR

INCLUDES: The best ways to use and enjoy the harbour – on it, in it and beside it. The harbour as a highway, with all its special destinations – the ferry wharf parks, harbourside restaurants, the islands, the secret places. Up the Lane Cove River on a vintage boat; to Parramatta on "The Cat"; and to Manly on the grand old ferries. The good things and the bad things about "the finest harbour in the world."

Sydney's Showplace

To the people of Sydney the harbour is a stage – the showcase where Sydney shows off to itself and to the world. Like Piccadilly Circus or Times Square, it is the place to meet, to strut your stuff, to compete, to party, to wave the flag, to let off the crackers. It's the amphitheatre where Sydney flaps its sails, the place where it all happens: on Boxing Day, as the Sydney to Hobart Yacht Race starts; on Australia Day; on New Year's Eve; as a welcome, as a farewell, or just on any regular Saturday afternoon, winter or summer – the best show in town is taking place on Sydney Harbour.

It can also be a secret place, a place where, even on a hot Sunday afternoon, there is somewhere still and private, where you can be alone with the Australian bush, whether sitting on a rock or rocking on a boat.

Sydney Harbour is one of the few places in the world that is as good as, or better than, the glossy postcards and brochures show.

WHAT AND WHERE IS IT?

Topographically speaking, the waterways of Sydney, of which the harbour is only a part, are a drowned valley – a place where the sea has pushed its way out to meet the bush, leaving deep fiords which touch practically every part of the greater Sydney area. These waterways reach to Parramatta in the west, Watsons Bay to the east; to the north, Pittwater and Palm Beach, and to the south, Taren Point and the Georges River.

The stretch of water usually described as Sydney Harbour, from the Harbour Bridge to the Heads is, in fact, Port Jackson. Sydney Harbour is a general description for all the waterways inside the Heads and includes Port Jackson, Parramatta River, Lane Cove River, Middle Harbour and North Harbour.

In this chapter, we will share with you our favourite harbourside places to eat and what to

"Go Walkabout with Sydney Ferries" *will give you all the times, duration of trips and help you access the walks around the ferry stops.*

visit and, most importantly, show you how explore them all in the most enjoyable way – by water.

THE HARBOUR HIGHWAY

One of the best things about Sydney is the public water-transport system. It is cheap, clean, efficient and, for a few dollars, it delivers some of the best experiences you can hope to have in Sydney. As Paul Theroux wrote: *"It is the journey that gives the destination heart."* Even for folk who have lived in Sydney most of their lives, like Balmain designer Sioned Fay, who never tires of catching the Balmain ferry to Circular Quay when she's heading for the Opera House: *"It is simply a magic moment. The sun is usually setting on the harbour, the water picks up the colours and half-lights of peak hour. Then there's the walk around the foreshore – could there be a better place to be in the world?!"*

Our advice is, when in Sydney, do what the savvy locals do: use the waterways as a delightful convenience rather than just a place to be visually admired. And, by the way, it is a popular myth that the waterways of Sydney only lap the shores of a few privileged suburbs – over 70% of Sydney's suburban areas have access to them.

LIVE A LITTLE – JUMP A FEW FERRIES

The easiest part of Sydney to get to and enjoy is the harbour and, were this book being written for any other traveller than an UnTourist, this would be a short chapter indeed. We would simply direct you to either Circular Quay or Darling Harbour and suggest you help yourself to the many attractive excursions on offer.

In truth, it is a good way to start – just as when going to New York for the first time, a Circle Line cruise around Manhattan Island is worthwhile for familiarisation – a way to get a feel for the whole before you discover the particular. So if you would like to have a good overall look at the harbour in an orderly way, you can take any one of the "whip-around" trips available. We favour the excellent tours run from Circular Quay by State Transit's Sydney Ferries. You can also connect up with the land-based Explorer bus trips which are equally informative. See chapters 13 and 14 or call State Transit for detailed information.

When it comes to accessing the harbour, the difference between Darling Harbour and Circular Quay is that Darling Harbour is where mostly private tour and charter boats moor, whereas the Quay is the main base for government transport ferries. Sydney Ferries Information Centre is opposite Jetty 4, at the Quay, so whatever you have in mind to do, it's a good idea to drop in there for extra information and timetables. State Transit offers two particularly useful products. One is the Sydney Pass, which saves time and money and allows you to avoid messing around with the ticket machine. The ticket machines at the Quay are perfectly easy to understand and use, unless you happen to be, like this writer, a bit mechanically challenged. If this is the case, just assume the air of a confused visitor (even if you happen to live in Pymble) and ask for help. The other excellent State Transit item to pick up while you are at the Information Centre is a small booklet called *Go Walkabout with Sydney Ferries*, which will give you all the schedules and duration of trips and will help you discover the walks around the ferry stops (see map, page 22). Wherever you choose to go, you will always end up back where you started, at the Quay.

BACKSTAGE, WEST OF THE HARBOUR BRIDGE

Visiting English businessman Peter Spedley, after taking the River Cat, a sleek twin-hulled, smooth and speedy ferry to Parramatta recently, burst into his bemused Sydney office with the dramatic announcement: *"The harbour doesn't stop at the Bridge!"*

As most of the tourist attention seems to stay on the more spectacular eastern part of the harbour, it is easy to get this impression. It is partly because very large cruise boats have difficulty in manoeuvring the smaller bays and estuaries. And residents don't much like a booming recorded commentary at closequarters, interrupting their peaceful neighbourhoods.

It was only a few years ago that the decision was taken to light the western side of the Harbour Bridge at night, despite the fact that well over 80% of Sydney's population has this aspect. Until then, only the east had the privilege of the light show.

For telephone numbers and addresses, see the yellow pages Directory at the back

The old working port of Sydney can be seen by taking a Darling Harbour Ferry from Jetty 5 at the Quay. However, it will first take a small diversion across to the northern shore, calling into the nostalgic **Luna Park** and then to the charming McMahons Point – all with wharf parks on or near them. (If you want to see more of this area, it is probably easier from **Lavender Bay** wharf. The little Hegarty's ferries are the only ones to go right into this wharf from Jetty 6 Circular Quay.)

From this northern shore, the ferry doubles back to the old working port area which starts around the southern pylons of the Harbour Bridge, past the finger wharves of **Walsh Bay**, now the home of some of Sydney's leading cultural groups. The Sydney Theatre Company and the Sydney Dance Company occupy Pier 4 (in the foyer there is a good little coffee shop). Upstairs, overlooking the harbour, is a very good restaurant called, appropriately enough, the **Wharf** Restaurant. Underneath, the space is shared by a great new performance space/night club called the **Starfish Club** – and about 30 to 40 fishermen who regularly come to enjoy fishing off the wharf.

Ferries arriving at and leaving Darling Harbour pass under the old **Pyrmont Bridge,** said to be the oldest working electric "swing" bridge in the world. It opens only on the rarest occasion, when there is some sort of yacht festival or other special event. Mostly it is closed so the people and the Monorail can cross it.

Darling Harbour is best reached by water. Not many Sydneysiders realise that you can ride any old craft, canoe or row boat in there and tie up to the promenade, have a coffee, get back in your boat and tootle off into the sunshine or the moonlight, as the case may be. Nor do many people realise just how much more can be got to from Darling Harbour – in addition to the Harbourside shops, **Maritime Museum** and the **Aquarium,** you can take in the **Chinese Gardens, Chinatown**, the cinema district, and the wonderful **Powerhouse Museum.**

WHARF PARKS & HARBOUR

HARBOUR PARKS

Regardless of which ferry you take – one to Mosman, to Manly or to Darling Harbour – you will notice that, with few exceptions, the ferry wharves are marked by small, well-kept little parks and gardens which we have high-lighted on this map. These are a bonus for ferry-jumpers as they usually have nice hardwood tables and chairs where you can read the paper or munch into a picnic.

FERRY ROUTES

HARBOUR BEACHES

NOTE: For public transport instructions telephone 13 15 00 and give the street reference supplied.

1 **Balmoral** The Esplanade via Military Rd.
2 **Camp Cove** Watsons Bay. Cliff Sreet or Pacific St via Hopetoun Ave or Old South Head Rd.
3 **Castle Rock** Balgowlah Heights. Walking track from Beatty St via New St.
4 **Chinamans** Mosman. McLean St via Parrawi Road
5 **Chowder Bay** Clifton Gardens. Morella Rd via Bradleys Head Rd.
6 **Clontarf** Clontarf. Monash Cres. via Heaton Peronne Ave.
7 **Cobblers** Middle Head Rd.
8 **Collins** Collins Beach Rd, Manly

via North Head Scenic Drive to Police Training College then a short walk. Best by private boat.
9 **Delwood** Lauderdale Ave, Manly.
10 **Double Bay** Beach St or William St via New South Head Rd.
11 **Edwards** The Esplanade via Awaba St, Balmoral.
12 **Fairlight** Arlington St via Lauderdale Ave, Fairlight.
13 **Fairy Bower** Marine Parade, Manly. (Ocean beach.)
14 **Flat Rock** Best by private boat Walking track from Killarney Drive, Killarney Heights. **Warning:** At weekends there are often water skiers here.
15 **Forty Baskets** Beatty St via New St, Balgowlah Heights.
16 **Gibsons** Salisbury St via Hopetoun Ave, Watsons Bay.
17 **Hermit Bay** Tingara St via Vaucluse Rd, Vaucluse.
18 **Kutti** Wharf St via Hopetoun Ave, Watsons Bay.
19 **Lady Jane** Walking track via Cliff St and Military Rd, Watsons Bay. Nude bathing allowed.
20 **Lady Martins Beach** Wolseley Cescent via Wolseley Rd, Point Piper.
21 **Little Manly Cove** Craig Ave via Stuart St, Manly.
22 **Nielsen Park or Shark Beach** Off Vaucluse Rd, Vaucluse.
23 **North Harbour Reserve** Harbour St via Condamine St, Balgowlah.

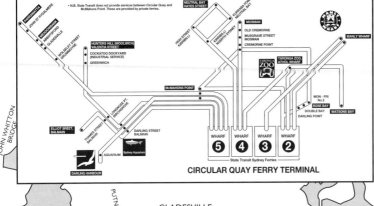

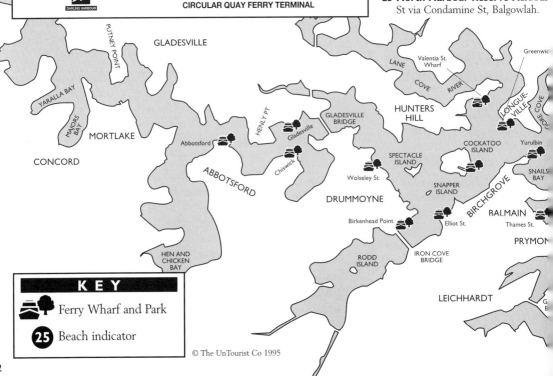

KEY

🛥🌳 Ferry Wharf and Park

25 Beach indicator

© The UnTourist Co 1995

24 Obelisk Chowder Bay Rd via drive along Middle Head Rd. Nude bathing allowed.

25 Parsley Bay Hopetoun Ave, Vaucluse.

26 Quarantine Manly. Guided tours only, call for bookings.

27 Reef Beatty St via New St or Manly Scenic Walkway track, or walk from Forty Baskets Beach, Balgowlah.

28 Sandy Bay Sandy Bay Rd, Clontarf.

29 Seven Shillings Beach Buckhurst Ave or Mervyns St off New South Head Rd, Point Piper.

30 Shell Cove Bogota Ave via Wycombe Rd, Cremorne.

31 Shelly Bower St via Darley Rd, Manly. (Ocean beach.)

32 Sirius Cove Sirius Cove Rd via Raglan St, Mosman, or walking track from Taronga Zoo Wharf.

33 The Spit Spit Rd.

34 Store Accessible only by boat.

35 Taylors Bay Difficult access from Illuka Rd, Mosman. Walking track from Bradleys Head Rd.

36 Vaucluse Wentworth Rd via Vaucluse Rd.

37 Washaway Cutler Rd via Woodland St, Clontarf. Walking track from Harbour St via Cutler Rd.

38 Whiting Ferry to Taronga Zoo Wharf. Walking track to beach.

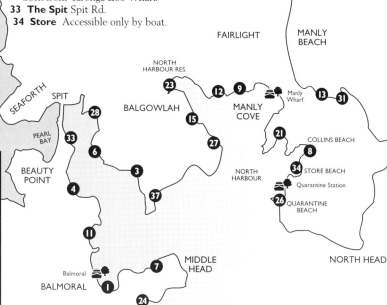

> One of our favourite stop-offs is **Thornton Park** at the **Darling Street** wharf. Here you can sit peacefully near the rose garden with its commemorative plaque to **William Balmain**, principal surgeon to the colony (1797-1803), taking in the spectacular postcard vista of central Sydney.

THE FISH MARKETS

If you don't mind a bit of a walk (about 15 minutes), you can also stroll from Darling Harbour to Blackwattle Bay and the Sydney Fish Markets (although the walk is a bit awkward, with overpasses rampant). It is much more fun to call a water taxi – as with many things in Sydney, it is a great experience to go to the Fish Markets by water. Considered one of the finest markets in the world, the Sydney Fish Markets are owned and run by the fishing cooperatives and the retailers within the markets. The two nations which seem to have the fish business sewn up in Sydney are the Greeks and the Japanese and at the markets you'll find a great mix of Greek and Japanese Australians working over the catch. A lunch of sushi with a Hunter Valley white and a cappuccino finish is par for the course.

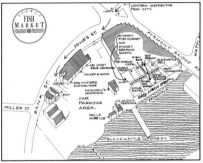

Within the markets there are some excellent fresh-produce stores – fruit and vegetables, a deli and a bakery. Doyles has a rest-aurant there, opposite the Italian cafe, and close to the sushi bar. Our favourite is Manettas, which has "a buy, cook and eat it" place Peter's, within its retail area in the main hall. Once you have selected your fish, they will cook it for you and, armed with a chilled local Chard-onnay and maybe some oysters, you can sit indoors or out by the fishing boats and enjoy the whole

The Fish Markets run

experience. The seagulls will pester you, so you may as well pass over their commission up-front in order to maintain the peace.

Features: The Oyster Co-op; net sales; fruit and veg.; bakery, Italian cafe, Doyles; grog shop; Sushi Bar; the deli; various fish displays and who owns them; car park; scissor man; tables and benches; auction rooms.

SEAFOOD SCHOOL

Fish eating and cooking is one of the few culinary categories which needs local knowledge. Knowing the difference between travella and travelly, or crayfish and lobsters, or how to cook parrot fish, or what is flake – the answers can make the difference between a memorable meal or a disaster. A great addition to the markets, for those who are prepared to invest the time, is the new Seafood School. Some of Sydney's top chefs – Tony Bilson, Chris Manfield and Serge Dansereau – are involved, and a call to the Sydney Fish Markets will give you the particular speciality which is being featured, be it luscious laksa or bouill-abaisse. To dig even deeper into the wonders of seafood, there is the Early Morning Breakfast Tour which inc-ludes a guided tour of the market where you will watch the Dutch Auction process. You then pick out your fish and go on to get all the information on cooking it. The finale is a great seafood breakfast. The cost is budget-level and includes free parking. There aren't many dates each month when this is on, so a call to the Sydney Fish Markets number for further details.

BALMAIN FERRY RUN

Balmain and its small neighbour Birchgrove are among Sydney's oldest suburbs. Unlike most of the Inner West, Balmain is very "old Aussie" and charac-terised by good food, old pubs and boats. Almost totally surrounded by water, Balmain can be reached via four strategically located wharves: Elliott Street; Darling Street; Long Nose Point and Thames Street. There is a good bus connection to the heart of Balmain from the Darling Street wharf.

Balmain was the main ship-building area for Sydney Cove and most of the old ferries were built there. There is still a strong tradition in wooden boats, although the boat builders are gradually being moved further west as the cost of land escalates.

🦅 THE 18-FOOTERS

At the turn of the century, these classic racing craft were made of Australian cedar. With their immense bowsprits supporting a great press of sail, the undecked "skimming-dishes" were unballasted, except for the weight of their crew. Spurred on by noisy on-shore supporters, small ferries loaded to the gunwales with shouting punters would follow the races – "follow" is a slight exaggeration as the average 18-footer would leave a ferry standing; "chase" is more appropriate.

Aluminium has replaced wood and Kelvar has replaced canvas but nothing much else has changed. English writer Jan Morris in her book *Sydney* (Viking, 1992) observes an elderly, white-hatted couple who settle on Bradleys Head, *"...and presently into our line of sight there burst the 18-footers of the Sydney Flying Squadron, which is really what our dedicated pensioners have been wait-ing for – not bower-birds or whistle ducks, but furiously fast racing yachts."*

If one were seeking a single experience that captures the feel of Sydney, maybe Jan Morris is right – it is the *"showy hedonism of its Sunday afternoon, the brutal force of the 18-footers, the mayhem aboard the gamblers' ferry boat, the white-hatted old lovers – the mixture of the homely, the illicit, the beautiful, the nostalgic, the ostentatious, the formidable and the quaint, all bathed in sunshine and somehow impregnated with a fragile sense of passing generations, passing time, presents to my mind a proper introduction to the feel of the place."*

The 18-footer Jean *off Long Noise Point in Sydney Harbour in 1944. From the book* Sydney's Flying Sailors, *by Margaret Molloy, available from the Sydney Flying Squadron.*

Although the heart of 18-footer sailing is still in Balmain (or so the locals seem to think), there are now clubs in Double Bay and Milsons Point. You can get a ferry run by the clubs and follow the 18-footer races in the harbour.

There's a bar on board, light finger-food and bets have, most certainly, been known to change hands. It's a great Sydney experience which we recommend highly.

Call **Australian 18-footers** at Double Bay about the race ferry on Sunday, and the **Sydney Flying Squadron** at Milsons Point about the race ferry on Saturday. They both welcome visitors and there are several convenient pick-up points around the harbour.

THE LITTLE HARBOUR ISLANDS

In the early history of Sydney, most of the real work took place in the area of Millers Point, Pyrmont, Glebe, Ultimo, Balmain and Birch-grove. The boats were built, goods were traded, cargoes were landed and loaded and, like every city in the world, these are the areas which eventually become the most interesting to people who seek out old city environments and honest architecture. Some of those interesting environments are, surprisingly, on the islands of Sydney Harbour.

There are – or were – 13 in all. Some, like **Berry, Bennelong, Glebe, Darling** and **Garden** are simply buried or are now joined onto the mainland. This leaves seven little islands for us to enjoy (**Cockatoo** is generally not open to the public). Four of them – **Goat, Snapper, Rodd** and **Spectacle** are west of the Harbour Bridge and three – **Fort Denison, Shark** and **Clarke** – are in the main area of the harbour.

(See island map over page)

1 **Goat Island** An old quarry with a wonderful convict-built village still intact. Limited access, by arrangement with the Waterways Authority.

2 **Fort Denison**, or Pinchgut, as it was known before 1855, is a convict-built fort constructed to defend Sydney from its potential invaders – the Americans were a major threat. Open to the public.

3 **Shark Island** Once a quarantine station, now a charming picnic place. Open to the public, however transport needs to be arranged.

4 **Clarke Island** A classic picnic place for Sydneysiders since 1800. Beautiful natural bushland. No regular transport.

5 **Garden Island** Originally a vegetable garden, now a naval base. Contains grand old

buildings and a fascinating naval museum. Limited access. Tours can be arranged.

6 **Bennelong Island** Now part of the site of the Opera House.

7 **Snapper Island** Though an interesting historical site, it is not open to the public. A naval training area and repository.

8 **Rodd Island** This pretty little island is open to the public and is a wonderful place for picnics. Its fascinating history involves Louis Pasteur, who used it as a laboratory. Sarah Berhardt boarded her pet dogs there while on tour. Private transport needs to be arranged.

9 **Spectacle Island** A Naval repository and museum which is really worth seeing. Transport can be arranged.

10 **Glebe Island** Once an abattoir, now a container terminal – inaccessible to the public.

11 **Darling Island** Long gone. Now buried under Piers 12, 13 and 14 at Darling Harbour.

12 **Berry Island** A great picnic place, even if it isn't an island any more. Access by Shirley Road, Wollstonecraft (North Sydney).

13 **Cockatoo Island** This fascinating island is generally not open to the public. Once a prison and more recently a large shipbuilding yard

NB: The management of these islands is undergoing a number of changes, so if in doubt, **Banks Marine** which specialises in Island Events will be happy to advise you on arrangements.

PARRAMATTA RIVER

Because of the poor quality of soil around the new settlement of Sydney Cove, Rose Hill (later called Parramatta), 30km inland, was quickly established as a farming community. The transportation of produce was via the Parramatta River, which officially starts at Long Nose Point. The first ship to be built in Australia was a ferry, the Rose Hill Packet. It was an oar and sail craft, colloquially referred to as "The Lump". Commissioned by Governor Phillip in 1789, it was designed to take passengers and goods to and from Sydney Cove and Parramatta. The trip took a week; the sleek new River Cats now do the trip in an hour.

By the mid-1800s, the ferries were ploughing up and down the Parramatta river (oars were out – steam was in). Then came the trains and the growth of the dreaded motor car. By the 1950s, the water traffic to Parramatta had dwindled to next-to-nothing. Industry had bought up the riverside land, and pollution and silting became a major threat to this once grand waterway. The day of reckoning arrived, and the results of the big clean-ups of recent years are clearly evident. The river-as-highway has come to life again.

Until the River Cats were introduced by Sydney Ferries in 1993, getting to Parramatta could be nearly as taxing as it was in the early 1800s – and about as slow. Parramatta Road is

Ian Kiernan AO, founding chairman, Clean-Up Australia Ltd and former round-the-world yachtsman, was inspired to action when he saw how dirty the world's oceans are becoming.

"When overseas visitors fly into Sydney over the harbour, they inevitably report how clean the water is and then how clean the city streets are. That is, in comparison with other cities. But we have to do better. Australia is unique in that its environment is subtle and delicate, and we must be sensitive to this. At the same time, I believe we can set an example to the world in how to look after a global environment. By 2001, I want all the Sydney waterways to be free of pollution so people can swim at all of its beaches. This will be by means of fixing point sources of pollution, as is happening with the waste water treatment plant at Taronga Zoo. We also need improvement to Sydney's stormwater drainage system and for people to stop carelessly discarding rubbish, even including cigarette butts – these are largely plastic. I would also like to see an improvement in public transport – one-passenger cars are wasteful and polluting."

not one of the most attractive or accessible parts of this fair city. The water trip to Parramatta is now a delight, and Parramatta itself will hold great interest for students of Sydney's history.

Sydney Rowing Club on Parramatta River *by Sydney foreshores painter, David McBride (see Directory)*

On the trip into the Parramatta River from Circular Quay, the ferry glides between Balmain and Greenwich, the old Naval shipyard at **Cockatoo Island,** the **Naval Museum** on **Spectacle Island** and **Snapper Island,** past the Birkenhead "factory outlet" shopping complex. By now you are between Drummoyne and Hunter's Hill, on the Parramatta River proper.

Under the Gladesville Bridge, before the Cat makes its way into the upper reaches of the river, there are a few landmarks which may be of interest. The strange column marking the rocks on the starboard side of the boat also marks the entry to what used to be Sydney's great rowing waterway. The memorial off Henley Point, badly damaged by a hit-and-run power boat in early 1995, is a memorial to the 1888 world champion sculler, Henry Searle. The column – or what is left of it – marks the end of the early Head of the River sculling events. There are a number of rowing clubs around here, including the **Sydney Rowing Club** at Abbotsford wharf which has a good restaurant and occasional jazz concerts. The restaurant is open every day for lunch and dinner (except Monday and Tuesday). This area also has some literary significance as it was the home of both Henry Lawson and "Banjo" Patterson. The **Banjo Patterson Cottage** restaurant, Gladesville, with its grand private wharf, welcomes river visitors. It is rich with mem-orabilia and serves fine fare in delightful surroundings. If you want to get there by River Cat and if you give the restaurant reasonable notice, they will pick you up from Abbotsford wharf.

Continuing up the river, past the old shipbuilding area of Mortlake and the Putney Punt, past the wonderful little boathouse, which was part of the Walker Mansion and now in Concord Repatriation Hospital grounds. Soon comes **Homebush Bay,** venue for Olympic City for year 2000. Once at Parramatta (see Chapter 4) there is an easy connection with the Explorer bus, which covers the historic spots – the fearful Women's Prison, Rose Hill Cottage, Elizabeth Farm and Old Government House.

LANE COVE RIVER

The Lane Cove River, also on the western side of the Harbour Bridge, gives access to a beautiful national park and passes through some of Sydney's loveliest northern suburbs – all within a few kilometres of the CBD. The best way to see it all is by the vintage ferry, *MV Reliance,* and your host is teacher, shipwright and captain, Bill Moseley.

From Darling Harbour, where the shallow-draft river boat departs, the journey goes past Luna Park, Goat Island, up past the fine waterfront houses of Hunters Hill and on under the Figtree Bridge to experience the serenity of an almost untouched river ecology.

The MV Reliance *in the Lane Cove National Park & Wildlife Refuge.*

From backstage harbour, on to the main performance space to the east of the Bridge. The Mosman ferry route runs past **Kirribilli,** Sydney home of the Governor General and the Prime Minister (different mansions, you'll be relieved to know), around past the grand old Royal Sydney Yacht Squadron, to **Careening Cove** and **Neutral Bay,** Cremorne, and on to calm and beautiful Mosman Bay.

🐦 MOSMAN BAY

Few of its gentle residents realise that Mosman started its life as a very smelly old whaling station and that Mr Mosman was a notorious whaler whose ships worked their killing-fields halfway around the world. In fact the early colony might have had an even more difficult time had it not been for the likes of Mr Mosman, the whale killer. It is said that the whaling industry supported the lifestyle of the settlers handsomely. No whiff of such an unattractive endeavour nowadays. This area is a great place to mooch around. There are many walks around the bay through the Cremorne Gardens (another leftover from Victoriana), past "The Barn" where Mr Mosman did his dirty business, on to the Mosman Rowing Club, which has an excellent seafood barbecue on the verandah overlooking the bay. Call first so you won't be disappointed.

From Mosman wharf, there is a walk across Curraghbeena Point to the Taronga Zoo, where another ferry can be taken to the Quay. Even if you aren't mad about zoos, the Sydney version is very special. The booklet *"Go Walkabout with Sydney Ferries"* also details a walk from Mosman Bay though to Bradleys Head and beyond. Bradleys Head juts out from the Mosman shoreline, interrupting the otherwise clear east to west run up the harbour. This makes it one of the finest viewing places on the harbour but, for the same reason, it has also been the scene of Sydney Harbour's three major dramas.

Mosman Bay Walk   *The Cafe Mosman – what a world away from whales*

THE INVASION OF SYDNEY

Between Bradleys Head and Clifton Gardens is **Taylors Bay,** a protected little beach and a popular anchorage. It was here, in 1942, the final dramatic scenes were acted out in Sydney's only invasion.

The American destroyer, *USS Chicago*, was at anchor off Garden Island. With the aura of heroes, the Americans had come to Australia's aid in World War II and, most would hold, saved it from a major Japanese invasion. In the autumn of 1942, Sydney was indeed attacked by Japanese submarines. At 5pm on May 31, four midget submarines carrying two torpedoes and a crew of two officers slipped through the undersea nets and slid into Sydney Harbour. They were detected at 10pm, and a general alarm was sent out. The *USS Chicago* started firing shells at the conning tower of one of the submarines which had been picked up in the searchlights. One of these shells hit the tower at Fort Denison. It wasn't until just after midnight that the invaders were able to get off two torpedos from their position near Bradleys Head. One torpedo ran ashore without exploding, but the other sank the converted ferry *Kuttabul* off Garden Island, killing 19 sailors. When the sun came up the next morning, three patrol boats battered the last submarine to pieces in Taylors Bay.

Six nights later, just as the shock was wearing off, another Japanese submarine surfaced off the Heads and fired 10 shells into the residential Eastern Suburbs. The majority failed to explode and, miraculously, there were only minor injuries.

Sydney never before or since has been invaded by another nation.

An interesting display of memorabilia from this part of Sydney Harbour's history can be seen at the Garden Island Naval Museum and the remains of one of the submarines can be seen at the Naval Repository and Museum on Spectacle Island.

THE ROLLING OF THE RODNEY

The bizarre happenings on board the *Rodney*, in 1938, also involved the American Navy. Young Sydney girls were out to farewell the glamorous Yankee sailors of the *Louisville*. The privately chartered little ferry was dangerously overloaded and unbalanced. Off Bradleys Head, the cheers turned to screams as it capsized, drowning 19 people.

GREYCLIFFE DISASTER

Bradleys Head was also the scene of an equally dramatic and even more tragic event in the summer of 1927, involving the little

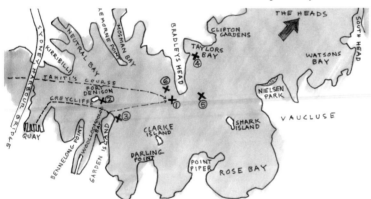

1 *Greycliffe* is struck by *Tahiti* 1927, 42 people killed
2 Fort Denisopn shelled by *USS Chicago* May 1942
3 *Kuttabul* sunk by Japanese submarine May 1942, 19 killed
4 Japanese submarine battered to peices
5 Japanese submarine fires on the Kuttabul and eastern suburbs
6 Rodney sinks 1938, 19 people drown

The collision of the Greycliffe *and the* Tahiti

wooden ferry Greycliffe. She was on her regular run from Circular Quay to Watsons Bay and was rammed amidships – virtually torn in half – by the mail steamer *Tahiti*, with the loss of forty-two lives. Many were school children coming home on what was called "the school ferry".

The Sydney Morning Herald captured the tragedy:

> "The greatest disaster that has ever occurred on Sydney Harbour took place yesterday afternoon about 4.30 o'clock, when the Union Steamship Company's Tahiti rammed and sank the Sydney Ferry Company's Greycliffe off Bradleys Head. The accident was accompanied by appalling loss of life. The latest reports last evening stated that 11 bodies had been recovered, 28 persons were reported missing and over 50 had been treated at Sydney Hospital for injuries received in the collision."

The Special Marine Inquiry ruled that fault lay solely with the *Tahiti*. It was estimated at the trial that she was travelling at six to seven knots above the speed limit for those waters.

Despite the foregoing, the Sydney Ferries service has an impeccable safety record, having carried many millions of passengers around the harbour of Sydney in safety since that tragic day in 1927, which is still remembered particularly by the older people of Watsons Bay.

CAMP COVE

The maritime history of Watsons Bay can be charted back to Captain Arthur Phillip's first encampment. The three small oar and sail pinnaces, being the exploring party from the First Fleet which remained moored in Botany Bay, made camp on what they named appropriately Camp Cove on the 21st of January 1788. It was from Watsons Bay he viewed "...one of the finest harbours in the world, in which a thousand sail of the line might ride in perfect security". Today, the village in the bay and its surrounding inlets and beaches Parsley Bay and Vaucluse is one of the delights of Sydney Harbour. It is a safe anchorage and a marvellous place to arrive by yacht, launch or ferry to take in the wonders of the city skyline. There's the Watsons Bay Hotel, where you can stay if you wish; there's the fish and chips, the foreshore walks under deep green fig trees and swimming at Camp Cove. The eateries and the pub are open every day and night. Ferries run from Jetty 4 at the Quay four times a day during the week – more at weekends – or you can pick up the Doyle's Water Bus, which runs a regular shuttle back and forth. You could be different and come by road. It is actually a great run along New South Head Road: the 324 and 325 buses run regularly from the Quay.

RESTAURANTS ON THE HARBOUR

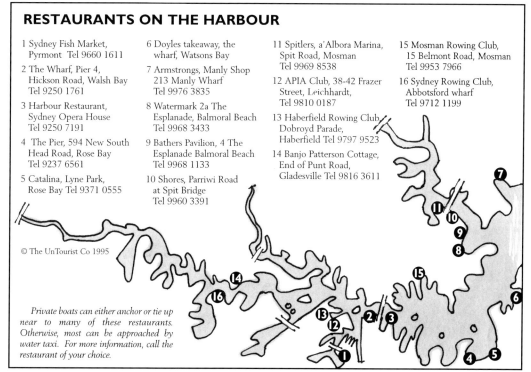

1 Sydney Fish Market, Pyrmont Tel 9660 1611

2 The Wharf, Pier 4, Hickson Road, Walsh Bay Tel 9250 1761

3 Harbour Restaurant, Sydney Opera House Tel 9250 7191

4 The Pier, 594 New South Head Road, Rose Bay Tel 9237 6561

5 Catalina, Lyne Park, Rose Bay Tel 9371 0555

6 Doyles takeaway, the wharf, Watsons Bay

7 Armstrongs, Manly Shop 213 Manly Wharf Tel 9976 3835

8 Watermark 2a The Esplanade, Balmoral Beach Tel 9968 3433

9 Bathers Pavilion, 4 The Esplanade Balmoral Beach Tel 9968 1133

10 Shores, Parriwi Road at Spit Bridge Tel 9960 3391

11 Spitlers, a'Albora Marina, Spit Road, Mosman Tel 9969 8538

12 APIA Club, 38-42 Frazer Street, Leichhardt, Tel 9810 0187

13 Haberfield Rowing Club, Dobroyd Parade, Haberfield Tel 9797 9523

14 Banjo Patterson Cottage, End of Punt Road, Gladesville Tel 9816 3611

15 Mosman Rowing Club, 15 Belmont Road, Mosman Tel 9953 7966

16 Sydney Rowing Club, Abbotsford wharf Tel 9712 1199

© The UnTourist Co 1995

Private boats can either anchor or tie up near to many of these restaurants. Otherwise, most can be approached by water taxi. For more information, call the restaurant of your choice.

MIDDLE HARBOUR

Ferries don't have regular routes into Middle Harbour. However, Sydney Ferries runs an excellent afternoon cruise which leaves from Jetty 4, Circular Quay at 1pm daily and goes straight up the main part of the harbour to just inside the Sydney Heads, past Middle Head and those beautiful areas so often painted by Ken Done (whose studio looks down on Chinaman's Beach), on to Balmoral, under the Spit Bridge and up to explore the upper reaches and grand waterways of Middle Harbour.

Balmoral, a residue from Victorian years and named after the Queen's castle in Scotland, is lovely part of Middle Harbour. The beach is netted and it is surrounded by nice restaurants, particularly Victoria Alexander's Bathers Pavilion which is right on Balmoral Beach.

At the Spit Bridge area where you can hire a boat and go exploring, there are also some good fish restaurants, a couple of which you can reach by boat. This is one part of the harbour, however, where pleasure must be restricted to either being *beside* or *on* the water rather than *in* it.

THE DARK SIDE

There is great enjoyment to be had in the quiet backwaters of the harbour, but swimming isn't one of them unless you have a protected pool or beach. It is in these beautiful upper reaches of the harbour waters that Sydney's worst shark attacks have happened. They don't happen very often – in fact, the last tragedy took place in 1963, in Sugarloaf Bay when a young actress was wading in less than a metre of water. She was dragged to her death by what was thought to be a two-metre grey nurse shark. Along the banks of these estuaries there are signs warning people not to swim – however it is amazing how they are ignored, particularly by visitors to the country. The accompanying map shows areas where you should avoid swimming – no matter how shallow the water.

Another special Sydney experience can be the "southerly buster", a sudden change in wind, usually on a hot summer afternoon. It can be particularly hazardous if you are out on the water. A southerly buster is caused by a sudden drop in pressure and is followed by strong winds, sometimes gusting to 50 or 60 knots and often accompanied by squalling rain. The good news about a "buster" is that it is usually over in an hour, or less, and that it dramatically reduces the temperature after a hot day.

Sydney Harbour has its traps for the unwary. So get some good "insider" advice from one of the experienced boating locals if you plan to take a craft out on the harbour. If in doubt, call the Waterways Access Line.

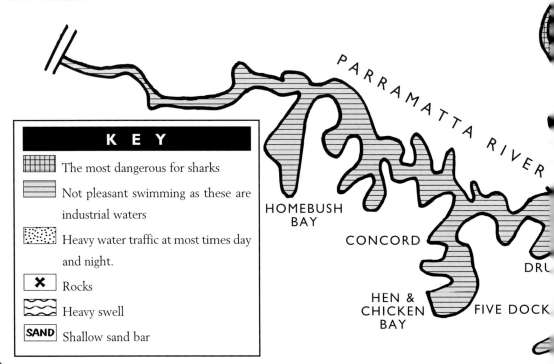

KEY

⊞	The most dangerous for sharks
▤	Not pleasant swimming as these are industrial waters
⋯	Heavy water traffic at most times day and night.
✗	Rocks
〰	Heavy swell
SAND	Shallow sand bar

PARRAMATTA RIVER

HOMEBUSH BAY

CONCORD

DRU

HEN & CHICKEN BAY

FIVE DOCK

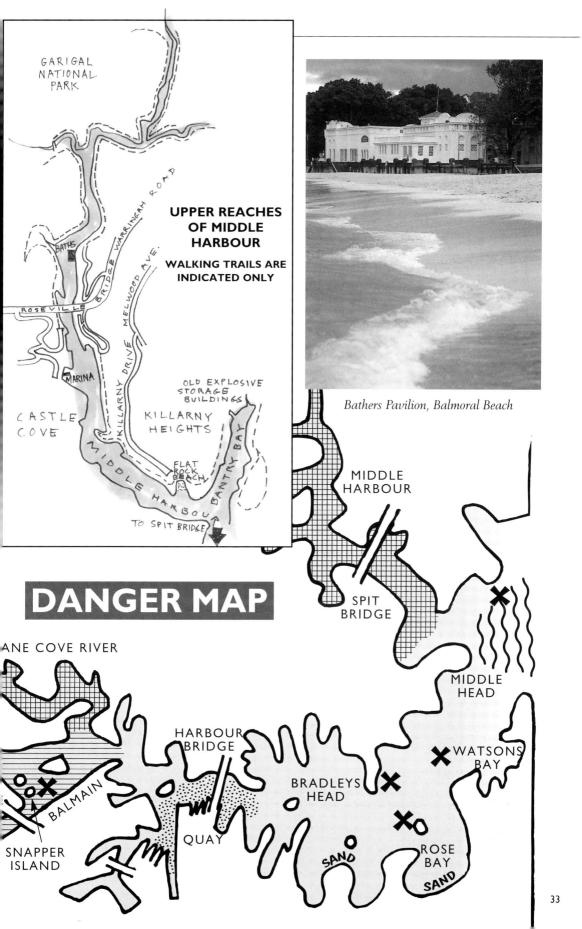

GARIGAL
NATIONAL
PARK

**UPPER REACHES
OF MIDDLE
HARBOUR**

**WALKING TRAILS ARE
INDICATED ONLY**

BATHS

ROSEVILLE BRIDGE

KILLARNY DRIVE

WARRINGAH ROAD

MELWOOD AVE.

MARINA

CASTLE
COVE

KILLARNY
HEIGHTS

OLD EXPLOSIVE
STORAGE
BUILDINGS

MIDDLE HARBOUR

BANTRY BAY

FLAT
ROCK
BEACH

TO SPIT BRIDGE

Bathers Pavilion, Balmoral Beach

MIDDLE
HARBOUR

SPIT
BRIDGE

MIDDLE
HEAD

DANGER MAP

ANE COVE RIVER

HARBOUR
BRIDGE

BALMAIN

SNAPPER
ISLAND

QUAY

BRADLEYS
HEAD

WATSONS
BAY

SAND

ROSE
BAY

SAND

33

MANLY

"Seven miles from Sydney and a thousand miles from care". The ferry trip to Manly is a great treat when the weather is calm. When the weather is rough, it is rather like taking the big-dipper at Luna Park, except more fun. The crossing of these seven nautical miles (about 8 regular miles or 13kms) tells much of the story of Manly. The beginnings are well known, although Governor Phillip's observation on the local Aborigines' *"confidence and manly behaviour"* came under question two months later when he caught a spear in the shoulder on Collins Beach. (See page 23) Today, **Store Beach** (the next beach south) is a popular stop-over for yachties and, next to that, there's another beach with access to **Quarantine Station**. The Station is surrounded by natural beauty and is redolent with a poignant history spanning 170 years. (For a guided tour, call Sydney Harbour National Park Information).

Sixty years after Governor Phillip caught the spear in the shoulder, the real estate developers arrived and the first of those was Henry Gilbert Smith Esq. He was probably Australia's first resort developer – the first one of that happy band who, on seeing a beautiful natural beach, have to "improve" it. Australia has had many of them over the past 200 years. The 1980s were the primetime for "improving on nature". However, back to Mr Gilbert who chartered the wooden paddle steamer *The Brothers* as a "come-on" to encourage potential buyers of his newly subdivided land.

The popularity of Manly grew and soon a regular weekly service was operating from the Quay to Manly. This regular service encouraged more development in Manly and the competition was so fierce between the boat operators that a cost-cutting war developed which almost brought them all to bankruptcy. At one stage, you could get to Manly for three pence which, even in those days, was a bargain. The problem was solved by a merger in 1896. In 1901, the locally designed and built forerunner to the modern ferry was launched. The *Kuring-gai* could carry 1228 passengers and had "The Electric Light". To *"serve at all times as well as the beautiful but inconsistent moon,"* read the advertisement. There followed the awkwardly named "K" ferries: *Kai Kai, Kuramia, Koom-partoo* and the ill-fated *Kuttabul* which, 20 years after her launch, was sunk by a Japanese torpedo.

Continuing in their alliteration mode, The Port Jackson and Manly Steamship Company then moved into the "B" series with *Binnarra, Burra Bra, Bellubera, Balgowlah, Barrenjoey* and the *Baragoola*. The '30s broke the naming pattern and the much loved *Dee Why, Curl Curl* and, the most magnificent of them all, the *South*

Steyne, were launched, complete with strolling musicians and 'refreshments' on board. The *South Steyne*, now fully restored, is permanently moored in Darling Harbour where you can check it out.

It was around 1930 when Manly was in full bloom. The '30s character and style of the grand old ferries was reflected in the architecture and mood of the suburb. No other place in Sydney was like Manly – nor is it now – but more of that later.

Some say the '30s marked the end of romantic Manly Ferries and maybe this is so, but the shiny new Jet Cats and newer ferries still give you a great ride, and the pleasures of the journey don't diminish with the years.

WHAT WONDROUS SIGHTS TO SEE

To return to the city from Manly, past the Heads with Watsons Bay still looking like a fishing village nestled under South Head, then to swing into the main harbour, whether in a ferry or under full sail on the run home, is always a special experience. This is the classic ride up the harbour... the water flecked with skiffs, the spinnakers unfurled, past the dress-circle suburbs Vaucluse, Rose Bay, Point Piper, Double Bay and Darling Point, with the grand old "coathanger" and the white sails of the Opera House centre-stage ahead.

Could it be that we have actually "improved" the harbour where Captain Phillip arrived with his huddle of settlers such a little time ago? And later, much later, when the giant *SS Queen Mary* in her war-torn battle-greys brought home her shell-shocked cargo of diggers – what a sight this harbour must have been to them. And for those Italian and Greek immigrants – what a feast. And for those in flight, the South Africans, Poles, Yugoslavs, Chilians, Chinese and Jews, a sanctuary. And for the teary-eyed, homesick young Australians in the '60s, after serving their statutory working holiday "at home" in Britain, gripping the railings of the great white P&O cruise ships *SS Orontes* and *SS Orion*.

And when, in 1988, the yacht *Blackmores First Lady* with Kay Cottee at the helm, arrived after 189 days at sea – the first woman in history to sail the world, unassisted, non-stop and alone. She sailed up the harbour in tears with what seemed like half of Sydney, there, on the water, cheering her home.

And to those who see the start of the Sydney Hobart Yacht Race for the first time – at last count, 100 yachts under full spinnaker. Or to see everything that will float out there in the "sail past", held each Australia Day, or on any early summer's morning, or bejewelled, at night, or anytime – what a show.

Sydney, 1874, drawn by A.C.Cooke

2 THE CENTRE

As is the case with all large city centres, environments and experiences can change immensely within a few blocks. Because of this we have divided Central Sydney into four neighbourhoods, each offering something different.

In and Around The Rocks

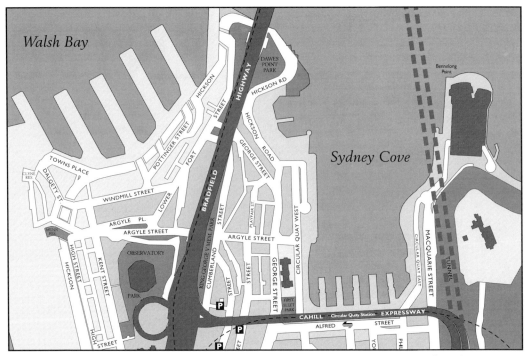

INCLUDES: *The environs surrounding the Opera House, Circular Quay and The Rocks form the showcase of Sydney and, therefore, attract more visitors (dare we say tourists?) than is ideal. And why not - the area's a stunner. The old Sydney pubs; special places like Observatory Hill; Millers Point; the Museum of Contemporary Art; and some curious little shops, nooks and crannies in and around The Rocks and the Quay make this area a must for even the strictest UnTourist.*

A good starting point is the **Observatory** on Observatory Hill, because it was astronomy that brought Captain Cook to Australia in the first place. In 1769, he sailed on the Endeavour with his team of scientists into the South Pacific to Tahiti to observe the transit of Venus across the sun. Then, sailing west, he discovered Australia's east coast.

Looking down from Observatory Hill today, it is easy to imagine, some 18 years after Captain Cook's discovery, Captain Arthur Phillip's joy at discovering a perfect natural harbour. At the water's edge of what he named **Sydney Cove,** he discovered a ledge of sandstone, some 18m wide, sitting up a bit above the high-tide mark. From the ridge, the water dropped steeply to five or six fathoms. Here was a natural harbour indeed – around which Phillip was able to construct a series of quays "at very small expense" and where, within a decade, one would see the more disreputable citizens of

Sydney Town carousing in and about The Rocks, as the nearby area was soon called.

Still standing on Observatory Hill, one can look down on the oldest suburb in Sydney, **Millers Point,** or "The High Rocks", as it was referred to in the 1800s, when it managed to maintain a certain bourgeois decorum even when, at the foot of the escarpment, The Rocks was at its most appalling. No doubt the gracious residents rarely looked down. Lord knows how they managed to ignore the smells wafting up from the open sewers and general filth below. Today, Observatory Hill is home to the **National Trust** and the **S H Ervin Gallery** with its regular exhibitions relating to Australia's cultural heritage. Best approach for both is via the Agar Steps, Kent Street.

In Millers Point, there are two great old pubs, the lusty **Lord Nelson**, at 19 Kent Street the oldest pub in Sydney, and the wonderful

Palisade, 35 Bettington Street. The Palisade now houses one of Sydney's best new restaurants run by Annie Parmentier, a chef who has the dubious distinction of having introduced sticky toffee pudding to the Antipodes from Mother England. (Incidentally, from the Palisade's "widow's walk" there is a much better overview of Sydney than from the Observatory.) Both of these old Sydney pubs are great places to stay, to eat, or just to hang out. But before we leave Millers Point, more details on the Observatory and an introduction to the nearby **Society of Australian Genealogists,** housed in an historic building moved stone by stone across the city from the Domain to 120 Kent Street.

At the **Observatory**, built in 1858, you can enjoy a hands-on experience with practically the whole universe, as today it is a museum of astronomy. Bookings are necessary for night visits which include guided tours of the building, films and videos. Open every night except Wed. Also open Mon-Fri, 2pm-5pm. Sat, Sun, school holidays, 10am-5pm. Admission free. Watson Road, Observatory Hill.

And at the **Society of Australian Genealogists,** for a few dollars, you can become a day member and have access to records allowing a search for your family tree. Volunteers will help you find any skeletons or saints. Open Tues, Wed, Thurs, Sat, 10.30am-4pm, l20 Kent Street.

At the base of the ridge, around the southern bridge pylon, are the **Walsh Bay finger wharves.** These wharves are very much part of the old working port of Sydney Cove. Pier 4, Hickson Road, is now home to the fine **Wharf Restaurant**, and two of Sydney's leading cultural groups, the **Sydney Theatre Company** and the **Sydney Dance Company.**

On the western shore of Sydney Cove is The Rocks proper – though given its improper history, that's hardly an appropriate description. The sailors would roll out of their vessels after months at sea and generally make up for lost time. There were opium and Pak-ah-poo dens (Pak-ah-poo was a form of Chinese lottery, like the ubiquitous Australian TAB, without the horses.) After the 1840s, The Rocks became crowded with commercial activity and notorious as the haunt of "The Rocks Push", larrikin gangs who bashed and robbed unsuspecting passers-by.

"SAVE THE ROCKS"

In the early 1970s, a decision was made to demolish large areas of The Rocks to make way for a high-rise development. Thanks to a new community consciousness about preserving our historical areas, combined with a series of campaigns run by Jack Mundey and the NSW Builders Labourers Federation, restoration replaced redevelopment and the historic Rocks survived.

Sydney's oldest public house licence for Sydney's oldest pastime is held by **The Fortune of War Hotel,** 137 George Street. Now for pub drinkers and eaters who like a flutter, there is a backroom full of TV screens, and the odds are telephoned in from the TAB. Before you blow all your dough, go upstairs for real Australian pub food (damper on weekends). The upstairs opens on to **Surgeons' Court** where the three ships surgeons who came with the First Fleet set up the first hospital in 1788. As they had no blankets and only a few past-shelf-date drugs, they made do with tarpaulins and native sarsaparilla.

If you fear one of your ancestors may have been subjected to this treatment, you can check nearby in the **NSW State Archives,** where a few dollars buys you a poster of those who made up the First Fleet, from captain to convicts, at 2 Globe Street (enter from George Street). A few doors back along George Street is the sleek and contemporary **Rockpool,** one of Sydney's best restaurants, 107 George Street.

For the **Aboriginal Arts and Tribal Art Centre,** find your way past a large red 80-year-old fire alarm, hydrant and key, safely enclosed in a glass case; upstairs there is a particularly good collection of Aboriginal art, much of which comes from Aboriginal co-operatives. Open every day, 10am-5.30pm. Level 1, 117 George Street. Nearby is the delightful **Russell Hotel** at 143a George Street, with the charming restaurant the **Boulders** at street level (particularly good for breakfast).

🐦 THE SCENE AT AND AROUND THE MCA

Just across the road is the **Museum of Contemporary Art,** one of Sydney's newest and brilliantly housed in a converted 1950s sandstone office block right at the water's edge of Circular Quay West. Excellently lit display areas on three floors house intelligently curated exhibitions and installations from the MCA's own collection, and from interstate and overseas, on various post-modern art movements, conceptual art, national themes and contemporary aboriginal art. Exhibitions change every six to ten weeks. Free guided tours by

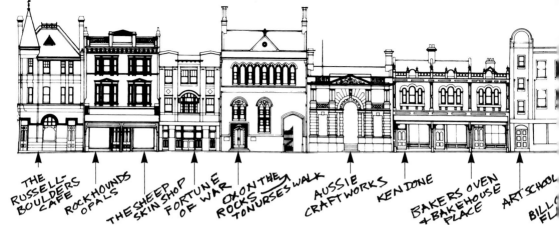

THE RUSSELL-BOULDERS CAFE · ROCKHOUNDS OPALS · THE SHEEP SKIN SHOP · FORTUNE OF WAR · OX ON THE ROCKS TO NURSES WALK · AUSSIE CRAFTWORKS · KEN DONE · BAKERS OVEN + BAKEHOUSE PLACE · ARTSCHOOL · BILLO FL

The Museum of Contemporary Art (MCA)

attendants who are all art buffs, practising artists or students. Entry fee. Open every day, 11am-6pm, 140 George Street.

The MCA has a fine indoor/outdoor **Cafe** – small and usually crowded. After a visit to the Museum, have a coffee waterside at the Cafe – there's no better way to get a grandstand view of the ferries and small craft that ply the Quay's bright waters, a kaleidoscope of blue, green, yellow and white against a background of green parks and white high-rises. Morning is the sunny time, shade after midday. Excellent coffee, imaginative snacks, adequate choice of wine/champagne, sedulous service. Open weekdays 10am-5.30pm; weekends, 9am-1pm. The **MCA Store** is a really good place to browse around for UnTouristy things to buy – you will be pleased to know that it bears no resemblance to the duty-free emporiums which litter The Rocks. Books, good craft things and some fine local jewellery are on show – we found the little Harbour Bridge brooch that appears on our cover at the MCA store.

The little stone house next to the MCA is the 1815 Cadman's Cottage – some say the oldest surviving building in Australia and now the visitors' centre for the NSW Parks and Wildlife Service. Definitely worth checking out.

Although there is a lot of tourist stuff to be avoided in the shops at The Rocks, there are also some special goodies to be found. **See detail on these in chapters 8 and 9.**

In 1980, a Sydney painter designed a simple screen-printed T-shirt that has since become a bit of an icon. **Ken Done** managed to capture the sheer joy of Sydney in that original T-shirt (12 were made to promote an exhibition of his paintings at the Holdsworth Galleries) and, during the past decade, he has gone on to spread that fresh, zesty Sydney sense of fun all over the world through his designs and paintings. Like most prophets in their own land, Done is taken for granted in Sydney. Artists aren't supposed to be rich and successful – Ken Done is both. You can still get the original T-shirt at **Done Art and Design,** 123 George Street, The Rocks, and at the **Ken Done Gallery,** 1-5 Hickson Road, you can see his pictures (and Ken in person sometimes). Or, if you can't afford the original (not Ken, the pictures), you can acquire one of his charming posters that so well depict happy, hedonistic Sydney. Sometimes things and people rise above the "tourist" categorisation, and we think Ken Done is one of them.

Around Campbell's Cove, there's the **Imperial Peking** restaurant with its good northern Chinese cuisine, **Bilson's** restaurant and the beautiful **Sydney Park Hyatt** – all with matchless views across Sydney Cove to the Opera House and beyond.

In an attempt to woo more locals into the area and to curb the touristy image of The Rocks, The Sydney Cove Authority has converted the marvellous old **Argyle Stores** building into a "shop within a shop" type of department store – called, we hope, the **Argyle Store.** At the time of going to press, the project was a still a bit vague around the edges. We will review this, among other things, in our **Events Update** service.

NOTE: For more detail on The Rocks history to the present day, call in at **The Rocks'**

ETO ES WALK / THE GREAT ROCKPOOL RESTAURANT / AKUBRA HATS OILSKINS GOOD KNITWEAR / PUB RESTAURANT / ROCKS CAFE / CHEMIST / NEWSAGENT / CAFE / POLICE STATION

Visitors and Information Centre to see its excellent graphic displays and pick up a free pamphlet for a thorough self-guided tour, 106 George Street.

CIRCULAR QUAY AREA

Semi-circular Quay, as it was originally called before the wharves "squared" it off, is a great space to check out – not just as a thoroughfare to the Opera House or The Rocks, but as a place in its own right. Its job, as Sydney's main ferry terminal, is to provide traffic access to the harbour. As if to lighten the workload, there are always plenty of buskers, busy restaurants and cafes, and a general feeling of bustling, good humour. **Rossini** right on the Quay, serves a hearty plate of pasta, a glass of wine and quite good coffee well into the early hours.

Just up from Circular Quay is **Macquarie Place Park,** off Loftus Street. There is more interest packed into this tiny park than you would have thought possible. Start with the **Obelisk**, erected in 1818 to pinpoint the centre of Sydney Town, and from which all public roads in the colony were measured. The Obelisk stands just 200m from the place where, on January 26, 1788, Captain Arthur Phillip stepped ashore to found the colony. Near the Obelisk is the vast anchor that is all that's left of one of Phillip's ships, *HMS Sirius*, which had scarcely arrived from England before she was wrecked on the rocky coast off Norfolk Island.

Next to the anchor, a drinking fountain with a cast-iron canopy admonishes you to "Keep the Pavement Dry". Should you want something stronger than water, right behind you is the **Custom House Bar** (in front of the **Renaissance Hotel**), where every fine day you can see a flotilla of blue-suited business executives from the Sydney Stock Exchange and hundreds of nearby offices and government departments exercise that inalienable Sydney-

siders' right – to stand outside and drink draught beer. Around the corner lies **Bulletin Place** where for many years Sydney's most ebullient weekly magazine saw the light of day. Now it boasts a fine oyster bar. Or have lunch for a tenner if you fancy such delights as Thai Surprise with Octopus Pizza.

The **Paragon Hotel,** 100 years old and done up in Art Nouveau style, is dedicated to the provision of ice-cold drinks and all the latest in gambling for the discerning punter. A great place for a relaxing afternoon if you've plenty of serious change in your pocket. Unfortunately, you can't stay overnight here, but there is an excellent restaurant, the **Paragon Cafe,** upstairs behind the handsome little balconies, 1 Loftus Street (just off the Circular Quay area).

🦅 🦅 SYDNEY OPERA HOUSE

It is hard for an old Sydney "insider" to look at the Opera House objectively. Not just because it is grand and all-pervasive – so is the Harbour Bridge – but because the notion of living in Sydney without it is unthinkable.

In 1973, when the Opera House was opened, many saw it as a cultural bridge, the catalyst that would fast-track Sydney in the performing arts world. Similar high expectations were held for the Harbour Bridge when it was first mooted by the great colonial architect Francis Greenway. Such a structure, he proclaimed, would *"bring magnificence, credit and glory to the colony"*. Perhaps a little overstated, but both expectations reveal the "catch-up-quick" character of a brash, shiny, new city like Sydney.

In the case of the Opera House the symbolic promise was delivered. When it opened, things seem to change – performers seemed to grow in stature within this wonderful new space. It was white, shiny, different, lauded, and it looked like a Picasso, not a Rupert Bunning. But, oh, what a spiky, painful birth.

1 **Concert Hall and Organ Loft** Home to the Sydney Symphony Orchestra and venue for a wide variety of performances by major Australian and visiting orchestras and choral societies. The white birch and brush-box wood-lined hall has great acoustics and seats 2,679. The grand organ, designed and built by Australian Ronald Sharp, is one of the largest in the world.

2 **The Opera Theatre** Seats 1547 and is home to the Australian Opera Company, now recognised as one of the leading and best-patronised opera companies in the world.

3 **Box Office Foyer** Bookings can be made and tickets collected here for all events at the Opera House. Depending on the performance, you can often get tickets at the last minute – but don't rely on it – the Opera House is a popular place. If you want to get information about forthcoming programs, the UnTourist Co has an Events Updates which gives you access to making your bookings up to twelve months ahead. See the yellow pages at the back of this book.

4 **Bennelong Restaurant** Now under the direction of the great Gay Bilson, it is undoubtedly Sydney's most spectacular restaurant. The setting, the food and the general ambience will dash all those old ideas of "the better the view, the worse the food". As you would expect, it's expensive.

5 **Playhouse** Originally designed for chamber music, then for recording, this small hall which seats 398, is now used for small-cast plays, lectures and seminars. There is always something of interest going on there.

6 **Drama Theatre** The Sydney Theatre Company and the Sydney Dance Company are the main companies using this 544 seat theatre. Incidentally, the rather low ceiling is made from "refrigerated aluminium panels" – not for the purpose of cooling down an over-excited audience, but for air-conditioning purposes.

7 **Library** The Dennis Wolanski Library of the Performing Arts contains books, libretti, scores, magazines, newspapers, programs, photographs and archival material relating to the Opera House itself.

8 **Car Concourse** You can drive in to drop-off and pick-up, but you can't park there.

9 **Northern Foyer** Kenneth Slessor wrote the poem Five Bells which inspired John Olsen's brilliant mural for the foyer with the amazing view of Sydney. It is often used for small concerts, as well as for champagne-drinking at interval.

10 **Harbour Restaurant**

We consider this to be well on the way to becoming the best fish restaurant in Sydney. Indoors and outdoors, it is open for lunch and for pre-theatre dinner.

11 **Concourse Bistro** More casual fare – Modern Australian cuisine with a Mediterranean influence. Open pre- and post-performance.

12 **Mozart Cafe** Great place to grab a bite in a hurry. Casual and imaginative food, before and after performances. It's on the same level as the box office foyer.

13 **Ice-cream Bar** Rich, wicked and wonderful ice cream and espresso.

14 **Oyster Bar** Great for a before-performance snack and one of our favourite places to eat Sydney Rock Oysters.

15 **The Car Park** Pedestrian entry and exit.

16 **The Main Gate** Check-point for entry.

17 **Car Park Entrance** Parking fee (around $16). It's wise to pay before the performance rather than after.

18 **Man-Of-War Steps** One of the great experiences of Sydney is to arrive at these steps by water-taxi to go to the Opera House. They have been in use for almost two centuries, having been put in place at the time of Governor Macquarie.

19 **Outdoor Sitting** Here are some particularly good places for sitting and taking-in the ambience of the area.

20 **Outdoor Entertainment** At the weekends in particular, you will hear some good bands and groups playing their hearts out.

Danish-born Jytte Thøgerson came to Australia in 1961 to work as a technical draftsman on Jørn Utzon's Opera House. "Jørn had a way of making you believe that wonderful dreams could come true," said Jytte, now the wife of top feature-film editor Nicholas Beauman. "It was a major excitement. We thought it was a fantastic site and we felt that the greatest building in the world was going to be created. Jørn, like the rest of us, was politically naive and we had no idea about the in-fighting going on. We all got a terrible shock when he was forced to go. But the dream did come true. He was right. What an amazing experience."

"They" (the government and bureaucrats) said that the architect Jørn Utzon had completed no drawings of the interior and that the concept was impracticable without major modifications. "He" (Jørn Utzon) said that there had been virtually no collaboration on the most vital items of the job, that he was through with it, and he didn't care if they pulled the Opera House down. He left and never saw it finished. Few may recall that Michaelangelo had an equally rough time with the Sistine Chapel. At least "they" didn't threaten to push Utzon off the scaffolding, as the Pope did to Michaelangelo!

Time, it would seem, retains the things of value and forgets the detail. The Opera House is now a special space for Sydney locals as much as it is for visitors. This icon is very much alive – the centrepiece of the performing arts in Sydney – and is itself the subject of a new opera *"The Eighth Wonder"*, by the Australian composer and lyricist team of Alan John and Dennis Watkins, which had its first performance in the Australian Opera's 1995 summer season. Venue: the Opera House.

The show on the outside of the Opera House is as good as the one going on inside – 360° of 3D action! With the city skyline and the Bridge providing the backdrop, the ferries pass to and fro to their stalls in the Quay. Meanwhile, on the proscenium, outside **The Harbour** restaurant, shiny first-nighters are promenading while the yachts glide and swoop, so close you can hear the flaps and clangs, the yells and curses. The smart subscribers are dining pre-concert at Gay Bilson's wonderful new **Bennelong** restaurant; backpackers with their picnics are lounging on the stone steps; uniformed school kids are trailing around the hip coffee-sippers at the **Concourse** restaurant, and the inevitable tourists, like a chorus of extras, are posing and clicking around the scene. It is all part of the great Sydney Opera House show.

For a small fee you can take a tour of the Opera House; it takes about 60 minutes and runs continuously 9am-4pm every day, except Christmas Day and Good Friday. The Enquiry Office, which is near the box office, has hand-outs on all the details and specifications of the building.

Uptown

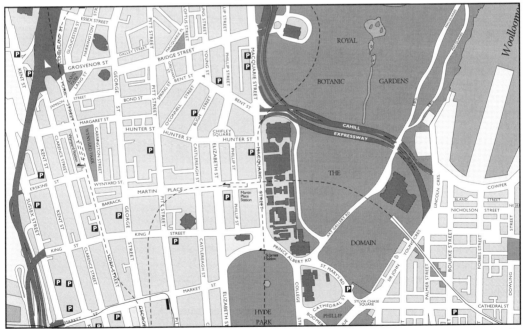

INCLUDES: *Posh old Macquarie Street, starting at the Conservatorium of Music; Library of NSW; Parliament House; Sydney Hospital; the Mint Museum; Hyde Park Barracks Museum; Queens Square; the Law Courts and St James Church; the Art Gallery of New South Wales; in and around the Domain; Mrs Macquarie's Chair and the Royal Botanic Gardens; Museum of Sydney; Martin Place... then to David Jones, Gowings and Uptown shopping.*

UPTOWN

On the edge of the Royal Botanic Gardens, just up from Utzon's House, the discordant overlay of scales will announce the **Conservatorium of Music**.

Another Francis Greenway building, it was designed (incredibly) as the Governor's stables and Offices for Lachlan Macquarie and built 1816-1819. Castellated brick, octagonal towers. Impressive. The building became the NSW Conservatorium of Music in 1913, but is now the Sydney Conservatorium, since it became part of the Univ-ersity of Sydney a few years ago. The concert hall is named for the first director, Belgian Henri Verbugghen, and that's where you get your free lunchtime concerts, on Wednesdays or, for a small ticket price, Fridays, plus twilight concerts – but check first because the days and programs vary. Open every day, 9am-5pm.

The inviting, airy **State Library of NSW** is on Macquarie Street at the top of Hunter. The 11-storey building is (naturally) a treasure-trove for readers, but it's a lot more than that. The building, completed only in 1988, is connected to the "old" State Library, housing the Mitchell and Dixson Wings. In the complex, you can see (free) old and new films in the splendid Metcalf Auditorium, and lunch or dine at the **Glasshouse Cafeteria.** There's a dandy bookshop, of course, where among other delights you'll find some of Sydney's best books about itself. Open Mon-Fri, 9am-9pm; Sat, 9am-5pm; Sun, 2pm-6pm. Closed major public holidays.

State Parliament House (next to the Library), seat of NSW Government since 1829, was once the northern wing of the "Rum Hospital", replaced now by Sydney Hospital. There's an especially eccentric plaque on the footpath outside. It says: "Proposed Parliament Buildings. The advent of Responsible Government in 1856 saw the first of three never-to-be-built schemes. For the 1888 centenary, *A FOUNDATION STONE ONLY WAS LAID* (italics ours)". Anyway, the present building is real enough, and worth a visit, especially when the House is sitting... or standing and shouting. Mon-Fri, 9am-1pm, 2pm-4.30 pm. Gallery seat bookings necessary when Parliament is in session.

For telephone numbers and addresses, see the yellow pages Directory at the back

Next door is **Sydney Hospital,** which seems always to be undergoing renovations. It was originally the central block of the Rum Hospital, so-called because rum was the favourite tipple of the early colonists, and also used as currency. In 1810, Governor Macquarie gave three locals the rum monopoly provided they built him a "splendid hospital". This they did, promptly.

The present sandstone Sydney Hospital was completed in 1894 by architect Thomas Rowe to replace the Rum Hospital, demolished in 1879. The plaque outside the hospital has this quaint dedication:

"Victoria, by the Grace of God, of the United Kingdom of Great Britain and Ireland, Queen, Defender of the Faith and so forth...."

Sydney Mint Museum

Still on Macquarie Street, one is treated to the treasures of the **Mint Museum,** housed in one of the oldest surviving buildings in Australia. It was established as a mint during the Gold Rush in 1851, and for 70 years or so, millions of ounces of raw gold were processed into currency and bullion. There's a dazzling gold-leaf curtain at the museum's shop, and visitors can mint sovereigns and try their hand at safe-cracking. Pleasant lunch facilities are available, indoors or in the courtyard. Open every day, 10am-5pm, except Wed, 12 noon-5pm. Entry fee. Queens Square, Macquarie Street.

Next door to the Mint is the **Hyde Park Barracks Museum.** This splendid building was designed in 1819 by Francis Greenway to accommodate fellow convicts. It was later used to house single female migrants. Visitors can arrange to sleep overnight in the reconstructed hammocks in The Barracks – but be warned, there is a longer waiting time than probably for any other accommodation in Sydney. You've quite a choice: simply stay overnight with a "mean" convict breakfast; stay overnight and sail away for a cruise on the vintage sailing ship, *Solway Lass;* OR, be "tried" at the **Justice and Police Museum** nearby (see below) and "transported on the *Solway Lass* and condemned to swing in a hammock overnight". A licensed cafe in Barracks Square is open Mon-Sun, 10am-5pm, light meals inside or outside. Museum admission free, hours Mon-Fri, 10am-5pm. Tues open 12pm-5pm.

In Queens Square at King Street is **St James Church,** Sydney's oldest church, built in 1822, and another of convict architect Francis Greenway's triumphs. This lovely church is overshadowed, but not overwhelmed by the nearby **Law Courts** building. It is a superb example of the colonial Georgian style, and its tall spire was a landmark for ships on Sydney Harbour. St James is often the venue for superb chamber music. Open Mon to Fri, 8am-5pm, Sat, 8am-6pm, Sun, 8am-4pm. Choral Eucharist every Sunday. You can hear wonderful music from the likes of the Sydney Symphony Orchestra, different choral groups and varying soloists. These are on an irregular basis, mostly on weekends, so telephone for times.

On Elizabeth and King Streets, the **Supreme Court,** was begun in 1820 and first used in 1828. It's another Greenway design, but there have been many changes and not much of his original building remains. The 14th floor cafeteria is open to the public on weekdays, and offers wonderful views over the city to Hyde Park and Woolloomooloo. The ground floor offers wonderful views, too, of bewigged barristers - male and female – on their way to serve justice. The courts are open to visitors Mon-Fri, 10am-4pm when they are sitting. Closed for lunch (except for the cafeteria) 1 pm-2 pm. Breakfast in the cafeteria 7am-9am; lunch 12pm-2pm and snacks 3pm-3.30pm.

The **Art Gallery of NSW** in the Domain is a constant joy any season, any year, with superb, stylish exhibitions. Established in 1874, the Gallery houses one of the finest collections of art in Australia, including European art from the Renaissance to the present, as well as Asian art from China, Japan, Korea and Southeast Asia. Aboriginal art includes examples of aboriginal culture through Western Dot paintings, Tiwi poles and the works of urban Aborigines. Special exhibitions are held frequently. Entry free, except for special temporary exhibitions. Open daily, 10 am to 5pm, closed Christmas Day, Good Friday, Art Gallery Road.

The restaurant in the Gallery is extremely pretty, a good spot to rest tired feet and contemplate gems bought from the fine library of reproductions, souvenir programs, catalogues.

🦜 ROYAL BOTANIC GARDENS

Around the **Art Gallery** are the **Royal Botanic Gardens** and the **Domain.** There are many entrances to the 30ha Royal Botanic Gardens with its wonderful picnic spots (some by the harbour). With help from the obliging people at the visitor centre (off Mrs Macquarie's Road entrance), you'll have all the information

Royal Botanic Gardens area, 1874

needed to enjoy the Gardens to the full. There are free guided walks Monday and Friday. Open daily 6.30am to sunset. The main entrance is the Woolloomooloo Gate on Mrs Macquarie's Road.

Hidden in one of the prettiest parts of the gardens, the charming **Botanic Gardens Restaurant** gives the impression of being suspended in a large pigeon loft over the fig trees at the bend in the creek. You can enter from Mrs Macquarie's Road and ask at the visitors centre, or approach from the back of the Conservatorium and walk through to the restaurant. Open daily for lunch only. At time of going to press, it was being run by one of Australia's finest chefs, Lew Kathreptis.

At the entrance to the Botanic Gardens across from the Mitchell Library, is this unforgettable memorial plaque: *Erected by the members of the desert mounted corps and friends to the gallant horses who carried them over the Sinai Desert into Palestine, 1914-1918. They suffered wounds, thirst, hunger and weariness almost beyond endurance, but never failed. They did not come home. We will never forget them. TO THE HORSES OF THE DESERT MOUNTED CORPS.*

Next to the Gardens, is a wide, free and wonderful "Common" for all, and has been since 1810. **The Domain** is used by office workers for hockey and football and netball games at lunchtime. Plenty of joggers there, too, using the well-marked fitness track.

One should try to visit the Domain on Sunday. That's when everyone with a cause appears at "Speakers' Corner" (like London's Hyde Park), and there's hardly a subject someone doesn't feel strongly and vocal about. Since 1820, cricket matches have been played regularly in the Domain.

One of the loveliest views of Sydney Harbour is from **Mrs Macquarie's Chair.** It is at the end of HER road, running down from the Art Gallery by the Domain. The Governor had the road built to a point where a sandstone rock ledge was carved as a seat for Mrs Macquarie. Today, we can all sit there, just like gentry. The Chair was completed in 1816, and we now have the bonus of the Opera House and the Sydney Harbour Bridge in our view.

On the corner of Phillip and Bridge Streets is the **Museum of Sydney,** opened in May, 1995 on the site of the first Government House. It is about yesterday's Sydney brought to life in today's technology. The three-storey building captures the visitor in dazzling ways: films, computer displays, paintings, documents, artefacts, diaries, talking trips through history. The displays include sketches from the National History Museum, London. It starts in the piazza, where a forest of "talking poles" symbolises the early encounters of Aborigines and Europeans, each guardedly watching the other. Inside, one looks down into a "display hole" with its wall of foundation bricks from the original Government House. The Museum of Sydney vividly portrays the dreams, fears and aspirations of the cultures who met here, and is an invaluable addition to the pleasures of Uptown Sydney. Sounds touristy? It's great. Call for information about regular events at the Museum. Entry fee. Open every day, 10am-5pm.

"Enter," says the brochure of the **Justice and Police Museum,** "the World of Police, Law, and Crime." Who could resist? Among other adventures, one can see bushranger Captain Moonlight's death mask, view mug shots of Sydney's early criminals (and their weapons), visit a 19th Century police station and participate in mock trials. It's realism itself, and although it won't frighten the horses, it will give one a bit of a chill. Entry fee. Sun 10am-5pm; Sun-Thurs in January (during Festival of Sydney.) Open for booked groups, Mon to Fri, Corner Phillip and Albert Streets.

In **Martin Place** (between George and Macquarie Streets) is the **Sydney Information Centre** (closed weekends!) near Castlereagh Street. In the same kiosk is **Halftix,** where you can pick up last-minute theatre tickets at half price – cash only, on the day of performance. One of the two **Dendy** "art house" movie theatres is in Martin Place. (The other is in George Street, past Town Hall.) And of course, there's the golf driving range, near the corner of Martin Place and Pitt Street. Strange as it may seem, this is true, and it's very popular too.

Trailblazers John and Merivale Hemmes opened their cleverly named **Hotel CBD** in the city. They converted a grand old bank building into a classic city club, though only a small part of it is for private membership. On the lower floor is a bar which, on Friday evenings, spills out onto the pavement with the young and upwardly mobile in mating mode. On the first floor, a restaurant, and on the floor above, a pool and games bar; on the floor above that, a club. If you've an insider friend who's a member, it's a great place to meet, or if you're going to the restaurant, club manager and fine jazz and blues singer, Brooke Tabberer, might invite you in if it's not too busy. Corner King and York Streets.

We spend a fair bit of time on Uptown shopping in chapter 8. However, a quick rundown: **David Jones,** the 1927 draper with "the silky service", menswear and food in the Market Street store and women's and children's fashion in the Elizabeth Street store); **Gowings** (men and boys forever have "Gone to Gowings") looks pretty boring from the outside but it is fast reaching cult status in Sydney, corner Market and George Streets; and the **Strand Arcade**, 412 George Street, with a myriad of fabulous Sydneyesque shops.

Downtown

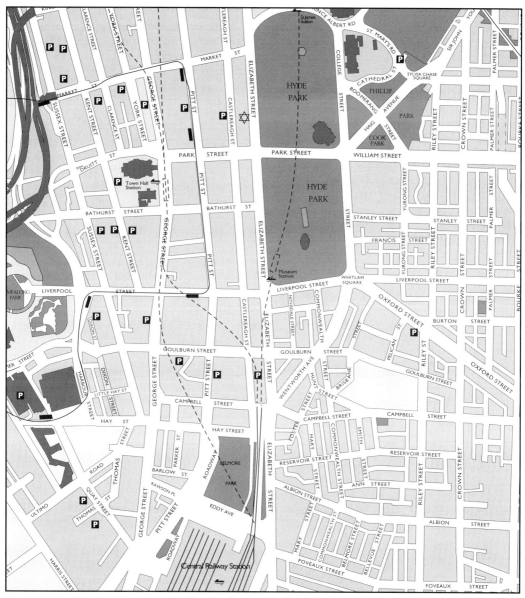

INCLUDES: St Mary's Cathedral; St Andrew's Cathedral; The Great Synagogue (Downtown is nothing if not ecumenical); the Capitol Theatre; Hyde Park; the Australian Museum; the Town Hall; the "Mr Eternity" plaque in Sydney Square; the Queen Victoria Building; and the cinema centre.

You've hardly left Uptown Sydney when you're Downtown, the area between Market Street and Central Railway.

St Mary's Cathedral's glorious stained-glass windows tell you its history, from the laying of the foundation stone by Governor Macquarie in 1821 through to the present day. St Mary's was destroyed by fire in 1865, and in its present form was opened in September 1928. A comprehensive brochure guides you through, with floor plan and descriptions of the windows, as well as data about the crypt, the choir, and the Catholic Returned Soldiers and Sailors Memorial. The brochure also notes that the planned spires have yet to be completed. College Street and Hyde Park.

A favourite place for a lunchtime break for office-workers is **Hyde Park** itself, which starts at the city end of Macquarie Street and runs through to Liverpool Street. At the Macquarie Street end is the highly ornate **Archibald Fountain,** given to the city by J F Archibald, one of the founders of *The Bulletin* magazine. And a particular UnTourist delight – the possums, more winsome than the ubiquitous pigeons and ibises. They come around the fountain area almost every day, especially near dusk. The Parks and Wildlife people suggest you don't feed them, and we implore you not to pat – they have a nasty love bite. Incidentally, here's another plaque: it's on the statue dedicated to Captain Cook, in Hyde Park. It reads, in part:

> "This plaque marks the site of a previous plaque which disappeared in November, 1991."

Some people will lift anything. Watch this space.

The clean and simple **Anzac Memorial** towering near the Elizabeth Street end of the Park is a revered building housing memorabilia of deeds of war. It was built for Australians to remember servicemen and women who died for their country and is well worth a quiet visit.

A magnificent building, the **Great Synagogue** is the Mother Congregation of Australian Jewry. It's in Elizabeth Street, facing Hyde Park, but it's so cleverly concealed among commercial buildings that it's hard to pick. The Great Synagogue's history goes back to convict days, when a handful of Jews arrived in the First Fleet. This edifice was designed by eminent non-Jewish architect Thomas Rowe, and was consecrated in 1878. Its Byzantine style, with Gothic touches, features a fine wrought-iron gate, the design of which is reflected in the stunning "wheel window" lighting the interior. In fact, the windows are all brilliant, with tens of thousands of "stars" shining from the ceiling. Worth a visit for many reasons. Conducted tours Tuesday and Thursday at noon include video and spectacular lighting effects. Closed religious and public holidays. Call for group bookings; otherwise, just bowl along on open days at midday. Entrance, 166 Castlereagh Street.

The **Australian Museum** is much more than dinosaurs, we're happy to report, although it does have Australia's largest natural history collection. It's a huge building, on five levels, where you'll see everything you could want to know about science today, as well as changing gem exhibitions, mining displays and many special exhibitions. Visitors will happily discover worlds they didn't know existed. One should be prepared to take a break occasionally, because the Museum seems to go on forever. And one wishes it would. Open every day except Christmas, 9.30am-5pm. Highlight tours daily at 11am, noon and 2pm. Some charges for special events, 6 College Street, corner of William Street.

The **Sydney Town Hall** is very large and very eccentric, and, like so many buildings of the mid-1800s, is of Italian Renaissance/Victorian/Disney style (we loved it then) in Pyrmont standstone. The foundation stone was laid in 1868, and the building completed in 1889. The sound of the clock, installed in 1884, is familiar to Sydneysiders. Every quarter of an hour, as the clock strikes, you see them checking their watches. Some of the world's finest performers have thrilled audiences in the wood-lined Centennial Hall, one of the grandest Victorian halls in Australia and a great favourite for musicians because of its fine acoustics. *"When you spike that thick wooden floor with your bass and draw the first note, it's like playing inside a violin,"* lyricised Brett Berthold, principal double-bass of the Australian Opera and Ballet Orchestra.

The great organ was built in London, its 8000 pipes shipped to Australia in 1890. At that time, it was the largest organ in the world. We're unsure just where it stands now, but it's certainly big... and grand. Oh yes, there are also City Council meetings in the first-floor chamber. Here the Lord Mayor presides "in full view of the public gallery". Bonus: Town Hall has a comfy, quiet, little brasserie on the ground floor – a good find in this area which doesn't have many. Enjoy. Corner George and Druitt Streets.

ETERNITY

It is not a towering edifice one sees from a distance – it's a small aluminium plaque by the waterfall on the lower level of Sydney Square (also known as Town Hall Square). It reads simply "Eternity" in the copperplate familiar to long-time Sydney dwellers. "Mr Eternity" was Sydney character Arthur Stace, a reformed alcoholic, who wrote the word "Eternity" more than half a million times on the footpaths of Sydney. When at his depths as a metho drinker

and cockatoo for minor criminals and gam-blers, he was inspired by a Baptist preacher in Darlinghurst, and began his mission of spreading the word "Eternity" throughout the city in yellow-crayoned, near-perfect copperplate. He performed his task at dawn for more than 30 years, but was rarely seen at his dedicated work. A touching memorial, this.

Sydney's great church architect, Edmund Blacket deserves most of the credit for the design of the handsome sandstone **St Andrew's Cathedral.** He is responsible for the twin west towers, built to a Gothic design, and the hammer-beam roof, the Bishop's throne and much of the interior. The foundation stone was laid by Governor Macquarie in 1819, a little way along George Street, well before the cathedral was built on the present site. (Lachlan Macquarie never knew an idle moment.) Construction on this site was completed in 1837, and the Cathedral consecrated on St Andrew's Day in 1868. Not surprisingly, it's classified by the National Trust. It's beautiful, inside and out. Free guided tours weekdays, 11am and 1.45pm are except for Thursday, 1.45pm only. There are Thursday lunchtime organ recitals between 1.15pm and 1.45pm on the 1866-built organ. Visitors are most welcome, as you can imagine. Sydney Square, corner of George and Bathurst Street.

First "completed" in 1898, **The Queen Victoria Building (QVB)** replaced the earlier Sydney markets. Covering a whole block between George, Market, York and Druitt Streets, it is a deadringer for the Crystal Palace in the Botanic Gardens which burned to the ground in 1888. It's also reminiscent of GUM, the "used-to-be-grand" but now awful department store complex in Moscow. The QVB project was a real job-creator. At the time, Sydney was in a recession, and the site's Byzantine architecture provided employment to many out-of-work craftsmen, stonemasons, plasterers and stained-glass window artists. It housed a concert hall, coffee palaces, office showrooms, and a variety of service-industry tenants. Later, the City Library was located there and, later still, the Sydney City Council. It was threatened with demolition in 1959 when most of the good things in Sydney were under such a threat. Pierre Cardin is often quoted as calling it "the most beautiful shopping centre in the world".

The restoration you see today was begun in 1984, the tender won by the Malaysian company Ipoh Garden, after a lack of Australian interest in the project. This welcome and unusual company was also responsible for the refurbishment of the old/new Capitol Theatre just down the road. Both buildings have remained the property of the Sydney City Council. The QVB is open seven days a week and contains some good local fashion on both the ground and the first floor. The **ABC Shop** on the first floor is also great. Here you can find books, videos and music that are just a bit different – particularly Australian stuff. As you get higher up, you find yourself immersed in tourist land. If you go right down to the lower ground floor, you are smack-bang into a somewhat pedestrian area. So stick to the middle ground.

"The Capitol – Australia's Greatest Theatre! Staggering in its immensity! Enthralling in its beauty! Astonishing in its entertainment!" Wow! In 1928 hyperbole was the order of the day. *"Imagine yourself seated in a beautiful old world Florentine garden; above the blue Mediterranean sky, stars twinkle."* And twinkle they do, in the $35 million resurrection of the 2000-seat, 100-year-old **Capitol Theatre** (the building has been around, pre-theatre, since 1893).

The new/old Capitol fills the need for a large lyric theatre in Sydney, and those involved with the meticulous restoration and extensions were able to utilise the original 1200 drawings and notes of John Eberson who designed the "atmospheric cinema". An atmospheric cinema or theatre, just in case you didn't know, was one that *"captured an outdoor courtyard or amphitheatre experience under a brilliant sky, including themes from Egypt, the Mediterranean and equatorial Asia".* (There's a modern one in Munich decked out like a motor car with the screen being the windscreen, etc). At any rate, the new/old Capitol is terrific, and now Sydney has a viable and fitting place to hold the 45th revival of *Oklahoma* or the Australian version of *Les Missaigon.*

The neighbourhood surrounding the Capitol is an international feast of plenty: the theatre is directly opposite **Kampung Malaysian, Wing Hing Barbecue** and **Wai Wong BBQ & Butcher.** At the back is the wonderful Czechoslavakian **Cyril's** delicatessen and the nomadic **Roma Cafe**, which has finally found a permanent home for its luscious goodies – both of these establishments have been a tradition with Sydney foodies for 40 years. The Capitol Theatre is on the eastern boundary of Chinatown, Campbell Street, near George.

Like the Capitol Theatre, **Paddy's Market** is on the fringe of Chinatown. These markets operate Saturdays and Sundays and are located in Haymarket, between Hay, Ultimo and Quay Streets. In the 1800s, they were the main markets in Sydney but now, like many markets, one comes across a whole lot of junk there. Still, there's some great stuff – particularly the fresh food.

The last stop downtown (before it becomes the Inner West) is Australia's first university, the **University of Sydney.** Built on rising ground to the south of the city, with its main quadrangle in the neo-Gothic style, the university is host to more than 30,000 students over numerous scattered campuses. An interesting place to visit (more in chapter 10).

The grand old Capitol Theatre which opened in 1928, was fully restored in 1995

In and around Darling Harbour

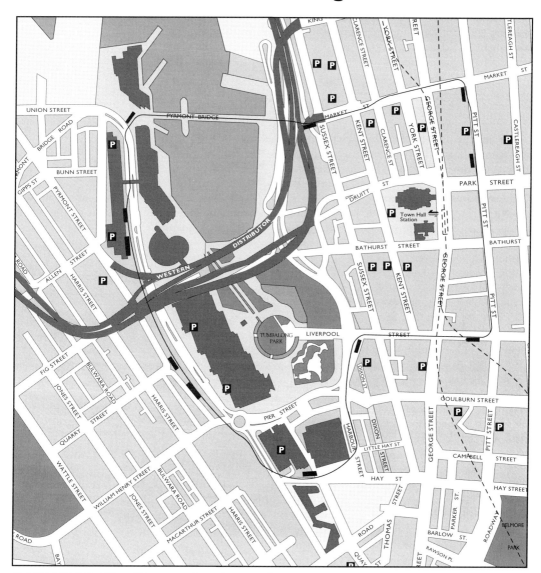

INCLUDES: The Chinese Gardens; Chinatown; Darling Harbour; The Aquarium; Maritime Museum; Powerhouse Museum.

🦅 CHINATOWN

Sydney's original **Chinatown** was in The Rocks area, and a sinful little spot it was. As Chinese merchants and traders became more affluent, they moved out to more salubrious areas such as Rose Bay and Carlingford, where they grew their vegies and imported other goods (among other things, they made a killing on bananas from Fiji). By 1880, the old Chinatown in The Rocks had all but gone, except for a few Pak-ah-poo shops and opium dens, having re-established down the southern end of the city, closer to the central markets (Haymarket), which started not far from where the Queen Victoria Building stands now. (Incidentally, one Quong Tart, who came to be a well-respected businessman within the Sydney community, eventually ran a tea-room in the pre-refurbished Queen Victoria building until, tragically, he was bashed and died. His spirit is still said to be lurking about there.) Gradually the Chinese commercial traders moved into Haymarket and stayed there.

Most big western cities have their Chinatown, and Sydney's is said to be among the best, with its restaurants, takeaways, produce stores, craft fashions, and furniture shops all doing a bustling trade night and day. Most of our early Chinese immigrants came from Guangdong province, and the cuisine is mostly Cantonese. If anything, Sydney's Chinatown is more typically "overseas" Chinese, rather than authentically representative of mainland China.

Our insider friend for Chinatown is businesswoman Hong Li, now an Australian but originally from Peking. We became friends at our favourite Chinatown restaurant, the **Chinese Noodle Restaurant** – or, in Chinese, the **Xibei** (literally, "west north"). Hong brings clients from Peking here when they are feeling homesick for their own cuisine. The restaurant is tiny, always busy and the moment you enter it you are in China – a pot of tea arrives on the table the instant you sit down and no one (not even the waiters) speaks much English.

When he has finished making his noodles (you can watch through the glass to the kitchen), Xiao Tang Qin will entertain you by playing both Chinese and Western music on his *er-he*, the two-string Chinese instrument.

The official address of the Chinese Noodle Restaurant is LG7, 8 Quay Street, Haymarket. However, this won't do you any good, because no one speaks English and you can't find this address as it's far too complicated. The best way to get there is from Thomas Street (left-hand side heading toward Hay Street). About halfway down, you pass the **Burlington Supermarket** (excellent for every kind of Chinese food imaginable); then comes the **Prince Gallery,** an arcade of shops where the restaurant can be found to the left of the escalator, on the ground floor.

Foodie Hong Li also recommends **Super Bowl,** 41 Dixon Street (a mall rather than a street), a popular place with older Chinese, that's also a good restaurant to visit late at night for a snack (it stays open until 2am). Hong

suggests the *congee* (a soup made from rice) with seafood or other meat choices. Hong takes her friends for *yum cha* to **Silver Spring.** There is nearly always a queue, and when you arrive you will be given a numbered slip until there is a space available. It's worth being patient because the food is fabulous and there is plenty of variety. On the edge of the ongoing expansion of the Chinatown area, Silver Spring is on the 1st Floor, Sydney Central Complex, cnr Hay and Pitt Streets. A vegetarian, Hong Li is enthusiastic about **Mother Chu's Vegetarian Kitchen** where the food also tends to lean more toward the northern style, 367 Pitt Street.

And if you are not feeling well, or if you want to continue in good health, Hong recommends a visit to Dongsen Li, a traditional Chinese

Xiao Tang Qin playing his er-he

herbalist and acupuncturist. He was trained in China and his family have been doctors for several generations. He is also academic adviser to the Sydney College of Traditional Chinese Medicine. You'll find Dongsen Li at the **Pacific Herbal Clinic,** a shopfront with traditional Chinese herbs and medicines in jars and drawers available over the counter. Shop 3, 37 Ultimo Road, Haymarket.

The SMH Good Food Guide has regularly chosen the **Golden Century** seafood restaurant as the best Chinese restaurant in Sydney – we like it too. Classic Cantonese, it specialises in fresh (that means alive) seafood at 393-399 Sussex Street, Haymarket.

DARLING HARBOUR

The back door to Sydney – 1874

In the 19th Century, **Darling Harbour** was called "the back-door" to Sydney because it had easy access to the centre of the city and it was where all the serious trading took place. It was the tradesman's entrance. Since an estimated $1.8 billion was spent to fast-track it into "a place for the people" for the Bicentennial, there has not been much sign of serious trading in Darling Harbour and access is far from easy. It is considered by the locals to be "a place for the tourists". There are periodic bleatings about Darling Harbour – the cost, the lack of trading. This will no doubt continue until the place becomes less touristy and more real and until the powers-that-be stop adding more tourist attractions, get more people to live there, and add a proper transport terminal on the city side.

Until then, to get to Darling Harbour you can walk down from Town Hall and cross over Pyrmont Bridge, an extension of Market Street. However it is easy to get lost, so we suggest the best way is to take the Monorail from midtown or catch a ferry from Circular Quay. For drivers, Darling Harbour has the best and roomiest parking anywhere in the city area. It's well signposted, well-lit and not too expensive.

Darling Harbour contains a great **Maritime Museum** and **Aquarium**, a hugely successful **Exhibition and Conference Centre**, the charming **Chinese Gardens** and some terrific boat shows, both official and unofficial. It's a nice place to just mooch around and watch the goings-on – mime artists, jugglers, clowns – all that pleasant "festival market" stuff.

Darling Harbour will blossom when it is given a real job, the job our early citizens gave it – that is, being the back-door to Sydney. After all, it is a strong Aussie tradition to invite favoured visitors through the back-door.

The **Chinese Gardens** were a gift to Sydneysiders from the people of China. A small admission charge buys you a delightful stroll among the exotic shrubs, winding paths and mini-pagodas, to the sound of waterfalls and tinkling wind chimes. Harbour and Pier Streets.

SYDNEY AQUARIUM

First, the no-nos. No set feeding times, no performing animals, no need to fret about dolphin nervous breakdowns and seal jitters. There are 5000 creatures there, representing 350 species of fish, marine mammals, molluscs, shellfish, sharks, rays, inter-tidal plants and animals – the list goes on and on in what the proud owners assert is *"the world's most spectacular Aquarium"*. There are three massive floating oceanariums for marine mammals, Sydney Harbour species, and the Open Ocean. You take moving walkways through acrylic tunnels under the harbour aquarium for a scuba diver's view of the wide variety of harbour habitats – wharf piles, seagrass beds, kelp

Aquarium finger-food service

forests, rock reefs, sandy flats and open waters. Australia's marine and freshwater habitats range from full tropical to Antarctic, so 50 tanks is none too many. You'll find displays of fish of the Far North, the Great Barrier Reef, the Murray-

Darling river system, and animals and plants from mangroves and rocky shores. There are also five aquariums with hands-on viewing controls through microscopes, and a touch pool, together with two (definitely *not touch* pool) crocodile displays.

Sydney Aquarium is committed to providing sanctuary to all seals injured or abandoned along the NSW coast. They are rehabilitated, then released into the wild (the Seal Sanctuary closes at sunset). The marine mammal pool is large enough for dolphins and small whales, too, should the need arise. The complex is provided with 11 soundtracks of natural sounds, and almost three-million litres of water in the two oceanariums are filtered every hour and a half for maximum clarity and purity. Entry fee. Open every day, 9.30am-9pm, Aquarium Pier.

The **Darling Harbour Olympic Showcase** is open all Darling Harbour hours. The old Manly ferry **South Steyne**, her brass and luxurious woodwork gleaming, her red carpet rolled out, hosts this upbeat display of audiovisual bragging about the forthcoming Sydney Olympics. There are some exciting sporting videos, some good-looking multi-lingual charmers to respond to your enquiries about Year 2000. Further ahead around the Harbour rise the graceful white

hangers and columns of Philip Cox and Partners' spectacular ship-like **Convention and Exhibition Centre**, usually host to some interesting goings-on, though these may not always be open to the public.

THE NATIONAL MARITIME MUSEUM

Where else in Australia, the island continent, could it be but around the bay from where the First Fleet came ashore in 1788? On the northwestern corner of Darling Harbour, abutting the old working-class suburb of Pyrmont, this huge site, complete with light-house, is best accessed by a walk across Pyrmont Bridge from the city, or by the monorail if you want a high-angle view. *"Our approach"*, wrote AMM Director Dr Kevin Fewster, *"has been to tell the stories of people – sailors and explorers, colonists and migrants, waterside and fisheries workers and people using the sea for their recreation."*

The ships, though, are the eye-grabbers, whether moored at the quay like *HMAS Vampire*, the ex-RAN Darling Class destroyer, with former naval persons to guide visitors, or kept indoors to save them from further weathering, like America's Cup victor *Australia II*, fully-rigged but now revealing her secret weapon, the famous winged keel. A more

Akarana, *The Maritime Museum's oldest vessel, built in 1888*

"Visit to the Antipodes"
1846
Travel accounts became best-sellers of their day, as education spread literacy among the population.

poignant sight is the little *Tu Do*, which brought 33 Vietnamese refugees on a perilous voyage through shark-infested waters to Darwin in 1977.

At opposite ends of the technological scale are a Westland Wessex Mk 31B former Naval helicopter and a Kaiadilt raft and paddles of mangrove wood, hibiscus bark and twine from the Mornington Peninsula. These vessels are just five of the Museum's 12,000 registered acquisitions, which include an astounding array of personal items, such as the kit of a 15-year-old cadet from the training ship *Tingira*, a World War II service-issue condom tin, and the death mask of a 19th-Century naval commodore. Entry fee. Open every day (except Christmas Day), 10am-5pm.

Before you leave things maritime, you might care for a hands-on sailing lesson with **Sydney by Sail**, setting out from the Maritime Museum. Sessions are under the guidance of Australian Yachting Federation instructors, headed by Matt Hayes. All lessons are good value – the introductory course of 90 minutes particularly so.

The glasshouse **Harbourside** building is a lively and multifarious shopping mall liberally laced with eateries and drinkeries offering everything from carveries, vegetarian thingos, seafood crepes and falafels. As this sort of feedbag food goes, it is fine – in fact, it is quite good. As so often happens in areas that attract a lot of visitors, people get a bit careless and, as a result, the main restaurants are really not good examples of the best of Sydney eating. What is truly great eating in Darling Harbour, however, is a **Fruit Frenzy** in the **South Pole** ice-cream shop at the main entrance. Here they whip up wonders with chilled fresh raspberries, banana, passionfruit, strawberries, kiwifruit or rhubarb – all mashed into ice-cream or whipped yogurt (your choice) in a waffle cone. One of the world's great cheap thrills.

THE POWERHOUSE MUSEUM

Ken Done, graffittist, at work on the walls of the Powerhouse Cafe

A stroll from Darling Harbour is the wonderful **Powerhouse Museum** with its host of things to see and do. In the decorative arts gallery, you can design your own historic gown or tea pot on touch-screen computers. In other parts of the museum, try shearing a sheep, test your body's electricity or brew your own beer on computer. You can see the largest suspended

How to get to the Powerhouse from Darling Harbour

aircraft in the Southern Hemisphere (a Catalina flying boat). Visitors also get to explore the world of cinema in the 1930s, or see what changes in style we have experienced over 300 years. Exhibitions are many, varied and changing and practically every aspect of the development of society in Australia is covered. Walk there from the southwest corner of Darling Harbour, or take the Monorail to Haymarket station, Tramway, Sydney. Discount car parking all day if you bring your ticket to the Museum for validation. Entry fee. Open every day (except Christmas Day), 10am-5pm, 500 Harris Street, Ultimo.

Poster in Kings Cinema, 1930's

Bondi in Winter

3 EAST

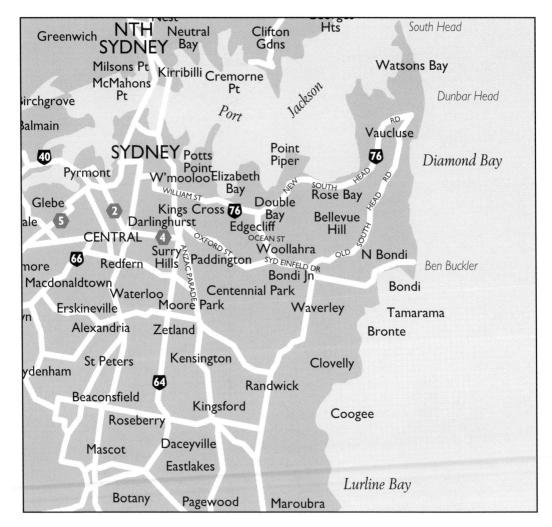

The high life and low life of Sydney

In the beginning, as the new settlement struggled to life...

"...the boat crews found a place where fresh water ran into an anchorage down a gentle declivity in the bush in a small snug cove on the southern side. A stone bridge was built over it, forming a rough boundary between the more disreputable quarters on the west side and the more respectable establishments on the east side."

Captain Watkin Tench, February 1788 – about the Tank Stream water supply.

And so, to this day, in some quarters, the same sentiment about east and west of the city still prevails.

"....All the nice people live in the East, darling"

Double Bay dowager, March 1995

The Eastern suburbs of Sydney contain more good places to stay and more good places to eat than any other area of Sydney – regardless of budget. However, in order to get to the nice suburbs you have to travel through some of the more disreputable ones closer to the city. It's all part of the high-life and the low-life of Sydney's East.

To enter the portals of the East, you have a choice of two rather infamous streets. **Oxford Street** – considered by the brave constabulary to be one of the toughest beats in Australia – runs from downtown Wentworth Avenue through to Paddington and Bondi, leaving a trail of 70 pubs, pick-up clubs and dives in its wake. By Paddington, however, Oxford Street has shuffled off most of the grunge and, by the time it reaches Bondi Junction, it is downright respectable.

The other entry to the East is via **William Street,** famous for its hire-cars and hire-girls. It takes you straight to the flashing neon heart of wicked Kings Cross, where it gives way to Darlinghurst Road and New South Head Road and leads to the wealthier suburbs of Double Bay and Vaucluse.

KINGS CROSS

Kings Cross used to be quite a genteel place in the Victorian era – fine carriages with the horses slipping down the steep slope of William Street on cobbles, headed into town. With its gracious houses, even a theatre, it was considered an attractive, middle-class family suburb. Parts of it are still tree-lined and charming (though not really family). The northern end of **Victoria Street** is delightful, with its flame trees and fine old houses, some of which have been converted into small hotels and excellent restaurants. For this legacy of the past, we can thank a group of tough unionists led by Jack Mundey. In order to protect the area from developers, who planned to demolish the old buildings in the name of "progress" in the 1970s, they conducted a determined campaign which at times was on the fringe of violence. Local residents applauded and assisted the unionists in their now-celebrated Green Bans.

If you were seeking to identify one area having both the very worst and the very best of Sydney, you would probably settle on **Kings Cross**. Here, you will find a complete patchwork of demographics. There are the dignified dowagers from **Potts Point** trying to ignore the drunks and addicts who have passed out by the **El Alamein** fountain in Fitzroy Gardens; there is a sideshow of prostitutes on their beats at the hire-car end of William Street; there are gawking backpackers (the Cross is Sydney's backpacker centre); there are the sleazy middlemen operating around the many bars and "Adult Shows" (a local euphemism for sex shops); the cappuccino journalists at **Bar Coluzzi;** a tableau of disoriented Aborigines up from the 'Loo (Woolloomooloo), the area that straddles the inner harbour at the fringe of the Cross. Occasionally you even see small children, although this is rare – the Cross is not for kiddies.

Tucked into Hughes Street is **The Wayside Chapel,** "the biggest little church in the world". In every city in the world, you find these pockets of goodness, and this is Sydney's. Visitors to all the activities of the Wayside Chapel are very welcome and any contributions are gratefully accepted. Somehow it seems appropriate that, at the time when one is travelling, sightseeing and experiencing new pleasures, one might feel like sharing a little of that good fortune to help the committed volunteers of the Wayside Chapel.

Every few years there is a big campaign to "clean up the Cross" – not from the rubbish but from the sin. There will be the inevitable real estate-driven headline: "The Resurgence of the Cross" or "Tourism-led Recovery". The campaign soon fades away, however, and the Cross sets its own pace again. For a visitor though, no matter what's happening the Cross, it is definitely not boring.

POTTS POINT

Trying to distance itself from Kings Cross, but bordering on the north is Potts Point, a quiet, rather dignified little suburb having some of the best accommodation and eateries in Sydney and, we believe, a lot to commend it as a base during your visit.

We took a vote at the UnTourist Co as to what would be our preferred base were we visiting Sydney and the winner was Potts Point. The reasons varied. There are some great small and stylish hotels, apartments and hostels as well as some of Sydney's best restaurants in and around the area. Regardless of whether you have an open cheque book and are past the half-century mark, or whether you are 19 and on your first post-school trek with empty pockets, the area has the things you want when you are in a new place. You are close to the centre of the city, as well as being in one of the more *avant garde* areas.

Potts Point is that gentle, charming, tree-lined neighbourhood bordered by sinful Kings Cross, arty **Darlinghurst,** posh **Elizabeth Bay** and the mixed bag of Woolloomooloo. From this area you have easy access to both the central areas of Sydney and the eastern and southern suburbs. It is also where most of the hire cars, taxis and buses are. It is en route to the airport and, if you've ever tried to get across peak-hour Sydney in a hurry to catch a plane, this is a definite asset.

Within a few blocks of Potts Point, you will find wonderful small hotels like the **Regents Court** and **Simpsons,** and outstanding restaurants like **Cicada, Darley Street Thai, Wockpool,** and **Mezzaluna**.

Because the Eastern suburbs has always had more than its fair share of Sydney's money it has, consequently, had a fair share of the grand houses and estates. **NSW Historic Houses Trust** has a great deal of free information for visitors on beautiful old **Elizabeth Bay House,** 7 Onslow Avenue, Elizabeth Bay. It is often the venue for small chamber music concerts. (Further on, towards Watson's Bay, there is **Vaucluse House,** Wentworth Road, Vaucluse with its wonderful gardens and Tea Rooms which are more than tea rooms.)

WOOLLOOMOOLOO

Rubbing up against Potts Point to the west is Woolloomooloo, the site for a government housing scheme in the 1970s. Today, it seems to be a strange combination of good pubs, trendy offices and low-rent houses – all liberally covered in graffiti. On the waterfront are the historic finger wharves, now on the drawing board for conversion into high-rent housing and other appropriate facilities. The smart money says that the low-rent ten-ants will be moving on to greener, or cheaper, pastures when all this evolves.

The 'Loo has a good feeling about it, even if you get the impression that it is in transition – but then it seems to have been in transition for the past 50 years.

A special place to visit in the area is **The Tilbury Hotel.** By day it is just another good Woolloomooloo pub, but at night it transforms itself into one of the best entertainment venues in town. It specialises in real talent, be it an old talent revived or a new talent discovered. The style could be described broadly as cabaret but regardless of your musical tastes or standards, the Tilbury will deliver a great evening, corner Nicholson and Forbes Street (see Directory).

On the western side of **Woolloomooloo Bay,** there is a pleasant walk which takes you right through the **Botanic Gardens,** past

The Tilbury Hotel presents
Bader, Biggins & Hyde
in
Never Say CAN'T
RETURN SEASON
BY DEMAND ONLY!

TILBURY
January 2nd
358
BO

Gerald Turner
"This moment..."
Devised by
David Mitchell and Geraldine Turner.
Musical Direction by
Brian Castles-Onion.
Jan 30 to Mar 4

Umbrella Events and The Tilbury Hotel presents....
David Campbell
direct from his triumph in "Only Heaven Knows" at the Opera House and Mardi Gras

Nowadays
the concerts
A Special Encore Season of 8 Shows
9 Shows July. 22 - 31 May, 1995
The Tilbury Hotel
Cnr Nicholson & Forbes Sts.
Woolloomooloo.
Bookings: 358 1295

Mrs Macquarie's Chair and on to the **Opera House** and **Circular Quay.**

If you are strolling around this area, you come across the **Boy Charlton Pool** on the western shore of Woolloomooloo Bay, previously called the Domain Baths and now the venue of the annual Gay Swimming Carnival. The pool is named after one of Australia's greatest swimmers, Andrew "Boy" Charlton who, in 1924, beat the world champion Swedish swimer Arne Borg in the then world record time of 5 minutes, 11.8 seconds. (He came third in the Olympics of that year, the winner being Johnny Weismuller.)

Harry's Cafe de Wheels – or, since mid-1995, more accurately **Harry's Cafe de Bricks** - has long been a Sydney institution. Now permanently adhered to the roadside on the Woolloomooloo Bay waterfront, Harry's does a brisk trade in pies with the after-theatre or movie crowd and at all hours with the naval lads of the nearby base **HMAS Penguin.** Yes, you're right, it is strange that a large part of the Australian Navy should be moored right in the centre of Sydney. And what about the five-storey car park that enjoys some of the best water views in Sydney's east? Ours not to question why, etc.

DARLINGHURST

Most times, but particularly on Saturday mornings, the cappuccino strip running from the top of William Street south along Victoria Street is where you will find the best coffee outside Italy – well, maybe Leichhardt. **Bar Coluzzi** is the most famous, but the others aren't far behind. You may be sitting on an upturned milk crate on the pavement but that's okay. Open every day at 5.30am, 322 Victoria Street. If you can find it, the skinniest coffee bar ever is **Box.** One blink and you'll miss it, so watch out for the child-like scratching "Box" on the wall. Home to the ultra-chic coffee crowd, open every day from 7.30 am, 28A Bayswater Road, Kings Cross.

Almost opposite Bar Coluzzi on Victoria Street is the back entrance to **St Johns Anglican Church** (main entrance, Darlinghurst Road) which has an "on the house" sausage sizzle every month for anyone who would like to come. Even if you don't catch Rev Bill Lawton's special hospitality, the old stone church and its delightful garden is worth a visit.

Darlinghurst Road runs south from Kings Cross through the suburb of – you guessed it – Darlinghurst which has more cafes and places to eat, closer together probably than in any other suburb in Sydney. Like **Burgerman** the gourmet hamburger shop, 116 Surrey Street; **bill's** (ostentatiously always lower case "b") for healthy breakfasts, 433 Liverpool Street; the eccentric **Le Petit Crême,** 118 Darlinghurst Road and **Fishface,** 132 Darlinghurst Road.

Popular week-night watering hole for Darlinghurst locals is the **Green Park Hotel.** This is the place for a fast game of pool, or to meet some friendly locals who take in loud music with their drink, 360 Victoria Street. Popular with value-conscious movie buff locals with a vegetarian bent – **Govindas** where you watch your movie lying on a huge body pillow after your all-you-can-eat

For telephone numbers and addresses, see the yellow pages Directory at the back

vegetarian meal. The restaurant opens at 5.30pm and the first feature starts at 7pm, the second at 9.15pm. 112 Darlinghurst Road, Darlinghurst.

On the corner of Darlinghurst Road, and Forbes Street is the old Darlinghurst Gaol, or "Starvinghurst" as one of its famous inmates, our celebrated writer Henry Lawson, used to call it. It is now a centre for training operated by TAFE college. Inside this interesting sandstone complex is an area used as a performance space and exhibition centre.

Opposite the gaol is the **Sydney Jewish Museum** – an interactive museum where the survivors of the Holocaust now living in Australia (and there are many) act as guides. This museum is home to Australia's Jewish History and the Holocaust. Entry fee, Mon-Thurs 10am-4pm, Fri 10am-2pm, 148 Darlinghurst Road.

Moving away from the Cross and Darlinghurst, south toward **Oxford Street,** the grand old 1842 **Darlinghurst Courthouse** looks disap-provingly across to Taylor Square, marking the end of inner East Sydney and, more importantly, sitting smack dab in what is considered to be the centre of Sydney's gay scene, the spot that's the focus of activities for the annual **Sydney Gay and Lesbian Mardi Gras.** During Mardi Gras time, which is usually in early March, it's hard to get room to swing your false eyelashes around Taylor Square.

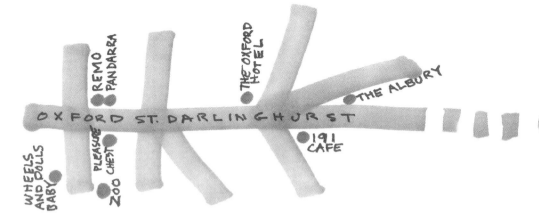

Map labels: REMO, PANDARRA, THE OXFORD HOTEL, THE ALBURY, OXFORD ST. DARLINGHURST, 191 CAFE, WHEELS AND DOLLS BABY, PLEASURE CHEST, ZOO CHEST

GAY AND LESBIAN MARDI GRAS

From a motley, illegal little street demonstration in 1978, the Mardi Gras has grown into possibly the largest night street parade in the world. Far from being illegal, the organisers now get public support and encouragement from the prime minister, the state premier, the lord mayor, and many senior politicians and leaders of the community. Only a cynic would suggest that this remarkable change in fortune has to do with the sheer size and hence voting power of Sydney's homosexual community. In 1995, Prime Minister Paul Keating suggested that the event *"provides a wonderful opportunity for gays, lesbians and the wider community to celebrate the great tolerance and diversity of our nation"*.

Probably true, but the real reason why the event has become so popular, in such a comparatively short time, is that it is such a great show.

Theatre, dance, art and photography, sports events, cabaret – all flowing on from a highly witty, and graphically spectacular parade stretching halfway through the centre of Sydney with what seems like a quarter of its population marching, another quarter lining the streets, while the rest are at home muttering disapproval or watching it on television. As a consequence of all this gaiety, this particular strip of Oxford Street, from Bourke Street through to Paddington has been dubbed The Pink Precinct.

Young Megan Hall, a Darlinghurst local, strutted us along Oxford Street to pick out some of the highlights. At 82 there's **Remo,** the eclectic general store where Remo Giuffre sells only the best of everything, be it a wooden

"... the great tolerance and diversity of our nation"

Clover Moore MP for Bligh and devoted constituents.

clothespeg or a hand-crafted silver watch. It also has a "best of everything" coffee house where, not surprisingly, you can get great snacks. Across the road and a few doors up at 259 Crown Street is **Wheels & Doll Baby** – outfitters to the stars. Denim, leather and latex – as long as it's

tight. At 96 Oxford Street is the one-stop cowboy shop the **Pandarra Trading Co.**

PADDINGTON

At 180 Oxford Street, Paddington is **Hot Tuna** – Australia's hottest surf-turned-fashion label; at 339 Oxford Street, Paddington is **Dinosaur Designs** beads, bangles and stuff – and so it goes. For those who are born to shop, with a taste for the unusual, Oxford Street is worth a visit. But to walk, if you are over 25, can be quite taxing – it's a long street. If you are looking for more slightly off-the-wall exotica, you'll use up less shoe leather on Glebe Point Road, Glebe, Chapter 8.

If you make it to **Victoria Barracks** opposite the Women's Hospital, Paddington, you'll be safe from temptation for a while. The Barracks is one of those rare historic buildings still being used for the same purpose for which it was built in 1841 – to house the Army. In many ways, the building of Victoria Barracks created the character of Paddington which was then an isolated village. Because it was considered at the time a pretty big project, the workmen (many of whom were convicts) built and lived in tiny houses near the area around McLaughlan and Spring Streets. Paddington is filled with little streets with rows of identical houses, with only the grandest decorated with the famous "Paddington lace" – intricate cast-iron worked balustrades and fretwork which was brought to old Sydney town from England as ballast in the holds of sailing ships.

By the time you reach the heart of Oxford Street, Paddington, you'll feel like a good coffee. Try the **Sloane Rangers Cafe** at 312 Oxford Street or **New Editions** bookshop and tea rooms at 328.

Behind the Victoria Barracks lies the **Moore Park** complex consisting of the Cricket Ground (the legendary SCG), the Football Stadium and the Showground for years to the Royal Agricultural Society's Royal Easter Show, pop concerts, opera spectaculars, other celebrations and now, Twentieth Century Fox movie studios.

At the top of Oxford Street in the grounds of the local church is one of the best markets in Sydney. The **Paddington Bazaar** with its 250 stalls of old wares, paintings, original new and trendy vintage clothing, jewellery and toys. This is a market which has managed to avoid the commercial exploitation which erodes so many similar places. The locals eat there, sing there, shop there and just strut around. Open every Saturday 10am till about 4pm, 395 Oxford Street.

CENTENNIAL PARK

At the point where Oxford Street, Paddington, meets Queen Street, Woollahra lies the entrance to **Centennial Park,** probably the most loved and used park in Sydney. Bicycle riders, equestrians, joggers, walkers, kite-fliers, skate-boarders and families picnicking by the duck pond or just motoring along the Grand Drive at a Sunday pace – they're all there. If you would rather just see the action rather than participate, try the delightful **Centennial Park Cafe,** corner Grand and Parkes Drive.

Just inside the entrance gates to **Centennial Park** is a statue of a 19th Century footballer. On the base of the statue, beautifully carved in bronze, is a heavenly game of footy – truly heavenly, played by angels and cherubs, and complete with a cherub keeping score. A very different game from the head-bashing, bone-crushing Rugby League played in Sydney today.

It was Lord Carrington who, in 1888, harnessed the enthusiasm of Henry Parkes, the then Premier of NSW, to create the present park. It was inspired by London's Hyde Park and The Serpentine, and is used by its Sydney citizens in a similar way.

There is the **Bird Sanctuary** with its beautiful wrought-iron gate, the turn-of-the-century **Avenue of Palms,** the formal rose garden near the ponds, and **Lachlan Swamps,** where nearly 100 species of birds nest, at peace with their surroundings.

Cared for by the locals through the **Centennial Park Trust,** the majority of the 220ha area was originally a market garden. It also provided a vital link for Sydney's water supply which, oddly, is the reason why there is still access to the city via the Centennial Park "swamps".

In 1824 the original water supply to Sydney Cove, the Tank Stream, became polluted and the then Chief Surveyor and engineer extraordinaire John Busby with his sons and a team of convicts were called in to fix the problem. They drained the swamps in the area, dug out a quarter of a million cubic feet of soil, built a tunnel to Hyde Park and put in place a pump with a capacity to pump over two million litres a day. **Busby's Bore,** as it was named, supplied Sydney with water until 1859. No mean feat!

Waverley is not a suburb of Sydney with a particularly high profile – in fact, other than its cemetery with its magnificent ocean view, it is hard to find much to say about it at all. However, would you believe, in 1869 it was the site of the little known **Battle of Waverley** which was to have significance for the later use by the public of Centennial Park.

One of the protagonists of the infamous 1869 battle was the Mayor of Waverley, Llewellyn Baglin, who could see no reason why his constituents could not use the area known as Lachlan Swamps as an access point to the city.

The Mayor of Sydney, Charles Moore, however, had every reason to protect the area from trampling horses, hooves and citizens' boots as it was right on the site of Busby's Tunnel which provided Sydney with its main water supply. On the strength of this, and in the general interests of greater Sydney, Mayor Moore barricaded their way. In response, the Waverley residents, led by their defiant mayor, knocked down the offending structure.

The plot escalated and Moore, not to be outdone by a bunch of country hicks, hired some vigilantes. The angry residents then set fire to the bushes in which the hired guards were lying in wait to arrest them. It was then definitely on for young and old and, after a bit of skirmish, Moore's guards were finally routed by the women of Waverley, brandishing "household implements".

The Centennial Park and Moore Park Trust is entrusted to carry out Lord Carrington's dedication at the opening ceremony on Australia Day 1888...*"to take as much interest in it as if, by your own hands, you had planted the flowers".*

WOOLLAHRA

The Centennial Park main entrance faces Woollahra's famous **Queen Street** with its claim to be "Antique Alley". Not your "Wow, did I pick up a bargain" type of antique buying – more the "right pedigree and right price" type of antique buying.

Woollahra is a charming, quiet residential neighbourhood – in fact it has for many years enjoyed the privilege of being the most expensive suburb in Sydney. It is not a showy place, however, unlike some other suburbs in Sydney where the many millions spent are there on the facade for all to see. Woollahra is more

Centennial Park, via the battlefield of Waverley

Double Bay Village

style than show and, because of this, we searched high and low to find somewhere our visitors could stay. We were particularly pleased when we discovered the likes of the charming **Hughenden Boutique Hotel.** The restaurants, the cafes, the shops are all enjoyable – and there is the local pub, the **Woollahra Hotel** with its excellent **Bistro Moncur.**

DOUBLE BAY

Double Bay is Woollahra's harbourside neighbour, and it is a suburb you should also consider as a base during your stay in Sydney. Double Bay ("The Bay" or "Bay Bay") 20 years ago was the hottest and most chic, place to be in and to be seen in. But during the late-80s, when conspicuous luxury, status labels and general glitz were starting to be considered outre, Double Bay (or Double Pay as it was often called) started to go off the boil. Not only did the retail trade start to slide with customers seeking less-predictable and more value-for-money-places, so did the real-estate values, for the same reason. Double Bay started to look unloved.

The good citizens of the area got to work to put The Bay back on its pedestal. Double Bay now seems to move with a new vitality – more trees; new sidewalk cafes; the storybook cul de sac which is **Transvaal Avenue** (cute little houses for nearly a million each); the beautiful

Zigolinis restaurant at 2 Short Street; more hairdressers per square inch than any other area in Sydney; the wicked **Bon Bon** chocolate shop; the equally wicked **Riviera** ice cream; and the new addition that made the biggest difference – a grand new hotel in Cross Street, the **Ritz-Carlton.**

This fine hotel is the only hotel we would put in this special category outside the centre of Sydney, where its rival is its Macquarie Street sister establishment of the same name. In the relatively short time it has been on the Double Bay scene, it has become *the* scene, rather like the manor house of the village. It also has one of the best Sunday brunches in town according to local Sunday-brunch expert Russell Morgan and his opera-singer wife Jennifer McGregor.

In earlier Double Bay days, the focus was the **Cosmopolitan** and **Twenty One** in Knox Street. This was where the middle European folk would settle down on the side walk with their coffee, sacher torte and a game of chess. Many of these people, who had such an important influence on Double Bay, were the fortunates who escaped Nazi persecution in Europe.

They came to Sydney and settled in Double Bay, Bellevue Hill and Bondi. Ruth Fischer, our

insider guide to these areas, whose parents took refuge in Sydney in 1941, led us through Double Bay and on to **Hall street,** Bondi Beach.

BONDI BEACH

At 61 Hall Street you'll find the traditional **Hakoah Club.** You don't have to be either Jewish or a member to enjoy the matzo ball soup and goulash. Just flash some identification (**passport** or driving licence), and you will be welcome to play the pokies or maybe a game of cards.

Stark's Kosher Deli and the **Centre of Kosher Meats** further up Hall Street, Bondi, have a comfortable, almost old-fashioned atmosphere. There are many Russian Jews in Bondi – they tend to come from Odessa which has a similar environment so they feel quite at home here.

Savion, the Israeli restaurant, with its always-fresh and tasty take-away at the north end of Bondi Beach, is within walking distance of the beach on the corner of Wallis Parade and Wairoa Road which runs perpendicular to Bondi Golf Course.

Bondi Beach should not be confused with **Bondi Junction,** Bondi has the beach and is hip – Bondi Junction has shops and is not hip. For those who, through the disadvantage of either age or distance, or both, are not aware of local Bondispeak, don't be overly concerned when you hear locals talking in negatives. On Bondi's beachfront, everything that is bad is good –

got it? A "wicked" night shooting pool at the **Pavilion Hotel;** a "hell" afternoon surf; buying a "mad" midriff at **Purl Harbour** – these are all very good things.

To have a real feeling for Bondi you have to go back to its pre-hip days. That was about 1950, when roast chicken and flavoured ice-cream were special, the beach culture at Bondi was hot but, lord knows, you didn't consider living there.

Even as late as 1992 Jan Morris observed of Bondi that *"its dull and shabby promenade was one of the great disappointments of Sydney".* But things had started to happen to Bondi in the late eighties that Ms Morris didn't notice. The food culture was replacing the beach culture and the style-seekers moved in with it. English writer Paul McGuire would have been pleased. In 1939, after a swim at Bondi he wrote: *"But I wish Australia could do one a reputable café crème".*

Around 1920 – this was Bondi's prime. It was about 10 years after Mr Gocher's defiant act of swimming openly, on a public beach, for all to see, in the forbidden daylight hours between six in the morning and eight at night. (The public beach was not actually Bondi but Manly, but it was plucky Mr Gocher who showed the way for Sydneysiders to embrace their surf.)

So began the build of the beach culture: the parade of the lifesaving heroes in their little red and yellow caps, with toes stabbing the sand as

they posed for newsreels and posters, and the office workers rushing to the waves at the weekend by tram, hence the expression "shooting through like a Bondi tram", meaning speed and physical freedom.

The Bondi Pavilion with its dressing rooms for 5000 people, Turkish and hot baths, shops, a gymnasium, a grand ballroom, a theatre, a large dining and banquet hall and private sun-bathing lawns provided permission to indulge. Bondi Beach was the place to be. But in-the-surf – the land was all but ignored.

It is only within the past 10 years that Bondi Beach *the place* has been "discovered". And now that shabby promenade sparkles with sharp-looking people at all hours. There are some great restaurants and a few very good places to stay. The shops are cornucopias of fresh seafood, yummy ice-creams, pastries and yes, Mr McGuire, you could get a sensational café crème – at two in the morning if you'd wish.

We think Bondi deserves more than a day visit – it makes a great place to stay and our favourite is **Ravesi's.** While you're there, the walk from **Bondi** to **Bronte** makes for a breathtaking trip to savour the real sights of Sydney's famous beaches (see Chapter 10). On Sundays, between 10am and 4pm, visit the **Bondi Beach Markets** at Bondi Beach Public School Campbell Parade. The famous and sexy **Bondi Lifesavers** in their red and gold caps and cossies (swimsuits) train at different times each day. For more information, call the **Bondi Surf Club.**

Coogee Beach, a few beaches south from Bondi, has recently had a revival which is worth acknowledging. A good swimming rather than a vigorous surfing beach, Coogee is only a fraction the size of Bondi, and the beach and surrounding area are much more intimate. Traditional Aussie beach-side suburbia and shops rest easily with the changes which have improved the beach-front park and added some acceptable new apartment buildings. The 1995 architectural Greenway Award for Conservation Adaptive Re-use, won by Wylie's Baths, confirmed the sensitive direction of refurbishment efforts in Coogee. Not too much yet in terms of top places to eat – though several of our local insiders say the **China Bowl** on Beach Street is worth a visit, though check in early on Saturday and Sunday for midday yum cha. In late 1995, renovations to accommodation at the **Coogee Bay Hotel** were well under way, and the **Holiday Inn** also has merit. It is useful to know that Coogee is easily accessible from Sydney airport.

Heading north again to visit the outer eastern suburbs, the way to go is via **New South Head Road**. After passing through Double Bay, the next residential water view areas are **Point Piper, Rose Bay** and **Vaucluse.** At the end of New South Head Road is the village of **Watson's Bay.**

🐦 WATSON'S BAY

**Reminiscing in and around Watson's Bay -
by a past resident, Jacqueline Huié**

When you have lived in, and loved, a place – going back years later is not a good idea. Particularly if, in the 40 years since you left, the place has become a bit of a tourist mecca, and the tossing and turning of your life has moulded you into a dedicated UnTourist. I managed to postpone the visit for as long as a person writing a book about Sydney could. I need not have carried on so – the whole area in and around Watson's Bay

death, then commuted to transportation for life. And he ended up owning Vaucluse House. Mmmm.

The area has managed to hold hard to its very essence thanks to a lot of caring and, no doubt at times, stroppy residents.

So, sure maybe, **Doyles** isn't the same as it was when it was smaller, and the old cinema in the main street, Military Road, which thrilled us all by serving (very sophisticated) coffee at interval, has now become the **Car Museum** and the fine little **Picnic** cafe next door is where a block of flats used to be. It serves, arguably, the best food at Watson's

Author (centre) with mother and friends, Watsons Bay, 1960

is still wonderful. The heavy dark figs in the park still hang over the stone path, which leads you around **Alf Vocklers Pool**, the **Vaucluse Sailing Club** where the famous VJs were developed, and then to Parsley Bay and wonderful **Vaucluse House**. I often wondered about Vaucluse House and its first owner Sir Henry Browne Hayes, a large landholder and the Sheriff of the County, who "abducted an hieress" in Cork around 1797. The heiress, a certain Miss Pike, was indeed abducted in the dead of night but whether for lust or lolly, we will never know. The spirited Sir Henry was declared an outlaw, with a thousand guineas set upon his head, which he managed to split with his informant. He was tried and sentenced to

Bay. Some of the houses are a bit grander, but overall it feels the same, rather like a fishing village. Which of course it was, as well as a place for whalers – and the first centre of bureaucracy in Australia. In the early days of the settlement, a base was created at Watson's Bay for the pilots and customsfolk to clear papers before entering or leaving Sydney Cove.

In fact, Watson's Bay was the first of everything in Australia because it was here, in dear **Camp Cove**, where Phillip, exploring from Botany Bay in his three pinnaces (with my great-great-great-great-great grandfather on board one), made his first camp. He chose well. Camp Cove is probably the loveliest of Sydney's 70 beaches.

But I am jumping ahead. As you approach the village down Old South Head Road – a road built "in record time" by a company of soldiers. There is a plaque in the south-west corner of the park which registers this fact with, one feels, almost surprise. As discipline and obedience were not the order of the day in Sydney Town at the time, it probably was a surprise to have anything done in record time.

Anyway, on the highest part of the road, on the left before you pass Greenways 1981 lighthouse and the **Signal Station** there is a

anchor in Watson's Bay; the omnipresent wreck of the *Dunbar* (1857 and all souls lost -but one); **The Gap** where so many others have jumped to their deaths since; the *Dunbar's* anchor (now outside Dunbar House in the park); and the *HMAS Watson* on South Head, beside our house. The mural also showed the old tram that would career terrifyingly down the hill toward the little stone church with its memorial *Dunbar* Gates where two of my son's were christened and the old Ozone fish cafe which then became Doyles. Tim Doyle (who now

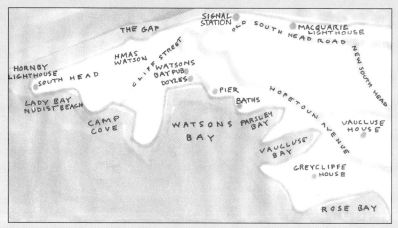

house which once was a pub. The "boys", including the older Doyles, at the **Watson's Bay Hotel** (which is a great place to stay), used to retell their grandfather's tales of the pilots up there on the verandah, shickered to the eyeballs, with spyglasses wavering to sea, waiting for some speck of an approaching boat which might pay their next rum bill. When the speck was sighted, the race was on.

There is a photo in the main bar of the Watson's Bay Hotel which shows all the old regulars having their "heart starter" in the backyard of Ted Page's house. John Doyle recalled – Ted's ghastly, featherless, 100-year old parrot, which imitated the sound of his gate-hinge opening. The Pages lived in *Do Me* which was next door to our tiny stone house.

I painted a mural for my eldest son, John, which I am sure was itself painted over years ago. It showed the old Captain Cook pilot boat, the pretty one, with the raked lines, at

runs Doyles at the Quay) was our butcher's delivery boy. The Doyle family are now the fishing aristocrats of Sydney. Wherever there are fish to be eaten, written about, caught, transported or cooked, there will be one of Ma Doyle's young lads on to it. They have the pub, and the takeaways and the two fish restaurants, the big Doyles On The Beach and Doyles Wharf Restaurant. The Doyles are old-style fish cooks, which means that you won't find first class Modern Australian Cuisine there (although the smaller Wharf Restaurant would be ideal for just that), so go for the fish in beer batter, the mussels, oysters, lobster – or the simple takeaways. Maybe sit on the beach, lean up against the upturned rowboats, with a glass of wine, watch the dogs dig sand holes, look at Sydney and be glad you are where you are. Things don't change, apart from the fact that it's a little harder to spring up from a prone position these days. Will someone refill my glass please?

The United Nations of Haberfield
Public School (see page 75)

4 WEST

INCLUDES: The avant-garde Inner West to the Outer West where an innovative grassroots culture is brewing – the West is the melting pot where most of Sydney lives, where there is a smorgasbord of things to see, eat and do: Italian Leichhardt, Lebanese Dulwich Hill, Greek Marrickville, Portuguese Petersham, Asian Cabramatta, the Aussie "island" of Balmain and, the place where it all started, the old English capital city of Parramatta.

71

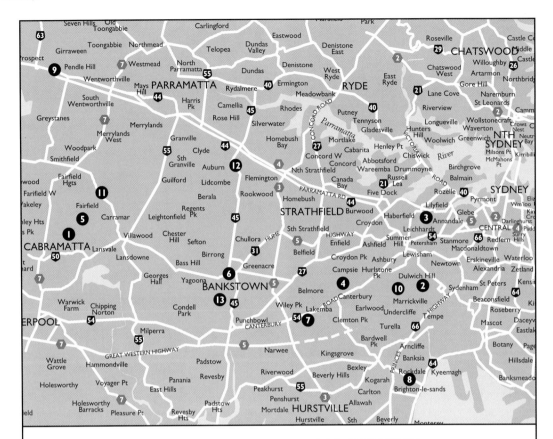

INTERNATIONAL STOPOVERS – NO VISAS REQUIRED

There are many nationalities spread over and integrated throughout Sydney, however, this map shows major ethnic community clusters by suburb in the West.

1 **Cabramatta** – Cambodian, Laotian, Vietnamese

2 **Marrickville** – Greek and Vietnamese. Great food shops and restaurants

3 **Leichhardt, Haberfield** – Italian. Sydney's little Italy

4 **Campsie** –Korean. Kim-chi noodles

5 **Cabramatta, Fairfield** – Laotian Buddhist temples

6 **Bankstown** – Latvian, Lithuanian

7 **Lakemba** – Lebanese, Egyptian. Often called the Muslim heartland of Sydney

8 **Rockdale** – Macedonian. Great bakeries, St Petka Church

9 **Pendle Hill** – Maltese

10 **Petersham, Marrickville** – Portuguese. Small community near intersection New Canterbury Road and Stanmore Road

11 **Fairfield** – South Americans

12 **Auburn** – Turkish.

13 **Bankstown, Cabramatta** – Vietnamese. They tend to live in Bankstown, but their businesses in Cabramatta have given rise to the notion of "Vietnamatta"

West of the Bridge, South of the River

No area in Sydney represents both the past and future of Sydney as accurately as the Western Suburbs. Not only is this vast area west of the Harbour Bridge and south of the Parramatta River arguably the most interesting in Sydney, it *is* Sydney. Certainly in demographic terms – 80% of Sydney people live there. Even though there are fewer high-income earners in the area, more people are building new homes there. The West is big and getting bigger – this is where the awesome Sydney suburban sprawl is happening.

SYDNEY GOES ETHNIC

Having originally duplicated British society so absolutely, Sydney, in the latter part of the 20th Century started taking its social leads more from Southern Europe and Asia, whose emigrants to Sydney were settling mostly in the Western Suburbs.

Mediterranean eating and drinking styles arrived and, with their outdoor tradition of barbecues and picnics, Sydneysiders comfortably and quickly adopted al fresco styles of eating. Fashion became more casual, with inspiration coming from ethnic style and fabrics. Foreign terms crept into the everyday culinary language: "cappuccino", "pasta", "croissant", "falafel", "al dente", "focaccia". The invasion of the mouth had begun. It was okay to be ethnic.

Real estate was affected. Smart Sydney discovered the advantages of shopping, eating and living in suburbs which had been settled by these "new" Australians. The real-estate prices in places like Newtown, Leichhardt, Marrickville and Dulwich Hill started to rise; fashionable apartments were converted from importers' warehouses; Double Bay shopped at Bondi Junction; Balmain shopped at Leichhardt; Hunter's Hill at Ryde. The message was loud and clear – check out where the Italians buy their pasta, the Greeks buy their olives and the Chinese buy their vegetables – that was the place to be, and to be seen.

THE ARTS

The avant garde status of the West is not all food, nor is it all "happening" in the Inner West. Sydney cultural doyen and recent head of the Australia Council, Donald Horne, writes of the exciting new grass-roots cultural transformations taking place in the far west of Sydney in an article which appeared in the *Sydney Morning Herald*, March 1995:

"If anywhere is a 'new 'Australia confronting old stereotypes, it's west Sydney."

The level of community commitment to both graphic and performing arts out west has blossomed over the last decade. Even David Jones, the conventional department store in Parramatta has hosted shop window theatre art, replacing its normal window display. At **Parramatta's Riverside Theatre** complex (an easy stroll from Parramatta wharf to the corner of Church and Market Streets), you can see and hear a comprehensive cross-section of the performing arts – both national and international. Call for bookings and enquiries. On the other hand, places such as the **Wollondilly Heritage Centre** and the wonderful new **Casula Powerhouse** are acting as crucibles for creative talent from all over the area.

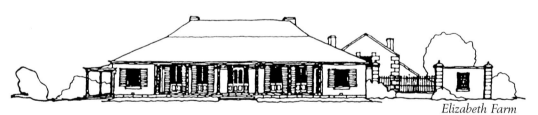

Elizabeth Farm

PARRAMATTA, THE COLONIAL CAPITAL

It was very different at the beginning. Poor, long-suffering, snobby Mrs John Macarthur, stranded in this uncivilised outpost wrote in 1810 to her genteel friends at "home" in England, explaining that Parramatta meant "head of the river". No doubt she could not cope with the reality of living in a place called "where the eels lie down".

Although thought of by Sydneysiders as a suburb, in 1938 Parramatta was declared a city in its own right. Which seems only right and proper as in 1791 the capital of New South Wales was considered to be Parramatta, or as it was originally called, Rose Hill.

"Sydney [Sydney Cove] has long been considered a depot for stores, it exhibits nothing but a few old scattered huts and some sterile gardens, cultivation of the ground is abandoned and all our strength transferred to Rose Hill", so wrote one of Governor Phillip's marine captains in his diary.

Over the years Parramatta has been both blessed and cursed by the fact that it started as the colony's farming community. Blessed, because as the urban concentration moved back to Sydney in the early 19th Century and there was not so much development pressure on the land. As a result, many more of the original buildings survived the dreaded bulldozers. Cursed, because, being a farming community, there were plenty of open spaces in between the wonderful old buildings which were soon filled up with opportunistic and careless development. As a result, Parramatta today is a bit of a mixed bag.

For this reason, one has to be led around in order to pick out the interesting bits. Being the "Cradle City", Parramatta can lay claim to many "firsts" and "oldests", which may or may not interest you – the first gaol, the oldest house, the first land grant, the first vineyard, the oldest military establishment, the first brewery (legal that is), the first ferry, and so on and so on. Two of the most outstanding places to see are both National Trust properties – **Old Government House,** with its important collection of early Australian furniture, (bottom of Pitt and Macquarie Streets) and **Experiment Farm Cottage** on the site of Australia's first land grant, 9 Ruse Street.

We recommend the best way to get the best out of Parramatta is to take a trip up the Parramatta River on one of the sleek River Cats which set out from Circular Quay. When you arrive there, play tourist for a change and pick up an **Explorer** bus from the wharf at Parramatta. The guides are full of knowledge and you can check out the great old houses in comfort. You may alight to see what interests you, then let the next bus pick you up for the next set-down – or head back to catch the River Cat back to the city.

For a place that started as Sydney's breadbasket, Parramatta is a bit light on for outstanding or interesting places to stay or eat (could the dearth of good eateries be because Parramatta has not been settled much by recent immigration?). However, don't despair – insider local businessman, Lionel Marz, recommends **Courtney's Brasserie,** (Modern Australian), 2 Horwood Plaza; **The Indian Affair** (north Indian), 79 Macquarie Street and **Barnaby's**

Riverside, (Modern Australian), in a lovely old sandstock brick house by the River.

Parramatta **Visitor Information Centre** is at the corner Church and Market Streets.

CABRAMATTA

"Vietnamatta" is the stereotype, rather than the real picture, of Cabramatta as the Vietnamese are more likely to reside in Bankstown. Many of their businesses are in Cabramatta which is, in the most part, run by Chinese, Cambodians and Laotians. In the past few years Cabramatta has been beset by drug-trafficking problems and it is wise to be cautious in the area, preferably visiting in the day-time or in the company of several friends.

A day trip to Cabramatta will make you feel like you've been transported to Asia. It has Australia's largest Asian shopping and restaurant complex. Getting there is a 40-minute drive from the centre of Sydney along the Hume Highway. By train from the city centre on the Liverpool line, it takes only 45 minutes.

To explore the ins and outs of this Asian settlement is great fun. You'll discover a world of great variety – from a colourful bazaar of weird and wonderful fabric to bargain-priced gold jewellery, exotic fruits and vegetables.

Shopping at Cabramatta is good every day of the week but it's probably best to head there on a weekend, when the locals come out in droves. Spend some time sitting in the Freedom Plaza taking in the Chinese Gateway, statues, banners and buskers which complement market arcades overflowing with people and produce.

THE ROOTY HILL RESORT

Welcome to the Rooty Hill Resort with its view over the railway. The eight-storey hotel, with its location in the heart of one of Sydney's most unfashionable suburbs, is owned by the adjacent Rooty Hill RSL. This self-styled "Last Vegas of the West" has a weekend occupancy rate of around 95%. Nearby is the Eastern Creek Grand Prix Raceway and Australia's Wonderland – but don't worry, it is also close to the **Featherdale Wildlife Park** and is halfway between the city and the Blue Mountains. For an experience of a genuine piece of suburban Australiana, this could be it. Sherbrooke Street (cnr Railway St).

One of the most popular restaurants in Cabramatta is **Tahnh Binh.** House specialty, *chao tom* (sugar cane prawns) and *ga kho to*, fish cooked in an earthenware pot. Open every day, breakfast, lunch and dinner, 56 John Street.

Call in for a delicious traditional bowl of beef-noodle soup at **Pho 54.** Or try *bun bo xao*, a warm beef salad with bean sprouts, mint, lemongrass, chopped peanuts and rice vermicelli. Open every day for lunch and dinner. Shop 2/54 Park Road, Freedom Plaza.

As well as offering Thai and Chinese dishes, **Camira** serves sweet and sour *samlor mchou*, an aromatic soup containing the Cambodian herb moam, fresh basil, mint and a choice of seafood or fish. Open every day, 50 Park Road.

For sale at **Hong Kong Children's Fashions,** miniature evening numbers in black lace, gold lamé and sequins to transform the kids into Liz Taylors and Dolly Partons. It may not be your cup of tea, but it's worth having a look. Among all the frou-frou are some reasonably priced cute kids' gear and unusual shoes. Open every day, 2/68 John Street.

You can't go past the traditional Chinese wedding clothes on display at **Hong Kong Wedding House** for their painstaking detail. Clever brides from all over Sydney head here to have that perfect Valentino gown recreated for a fraction of the cost. Open every day, 1st floor, 24-32 Hughes Street.

Cabramatta is known for its wide range of well-priced fabrics, buttons and trims, and **Hai Ha Fabrics** offers possibly the widest selection of dress fabrics in all Sydney. Open every day, 45 John Street.

BICENTENNIAL PARK

On the Parramatta River, in what we will describe as the mid-west, is Sydney's Bicentennial Park, right beside Homebush Bay, the Olympic Games Village site. This sanctuary for wildlife is set up as a field study centre for the eco-systems of the area. You get there by taking a train to Strathfield, then the No 401 bus.

A group of young enthusiasts from the inner west suburb of **Haberfield** (it is, incidentally, architecturally a classic Aust-ralian Federation suburb, yet has a marvellous mix of nationalities as residents), visited the Park and gave us their report:

OUR EXCURSION by school classes 2T and 2F Haberfield Public School

Nell: *On thursday 2T and 2F went to Bicen-tennial Park, and when we got off the bus we went into a tower and learned many things about life in the Wetland. It was fascinating....*

Libby: *It was humungus. When Carly and I were halfway to the top, Carly said "I want to go back". So did I. I only went up because I couldn't get down. Carly could though.*

Julia: *Someone gave the Ranger a turtle to look after. There was fish and crabs...*

Monika: *We went bird-watching with binoculars.*

Carly: *Ranger Fiona took 2F to the boardwalk...*

Genevieve: *Monika tasted a leaf.*

Cheng: *on the boardwalk there we caught fish and water bugs...*

Sophia: *We saw Golden Orb spiders...*

Anthony: *We walked on the boardwalk through the mangroves and we went fishing with fishing nets...*

Tom: *I saw a spoonbill...*

Elizabeth: *We went back to the park and cleaned up...*

Sarah: *It was fun, then we went back to school.*

By Cheng　　　*Natural Scientists from Haberfield Public School at work.*　　　*By Julia*

AUSSIE HEARTLAND SUBURBS

Areas like **Ashfield, Marrickville, Dulwich Hill** and **Petersham** were once heartland average Aussie suburbs, where anyone with a foreign accent was looked on with suspicion, when 6pm was closing time for the pubs, giving rise to the "six o'clock swill". It was the era of cooch grass, cooing doves, "ham and beef" shops and staunch RSL members. That was when RSL clubs were for returned soldiers, and before they became the casino-like edifices they are today. The crossover into contemporary ethnic Australia can probably be pinpointed to the late '50s when Sydneysider John O'Grady wrote *They're a Weird Mob*, a humorous book about Western Suburbs Italians and Australians getting to know, and actually *like*, each other, even though it would be another decade before the derogatory *"wog"* description of immigrants began to fall out of daily use.

Culinary temptations from Abla's Pastry

These days, the cooch grass and the doves are still there, and the ubiquitous lawn mowers still emerge at weekends, but the average Aussies now – as well as

Maurice from the Dulwich Hill Roaster

O'Brien, Campbell and Smith – have names like Sidoti, Malaxos, Ng and Malouf.

Today **Petersham** has a small Portuguese community focused around New Canterbury and Stanmore Roads. There are some good cafes and pastry shops plus the Portuguese Community Club which has good food. Visitors are welcome. Open every day for lunch and dinner, 100 Marrickville Road.

In **Marrickville,** there are still many "old" Aussies, but most of it is a potpourri of Asians and Greeks, well represented in shops and restaurants. There are some great Greek bakeries, like **Athena Cake Shop,** 412 Illawarra Road and the **Hellenic,** 371 Illawarra Road. There's also a fine taverna, the **El Greco,** enthusiastically supported by the Greek community, 362 Canterbury Road. Marrickville is also home to **Paesanella Cheese Factory,**

37 Gerald Street, where the late Umberto Somma introduced locally made fresh Italian cheeses and made mascarpone a household word. It's open Sun-Fri in the mornings to the public.

The Vietnamese focus in Marrickville is on Illawarra Road and our favourite restaurant there is the **Bac Lieu,** 302 Illawarra Road.

As for **Dulwich Hill,** there are two strong motivations for going there, and they are both Middle-Eastern. The first is a produce store, the **Dulwich Hill Roaster,** where Maurice Hazim sells the freshest and the best beans and nuts, imported and roated by his brother, Samir, corner Pigott Street and New Canterbury Road. The second, and the most dangerous, is the diet-threatening Lebanese pastry shop **Abla's Pastry,** another brother act just up the road. This palace-of-pastries used to be called Sedaka's, but, regardless of the name change, the temptation is the same. It also has great ice-cream and solid, black, sobering coffee, 425 New Canterbury Road.

LITTLE ITALY, LEICHHARDT

While there is a strong Italian community in Leichhardt, the Italian influence is all over Sydney. In fact **Buon Ricordo** has been nominated by the city's Italian Lord Mayor Frank Sartor as the best Italian restaurant in Sydney, but it is nowhere near Leichhardt – it's in Paddington.

Insider local Linda Browne says that Leichhardt abounds in cafes, restaurants and friendliness. It's a comfortable suburb, where "old" Aussies and Italians have made an agreeable cultural marriage – in many cases literally, mutually fussing over the quality of the focaccia or barracking together for the Tigers or choosing their vegies in the same market.

Approaching from Parramatta Road, just before you start into Norton Street, try a visit to a traditional Italian *bonbonniere* (which means keepsake). **Lucky Tom's (I)** is a treasure-trove of traditional Italian wedding trinkets. It's also

home to some incredibly kitsch pieces, from a Vatican lamp to a metre-high ornate indoor fountain with garish fluorescent optical fibres that light up at night. Open Mon-Sat, 379 Parramatta Road.

Call in for an espresso and biscotti at **Rugantino's (2),** formerly the local funeral parlour. They bake their own Italian breads which are literally worth dying for, 13 Norton Street. **Bar Baba (3)** is the haven of Leichhardt's coffee aficionados. You can't go past their *tremazzini* (a delicious Italian club sandwich of home-made bread, tuna, olives, egg and provolone. Wash it down with a *cafe latte*, 31 Norton Street.

See and smell and savour the finest display of Italian produce in Leichhardt at the **Norton Street Market (4).** The best olive oils, balsamic vinegars, olives, Italian salamis, cheeses and breads this side of Roma. Open every day, 55 Norton Street.

The **Cafe Gioia (5)** is not your average cafe. With a little Italian ingenuity and lots of stucco, tiles, dimpled cherubs, fountains and over-the-top styling, a former petrol station has been converted into an oasis in the hub. Younger Italians meet here to drink coffee and cruise. Open every day, 126A Norton Street.

Call into **Bar Italia (6)** to sample on site its mouth-watering gelati which is sold to every self-respecting cafe in Sydney. Sit in its leafy green courtyard and you'll feel you've been transported back to the old country, 169 Norton Street.

MORE LEICHHARDT TREASURES

At **Raffan & Kelaher Auctioneers,** you can pick up anything, from a funky hot pink '60s velvet tub chair to a terrific Italian cappuccino-maker for a ridiculous $12, 42 John Street.

In one of the fastest growing gay areas in Sydney and reflecting the West's interest in the arts, the **Leichhardt Hotel** cleverly combines the two, boasting a florist shop, art gallery and working space for painters, print-makers, photographers and sculptors. Predominantly a lesbian hotel, it's closed on the eve of the Gay Mardi Gras, but you can witness the fabulous leather-clad Dykes on Bikes roar off for their night of nights, corner Balmain Road and Short Street.

Get soccer-mad with the Italians by indulging in a *bierra*, or a Campari and soda at the **Apia Club.** Open to the public, it's best to head down on a Saturday when Tele Italia shows soccer matches live from Italy. Frazer Street, Leichhardt.

If you are anywhere near the area in May - don't miss the **Leichhardt Festival** with all manner of stalls set up along the length of Norton Street. Enquiries, Leichhardt Council.

GLEBE

Sandwiched between Leichhardt and the city, is the fine old suburb of **Glebe,** which has more than a touch of serendipity. It also has some of the more interestingly named shops and cafes in Sydney. Up the Parramatta Road end of the main drag of Glebe Point Road, you have the cafe **Badde Manors** at No 37; **Half a Cow** – music shop and more at No 85; the **Valhalla Cinema** – the '30s picture-palace with arthouse movies at No 166. The largest and, in our opinion, the best natural food market in the country is **Russell's** at No 53 Glebe Point Road. For cross-cultural food and homegrown exotics – **Darling Mills** – considered to be one of Sydney's top restaurants, 134 Glebe Point Road.

Away from Glebe's main shopping and restaurant area is the famous **Harold Park Hotel,** once a popular venue for Australian writers to give readings from their works. The hotel still has strong literary associations, but no more sessions open to the public. However, these days you can participate in *Politics in the Park* each Friday night. A political issue of the day is discussed, often with well known politicians leading the debate, 115 Wigram Road.

THE OLD BOATS OF SNAIL'S BAY – AN EXPERT'S VIEW

Nick Swanton is 12 years old and he's mad about boats. He put together this report for us on his favourites around Balmain, where he lives.

For many years, Snails Bay has been used for shipyards, sailing, boatyards and mooring barges. That's why I like living and mucking about here. From Birchgrove Oval, you can see all the old boat sheds, some of which have been renovated.

These are some of my favourite boats.

Gool Gool - she's on the jetty at the bottom of Grove Street. Previously a "dogboat" operated by the MSB (Maritime Services Board). These boats were used to collect rubbish (including the occasional dead dog) out of the harbour. The narrow design was so the boats could move between piles under wharves. An upside-down bucket on the waterfront lawn of a house indicated to the driver there was some rubbish to be removed – with a few beers underneath the bucket for their trouble.

Gool Gool

Lithgow

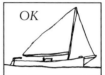
OK

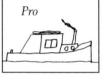
Pro

THE AUSSIE ISLAND OF BALMAIN

Despite being part of the multi-cultural West, the Balmain Peninsula is as "old" Australian today as it was in 1880, when there were 41 pubs in the neighbourhood – that was around one pub per 366 residents. In fact, it is probably more Aus-tralian now because in 1880 they were mostly recently transplanted Anglo-Celts.

Even though the pubs have dwindled down to a paltry 24, they are fine establishments, each and every one, even if they are "born-again" pubs, serving trendy cuisine rather than a schooner and pie. In fact, Balmain and its smaller neighbours, Birchgrove and Rozelle, are arguably the most Australian suburbs – and the leading pub suburbs – in Sydney. Before we leave the pub scene, there are a few which deserve a special mention in this chapter.

Built in 1867, the **Dry Dock Hotel** (nee Dock Inn) is the oldest continuously-operating hotel in the area. Its success was no doubt due to the fact that it was the watering hole for Mort's Dock, which was where the main ship-building action was in the mid-1800s. In recent years, it was the first to have entertainment, then the first to open a beer garden. Today it has one of the best pub restaurants in the area. Corner of Cameron and College Streets.

More histrionic than historic, **The Cat and the Fiddle** is a great entertainment venue. Like the Tilbury in Woolloomooloo, it concentrates on the unusual and the unusually talented. *Opera in the Pub*, with stars of the Australian Opera belting out Verdi and Puccini at the bar is a memorable program. Call for details, 456 Darling Street.

The **London Hotel** (1870) (nee Golden Eagle/Circular Saw) does a great trade on Saturdays as it is across the road from the popular Balmain markets held in the grounds of St. Johns Church, also a regular venue for young Japanese couples to have their "authentic Aussie weddings".

The London, among other distinctions, has the benefit of being the "local" for the UnTourist Co.

The old watering hole, the **Riverview Hotel** (built 1880), has fallen foul of renovation and looks a bit ersatz. However, it has a fine sporting heritage (the name referred to the Head of the River rowing classics which dominated this part of Sydney in the late 1800s). It was also a boxers' pub for years and locally it is still referred to as "Dawn Fraser's pub", even though Dawn sold it many years go. Any time, any day, you'll find the journalists, the shipwrights and the old Tiger supporters holding up the bar at the Riverview. Good food and regular trad jazz, 29 Birchgrove Road.

CHEZ OSCAR AND LUCINDA

Balmain had periods of grandeur. In the mid 1800s, the wealthy from Sydney Cove chose to build country properties there. This was the time and the setting for Peter Carey's *Oscar and Lucinda* and during those days, it was a day's ride by sulky from the settlement at Sydney Cove. Carey himself lived for many years in Louisa Road, close to Lucinda's "piebald" house on Long Nose Point.

If you look carefully at Balmain's now fabulously expensive waterfront residences, you will notice that most of them were built facing the road rather than the water. Today, with add-on picture windows, bold verandahs and sweeping lawns to the waterfront, these residences are now worth millions of dollars. But for nearly a century after Oscar and Lucinda's time, Balmain was very much a working-class suburb.

After the arrival of Mort's Dock in 1850, the folklore has it that many Balmain residents operated on the fringe of the law, with involvement in illegal SP bookie joints, illegal two-up schools (still illegal in Australia except for ANZAC day), and the odd "Robin Hood" thefts from factories and docks. But, as one of the Balmain old-timers told us:

> *"Even though, back in the '30s, the property of the bosses was fair game, it wasn't until the '60s, when the middle-class began to arrive in Balmain, that a bloke had to lock his front door."*

THE UNDERDOG TRADITION

In the mid-1800s the famous bushranger Captain Thunderbolt (real name, Frederick West) escaped from the gaol on nearby **Cockatoo Island** and found sanctuary with the locals in the Balmain bush. He was eventually discovered and shot dead in 1870. Over the years, Balmain has earned its champion-of-the-underdog ribbons many times over, an essential characteristic for anything which is quintessential Australian. This anti-establishment streak is reflected in many – though not all – of its famous sons and daughters.

There was Balmain shopkeeper and feisty Labor Prime Minister, William Morris "Billy" Hughes; the much-loved Governor General Sir William McKell; and Dr H V Evatt, who won the Balmain seat for Labor in the '50s, and later attained notoriety (or honour, depending on your point of view) for successfully supporting the "no" case against the banning of the Communist Party. In 1975, a Balmain boilermaker's son, Governor General Sir John Kerr, sacked the elected Labor government of Prime Minister Gough Whitlam. "Balmain boys don't cry," announced NSW Premier and true Balmain son, Neville Wran at a Royal Commission which attacked his reputation. Three times Olympic gold medal champion, Dawn Fraser, who's had the swimming pool off Elkington Park named for her, is claimed as "our Dawn" by Balmain locals.

Even today, despite the new money and the swish cafes, there is a certain inverted snobbery about Balmain which borders on eccentricity. Its citizens' laid-back – some would say scruffy – style of dress is worn as a badge of honour. This characteristic is best exemplified in the excellent **Chester's Cafe** which is set among junkyard trash – or bargains – depending on your point of view, at the **Tin Shed**, 148 Beattie Street.

Balmain is a great place to stroll around – there are plenty of good cafes along Darling Street (**Omnivore** at 333 Darling Street serves all three meals – deliciously) and one of the best restaurants in Sydney, **Tetsuya's** (it's been voted among the best for several years running) is at 329 Darling Street. **Victoire** is arguably one of the best French bakeries in town, 285 Darling Street. And don't miss the **Balmain Markets** at St. John's Church on Saturday – we consider them the best in Sydney.

The Balmain Association takes great pains to preserve the history of Balmain and to welcome visitors. The local historian is **Kath Hamey**, who conducts walks around the area, including a visit to the old Balmain lockup and a Balmain Pub Crawl. Call or fax her for enquiries.

The little Aussie island village of Balmain will charm you; it is one of the few "old" Aussie suburbs left in Sydney.

Captain James Cook, having arrived in his barque Endeavour jumped ashore for a comfort stop at Kurnell on April 29th, 1770.

5 SOUTH

INCLUDES: Captain Cook's historic stop in Botany Bay. Two of the many great ways to see the Royal National Park – up the Hacking River on the little MV Tom Thumb III or a short excursion by Parklink tram. Surprising Cronulla, larger-than-life Sylvania Waters and the secret upper reaches of the Georges River. Oyster farmers' tips on where to get the best – and zany King Street, Newtown.

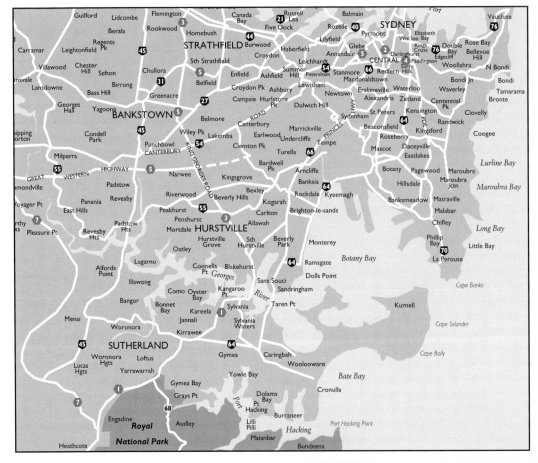

The Secret South

The South was the first place discovered by Captain Cook, in 1770, but the last place to be discovered by the Sydneysiders of today. If you think there are great waterways around the centre and north of Sydney, wait until you see the South. And if you think the North Shore is "leafy", have a look around Sutherland Shire. Eye-openers.

"Picnics, swimming and fishing on the Georges River in the family runabout, catching yabbies in the upper reaches of the Woronora River, travelling to Cronulla for surfing and sailing, and to the Royal National Park for boating and bushwalking – these are my most vivid memories, and the wildflowers in the Park in springtime were a special treat." says fifth generation resident, Gwen Chater.

"And there were tennis clubs, youth-groups, musical and theatrical societies. It was an ideal life in so many ways. Everything is still available, just as it was then, but more activities have developed over the years with the growth of population. We have our own symphony orchestras, numerous drama and musical societies, craft groups of all kinds, and a great variety of clubs and organisations. The entire community shares so much."

Some other people who were here before you and Gwen: Captain Cook, botanists Joseph Banks and Carl Solander and, of course, Le Compte de Laperouse. In more recent times, others who have lived here were artist Elioth Gruner, seven times winner of the prestigious Wynne Prize for landscape painting, and writers like Christina Stead, Clive James, Kathy Lette and Miles Franklin, author of *My Brilliant Career* who also wrote passionately about the South in *Back to Bool Bool*, under the pseudonym of Brent of Bin Bin: *"Botany Bay in the distance was the old Madonna blue; Cronulla's sands gold-tinted snow; the white fountains that are never still on the quietest Southern Pacific Day played about the feet of Cape Banks and Bare Island...."* Blackwood, Edinburgh, 1931.

Franklin also wrote about the nearby *"agglomerations of Erskineville and Newtown"*. And indeed, you still have to pass through Newtown on your way to the south, on Route 66, the Princes Highway. The highway is also called King Street as it passes through Newtown and is today considered one of the zaniest streets in Sydney. Miles Franklin, who concealed her gender in order to be accepted as a writer, would no doubt have been amused by the Newtown of today.

For telephone numbers and addresses, see the yellow pages Directory at the back

1 **Gould's Book Arcade,** 32 King Street. Filled from floor to ceiling with new and second-hand books. You may find that elusive title you've been searching for. Open from early till late.

2 **Newtown Hotel,** 174 King Street. If you feel like a spot of drag, drop in for a sparkling night of sequins and song.

3 **Newtown Markets,** Burland Hall, 220 King Street. A market reminiscent of a '60s time-warp.

4 **Kilimanjaro Restaurant,** 280 King Street. Pungent aromatic food is piled high on traditional wooden platters and served by beautiful Africans adorned in traditional tunics and fezzes.

5 **Newtown High School of Performing Arts,** opposite 381 King Street. Showcase concerts are regularly open to the public.

6 **Newton's Restaurant,** 403 King Street. During the day Lawrence trains young chefs and budding restaurateurs – many of them former street kids. At night, these poised and polished students turn on service and food that belie the tiny prices.

7 **Desperate Living,** 415a King Street. It's hip, it's hot and it's classic '60s decor at its best.

8 **All Buttons Great and Small** 419a King Street. Stand out from the crowd with Italian jewel encrusted domes or whimsical handmade animal buttons.

9 **Off The Rails,** 429 King Street. You'll be delighted with all the paraphernalia from the glorious

The Imperial Hotel, Newtown is where some of Priscilla, Queen of the Desert *was filmed.*

golden days of travel. (Note – is moving to 160 Salisbury Road, Camperdown.

10 **Dino Store,** 453 King Street. A toy store with a difference. The mini-archaeologists embark on an expedition through the rear of the shop which has been transformed into a pre-historic jungle.

11 **Aviamentos - Ribbons & Braids,** 457 King Street. This little haunt is visited by every designer, interior decorator, fashion enthusiast who's in the know.

12 **The New Theatre,** 542 King Street. A happening fringe-theatre venue.

13 **Imperial Hotel,** 33 Erskineville Road (runs off King Street), Erskineville. This is the pub where memorable scenes from drag flick, *Priscilla, Queen of the Desert* was filmed.

14 **Amera's Palace,** 12A Enmore Road. Swing your hips and sign up for your first belly-dancing class.

15 **Polymorph Body Art Gallery,** 82 Enmore Road. Polymorph is thriving with the latest demand for pierced navels, eyebrows, noses, nipples and other more interesting and – dare we say – more painful places.

16 **Alfalfa House,** 113 Enmore Road. Carries bulk organic/biodynamic whole foods and members are able to trade work for discounts.

18 **Wizard of Od,** 115 Enmore Road. Has a cult following for its re-vamped, re-dyed and re-cycled fashions.

JUST OUT OF NEWTOWN...

...try the **Tempe Tip** for something far more down-to-earth. Tempe Tip is properly called the Salvation Army Red Shield Industries. Everyone should experience a trip to the Tip to find treasures and leave trash – your trash will be someone's treasure and vice versa, and all in a good cause. By train, alight at Sydenham Station and it's a short walk to 7 Bellevue Street, St Peters.

BOUND FOR BOTANY BAY

To reach the rather hallowed spot of **Captain Cook's** landing place at Kurnell, Botany Bay, travel via Captain Cook Drive from Taren Point or Cronulla. (Half the places to see and things to do in the South seem to be named Cook or Endeavour or Banks or Solander.) **The Discovery Centre** at Captain Cook's Landing Place is a fine exhibition centre; it tells the story of Cook's exploration of the area, which led to the colonisation of Australia. The exhibits include "Eight Days that Changed the World", with artefacts, relics, pictures and texts. In the Centre are "Wetlands Reflections" focusing on the richness of Botany Bay's wetlands, where a great variety of birds and flora are protected by the NSW National Parks and Wildlife Service.

Because of the historic significance of the landing site at Kurnell, 100ha of land were set aside for public recreation in 1899, and the park was proclaimed an historic site in 1967. With Bare Island and La Perouse, it became part of Botany Bay National Park in 1988. Today, 436ha provide facilities for picnics and barbecues, bushwalking, fishing and bird watching. Park open 7am-7.30pm; Discovery Centre open 9.30am-4pm Monday to Friday, 10am-4.30pm weekends and public holidays. Entry Free. Captain Cook Drive – to Kurnell.

On the opposite side of Botany Bay from Kurnell is **La Perouse.** It's a park now, with a museum, located in the 1882 cable station. Le Compte de Laperouse (that's the way he spelled it, and the way the museum does now), was a great and gentle man. He was commissioned by King Louis XVI of France to undertake a scientific voyage of the Pacific region. By a remarkable coincidence, Laperouse and his two ships sailed into Botany Bay on the 26th of January, 1788, just six days after the arrival of the

British settlers on the First Fleet, and the very day Phillip was establishing the Sydney Cove colony at Port Jackson. The Laperouse expedition stayed in Botany Bay only briefly, and after six weeks sailed toward New Caledonia never to be seen or heard of again. More's the pity, we say. To get to La Perouse, travel along Anzac Parade right to the end.

Laperouse Museum is open daily, small entrance fee. Bookings essential for guided tours which are available in English and French. On Sundays, you can see Aborigines giving boomerang-throwing demonstrations and there is also a Snake Show, which is very educational, if you like that sort of thing. End of Anzac Parade, La Perouse.

On Saturday and Sunday, there are regular boat trips from La Perouse Park to **Bare Island** and its Fort. The island is now connected to the mainland by a causeway and the Fort was built in 1885 as part of the Colony's defence-works against the Russians. A wild idea.

La Perouse has often been described as a lonely, windswept area with humpy housing. Today, it is a lonely, windswept area with no humpy housing. The aboriginal humpies have been replaced by solid suburban dwellings, but the wind still blows across Botany Bay with quite a force. Down from the Museum and right on the beach is the **Boatshed Cafe** – a nice-looking cosy waterfront cafe with a big verandah. The outlook is over Frenchman's Bay, where Kurnell refineries don't intrude at all – well, maybe a bit. You can arrange boat hire here, too. Room for improvement in the food department.

Lydham Hall was built in 1860 on the highest point of land overlooking Botany Bay. It is a fine example of the transition of simple Georgian-style architecture to the more elaborate Victorian-style. It has been faithfully restored and was the childhood home of writer Christina Stead. It was at one time the residence of her father, David Stead, fisheries expert and naturalist - who, incidentally, gave the suburb of Banksia its name, after Sir Joseph Banks, naturally. Open Saturday, Sunday and public holidays from 2-4pm. Entry free. Group inspections by appointment with curator. 18 Lydham Avenue, Rockdale.

At **Kareela,** on the Georges River which feeds into Botany Bay, is the **Joseph Banks Native Plants Reserve.** Sir Joseph Banks and Carl Solander collected many specimens of native flora to send to London for the delight of the English. At the reserve are displays of flowers and fruit of native plants from all over Australia demonstrating the way they grow in local conditions. The Reserve includes a charming scented garden as well. There is also a "warm" rainforest for tropical plants and a cooler one of temperate rainforest trees. The reserve offers many delights that the Royal Botanic Gardens in town could envy. Off Manooka Place via Alpita Street and not far from the airport, it's open 7am-3.30pm Mon-Fri; l0am-5pm weekends and public holidays (closed Christmas Day and Good Friday). Another plus for this charming place is the **Kareela Golf Club.** Not just for the golf – for the oysters. This is one of the recommendations we got from the Oyster Farmers' Association. If you go for a meal (no hardship) you can book in at the club as a day member.

UNEXPLORED TERRITORY

The Georges River cruises on the *MV Bass* and *Flinders* or *MV That's Life* wind right up into the upper reaches of the Georges River to places like Como and Lugarno, which are like unexplored territory to most Sydneysiders. **Riverboat Cruises** depart from **Sans Souci Wharf,** Sans Souci Park. Varying prices for coffee and lunch cruises, of one-and-a-half or three hour duration. The cruises are good value, the finger food generous, and the lunches rich

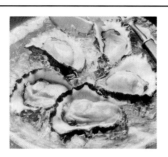

OYSTERS - WHERE TO ENJOY THEM

We have mentioned a couple of these eating places in other parts of this chapter on the South; however, for oyster-lovers, here are the recommendations of the Oyster Farmers' Association (and who knows better): **The Black Panther** (great name for an oyster restaurant!) 1260 Princes Highway, Engadine; **Staplyton's Restaurant,** 782 Princes Highway, Sutherland; **The Beached Brasserie,** (overlooking Cronulla Beach) 20 Gerald Street, Cronulla; **Kareela Golf Club,** (near the Joseph Banks Native Plants Reserve.) Bates Drive, Kareela.

STAYING IN THE SOUTH

It's not easy yet to find our special UnTourist-style places to stay in the South. However, our pick is the **Novotel** in the Botany Bay area, at the corner of The Grand Parade and Princess Street, Brighton-le-Sands. It has a well-equipped gymnasium, as well as restaurants and a pool. Fine views across Botany Bay. And, in the deep south, **The Kingsway,** on Cronulla Beach, is another hotel with spectacular views. You're close to the National Park here, too.

and satisfying. And all the while you're treated to some spectacular views, lush country, picnic grounds (well-patronised) and very expensive houses indeed.

Best fun of all must be the overstated **Sylvania Waters** of BBC/ABC TV fame. This canal subdivision, similar in taste to Gold Coast and Florida developments, is the largest privately owned waterway in Sydney. In 1963, one James Goyem acquired the land by purchases from various oyster farmers, and called it "Sylvania Gardens". Yes, "overstated" is the word, and most residents of Sylvania are more than a little embarrassed about the whole thing, especially since the documentary a few years ago created headlines and comment all over the place. Two of its most famous residents, Noeline and Laurie Donaher, were stars of the show.

An aside: A crew member on the Riverboat cruise told us that friends of his went to a costume party as Noeline and Laurie. "She lent us some clothes," the friend said, "and he lent us some of his racing gear. I asked if I could borrow her blonde wig. That was a mistake, as she told me that her blonde hair was in fact all her own." Noeline is real, from top to toe, and long may she prosper.

On this cruise you also pass many oyster farms. Georges River oysters are the most famous of the famous Sydney rock oysters. Oyster farming is a million-dollar industry begun as early as the l880s, and the industry continues to improve in value and production.

THE 'REAL' SOUTH

And now for your visit to the real South. According to the (Sutherland Shire) locals 'the real' starts south of Botany Bay. They certainly wouldn't claim Newtown.

Sydney people who don't live in the South tend to think of **Cronulla** purely as a beach but, as we discovered, it has much more to offer than surfing. Cronulla Beach is famous for two things: the great surf, and the book and film *Puberty Blues*. Kathy Lette is responsible for the book. She, with co-author Gabrielle Carey, recounted some of the more fascinating teenage doings around the area in the 1970s. Cronulla is an attractive, secluded beach, with nice buildings, sheltering trees and the minimum of "beach tat" around the surfing area. Overlooking the beach is the **Beachside Brasserie** (another "best oysters" tip from our Oyster Farmers Association mate). It is the only Sydney beach you can get to by train, and it is on the suburban rail system on the Illawara line which departs from Central Railway Station.

Other lovely beaches near here are **North Cronulla, Wanda** and **Elouera.** But there are many more joys in the Cronulla area because it faces both out to the open sea and into Port Hacking, mouth of the Hacking River – a marvellous stretch of water winding up into the Royal National Park.

The Cronulla Marina, on Port Hacking, is a special little place. Small and sheltered with an old-fashioned boatshed feel about it, it has the statutory Aussie cafe serving instant coffee, iced doughnuts and lamingtons. Above it there is the pleasant looking **Mariners Cove Restaurant** which caters for local weddings. It is open to the public, but not for lunch Saturday and Sunday.

The Cronulla Marina is the base for the **Cronulla National Park Ferry Cruises** with its two sturdy little wooden ferries, the *MV Tom Thumb III* and the *MV Curranulla* which moor at the wharf ready to take you across to the village of **Bundeena,** or up the Hacking River to the wondrous **Royal National Park.**

The Marina is also the base for **South Pacific Seaplanes,** and you can arrange charter flights to and from wherever. From the South Pacific Seaplane base, you can also hire an open "tinnie" with an outboard motor, or a houseboat which has full facilities – four double-beds and two single-berths, plus gallery and utensils.

Now to the cruise, which is probably the most practical and enjoyable way to see and explore the superb bays and inlets of **Port Hacking** and the Hacking River.

The little *MV Tom Thumb III* (named for Bass and Flinders' craft) takes a leisurely three-hour trip up the Hacking River from Cronulla and is a charmer. A real, honest 48-foot wooden boat that carries only about 50 passengers – there's coffee from an urn on a table with a checked cloth, and you help yourself to handfuls of biscuits. Wonderful old photographs and

MV Tom Thumb

maps tell you who's been there in years past and where you are now. No pretension and plenty of warmth. The boat, incidentally, is six times the size of the original eight-foot *Tom Thumb* in which Bass and Flinders explored and mapped much of Australia's eastern coastline.

Cruising is on one of the "most unspoiled waterways in the world',' as the boat owners boast, Port Hacking and the Hacking River. It is indeed unspoiled, because on the south side is the majestic **Royal National Park.** On the north side the boat goes in and out of wonderful bays and past a diversity of homes – some gently blending, others standing out less gently in the sylvan surroundings. Overall, it's a beautiful cruise indeed.

MV Tom Thumb III departs Sunday, Monday and Wednesday 10.30am, returning at 1.30pm. For information, call Cronulla and National Park Ferries Cronulla Marina at Tonkin Street Wharf near Cronulla Railway Station.

THE WORLD'S FIRST NATIONAL PARK

Well, it's the South's back garden, and it's hard to believe that any place so tranquil could be controversial, but the Park is, in a (gentle) way. Is it the world's oldest? Or is it second to the USA's Yellowstone? Here are the facts, as stated in the Park's brochure: *"Our Royal National Park was gazetted in 1879 as 'The National Park'... this was the first application of the term to a public reserve. Although Yellowstone was established in 1872, it was not officially designated as a National Park in legislation until 1883, four years after its Australian counterpart."*

The Royal National Park (it's 15,014ha) can therefore lay claim to being the world's first National Park – and it does.

The Sydney Tramway Museum is a bit further afield, at Loftus, which can be reached by train from Arncliffe, or indeed from the city (the Waterfall Line). It's a "hands-on" experience, with a great display of vintage trams, as well as a selection of electric trams from other Australian centres as well as from San Francisco and Nagasaki. And you can actually ride on them. There's a trip to the Royal National Park by the Parkline tram too. Museum entry fee can include tram rides. Group concessions available. Corner of Princes Highway and Pitt Street, Sutherland Shire.

BUSHFIRES

A word about the horrifying bushfires that swept much of the South and the Royal National Park in the tragic days of January, 1994. They began on the 5th of January in the National Park, and quickly escalated. On Thursday, the 6th, fires swept past Bundeena and Maianbar in the Park, and on Friday caused loss of homes in Bangor. The fires devastated housing and other buildings and reserves in Como, Bonnet Bay and Jannali.

One hundred and four Sutherland Shire homes were totally destroyed, as well as a church, Como West Public School, part of Jannali Public School and a kindergarten. A further 38 homes were severely damaged. An appalling 98% of the National Park was burnt out – more than 14,500ha. The Shire's 13 Bushfire Brigades, the NSW Fire Brigades, and NSW and interstate fire services, Police Central District Ambulance, welfare services and civilian volunteers gave unstinting service.

Assistance came not only from all parts of Australia. Sutherland Shire's Japanese sister city, Chuo, gave a total of $23,000 to local bushfire victims, from the Chuo Council, individuals and students. The fires were not reported extinguished until Friday, January 14.

We are happy to report that regrowth has been remarkable in the Royal National Park.

THE ROYAL NATIONAL PARK

There is bushwalking, swimming, sightseeing, bicycling, camping, fishing or boating. Or simply enjoying the spectacular coastal cliffs, woodlands and surf beaches. There are something like 700 species of flowering plants, and memorable waterfalls, cascades and rockpools.

The legacies of Aboriginal culture are here, too, in rock engravings, charcoal drawings, axe-grinding grooves, hand stencils. For hundreds of generations, the land had been occupied by the Dharawal tribe, who fished the coast estuaries and streams, and supplemented their diet with vegetable and animal foods from the bushland. (These Aboriginal sites and artefacts are protected by the NSW National Parks and Wildlife Service.)

The **Visitors Centre** at Audley is very helpful. To get there you take Route 68 and, heading south, just past Engadine, turn right off Princes Highway. Audley, by the way, was the first English settlement in the Park and it has information about camping and boat hire – canoes, rowing boats and paddle boats. For further information, contact the South Metropolitan District office of the **Parks and Wildlife Service**, Monday to Friday, or the Audley Visitor Centre 9am-4pm daily.

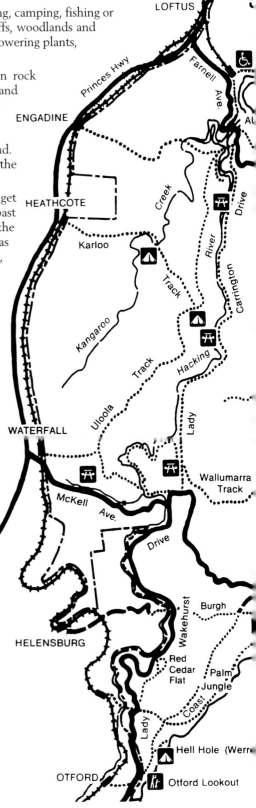

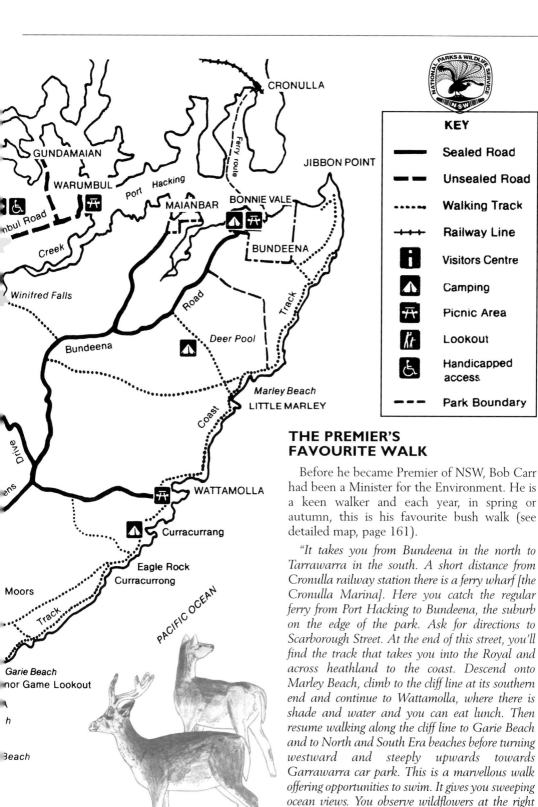

KEY

——————	Sealed Road
— — —	Unsealed Road
······	Walking Track
+++++	Railway Line
ℹ	Visitors Centre
⛺	Camping
⛱	Picnic Area
🚶	Lookout
♿	Handicapped access
– – –	Park Boundary

CRONULLA

JIBBON POINT

GUNDAMAIAN

WARUMBUL

Port Hacking

MAIANBAR

BONNIE VALE

BUNDEENA

nbul Road

Creek

Winifred Falls

Road

Bundeena

Deer Pool

Track

Marley Beach
LITTLE MARLEY

Coast

Drive

ens

WATTAMOLLA

Curracurrang

Moors

Eagle Rock
Curracurrong

Track

PACIFIC OCEAN

Garie Beach
nor Game Lookout

h

Beach

Scale

```
|————————————————|  km
1        2        3
```

THE PREMIER'S FAVOURITE WALK

Before he became Premier of NSW, Bob Carr had been a Minister for the Environment. He is a keen walker and each year, in spring or autumn, this is his favourite bush walk (see detailed map, page 161).

"It takes you from Bundeena in the north to Tarrawarra in the south. A short distance from Cronulla railway station there is a ferry wharf [the Cronulla Marina]. Here you catch the regular ferry from Port Hacking to Bundeena, the suburb on the edge of the park. Ask for directions to Scarborough Street. At the end of this street, you'll find the track that takes you into the Royal and across heathland to the coast. Descend onto Marley Beach, climb to the cliff line at its southern end and continue to Wattamolla, where there is shade and water and you can eat lunch. Then resume walking along the cliff line to Garie Beach and to North and South Era beaches before turning westward and steeply upwards towards Garrawarra car park. This is a marvellous walk offering opportunities to swim. It gives you sweeping ocean views. You observe wildflowers at the right time of year. In the right season, you might spot a passing whale. It's a tough but manageable 13km walk, tough because you'll know you've done a hard slog by the end of it. And you will have to arrange to be met by a car at Garrawarra."
(METRO, Sydney Morning Herald, October 1994.)

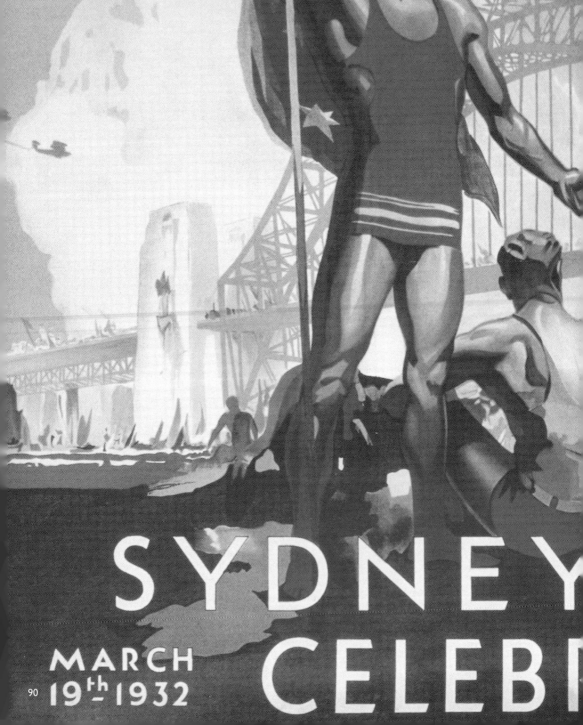

SYDNEY
CELEBR

MARCH
19th 1932

90

6 NORTH

INCLUDES: Sydney's "coat hanger"; Luna Park; joys of the Inner North Shore; the Zoo with the view; shopping at Mosman; The Spit; the Northern Beaches; Manly; the great Ku-ring-gai National Park; and the great water playground of Pittwater.

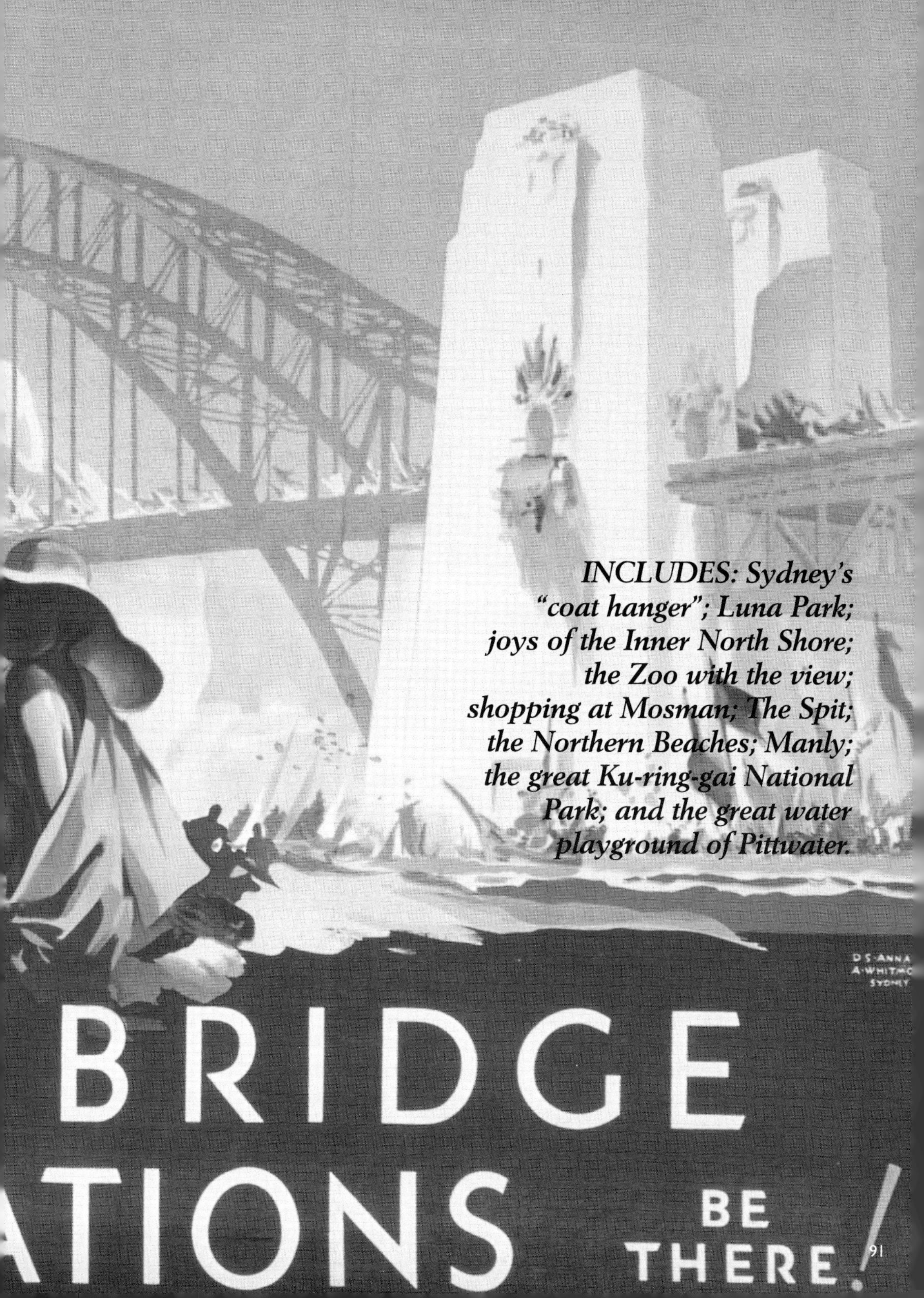

D S · ANNA
A · WHITMO
SYDNEY

BRIDGE
ATIONS BE THERE!

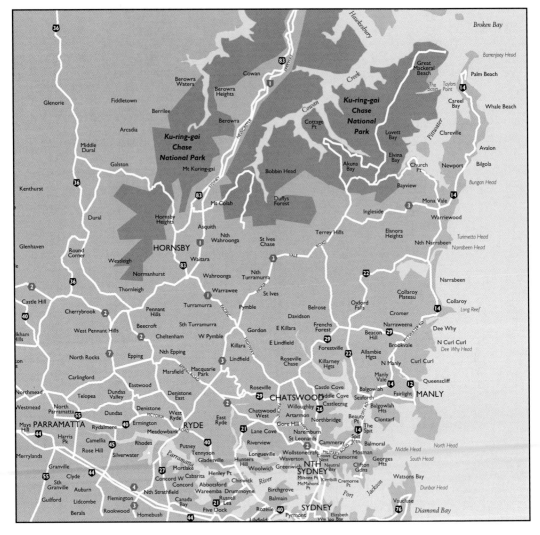

Over the Bridge and Far Away

The northern areas of Sydney are, in the most part, pleasant, conservative, green (environmentally, not politically) residential suburbs, and the people who live there love them.

We are told that the original inhabitants of the Northern Shore, the Gu-ring-gai Aborigines, expressed their commitment to the area by patronisingly naming the southern shore of Sydney Harbour "the other shore". The wonderful 14,838ha Ku-ring-gai Chase, only 24kms from the centre of the city, is named after them.

People think nothing of travelling to outback Australia seeking Aboriginal pre-history, yet there are over 2000 rock engravings in and around Sydney – the richest near-city heritage in the world, and few residents are aware of their existence. The best of these engravings are in the northern suburbs, as we will show you later in this chapter.

THE COATHANGER

To write about the North Shore without first focusing on the Harbour Bridge would be careless, as one begot the other. In fact, many Sydneysiders still refer to the northern suburbs as "over the Bridge".

There are those who date Sydney's first buds of maturity from the time the Sydney Harbour Bridge opened, possibly because it was Australia's first world-class architectural icon and it is still the longest single-span bridge in the world. The Bridge dominated the city as its tallest point from 1932, when it opened in the midst of the Great Depression, until 1967, when Australia Square (which is round), was built. Now that too has been overshadowed by a number of anonymous-looking office blocks.

The opening of the Harbour Bridge is one of the great Sydney folk tales, told and retold from grandparent to grandchild. A gathering of pompous dignitaries, representatives of King and country and the media in force, all concentrated on the long-awaited event, as did the excited citizens of Sydney who had watched with cynicism and doubt as the giant span crept to its closure.

The moment arrived.

The State Premier was about to cut the ceremonial ribbon when an Irish horseman with a Dutch name, DeGroot, wearing an Australian Army uniform and a rather racist attitude, beat him to the act and sliced it through – *"In the name of the decent citizens of New South Wales!"*

It appears that he and his super-right-wing colleagues thought the then Labor Party Premier, "big feller" Jack Lang, was not the appropriate person to represent *"A people of pure British stock"* in this symbolic event. For more than 60 years, until the Harbour Tunnel was constructed, the Bridge had the sole structural franchise to move the good citizens of Sydney north and south across the harbour.

Regardless of whether you are travelling north or south, the navigational skills and level of concentration demanded of the driver are at brain-surgeon level in order to avoid ending up in Hornsby when you were aiming for Roseville. This applies to savvy Sydney residents, so the visitor has little chance of an uneventful crossing.

We recommend, therefore, that first-time visitors would be well advised to walk, bicycle, take a cab, a train, a bus, or, as our chapter on transport suggests, cross by ferry when possible.

Despite the recent challenge from the uncharismatic Harbour Tunnel and the older, more artistic contender, the Opera House, the Bridge certainly stands as Sydney's most familiar and integrated monument.

One of the main reasons for this is that it is omnipresent. Unlike the Opera House, at which you sneak a glance from certain angles of the city's skyline, the Harbour Bridge seems to pop up everywhere, which is rather handy because, as it runs broadly north and south across the city, it becomes a convenient compass in times of uncertainty. Unless, of course, those times are when you are actually approaching, crossing or leaving the Bridge on one of its many fettuccine-like lanes – at these times, your compass tends to fail you.

The inner North Shore has many pleasures for the traveller, all announced by the cavernous mouth of Luna Park, which sits guarding what is arguably the most valuable 12.5ha of land in Australia, the subject of a great deal of wheeling and dealing since its beginnings.

LUNA PARK – "JUST FOR FUN"

Part of the Sydney landscape since 1935, Luna Park has had an eventful history as the playground of Sydney children and their enthusiastic parents. It was closed down by the war, then by a dreadful fire, wear, tear, abuse and finally by poor trading and a noisy and costly Big Dipper.

It has had many owners, but the development potential of those valuable hectares wound up to fever pitch during the entrepreneurial '80s when the state government stepped in just in time to stop a five-star Luna Park luxury hotel and 200-berth marina being built on the site.

During the '90s, Luna Park was renovated superbly, complete with fairy floss, ferris wheel, and a very expensive and contentious Big Dipper. As often happens in these developments, the most successful part is the cheapest – the old Coney Island with all its funny mirrors, the Turkey Trot, the original wooden slides, and all the wonderful old graphics lovingly replaced by friends of Luna Park, like Martin Sharp and Sam Marshall. Unfortunately Luna Park is currently closed and its giant face is harbour decoration only.

LAVENDER BAY

Lavender Bay and Luna Park are natural enemies. One is quiet, reflective and residential; the other noisy and vigorous. One complains that its neighbour is too loud and vulgar; the other responds with complaints about *them* being too stuffy and intolerant. It has been going on for years and will no doubt continue for many years to come.

The little Hegarty's Ferry, from Jetty 6 Circular Quay, goes right into the Lavender Bay wharf. This charming, unpretentious area at the foot of the slick high-rise of North Sydney is a particularly pleasant place. In fact, there are some lovely walks in the area. You can stroll through the overhanging fig trees, enjoying the lush natural gardens, sparing a thought, perhaps, for Lavender Bay's wicked past.

In 1830, it was called Hulk Bay. The rotting convict hulk *Phoenix* was moored in the bay. Its pathetic living cargo was worked, in many cases, to death, building the handsome stone buildings on nearby Goat Island. What an irony that peaceful Lavender Bay should be named after George Lavender, the *Phoenix's* overseer.

MCMAHONS POINT

McMahons Point is the site of the first cross-harbour ferry service in Sydney. It was run by a Jamaican who was first called Billy Blue (it is highly unlikely that this was his real name), later nicknamed The Old Commodore. It is also said that he was a confectioner in London and got caught with his fingers in the "lolly" jar and was thus transported to the colony. It all seems a bit vague; however, one thing appears to be clear – Billy Blue existed and he did run the first ferry, albeit oar-powered. If this is ever disproved, then there will be a whole lot of streets, parcels of land and establishments that have to do a quick name change around the Blues Point area.

The inner north is an attractive place to make your base in Sydney. Expatriate Sydney/New Yorker Susan Talbot, whose favourite place to stay is the Harbourside Apartments on McMahons Point, says: *"On this side of the Harbour you get to gaze at the classic Sydney skyline. When you stay on the city side, all you get to see is the North Shore."* She has a point.

One of the great advantages of staying in the lower North Shore is that McMahons Point, Milsons Point, Kirribilli, Neutral Bay, North Sydney, Cremorne and Mosman are all serviced by regular ferries which take you straight to the Quay in the centre of town – making travelling a pleasure rather than a drag.

In North Sydney we discovered the private little **McLaren Hotel** in, surprise, surprise, McLaren Street.

A director of the hotel, Chris Fairbairn, gave us some more insights into the area:

"There is a wealth of really interesting old buildings and a genuine village feeling running down to the harbour from North Sydney to McMahons Point, particularly as you walk through Lavender Bay Park. We have good food markets over the weekend. All the locals seem to gather at them. There are 105 places to eat in this area, so you won't go hungry. The 'watering holes' are special – The Rag and Famish, The Greenwood Hotel and Pennys – there are plenty of squash, golf and health clubs and the Walker Street Cinema is our local art movie house. North Sydney laboured under the image of a commercial/business district, with no soul, for years, but it's really a great place to live now."

NORTH SYDNEY HIGHLIGHTS

North Sydney Noodle Market, Friday nights summer, Sunday lunchtime winter, in the park between the Council Chambers and Stanton Library in Miller Street; **North Sydney Markets,** second Sunday each month at Miller and McLaren Streets; **Don Bank Museum,** historic timber-slab cottage, 6 Napier Street; **Mary McKillop Place** for Australia's first saint (at the moment just blessed), 7 Mount Street; **North Sydney Oval** dates back to 1867, Miller and Ridge Streets; **North Sydney Olympic Pool,** favourite haunt of Northside families, Alfred Street South, Milsons Point; **Indian Empire** for cuisine and view, Walker and Lavender Streets; **Thomas Street Cafe** – read the Sunday papers in the sun, 2 Thomas Street; **Fare Go Gourmet,** high-quality local produce and dreamy desserts, 65 Union Street; **Kirribilli Market,** once a month, Bradfield Park North, Alfred Street, Kirribilli.

SOME FOOD GEMS

Before we head further north, we take a detour away from the grand water frontages to point out a few particularly good food shops in the neighbouring suburbs of **Willoughby** and **Chatswood** – they are Italian, Iranian and Chinese (we are nothing if not eclectic). Both of these suburbs are sandwiched between the **Pacific Highway (Route 1)** and **Eastern Valley Way (Route 26).**

A unique shop and the North Shore's crown jewel among bakeries – **Il Gianfornaio.** The Italian bakers, imported from Rome, turn out a wondrous assortment of breads. Call in for the best cappuccino on the northside; you won't be disappointed. Closed Sundays, 414 Victoria Avenue, Chatswood.

The Iranian shop **Darya Deli** is full of the most wonderful aromas, from roasted nuts to the freshly baked baklava, halva and sweet honey pastries and lots of other Middle Eastern specialties. Open every day, 331 Penshurst Street, Willoughby.

If you are after a new foodie fix, head to **Omar Khayyam** for excellent food often accompanied by traditional Armenian musicians. Lunch and dinner, every day, 417 Victoria Avenue, Chatswood.

The Burlington Centre, originally only in Chinatown, now has a northside store. Filled with every conceivable Asian delicacy. Open every day, 258 Penshurst Street, Willoughby.

NORTHERN CURIOS

At nearby **Northbridge** (best approach is along Miller Street which runs into Strathallen Road), there is a full turreted mock medieval (or is it mock Gothic?) stone bridge, a developer's fantasy. The next surprise about average suburban Northbridge is that once you get into the shopping area on Sailors Bay Road, you realise that it is noticeably Japanese. It has, in fact, the best Japanese supermarket in Sydney, **Tokyo Mart,** 27 Northbridge Plaza, Northbridge. For some reason a little Japanese community has sprung up in suburban Northbridge. So if you want to buy or eat Japanese, go straight on from the mock-German-Gothic bridge in the typical Sydney middle-class suburb of Northbridge, and there you have it! And while you're there – **Antico's** in the same Plaza, is considered Sydney's best fruit and vegetable shop.

Nearby **Castlecrag,** once a ravaged wasteland, was turned by the celebrated American architect Walter Burley Griffen into a showcase for his domestic dwellings and "garden suburb" vision. (Burley Griffin is most noted for his 1911 master-plan for Canberra.) His Castlecrag homes are readily identifiable, usually built from rough-hewn native stone, set in heavy walls with detailed windows. His trademark flat concrete roofs were designed to meld with the craggy tiers of cliffs and boulders. It's worth cruising the streets – The Bastion, The Parapet, The Bulwark – to see what remains of one man's vision of a unique Australian architecture. Walking tour sheets are available through **Willoughby Council** (see Directory).

MOSMAN AND THE ZOO WITH A VIEW

For the indulgent who are born to shop, **Military Road** through Neutral Bay, Cremorne and Mosman is a most rewarding direction to follow – in particular, the shopping strip between Spit Junction into the "Zoo street" (Bradleys Head Road). This area is, in our opinion, the best fashion strip in Sydney – that is, if you are over 30. (We deal with this strip in greater detail in Chapter 8).

"OK. Tell the agent we'll take it."

No zoo in the world enjoys such a wonderful setting. Nestled in virgin bushland and perched on the edge of the Mosman clifftop, it looks down across Sydney Harbour. You can get there by bus or car but we strongly recommend the ferry ride to Taronga Park wharf below the Zoo. There's an amusement-park style cable car which lifts you up to the Zoo. It is worth the trip for the ride – even if you aren't that crazy about zoos. Entry fee. Open every day of the year, 9am-5pm. Now also has evenig openings so night animals can be viewed in their normal hours. Bradleys Head Road, Mosman.

BALMORAL BEACH, THE SPIT

Nearby Balmoral Beach, with its charming swimming beach and bathing pavilion is special. It is a place to spend a day very happily. There are performances by the Sydney Theatre Company here during the January Sydney Festival – "Shakespeare by the Sea" and concerts in the Rotunda. For information, call the **Mosman Council.**

Take a stroll along the Esplanade, take a dip in the harbour baths (with protective netting), or lunch under the Rotunda. You can even hire a windsurfer and take to the seas. You'll notice the majestic **Bathers Pavilion** perched on the seafront. The restaurant of the same name is excellent. If you'd prefer a casual light meal call into their refreshment rooms for coffee, divine cakes and icy cold drinks. Special feature – breakfast on weekends and public holidays. Open every day, 4 The Esplanade, Balmoral Beach.

There's also an excellent seafood restaurant, **Watermark,** almost on the sand at Balmoral Beach. It's particularly good for its many varieties of oysters. Open every day, including breakfast, 2a The Esplanade.

Spit Road, as it continues down to Middle Harbour and **The Spit Bridge,** is spectacular. Restaurants at The Spit with great views and food to match – **Shores,** Parriwi Road at Spit Bridge, and **I Canottieri,** 81 Parriwi Road.

A bit beyond the Spit Bridge, the road forks, one direction going to **Manly** and the other to **Pittwater** – both very special places in Sydney and places which, we believe, make great accommodation bases for a visitor.

The South Steyne, circa 1965

MANLY

Manly's claim has always been, "Seven miles from Sydney and a thousand miles from care". The corny phrase still works today as it did in Manly's heyday in the '30s, mainly because there is still an amusement-park feeling about the place. Peppered with ice-cream-eating day visitors, the very permanent, conservative retirees seem to mix it up with the very temporary surfies quite amicably. Manly seems to keep its festive and holiday feeling all year round, mainly because the surf is active most months of the year. In fact, to take a ferry ride across the Heads to Manly on a really wild day when the sea is up is something to write home about. Until the turn of the century, there was a man with a dinner bell who would ring it on Manly Beach to declare the end of permitted public bathing times which were only in the early morning and after dark. The local newspaper proprietor put a stop to that in 1902 by entering the surf, appropriately clad in neck-to-knee swimmers (some accounts have him in full morning dress), defying the law and setting the scene for the future.

Manly was given its name by Captain (later Governor) Arthur Phillip in 1788 when he noted a sighting a number of "manly" looking Aborigines on the shores of what he later called Manly Cove. This turned out to be a prophetic observation as Manly hosted the beginnings of such manly pursuits as body surfing, surfboard riding, surf lifesaving and, in the past decade, macho events like the Australian "ironman" competitions.

We like to eat at **Armstrongs Brasserie** at Manly Wharf and watch the comings and goings. Then there's **The Daily Grind,** great little coffee house that discourages tourists, so you should feel right at home, 29 Belgrave Street. There are two worthwhile oceanside restaurants at Shelly Beach – **The Bower** (what a magic view!), 7/9 Marine Parade, and **Le Kiosk** at Fairy Bower, end of Bower Street, Shelly Beach.

Manly has a good **Visitors Information Bureau** on North Steyne and they can give chapter and verse on the various walks of the area.

PITTWATER

*Where the dolphins
and whales play*

Vast expanses of clear blue water, lumbering pelicans feeding on the shores, natural bush inlets and islands to explore as well as all the creature-comforts – great restaurants and places to stay – this is Pittwater. For the UnTourist who wants to spend some time close to some of the undeveloped waterways of the Sydney area, yet have access to plenty of civilised things to eat, drink and do, this area has to be a serious option.

Pittwater, in the waters of Broken Bay, is under an hour's drive from the centre of Sydney – it takes a bit longer by bus, although in the peak traffic times, it is sometimes faster than by car. You can actually get from Manly direct to Pittwater by catching a No 12 bus from Manly Wharf which will take you to Pittwater via the great northern beaches (see Chapter 13 for details).

You can also fly there with **Sydney Harbour Seaplanes** regular charter flights from Rose Bay to Palm Beach if you wish. This is, not surprisingly, more costly than the bus, but what an experience – flying straight up the coast, along the edge of land and sea.

Most of the Pittwater communities like **Palm Beach, Whale Beach, Bilgola, Newport** and **Avalon** began with holiday homes for wealthy families. Many are now permanent homes for a large portion of Sydney commuters as well as more than the average share of writers, painters, film actors and directors.

The village of Avalon, with its charming little coffee shops and cafes has traditionally been a painters' retreat. **The Cafe for Obscure Avalon Painters** is at 1 MacMillan Court, Avalon Parade.

According to savvy local Frenchman Jean Luc Clavel, Gilles Hinkel's patisserie **La Banette** at 28 Avalon Parade makes the best petits fours outside Paris.

Captain Phillip sailed north to **Broken Bay** and Pittwater in 1788, only six weeks after landing in Sydney Cove, to seek out more arable land for growing produce for the new British colony. After entering the first stretch of water, he enthusiastically penned yet another of his "I've found the best harbour in the world" letters to Lord Sydney back home in England: *"...the finest piece of water which I ever saw and which I honoured with the name Pitt Water......it (could) contain all the Navy of Great Britain."* Eventually, land along the nearby Hawkesbury River provided vital produce for the colony, produce which was shipped down the coast, giving reason for early settlement in the Pittwater area.

At one time the Pittwater and the **Hawkesbury** area were renowned for their ferocious sharks and there are many blood-curdling tales of the fearful fate that awaited a careless sailor. These days people swim off the local beaches with no concern and there have been no shark attacks that anyone can remember.

True to our philosophy of seeing Sydney by water whenever possible, we recommend the **Palm Beach Ferries** as a great way to see a lot of the surrounding waterways and a way of accessing the **Ku-ring-gai National Park** (alight at **The Basin**). The service is owned by the Verrills family who were early settlers in the region and know it like an old friend.

It is not unusual to find one of the Palm Beach Ferries veer off its regular course to follow the dolphins when they come to frolic in Pittwater. As this book was going to press, two Southern Right whales swam up into the Hawkesbury

continued page 100

KU-RING-GAI CHASE NATIONAL PARK

The wonderful Ku-Ring-Gai Chase National Park is a world unto itself. Broken Bay is comprised of three major waterways – Pittwater, Hawkesbury River and Brisbane Waters – which all converge at Lion Island at the entrance to Pittwater.

KEY

N

Ku-ring-gai Chase National Park

Park entry

Aboriginal site

BBQ facilities (other than at major picnic areas shown on map)

Lookout, vantage point

Trail, walking track

0

Kilometres

ABORIGINAL ROCK ENGRAVINGS

There is magic at the 2000 Aboriginal rock engraving sites around Sydney. Often sited on the top of hills with panoramic views, they clearly have great environmental significance. One of the most accessible and the best of these is on the **Basin Trail,** off West Head Road. It has been lovingly presented by Parks and Wildlife, with diagrams to clarify the drawings. You can get to it by a short walk from West Head Road. (See symbol, top right hand corner of map). Sadly, there is little knowledge of their meaning, though clearly the drawings depict animals, people, weapons, hunting tools and, no doubt, heroes and Dreamtime gods.

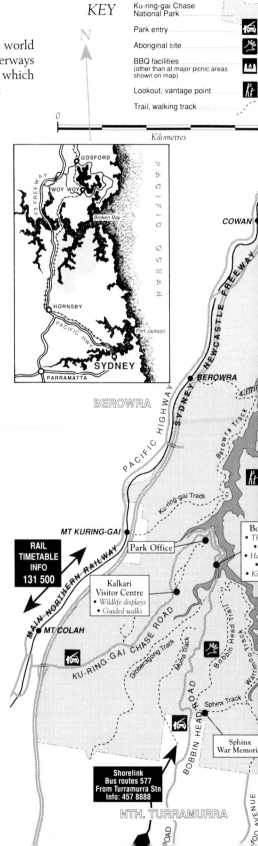

GOSFORD

F3 FREEWAY

WOY WOY

Broken Bay

PACIFIC OCEAN

COWAN

HORNSBY

PACIFIC HWY

Port Jackson

SYDNEY

PARRAMATTA

NEWCASTLE FREEWAY

SYDNEY

BEROWRA

BEROWRA

Berowra Track

PACIFIC HIGHWAY

Ku-ring-gai Track

MT KURING-GAI

Park Office

RAIL TIMETABLE INFO
131 500

MAIN NORTHERN RAILWAY

Kalkari Visitor Centre
• Wildlife displays
• Guided walks

Bobbin Head Trail

Warrimoo Track

KU-RING-GAI CHASE ROAD

MT COLAH

Gibberagong Track

Mirra Track

Sphinx Track

BOBBIN HEAD ROAD

Sphinx War Memorial

Shorelink
Bus routes 577
From Turramurra Stn
Info: 457 8888

NTH. TURRAMURRA

AVENUE

BANDICOOTS

The existence of this cute little critter, the long-nosed bandicoot, is now under threat. Once it was abundant in the backyards all over suburban Sydney. A community project in the Pittwater region is working towards ensuring these native animals remain part of the neighbourhood.

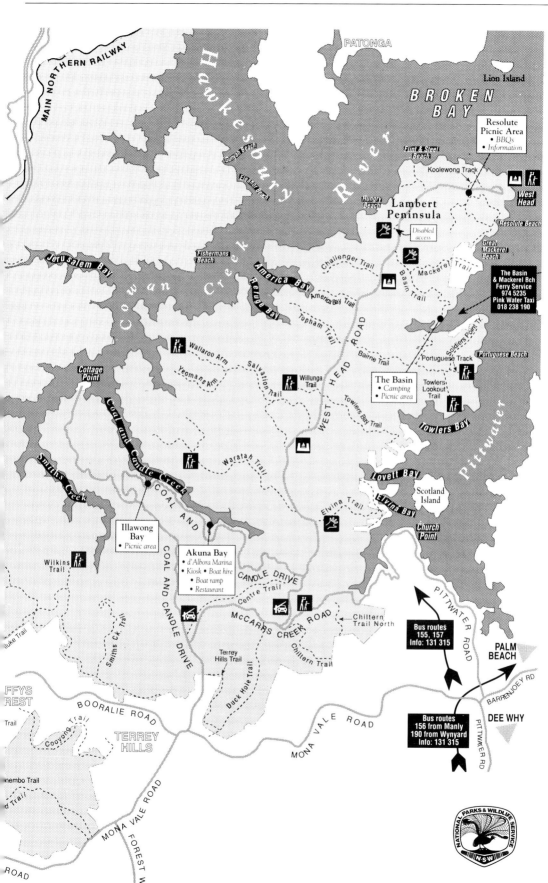

PATONGA

Lion Island

BROKEN BAY

Hawkesbury River

Main Northern Railway

Gunyah Beach

Eleanor Creek

Resolute Picnic Area
• BBQs
• Information

Flint & Steel Beach

Koolewong Track

WEST HEAD

Hungry Beach

Lambert Peninsula

Disabled access

Resolute Beach

Great Mackerel Beach

Fishermans Beach

Jerusalem Bay

Cowan Creek

America Bay

Refuge Bay

Challenger Trail

Basin Trail

America Bay Trail

Mackerel Trail

Topham Trail

The Basin & Mackerel Bch Ferry Service
974 5235
Pink Water Taxi
018 238 190

Soldiers Point Tr.

Portuguese Beach

Wallaroo Arm

Yeomans Arm

Salvation Trail

Willunga Trail

Bairne Trail

Portuguese Track

Towlers Lookout Trail

The Basin
• Camping
• Picnic area

WEST HEAD ROAD

Towlers Bay Trail

Towlers Bay

Cottage Point

Smiths Creek

Coal and Candle Creek

COAL AND

Waratah Trail

Elvina Trail

Lovett Bay

Scotland Island

Elvina Bay

Church Point

Illawong Bay
• Picnic area

Wilkins Trail

Akuna Bay
• d'Albora Marina
• Kiosk • Boat hire
• Boat ramp
• Restaurant

COAL AND CANDLE DRIVE

CANDLE DRIVE

Centre Trail

McCARRS CREEK ROAD

Chiltern Trail North

Bus routes
155, 157
Info: 131 315

PITTWATER ROAD

PALM BEACH

FFYS REST

Trail

BOORALIE ROAD

Cooyong Trail

TERREY HILLS

Smiths Ck. Trail

Terrey Hills Trail

Duck Hole Trail

Chiltern Trail

MONA VALE ROAD

Bus routes
156 from Manly
190 from Wynyard
Info: 131 315

BARRENJOEY RD

DEE WHY

PITTWATER RD

nembo Trail

d Trail

MONA VALE ROAD

FOREST WA

ROAD

NATIONAL PARKS & WILDLIFE SERVICE
N.S.W

River for the day, and we confess, we stopped work in our Pittwater office to go-see.

Palm Beach Ferries runs all kinds of trips in the area – check out the one that stops at Cottage Point for lunch. Peter also operates, and usually drives, the local Pittwater Water Taxi.

From **Palm Beach Wharf** (Pittwater side of Palm Beach) you can take a round-trip ferry, which takes about three-quarters of an hour, and calls in first to Coasters' Retreat (private residential) and The Basin (camping), Currawong (cottages for rent), Mackerel Beach (private residential), and then back to Palm Beach Wharf.

(Left to right) Peter, Mark and Max Verrills

SMUGGLERS AND LAW-MAKERS

Coasters Retreat was once known colloquially as Smugglers Cove. The coasters (merchant vessels) that plied the waters between the farms along the Hawkesbury River and the colony at Sydney Cove often sheltered here. But this was also where they were often waylaid, especially if they were known to be carrying rum which, for a while, was used as currency in the Colony.

The Basin has figured prominently in the making of Australian history. On Easter weekend 1891, a meeting of colonial leaders met on board the *SS Lucinda* which was anchored there. Here, they began to draft a key report which would lead to the breaking of the deadlock over contentious issues, thus paving the way to the formation of the Australian Constitution in 1901. Now The Basin is a popular camping site run by National Parks and Wildlife. There are also many moorings for visiting boats and good swimming.

Currawong, on the same ferry run and named after the sweet-sounding but predatory black birds which frequent the area, has a number of cottages owned by the Trades and Labor Council of NSW, which represents the trades union. The cottages were, many years ago, given by a benefactor to the "workers of NSW" to ensure that not just the rich and privileged but the workers too could enjoy a bit of paradise. While union members still have booking priority, non-members are also welcome and booking ahead is essential.

ON, AROUND, IN AND UNDER THE WATER

There are a number of places to stay in Pittwater which range from the spectacular **Jonah's** at Palm Beach to the water-based **Pasadena** at Church Point. There are plenty of places where you can hire boats in the area. Little "tinnies" around the Palm Beach Wharf from **Gonsalves** and "tinnies" and cabin boats from **Barrenjoey Boathouse,** Governor Phillip Park. Fine wooden Halvorsen cruisers in which you can explore the upper reaches of the Hawkesbury River as well as Pittwater, from the **National Park Hire.** Benateau yachts for some of the best sailing in

Carmel's Cafe at Barrenjoey Boathouse

Australia from the **Royal Prince Alfred Yacht Club** in Newport.

There are charming and good restaurants and cafes on, or by, the water's edge – **La Palma,** 1108 Barrenjoey Road, Palm Beach and the **Ancora Cafe** next door; **Church Point Top Room,** above the store at Church Point wharf; **Deckside At The Quays** marina, 1086 Pittwater Road, Church Point. There's fishing galore and plenty to explore. If you want to experience the wonders of the area in a more organised way, local film identity **Kit Moore** will put it together for you in the **Palm Beach Experience** (see Directory).

But before we leave this great place – on the road to Palm Beach (the beach itself is clean, classy and wonderful), there is a turn-off into **Governor Phillip Park,** which takes you to the headland guarded by Barrenjoey Lighthouse. In the Park you will find the **Barrenjoey Boathouse** where there is scuba diving, boat hire and the pelicans which do a very good, though not very elegant, imitation of the little sea plane lumbering into the wharf. **At Carmel's Cafe,** Carmel serves good basic tucker. "If they want flash food, they can go to Jonah's. This place won't change". Good on you, Carmel!

ENDANGERED SPECIES

It is the 21st Century. You are on the way to spend the day on the Pittwater Peninsula.

As you approach the area, you are confronted by boom gates. A ranger bars your way. You explain that, no, you have not booked ahead. You are told the visitors' quota has already been met, and you can either wait and replace others as they leave, or, you can take a booking ticket for another day. You are extremely cross.

Try this alternative.

It is the 21st Century. You are on the way to spend the day at Pittwater.

Around Newport, you park in the giant Private Vehicle Storage Centre, and transfer to the shiny People Mover (only large-capacity tour coaches and card-carrying residents are allowed on the road). The little cafes and boutique hotels have long gone, replaced by more practical 500-seat Visitor Food Barns and large, affordable short-stay accommodation along the Peninsula headlands. These

successful Council initiatives have gone a long way to contain numbers of day-trippers and lengthen the overnight visitor stays.

The new, extended wharf with its excellent public facilities, services the continuous ferries which pull in beside the greyish sand.

The old-timers tell of how in 1995, the dolphins frolicked, the whales came to visit and the pelicans slept on the beach beside the fishermen.

It matters not whether the subject is Pittwater, Darling Harbour, Sydney or the Solomon Islands – it is easy to predict their fate. Either the visitors have to be catered for, or limited. We are prepared to wait our turn to go to a special restaurant or to get tickets for a popular recital. Why not wait our turn for a country or region? Special places in the world can still be saved from "death by love". But local governments and residents will need to have brave new policies to do that.

For those seeking accommodation with a difference – the 1819 Hyde Park Barracks hammocks are available.

7 PLACES TO STAY

INCLUDES: From the "I really can't afford it, but I want something wonderful", to: "I want something wonderful but I have to watch the budget" and "I want something wonderful but at a rock bottom price". Grand hotels and little personal ones; serviced apartments and Aussie pubs; guesthouses and backpackers hostels, escapes, camping and the very different – they are all here. And rarely a tour bus in sight – take your pick.

Bedding Down in Sydney Town

The generally held perception of Sydney is that unless you can afford to stay in a five-star hotel, then it is time to bunk in with friends or family.

As a result, finding a place to stay in Sydney when either your good taste or common sense (or both, in the case of most UnTourists) tells you to avoid the international glitzies or the cheap motels, makes a difficult chore indeed.

We are therefore quite pleased to offer you this assortment of over 60 places to stay which have been painstakingly culled to meet your UnTourist requirements. You will find that there are far fewer recommendations in the West and the South than in the Centre, North and East. That's because despite our rigorous ferreting , there is a dearth of good places to stay in both these areas.

The thing about UnTourists is that they tend to choose where to stay based on particular principles. Firstly, UnTourists prefer places with a local flavour and character. They are not keen on hotels or motels that present like international chains. Avoiding mass-market tourists is also important and they like to meet the locals and learn more about the best things to do from the source, rather from a tour guide or brochure. So, where to stay is really the most important decision they can make, regardless of whether there is a little or a lot of money to spend.

For regular tourists it is relatively easy to choose accommodation because they tend to think vertically and trust in the stars. Meaning that it is easy to confuse price with quality — they think that the lower the price, the worse the accommodation. Or they confuse style with luxury - eg they feel a four-star hotel is not as good as a five-star hotel.

We grade establishments in a different way. Firstly, to get into an UnTourist guidebook means that the establishment is recommended by us and has met our criteria (see The Guide to the Guide).

If an entry has a duck or two beside its name, then that means there is something extra special about it. Our Flying Ducks are awarded for inherent excellence and charm. The more ducks - the more inherent excellence and charm. We also take into consideration value for money, thus a hostel could have more ducks than a luxury hotel. Our symbolic use of $'s works as follows:

(per standard double, per night)

$	(Cheap and good)	$15 - $40
$$	(Budget)	$40 - $75
$$$	(Moderate)	$75-$150
$$$$	(Premium)	$150-$250
$$$$$	(Top)	$250 up

Important hint: Out of season, or for stays of longer than a few days means that you can usually negotiate a better tariff.

Location is indicated by N; North, S; South, E; East, W; West, C; Centre. See the Location chapters for more information on the areas.
Each entry can be read as follows:

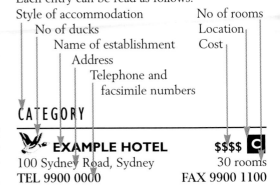

CATEGORIES

Small and Stylish Hotel; Grand and Special Hotel; Traditional Hotel; Aussie Pub; Guesthouse; Homestay; Bed and Breakfast; Hostel; Apartment; Camping; Very Different; Escape

THE SYDNEY OLYMPICS IN 2000

During the month of September in the year 2000, it will be hard to find places in the city of Sydney where you are not over-run by tourists. But if anyone can find them, we at the UnTourist Co can. The Olympic Information Centre is in the historic old South Steyne ferry moored in Darling Harbour. Tel. 61 2 9267 0099

SMALL AND STYLISH HOTEL

HUGHENDEN BOUTIQUE HOTEL $$$ **E**

14 Queen Street,
Woollahra 2025   36 rooms
TEL 9363 4863   FAX 9362 0398

The Hughenden is a welcome addition to Sydney accommodation. Small, stylish, comfortable and well located, this refurbished grand home and stables (c 1876) is set in one of Sydney's most prestigious streets, famous for its antiques shops. Fine pieces of furniture, large comfortable rooms and guest areas feature. The deluxe room and balcony is superb. The hotel has been popular with country people, especially during Easter Show time before the Fox film studios took over the Showground site. Fully cooked breakfast. On Saturdays the breakfast room becomes a popular cafe for day visitors. On Sundays this is where High Tea is served, between 1 and 4pm (pikelets, scones etc).

L'OTEL $$$ **E**

144 Darlinghurst Road,
Darlinghurst 2011
TEL 9360 6868   16 rooms

Step into the tiny foyer and you know you are connected to wit and style. Provincial furnished suites are air-conditioned; standard room rather small. There's a monthly exhibition of works by as yet undiscovered young artists. The deconstructed decor is carried through to the restaurant (which makes the Good Food Guide). On Friday and Saturday nights the bar at L'otel is so hip that it can hurt - models, megastars etc. Restaurant and cafe open from 7am to 12 pm daily.

PARK LODGE HOTEL $$ **S**

747 Dowling Street,
Moore Park 2016   23 rooms
TEL 9318 2393   FAX 9318 2513

Double glazing on the front rooms of this restored Victorian house keeps the traffic noise at bay and the very quiet back rooms look over an interesting landscape of haphazard inner city terraces. Only 15 minutes from the airport, and five minute taxi rides from King's Cross, the inner city et al. Pleasant inner courtyard. If you have a car (which you will have to park in the street), the approach to the hotel is via Thurlow Street).

RAVESI'S $$$ **E**

Cnr Campbell Parade and
Hall Street, Bondi Beach 2026   16 rooms
TEL 9365 4422   FAX 9365 1481

Ravesi represents the best of contemporary Bondi. Accommodation is well designed, comfortable and popular with visiting politicians and business people (and holiday-makers, of course). The ocean-view restaurant makes the Good Food Guide (and our list too) and the Hall Street side of the hotel is a Jewish gem (see chapter 3).

SIR STAMFORD HOTEL $$$$ **E**

22 Knox Street,
Double Bay 2028   72 rooms
TEL 9363 0100   **FAX 9327 3110**

Dark and dramatic decor is the hallmark of this small hotel set above a collection Double Bay's boutique shops. In the middle of Double Bay Village, the Sir Stamford is comfortable, stylish and has a great indoor pool beneath an atrium. Accommodation, many with four-poster beds, ranges from New York loft-style rooms to a studio with patio overlooking Double Bay and Bellevue Hill.

 McLAREN HOTEL $$$ **N**

25 McLaren Street,
North Sydney 2060   25 rooms
TEL 9954 4622   **FAX 9922 1868**

Boutique hotel in the heart of North Sydney, close to the harbour, northern beaches and with easy access to central Sydney. The entrance building is National Trust protected and there is a well integrated new wing. En suite bathrooms and hotel-style facilities, but with the friendliness that goes with smallness. Room cost includes breakfast. One grand suite with large balcony available.

RUSSELL $$$ **C**

143a George Street,
Sydney 2000   29 rooms
TEL 9241 3543   **FAX 9252 1652**

Built in 1887 in Sydney's original village, The Rocks, the Russell offers intimate charm and old fashioned hospitality. Individually decorated rooms in character with the building style; an excellent restaurant (The Boulders) below; a rooftop garden overlooking Circular Quay; a sitting room and balcony where you can read the papers, have a coffee, a drink, meet with friends. The recent addition of double glazing on the street-front rooms mutes most street noise on those lively Saturday Rocks nights. Ceiling fans for summer; heaters for winter. Sixteen rooms en suite, 11 shared facilities.

VICTORIA COURT $$$ E

122 Victoria Street,
Potts Point 2011   21 rooms
TEL 9357 3200   **FAX 9357 7606**

Small hotel on elegant, tree-lined Victoria Street at sufficient distance from the seediest parts of Kings Cross, yet handy to great places to eat, expensive and budget. The nearby backpacker hostels mean there is good, inexpensive and interesting food to hand. Restored from two elegant terrace houses built in 1881 (National Trust listed). Some have patios or balconies. Limited parking available.
Toll-free: 1 800 630 505

GRAND AND SPECIAL HOTEL

HOTEL INTER CONTINENTAL $$$$$ C

117 Macquarie Street,
Sydney 2000   133 rooms
TEL 9230 0200   **FAX 9240 1240**

Overlooking the Royal Botanic Gardens, the harbour and the Sydney Opera House, this grand hotel integrates the old state treasury building into the heart of its interior design. Part of this is the lobby lounge, a popular rendezvous for afternoon tea, pre-dinner drinks etc. The hotel has strong arts connections, expressed in

its Opera Club, first night parties and regular chamber music in the lobby. The Treasury Restaurant chef is Tony Bilson, one of Sydney's best. All the usual first class hotel facilities.

OBSERVATORY HOTEL $$$$ C

89-113 Kent Street,
The Rocks 2000   96 rooms
TEL 9256 2222   **FAX 9256 2233**

A member of Orient-Express Hotels group, the Observatory excels in drawing room comforts - an open fireplace, a library of leather-bound books, a collection of antiques, large comfortable chairs and top service. Its 20 metre heated pool is stunning, with its canopied ceiling, studded with stars, an appropriate reminder of the hotel's namesake nearby, the Sydney Observatory. Restaurant very good.
Toll-free: 1 800 806 245

PARK HYATT $$$$$ C

7 Hickson Road,
The Rocks 2000   158 rooms
TEL 9241 1234   **FAX 9256 1555**

Built of Sydney sandstone, this beautiful hotel snakes along the Harbour foreshore without imposing, yet managing to add its own imaginative presence to the surrounding icons of Sydney - the Opera House, Circular Quay and the Harbour Bridge, which is immediately behind. All rooms offer spectacular harbour views and most have private balconies. Luxury and service all the way, with prices to match. A quibble - the lobby decor has the brand "hotel", seen before.
Reservations (Aust): 131234
USA: 800 233 1234 London: 071 580 8197

RITZ-CARLTON, SYDNEY $$$$$ C

93 Macquarie
Street, Sydney 2000   106 rooms
TEL 9252 4600   **FAX 9252 4286**

Grandeur and intimacy go together in this fine hotel next to Sydney's financial district and opposite the Royal Botanical Gardens. The land on which the hotel is built was once part of the garden of Government House. In 1899 a sandstone building was erected and, before it became incorporated into the hotel, it was home to the NSW Department of Health. Opened in 1990, the Ritz-Carlton has a heated rooftop pool and all the usual services you'd expect from a top hotel. Impeccable standards of style, service and general ambiance.
Toll-free: 1800 252 888

RITZ-CARLTON, DOUBLE BAY $$$$ E

33 Cross Street,
Double Bay 2028   140 rooms
TEL 9362 4455   **FAX 9362 4744**

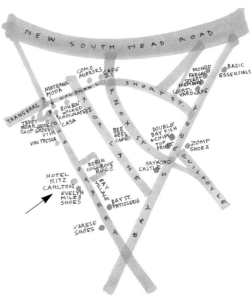

This is where celebrities from Madonna to foreign presidents often choose to stay. Like its sister hotel in the city, it has impeccable standards of style, service and general ambiance. If you arrive on a winter's day, the huge log fireplace in reception adds to your welcome. The daily buffet lunch in the Lobby Lounge is very popular with locals who usually include two or three of our rich and/or famous. Double Bay itself combines an easy sophistication with a local village atmosphere... and it's only 10 minutes from the city.
Toll-free: 1800 252 888

HOTEL — TRADITIONAL

CHATEAU SYDNEY $$$ E
14 Macleay Street,
Potts Point 2011   91 rooms
TEL 9358 2500   FAX 9358 1959

Conventional in style but exceptional in its setting and location, the Chateau Sydney has many rooms and some large suites with lovely harbour views to the north east. From the lobby it is a short step out on the patio which also over-looks the harbour. This is also where the swim-ming pool is. Friendly atmosphere and service.
Toll-free: 1 800 221 412 Telex: 22490 COMOTEL

HOLIDAY INN, COOGEE BEACH $$$$ E
Cnr Arden and Carr Street,
Coogee 2034   207 rooms
TEL 9315 7600   FAX 9315 9100

The ocean-view rooms with balconies and excellent room service tipped the balance for us in recommending a hotel with a very flourishing tourist group business – normally a turn-off to an UnTourist. The rooms are large, light and comfortable with all the usual big hotel facilities. There is a large swimming pool with its own fabulous view of the ocean. Because of its closeness to the airport, it is very popular with sporting teams who enjoy training on the beach.
Toll-free: 1 800 674 422 Telex: Z20723

MANLY WINDSOR HOTEL $$$ N
95 West Esplanade,
Manly 2095   53 rooms
TEL 9907 0688   FAX 9949 5587

With views overlooking Manly pool and across to the Sydney Harbour Heads, the Windsor is at the quietest end of Manly. All with balconies, baths and 24 hour service. Rooms without waterviews overlook suburban housing. Light, airy, fresh, – also has pool and spa. Three levels of accommodation. Continental or cooked breakfast. Corner conference room has best view of all.

RADISSON KESTRAL HOTEL $$$$ N
8-13 South Steyne
Manly Beach 2095   83 rooms
TEL 9977 8866   FAX 9977 8209

Tucked at the southern end of Manly Beach, the Radisson adds intimacy to its spectacular ocean views through the Norfolk Pines.

Grandest of all are the 4th floor suites with kitchenette, one with a huge patio . Aqua carpet throughout. Penthouses, three room suites. Pool, spa, sauna.
Reservations, toll free: 1 800 333 333

THE GRAND HOTEL $$ C
30 Hunter Street,
Sydney 2000   19 rooms
TEL 9232 3755   FAX 9232 1073

The heritage-listed Grand Hotel is one of Sydney's oldest hotels located right in the heart of the business district and is excellent value. It is built upon the TankStream (Sydney's water supply until 1826), is within easy walking distance of many of Sydney's major attractions and has a fully licensed and excellent dining room. Concierge on duty 24 hours, two bars, bottleshop and is minutes from all public transport. No breakfast available, but options nearby (we recommend The Boulders at The Rocks, 143 George Street, open from 7 am).

THE SEBEL OF SYDNEY $$$$ E
25 Elizabeth Bay Road,
Elizabeth Bay 2011   167 rooms
TEL 9358 3244   FAX 9357 1926

Famous for its friendly, personalised service, this boutique hotel has large rooms. Five rooms share bath and shower. Spacious newly-refurbished rooms and suites, many with great views over Elizabeth Bay. Rooftop swimming pool, sauna and gymnasium. The bar is the place to spot-a-celebrity and has long been popular with people in the film business.

AUSSIE PUB

COOGEE BAY HOTEL $$$ E
Cnr Coogee Bay Road and
Arden Street, Coogee 2034   40 rooms
TEL 9665 0000   **FAX 9664 2103**

A second floor ocean view room or suite is excellent value at this recently renovated Aussie Pub. The renovations cleverly enhance the original hotel and the best rooms have French-door access to a wide, open veranda and you feel you can almost touch the surf and sand. The hotel has popular live entertainment, so you should probably time your visit when the bands aren't in. Full English breakfast, under $10. A future development to the building will add apartments. Access to Sydney Airport is quick and easy.

🕊 DOYLE'S WATSON'S BAY HOTEL $$ E
1 Military Road,
Watson's Bay 2030
TEL 9337 4299   15 Rooms
Magnificent views over the harbour towards

the city from a large, common lounge room which serves basic, but very comfortable bedrooms. The hotel, with the only waterfront beer garden in Sydney, has been repainted inside, but still has all the character of the original and the locals still patronise the downstairs bar. The rooms have shared shower and toilet facilities. Daily rates include a continental breakfast and a free return trip to the city by Doyle's water taxi which runs regularly for patrons of the adjoining restaurants. Weekly room rates excellent value.

GLASGOW ARMS $$$ C
527 Harris Street,
Ultimo 2007   7 Rooms
TEL 9211 2354   **FAX 9281 9439**

Historic, recently renovated Glasgow Arms Hotel with its double-glazed windows is opposite the Powerhouse Museum and is a short walk to Darling Harbour, Chinatown, the monorail and CBD. Small, but attractively furnished rooms with TV, ensuites and tea and coffee making facilities and continental breakfast. Agreeable pub atmosphere. Lounge, bar and small restaurant and pleasant open leafy courtyard. Two double, one family, one twin and three single rooms.

LORD NELSON $$ C
19 Kent Street,
The Rocks 2000   6 Rooms
TEL 9251 4044   **FAX 9251 1532**

The best room on the top floor of this marvellous sandstone hotel is the corner queen bedroom which overlooks a delightful small triangle of grass set in a large space between a huge sandstone cut, the famous Garrison church and row of terrace houses. All but the cheapest rooms have TV phone and continental breakfast; bathroom facilities are shared. With a popular and busy bar below, quiet early nights on a Saturday seem unlikely and possibly unwanted anyway in this special and authentic area of the Rocks. The pub brews its own ales and there is a choice of five styles.

O'MALLEY'S HOTEL $$

228 William Street (Cnr Brougham Street),
Kings Cross 2010   15 rooms
TEL 9357 2211   FAX 9357 2656

Early 1900s' corner-pub well restored to period with contemporary comforts. It's close to, and contributes to, the local action - there's live entertainment every night in the bar and the hotel is located near the busiest part of the Cross. Terrific value for convenience. It has comfortable and attractive rooms and action-packed local atmosphere.

PALISADE HOTEL $$$

Bettington Street, Millers Point,
The Rocks 2000
TEL 9247 2272   10 rooms

A pub known for years to insiders who loved the marvellous setting on the cusp of The Rocks, and who wanted a cheap, attractive place to stay, the Palisade has begun to realise its potential. All grunge has been removed with paint and the careful restoration of original features like the wooden staircase and fireplaces. Facilities are shared (floor by floor) and the rooms are simply and pleasantly furnished, most with spectacular views of either the city or the harbour. The rooftop recreation area gives a 360 degree look at the city to the western side of the Bridge, Luna Park and up-River. Plans to extend to 17 rooms from original 10.

STEYNE HOTEL $$$

The Corso and Ocean Beach,
Manly 2095   53 rooms
TEL 9977 4977   FAX 9977 5645

Great value - Room 48, recently refurbished double with small ensuite, fully cooked breakfast included. Sit at a table set by a wide window and you can almost touch the beach and ocean. The rest is wide and creaky corridors, brown wood and cream walls, and tiny, friendly reception area – an Aussie pub experience plus. Some other ocean view rooms have balconies, but they are tiny. The Steyne has followed Australian beach hotel tradition since1865 when it was the first beautiful, simple hotel with verandah (see a photo in Ivy's Bar), through the 1930s when it was cloaked in brick with stingy balconies and tiny windows added. Still with its thirties look, gradually the inside is changing and a few rooms like 48 and its mirror image 47 are showing the way. If you want an early, peaceful night, probably best avoided on Saturdays as the Disco is below the best rooms. Some accommodation at the back for backpackers.

GUESTHOUSE

BROOKLYN $$

25 Railway Street,
Petersham 2049
TEL 9564 2312   5 rooms

In an area bereft of stylish accommodation, the Brooklyn wins out on location, general ambiance and value. Late Victorian guesthouse with four large bedrooms on the upper level, the front bedroom with a delightful balcony. Owner Angela is an enthusiastic bushwalker and the living room is usually occupied by interesting guests and good talk. Next to the Italian influenced suburb of Leichhardt. Share bathrooms; includes breakfast; no credit cards.

PERIWINKLE $$$

18-19 East Esplanade,
Manly 2095   18 rooms
TEL 9977 4668   FAX 9977 6308

This ideally located guesthouse on Manly Cove shows every sign of moving towards its full potential as fresh paint and ideas build up a warm, friendly environment. A variety of rooms with a variety of character – eg ground floor family room with bunks at the front; front double upstairs has best view, though is best as a single; upstairs west and north facing doubles have great charm. Buffet style breakfast. The Periwinkle is two Victorian houses linked together by upper verandah, forming an inner courtyard. The cosy and welcoming sitting room has a log (gas) fire. Antique Dutch, English country and other furniture throughout. Fourteen rooms with shared facilities. Coin phone. Prices negotiable for longer stays and during winter.

SIMPSONS OF POTTS POINT $$$ E
8 Challis Avenue,
Potts Point 2011   14 rooms
TEL 9356 2199   FAX 9356 4476

Set in a quiet, stylish street and restored from a stately Potts Point residence (circa 1892), Simpsons has large, spacious rooms, halls and stained glass windows plus "arts and crafts" decorations from the period. Continental breakfast, fresh orange juice, tea or coffee, croissants, brioches or pastries. Rooms range from standard to en suite with private spa. Special restaurant/accommodation package offered (except Sunday) so you can dine at one of the best restaurants in Sydney, Cicada, just across the street.

HOME STAY

SYL'S SYDNEY HOMESTAY $$$ E
75 Beresford Road,
Rose Bay 2029   5 rooms
TEL 9327 7079   FAX 9327 8419

Spacious new home with views of Sydney Harbour and only 10 minutes from CBD. Sylvia and Paul Ure have travelled widely themselves and have three children who attend a local bilingual school and share the hosting. They'll show you around Sydney and surrounding areas if you wish. Guests may borrow bicycles, golf clubs etc and leave luggage while travelling

elsewhere. Two double rooms, 4 single and a self contained flat with accommodation for up to six. All rooms have TV. British TV series "Wish You Were Here" recently featured Syl's.

BED AND BREAKFAST

BED AND BREAKFAST ON THE PARK $$$ E
2/50 Lang Road,
Centennial Park 2021   3 Rooms
TEL 9361 5310   FAX 9360 5717

Grand Edwardian house overlooking Centennial Park in one of the best addresses in Sydney (Australia's Nobel Prize winning author Patrick White used to live in Lang Road). Three guest bedrooms with either double or twin beds and shared bathroom. Country environment (horse-riding, cycling available in the Park) yet close to all the cosmopolitan attractions of Sydney.

BELLEVUE TERRACE $$ W
19 Bellevue Street,
Glebe 2037
TEL 9660 6096   3 Rooms

Set in a quiet street in a row of recently built inner-city duplexes, this friendly B & B offers fully cooked breakfast. Lisa knows her Sydney well (she came originally from Canada and is widely travelled herself). Walking distance from Darling Harbour, Powerhouse Museum, Chinatown; Paddy's Markets. Lisa is an excellent cook and will prepare meals by arrangement. No credit cards.

DARWINIA $$$ N
5 Sunrise Road,
Palm Beach 2108
TEL 9974 5604   2 rooms

Perched on a ridge which overlooks the ocean on one side and Pittwater on the other, Darwinia is redolent with local history and hospitality. Gabrielle's relatives, the Miles, once owned much of this headland. Self-contained accommodation overlooks Pittwater and includes verandah, a half billiard table, a pianola, plenty of books, tapes, CDs, TV. Separate bedroom with underfloor heating and a shower-with-view. Breakfast makings include fresh fruit. Impeccable. If you like, Gabrielle and husband Harl will show you the best local walks, restaurants etc. Golf course nearby.

LETHE $$

73 Cabramatta Road,
Mosman 2088
TEL 9908 3630 2 rooms

Small and impeccably kept Federation house owned by a recently retired couple, Lethe personifies the prestigious northern suburb of Mosman. The experience of this house and its attractive and friendly owners would give any visitor a real feeling for Australian middle-class living. The house is close to transport and there's a wonderful ferry ride across the harbour to the city centre. Soo serves a hearty English breakfast. Guest bathroom, use of lounge and TV.

TRICKETT'S $$$ W

270 Glebe Point Road,
Glebe 2037 7 rooms
TEL 9552 1141 **FAX 9692 9462**

Built last century by a wealthy merchant, then used as a children's court, this grand old 20 room mansion has seven bedrooms (plus separate shower and loos) set aside for guests. The main guest living room was originally a ballroom before becoming a courtroom. Spacious rooms, homely atmosphere, eclectic furnishings. Chinese temple in nearby street and set in an area of Edwardian and Victorian houses. Popular with Sydney University visitors; $5 taxi ride to city, walking distance to Sydney Fish Market and good restaurants.

HOSTEL

AVALON BEACH HOSTEL $ N

59 Avalon Parade,
Avalon Beach 2107
TEL 9918 9709 76 guests max

A good place to go to get out of the bustle of the city and to experience some of the northern beaches lifestyle in Sydney. Only 300 metres from the surf beach, Avalon Hostel has a good laid-back atmosphere. The usual backpacker facilities are here including a snooker table, plus the bonus of surfboards, boogie boards, and bikes for hire. They also can organise boating trips. Reservations are not essential but it is a good idea to ring in the morning to check bed availability. There is also a good example of that classic Australian institution – the RSL club, nearby. Office hours 8am –12noon; 4pm – 9pm Getting there: Catch the 190 (Palm Beach) bus from Wynyard in the city and get off at Avalon Beach.

BILLABONG HOSTEL, NEWTOWN $ W

5 Egan Street,
Newtown 2042
TEL 9550 3236 130 guests

Clean and quiet (Egan Street is off busy King St). Billabong has good facilities for guests and even has a small pool. Getting there: The hostel provides an airport pick-up service (9am – 9pm). Or you can get a bus from Railway Square (400 series run along King St.) to Missenden Rd. Egan St is also close to Newtown Station (King St). Experiences: Newtown /inner city restaurants.

COOGEE BEACH BACKPACKERS $ E

94 Beach Street,
Coogee 2034
TEL 9315 8000 157 guests max

Good location and friendly atmosphere - some rooms have views of beach/ocean. Getting there: 332 buses run to Coogee frequently from the city. Walk to the north end of the beach and head up the short steep hill closest to the water. Experiences: The beach, although not a true surf beach (Coogee is somewhat enclosed by headlands) is great for swimming. There are also beautiful cliff walks along the Eastern Suburbs. It is possible to walk north past Bondi and south to Maroubra.

EVA'S BACKPACKERS $ E

6 - 8 Orwell Street,
Kings Cross 28 rooms
TEL 9358 2185 **FAX 9358 3259**

Family owned and operated, Eva's is located in a small street around the corner from several of the Kings Cross Hostels on Victoria St. It is clean and friendly, has a wonderful rooftop garden and BBQ area, and has a good range of facilities for laundry and cooking. Eva's has 24 hour service and full security. Close to city, nightclubs and supermarket.

FORBES TERRACE, WOOLLOOMOOLOO $

155 Forbes Street,
Woolloomooloo
TEL 9358 4327   55 guests max

Quiet, new and located between Kings Cross and the city, Forbes Terrace is more modern and more upmarket in style than most backpacker places, and boasts a full range of facilities, including en suite for all rooms, TV, the whole caboodle.

HEREFORD LODGE YHA $

51 Hereford Street,
Glebe 2037
TEL 9660 5577   280 guests max

The best large YHA hostel in Sydney. Clean and well run, it has many pleasant features including a cafe, small rooftop pool, luggage storage, and Airport pickup. You can also pick up plenty of information on the travellers' grapevine here. Eating: The Hereford Lodge is located a short walk from the trendy Glebe Point Rd and so has plenty of cafes and restaurants in the immediate vicinity. Experiences: Glebe area, CBD.

LAMROCK HOSTEL, BONDI $ E

7 Lamrock Avenue,
Bondi 2026
TEL 9365 0221   45 guests max

A very friendly, well-managed house with full facilities for travellers (including bus ticketing). One block from the popular Campbell Parade and beach, and the only genuine hostel in Bondi. (There are a few other budget accommodation places if you are really stuck). Its proximity to the beach and the Bondi cafe scene makes it very convenient. It is also reputedly a good place for travellers to pick up work. Getting there: Buses run from the city to Bondi Beach.

MANLY BEACH RESORT BACKPACKERS $ C

Cnr Pittwater Road and Carlton Street,
Manly 2095
TEL 9977 4188   60 guests max

Fifty metres from Manly beach, and 30 minutes by harbour ferry from the CBD, this combination of backpackers and resort motel is very new. The usual backpacker facilities are here including a BBQ area and even a spa pool for guests. It might be a touch resortish for some UnTourists, but the location is very good for a stay in the city and a beach holiday. Getting there:

Ferry from Circular Quay (30 minute journey).

PLANE TREE LODGE, KINGS CROSS $

172 Victoria Street,
Kings Cross 2011
TEL 9356 4551   65 guests max

Good hostel – all rooms come with TV and fridge. Good location for Central Sydney and the Kings Cross area. Well managed and has 24 hour access. Getting there: 100m on right from Kings Cross train station. Experiences: Kings Cross area nightclubs and entertainment.

WATTLE HOUSE, GLEBE $

44 Hereford Street,
Glebe 2037
TEL 9552 4997   9 rooms

For warmth, friendliness, comfort and a taste of good Aussie hospitality, Wattle House is a winner. Aimed originally at the backpackers' market, Wattle House, which takes 28 guests,

has begun to attract a wider age range. Impeccably kept, little "extras" (individual bed lamps, linen, doonas, comfy pillows), a grassy, open garden, a "quiet" room with books, it has the atmosphere of a large family house. Off-street parking soon; tennis courts available. Has two doubles and a twin room. You'd better book in early. Office hours 9am -12pm; 6 pm- 9pm; 24 hour phone access for guests. Getting there: Kingsford Smith mini buses from the domestic and international airport will drop you to the door, or the big green and yellow buses will take you into the city from where you get any bus to Glebe along Glebe Point Rd.

APARTMENT

BALMAIN LODGE $$
Cnr Birchgrove Road and
Darling Street, Balmain 2041   35 apartments
TEL 9810 3700

Originally designed for inexpensive, longer-term lets, this attractive new building now fills a gap in the demand for short-term accommodation in the Balmain area. Well-carpeted rooms, simple but attractive equipment, food preparation facilities and utensils. Shared bathrooms. Excellent area for takeaway food. On the ground floor of the premises, Wok On Inn makes great noodle dishes and Fouronefive on the lower ground floor sells food, snacks and drinks.

DRUMMOYNE MANOR $$$ W
35 Marlborough Street,
Drummoyne 2047   26 apartments
TEL 9819 6166   **FAX 9819 7798**

Under 6 kilometres from Sydney CBD, near to historic Balmain with harbour ferries from nearby Drummoyne wharf. Drummoyne Manor has been converted into apartments from a grand house built in 1860 (National Trust listed). It has gardens and a small outdoor pool and spa. City buses within five minutes walk. All apartments with fully equipped kitchens are serviced daily. Larger suites available. Special rates for longer tenancies. Breakfast available, but self-catering recommended. Supermarket nearby.

HARBOURSIDE APARTMENTS $$$$ N
2A Henry Lawson Ave.,
McMahons Point 2060   82 apartments
TEL 9963 4300   **FAX 9922 7998**

The 16-storey Harbourside Apartments have it all - sensational harbour views; pool and garden facilities; a friendliness and service which gives a welcome, homely feel; location (seven minutes from the city by ferry or car); quiet environment, and value too. Prices are per apartment and range from studios to two bedrooms. Room service from Sails Harbourside Restaurant is available evenings up to 7.30 pm.

View from the Harbouside Apartments

MANLY WATERFRONT $$$$ N

1-3 Raglan Street,
Manly 2095   47 apartments
TEL 9976 1000   **FAX 9976 2226**

Four penthouses, 18 two-bedrooms and studios, all with balconies. Fully equipped, serviced daily. Spacious living rooms and cooking areas. Decor in pastel colours; security parking; pool on second floor; indoor/outdoor restaurant and bar. Top penthouse has 180 degree view from ocean around to Manly Cove with Sydney CBD on horizon. Toll-free: 1 800 222 060

MORGAN'S OF SYDNEY $$$$ E

304 Victoria Street,
Darlinghurst 2010   26 apartments
TEL 9360 7955   **FAX 9360 9217**

Converted from an old apartment building into studios and suites, Morgan's has an intimacy with its contemporary stylishness. Bedroom suites on Victoria Street with balconies and a view to the city and, to the right, into the heart of The Cross. Back bedroom suites look onto a quiet, narrow street of charming terrace houses. Tariff includes continental breakfast in the Victoria Room where you can read the papers looking out into a leafy inner courtyard. Self-catering facilities plus restaurant.

OAKFORD POTTS POINT $$$ E

10 Wylde Street,
Potts Point 2011   37 apartments
TEL 9358 4544   **FAX 9357 1162**

Manhattan-style studio and one bedroom apartments and penthouses at the best end of Potts Point, some with great views of the Harbour. Fully equipped, streamlined, comfortable, light furnishings, air conditioned, laundry facilities, outdoor pool and heated spa. Seven floors of apartments, seven minutes walk from Kings Cross railway station; 10 minutes by car or bus to city. Lower rates for longer stays. Studio, one bedroom, two bedroom, penthouse (3 bed). Toll-free: 1 800 818 224

QUAY WEST SYDNEY $$$$$ C

98 Gloucester Street,
The Rocks 2000   126 apartments
TEL 9240 6000   **FAX 9240 6060**

Spectacular views over the main action of Sydney Harbour; luxurious one, two bedroom suites and executive penthouse. Each suite fully equipped including CD player and with 24 hour room service. Swimming pool, whirlpool spa, bar and restaurant.

 **REGENTS COURT** $$$$ **C**

18 Springfield Avenue,
Potts Point 2011   34 studios
TEL 9358 1533   FAX 9358 1833

The two guiding principles in designing Regents Court were: that guests should not feel as if they were in a 'hotel' and that the rooms should feel comfortable to most without sacrificing any of the design's inherent style. In a quiet cul-de-sac in Kings Cross, the family-run Regents Court apartment hotel is comfortable, stunningly stylish and unpretentious. Large rooms with high ceilings, a muted palette of colours (teal carpet, khaki damask bedspread, mahogany panelling). Stainless steel kitchen, dining area to seat four. Beautiful incidental pieces of 20th century classic furniture. Delightful roof garden; home-made cakes and jams. Business facilities.

UNTOURIST APARTMENTS $$$$ **C**

243 Pyrmont Street,
Darling Harbour, 2000
TEL 9974 1326   FAX 9974 1396

Fully self-contained, serviced comfortable apartments in the apartment conversion of the historic, former Goldsborough Mort Wool Store (c1883) in the heart of Darling Harbour. Light and with city skyline views, each has 3.5 metre ceilings, huge, original iron-bark supports and tallow-wood floors. Available with one or two bedrooms, other options, these charming and convenient apartments can accommodate two couples or a family. Fully equipped kitchen. Access to swimming pool and sauna. Small shops, cafes, restaurant in building. Monorail station nearby. Toll-free: 1 800 066 818

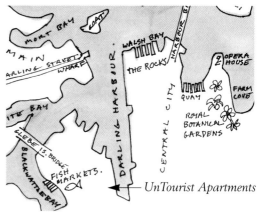
— *UnTourist Apartments*

THE YORK $$$$ **C**

5 York Street,
Sydney 2000   132 apartments
TEL 9210 5000   FAX 9290 1487

Within walking distance of The Rocks, the Opera House, Darling Harbour and the inner city, the spacious York Apartments have walk-out balconies, some with a view to the bridge and harbour and all fully equipped. Heated pool/spa in a rooftop garden and sauna; security parking included, supermarket shopping service six days a week. Recently refurbished foyer is grand indeed. Opposite small but attractive park and terminus for many suburban buses to the north and elsewhere.

CAMPING

In the greater metropolitan area of Sydney there are 15 excellent camping sites within National Parks. In the mountains – the Blue Mountains National Park; in the south – The Royal National Park; to the north – Kuring-gai Chase. For an excellent free booklet on where you can go to camp, or to bushwalk, call in at **Cadman's Cottage** Historic Site at 110 George Street, The Rocks, **TEL 9247 8861.**

VERY DIFFERENT

HOTEL 59 & CAFE $$ **E**
59 Bayswater Road,
Kings Cross 2011   8 rooms
TEL 9360 5900   FAX 9360 1828

Like a slice of Paris cut out and pasted incongruously between modern and quite ordinary apartment blocks, this small brown painted, characterful hotel sits atop a charming cafe (first rate coffee; light, healthy food; interesting clientele) and has modestly priced rooms. In its previous life it was a brothel. The nicest room is the dormitory (6 beds) which overlooks the quiet end of Bayswater Road and residential buildings. Other rooms rather small, but atmosphere very friendly, clean and tidy with pleasant, family-style lounge. Located next to Kings Cross; close to excellent restaurants, the city and easy transport. Continental breakfast except for cheapest stays.

HYDE PARK BARRACKS $ **C**
Queen's Square,
Macquarie Street 2000
TEL 9223 8922

If you are looking for something completely different, try an overnight stay in a hammock at Hyde Park Barracks (see photograph at opening of this chapter). They are what the early convicts slept in - 0.9 metres (three feet) wide and slung from bars or rails just 1.8 metres (six feet) apart. Overnight bookings for the Barracks can be made by family or school groups, at times to be negotiated. (Try well in advance). There are also special day "convict experiences", which start with sentencing at an "English Court" at Circular Quay, followed by "transportation" on a square rigger before a try-out of a Barracks' hammock.

SYDNEY STAR $$ **E**
275 Darlinghurst Road,
Darlinghurst 2010   10 rooms
TEL 0414 677 778

This old terrace house has simply furnished rooms, serviced daily, with sink and barfridge, TV and shared bathroom facilities. Stars on each room door add to the aura of stage dressing rooms in an old-time theatre. Very conveniently located for city and eastern hub access. No phones in rooms, but messages taken by Robert, who also prepares the continental breakfasts. Building next door under renovation will have 20 rooms available.

ESCAPE

THE BASIN $ **N**
Western foreshores of Pittwater,
access from Palm Beach wharf
TEL 9451 8124

Because of the surrounding points of interest, The Basin is one of the best camping sites in the greater metropolitan area. Camping area overlooks bays where there are netted and open swimming areas. Walking tracks through the Ku-ring-gai Chase National Park to Aboriginal rock carvings, intricate bays and panoramic views over Pittwater. Access is by ferry or water taxi. For ferry times, call 9974 5235 or for water taxi from Palm Beach 018 408 831 or 018 238 190.

BINDA COTTAGE $$$$ **N**
40 Kywong Road,
Berowra 2081
TEL 9456 1385   2 rooms

Accessible only by boat and set in lush bushland on the banks of Berowra Waters (part of the Hawkesbury River system), timber-built Binda Cottage can accommodate two couples in two loft bedrooms. (Sorry, no children under 12). Fully-equipped, breakfast provisions for weekend guests, boat with 5hp motor; board games, cards, snooker table. Four restaurants within 10 minutes by boat. An hour's drive by car from Sydney.

CURRAWONG BEACH COTTAGES $$

PO Box 4,
Palm Beach 2108   9 cottages
TEL 9974 4141   **FAX 9974 1328**

Twenty-three hectares on the beachfront owned by the Labor Council of NSW has nine self-contained cottages with water views. Includes tennis court, practice golf course, swimming beach, bushwalking trails. Each cottage has one bedroom with a double bed and small living room with a double sofa bed and a divan. Cooking and eating facilities. Need to supply own groceries; first morning ferry supplies bread, milk and newspapers. Excellent rates for mid-week use. Access by ferry or water taxi. Ferry timetable: 9974 5235 (also can provide water taxi).

JONAH'S $$$

69 Byna Road,
Palm Beach 2108   8 rooms
TEL 9974 5599   **FAX 9974 1212**

With one of Sydney's most spectacular outlooks, Jonah's is set on a clifftop above Whale Beach, about 45 minutes north of Sydney. Primarily a restaurant, Jonah's also has ensuite accommodation which makes it an excellent weekend getaway, or a means of exploring the northern beaches area without having to rush back to the city in the evening. Jonah's is one of Sydney's oldest restaurants (1929). Recent excellent renovations have optimised views, banished all the old mustiness, greatly improved the accommodation and the quality of the food has risen too. Weekend packages available.

PASADENA ON PITTWATER $$$

1858 Pittwater Road,
Church Point 2105   15 Rooms
TEL 9979 6633   **FAX 9979 6147**

A popular weekend escape with many locals, it has a magical view across Pittwater to Scotland Island and the Ku-ring-gai Chase National Park. The best rooms - all have cane furnishings, pastel colours - are the five on the waterfront. Number 9 is the best of the best. Only one apartment with bath, the rest have showers and all have a small fridge (not mini bars). The terrace restaurant attached has a spectacular setting with a wharf where small boats can lay alongside. To get to Pasadena is a special experience itself via Pittwater Road from Mona Vale. The road snakes between lovely bushland and a mud flat area reaching into the popular small boating waters of the area. Church Point Top Room above the mini market on the Church Point wharf is a must for breakfast.

The Greater Sydney Ensign reflects
Sydney's history and heritage and place
as a great sea port. It features the naval
cross of St. George, the stars of the
Southern Cross and the golden anchor,
crown and star, official ensign of the
City of Sydney.

8

THINGS TO BUY

INCLUDES: What you can buy where; the best shops and department stores; best places to buy everything from beads to beachwear, chocolates to chairs; local markets; specialist suburban shopping strips; bargains and where to get them; and mementoes of Sydney (tourists call them souvenirs).

Born to Shop

When it comes to things to buy, Sydney is a cutting-edge city – just how stylish it is, is a surprise to many visitors from other countries who naturally expect a place "way down under" to be somewhat behind the times. There were times, not so long ago, when Sydney folk would go to other countries with empty suitcases, buying up big – on sheets from Bloomingdales, shoes from Rome, fashion from Paris, cashmere from London, cameras from Hong Kong, carpets in Singapore. The list was endless, limited only by one's income and the capacity of the suitcases. This is no longer so and it seems that the only things Sydneysiders now appear to have on the "buy it over there" list are cashmere, sports shoes and cosmetics... that's probably all. The fact is there is not much you can't buy in Sydney; from the new and imaginative to the established and prestigious.

The shopping in Sydney, as with major cities in the world, is now internationalised – which is good news. The bad news is that in this worldwide market place, it gets harder to find those special things that are unique to the destination.

In this chapter we share with you the results of our fossicking around to find as many shops, markets, food, fashion, bits and pieces, as possible that are unique to Sydney.

EMMA CHISSIT?

Is Sydney an expensive place to shop? Well, yes, and no. Yes, it is expensive when compared with other Australian cities, probably the most expensive city in Australia. New Yorkers tend to think that Sydney is expensive; however, currencies fluctuate – in 1995, Germans thought it was cheap and in 1985 the Japanese considered it a bargain. So, at the risk of avoiding the question, the answer has to be – it depends. Whether it is cheap or expensive, the shopping environment is varied, interesting and up to the minute – mainly because with only three-million resident customers to fight over, and most of the world's major consumer trading companies represented, the competition in Sydney is fierce. This sort of competition usually means that traders find it hard to make a dollar but the customer does quite well.

Here is a general guide about pricing

LOCAL FARE, LOCAL FAIR

However far you travel,
However far you tour,
There's one thing in each foreign land
You'll swear you've seen before.
It's the local fare, the local fair,
For proper tourists everywhere.
See local treasures here displayed
And see the label "Hong Kong made".
The walking doll – a little jerky
Just like the one in Albuquerque.
Aren't those the rings you saw in Rome?
Have you that rosewood charm at home?
Those hats of every shape and size,
Bedecked with braid and doused in dyes.
Familiar note on all the beads,
"By local students strung" it reads.
– Or was that Boston? Mexico?
Can you remember, Billie Joe?
So have the fun of fairs, dear friend.
Of course it's not your travel's end.
The things to hold your
heart in thrall
Won't be on table, booth or stall –
You'll hear no spruiker
shouting wares
When you explore new
thoroughfares –
Just local history, simply told –
UnTourist traveller – there's the gold.
C. M. Ganong

MADE IN HONG KONG

BUDGET	$
MODERATE	$$
EXPENSIVE	$$$
BE WARNED	$$$$

WHERE TO SHOP

Shopping in Sydney fits into one of three groups. The Central Business District – CBD (we've included The Rocks here); regional centres or shopping malls, and the suburban "strips".

CBD Shopping here is contained fairly neatly in a square bordered by Park, George, King and Elizabeth Streets in the city centre. It is highly condensed, and the shops, arcades and stores concentrate mainly on men's, women's and children's clothing and accessories.

The best department stores are in the CBD and we have featured our favourites.

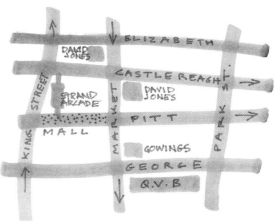

$$ TO $$$$ DAVID JONES

There are many more famous department stores in the world than David Jones – Harrods in London, Bloomingdales in New York, Les Galleries Lafayette in Paris.

But when you have seen them all, scraped away the exotic labels and made a cold comparison, David Jones in Sydney could just be the best department store in the world – especially the main store on the corner of Elizabeth and Market Streets where the vast, open, beautifully lit marbled ground floor invites the shopper first to a celebration, then, heaven forbid, maybe to buy.

Main staircase of the "new" 1887 George Street store

David Jones is more than a store to Sydneysiders – it is a tradition that spans almost the entire history of white settlement. Established nearly 160 years ago, the company, its trials and successes are reminders of the past – the Depressions, the Great Wars, the country droughts and floods, the golden years and heady boom times of the past century as well as this one.

There's always been great anticipation waiting for the David Jones' Christmas display – what its windows will be like, and what further magic can be worked on the main Elizabeth Street ground floor. And the principle of service to the customer, which includes sale-or-return, has never been an empty slogan.

The first store, established by the Welshman who gave it his name, opened in George Street in 1838. Its first extensive importations included "buckskins, ginghams, cassimeres, waistcoatings, silk, cotton ticks and daiper rugs – a very large assortment of slops". "Slops", the then current word (Old English) for ready-made clothing, and it was a term that lingered for decades.

By 1848, George Street had become a grand boulevard and was considered the first street in Sydney, "presenting an external appearance which London might well be proud of .... private residences, sale rooms, respectable shops, not to be excelled in any town of the same size in Britain".

Architect Morton Herman wrote of Sydney at that time in his 1962 introduction to *Sydney in 1848* (Ure Smith) *"....[Sydney was] a lovely colonial town of clean, chaste Georgian architecture. Whole streets were pleasant compositions of harmonious buildings... a beautiful Sydney that was, and never will be again."*

By the mid 1840s, David Jones was assured of its customers and on November 15, 1847 advised "Settlers and up-country Families visiting Sydney for their annual supplies" through *The Sydney Morning Herald* that there

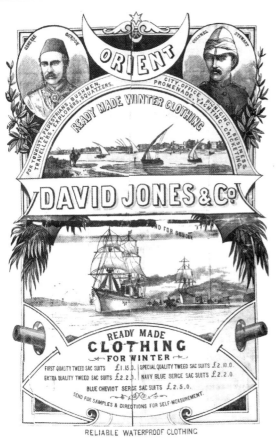

The well turned-out cricketers of 1883 – David Jones v the now defunct but fondly remembered Anthony Hordern & Sons.

David Jones, the founder, 1793-1873

Advertisement for winter clothing inspired by the Sudan War, 1885.

Former Primer Minister "Billy" Hughes in 1938 opens the new David Jones Market Street store.

was a new and enlarged department store for them. By then the city's population was around 40,000, and the vast interior was being further, if still sparsely, settled. In 1879 David Jones, already having a reputation as an innovator, offered shopping by mail, a boon to country people. Business boomed in the 1880s and more stores were opened.

In 1891 a Miss Santa Maria Baker of London took employment as a milliner at David Jones. Her annual salary was £165 and she was required "not to depart from or absent herself from the Company's premises without prior consent, nor was she to become addicted to intemperate habits".

In 1920 David Jones bought its current Elizabeth Street property taking over the Sydney Girls' High School building. The

pundits at the time said it was too far from the centre of town to ever be a success, but it soon became the new heart of retailing in Sydney.

In 1938, to celebrate 100 years of trading in Sydney, David Jones opened a new store in Market Street, opened by the famous "Little Digger", former Prime Minister, "Billy" Hughes. They also opened a Travel Service, which in those days, was for the very, very rich, or the very, very important. In the same year the inaugural flying-boat flight from Rose Bay to England took place. This David Jones store is now renowned for its excellent Food Hall – not as extensive as Harrods, mind you, but with a similar level of quality, and several fine sit-down counters for lunch and a morning or afternoon coffee break. Savvy locals love to shop here when they can.

$ TO $$ GOWINGS

The Gowings store on the corner of Market and George Streets now has a cult following that nicely rounds off a tradition of more than a hundred years of knowing how to win the customers of the day.

IN THE EARLY DAYS

When the notorious Darcy Dugan escaped from prison on his way to court in the late 1940s, he scrawled "Gone to Gowings" on the wall. When his story was splashed all over the front page of the newspaper, Gowings' managing director said to the staff: "If you see Darcy Dugan, give him a suit".

Like David Jones, the Gowings' story reflects the Australian retailing industry as well as forming an important part of Sydney's social history. And at a time when so many companies regarded as Australian icons are being taken over or sold off to overseas interests, most locals are delighted that Gowings continues to be a wholly Australian-owned company – now for four generations.

John Ellis Gowing was 21 when he arrived in Sydney in 1857. He was the son of a landed English family and one of his early jobs in Sydney was at David Jones. On the day Gowing Bros opened in 1868 in George Street, old David Jones made sure he was the store's first customer – what a world it used to be!

Gowings began as "gentlemen's outfitters" and so it continues to this day, a store where practical, well-made, well-priced gear for men and boys has always been available. For a while, women's wear was available too. One of the hallmarks of Gowings has been its lack of pretension and refusal to be caught up in merchandising fads. What you see in the windows and on the floor displays is what you gets. And it's a popular store for the well-heeled as well as the value-for-money crowd. Private-school boys have been outfitted here by their savvy mothers for decades.

Craig loved riding the bus home from Gowings

GOWINGS' TRADITION – LOCAL HISTORY

1920s – women employed largely behind the scenes; once married they had to resign.

1929 – the new Gowings building was built to the maximum height of 150 feet.

1931 – Mr Cheng's China Silk and Arts Goods took up a lease for £2 a week. The rent has gone up a little, but he's still there.

1930s – during the Depression, only married men were allowed to have full-time jobs. Nobody was fired from Gowings in the 1930s. However, in the early 1930s staff were only allowed to have their coats off until ten o'clock, even if the temperature was 110°F.

1941 House Rules included the instruction: UNDER NO CIRCUMSTANCES should the customer be sold higher priced goods than he, the customer, wishes to buy.

1942 – Staff notice: Re. *Married Men Being Called Up for Militia.*

If on our staff for one year give them a watch – value 5 pounds – and allow them 10s per week, to be paid monthly to their wives.

- There was the rat catcher who came to check the building who used to get rats from the tip, bring them into Gowings and plant them in the money tubes to keep himself in a job. They caught up with him when the store was rat-proofed.

- One salesman named Gibson eventually grew so old he would have to have an afternoon nap. The rest of the staff used to put him under the counter to have his rest on some blankets.

- In the 1950s, Ted Lanchester was managing director. His three rules for running a successful business were:

When you're on a good thing stick to it.

Don't waste money.

Always keep control.

That's pretty much as it is today.

125

Today's managing director John Gowing is a "new breed" manager. He's computerised the office and, aiming at the younger market, has created a 'cult' following for Gowings without alienating older customers.

With thanks to Stephanie Gowing for background information from her book, "Gone to Gowings".

$$$ QUEEN VICTORIA BUILDING

The building which marks the place of Sydney's original market, is now is the city's most contemporary department store. QVB covers an entire city block, bound by George, Market, York and Druitt Streets and was built during the 1890s Depression to replace the place where Sydneysiders first traded their wares in open markets. The Byzantine architecture was chosen so that many of the out-of-work craftsmen, stonemasons, plasters and stained glass window artists of the time could be employed. The project was a significant job-creator and when finished, it housed a concert hall, coffee palaces, office showrooms, and a variety of service-industry tenants.

In 1984 an intensive restoration program for the building began and every detail throughout the building was restored to maintain the integrity of the building including the arches, pillars, balustrades and the intricately designed tiled floors. Now, the QVB is, according to Pierre Cardin, "the most beautiful shopping centre in the world". And the people of Sydney and its visitors are very thankful.

The QVB is open seven days a week and contains some good local fashion on both the ground and the first floor. The **ABC Shop** on the first floor is also great. Here you can find books, videos and music that are just a bit different – particularly Australian stuff. As you get higher up, you find yourself immersed in tourist land. If you go right down to the lower ground floor, you are smack-bang into somewhat of a pedestrian area. So stick to the middle ground.

$$$ FLETCHER JONES

An uninspiring looking shop and their clothes won't make the fashion awards. But they still have old-fashioned ideas like "clothes should be made of good cloth, sewn carefully and the cut and fit should be paramount". Well-tailored basics – men's or women's. Fletcher Jones brand stretch jeans are really well cut. You won't see anyone in the store under 40. There are six stores in Sydney, the main one at 379 George Street.

$$$ STRAND ARCADE

The continuing existence of the historic Strand Arcade is due, in large part, to the passion Sydneysiders developed for their historic buildings in the 1970s – when The Rocks, Victoria Street, Kings Cross and a number of other historic places were about to be bull-dozed in the name of "development". This was the time of the famous Builders Labourers' Green Bans.

In the case of the Strand, the villain was a fire which nearly destroyed it in 1976.

Opened in 1892, the Strand was the last of the arcades built in Victorian Sydney and is now the only one remaining in its original form. The 1976 fire caused three million dollars, worth of damage, but newspaper campaigns gave voice to the people's sentiments:

"Please save the Strand, a gem among all those soulless city 'cigar 'boxes'" wrote Janice Beaumont in the *Daily Mirror.*

And so the decision was made to restore the

building with an authenticity which made it even better than before the fire. Today, it is a popular shopping area for visitors and Sydneysiders alike.

The story of the restoration is almost as heroic as the work of the Sydney Fire Brigade in saving the building.

- 252,000 mosaic tiles (replicas made by a Japanese company) were used throughout.
- For the cast-iron balustrades, the Department of Metallurgy specially blended a special free-flowing metal which would not bubble.
- A joinery shop of craftsmen with knowledge of the "antique" skills recreated the cedar shopfronts and other features. (Eventually 40,000 super feet of mostly Australian cedar was used, much of which was found at the home of an old man living in the suburb of Hornsby who had saved it for a boat he never got around to building).
- The painstaking restoration extended to each timber column on the staircases where there are 84 separate pieces of wood.

Shopping today in the Strand Arcade is a rewarding pastime with lots of little specialty shops to temp you. Look out for Rox Jewellery and Maggie Shepherd's shiney gear. Strand Arcade, 412-414 George Street, Sydney.

$$ TO $$$ THE ROCKS

There is much more "visitor" shopping in The Rocks than shopping by the locals. It can get downright touristy, but that shouldn't put you off the worthwhile places. Tucked down in the basement of what were the old Bond Stores at 80 George Street:

❶ METCALFE ARCADE has at least three unusual shops: **The Sydney Cigarette Card Company** (Shop 1) John and Meredith Studdert display a vast range of original and reproduction cigarette cards, from 50-card sets down to singles. And you can also buy old-time framed posters such as the Arnott's Biscuits parrot. **The Society of Arts and Crafts of NSW,** (Shop 2) A non-profit-making Society founded in 1906, the oldest established craft organisation in the State, this small shop features high quality individually made Australian work. The Society holds classes, and has demonstrations regularly on the first Sunday of the month. **Beads Galore,** (Shop 3) A specialty shop with a strong how-to message.

❷ LEFT-HANDED PRODUCTS Heaven for southpaws up a set of wooden stairs along this street of tiny shops, LHP is the only long-established shop for lefties in the Southern Hemisphere. Scissors; can-openers and vegie peelers; address and phone books; hand-held calculators, watches. House speciality: left-handed matches, 29A Playfair St, The Rocks.

❸ AUSTRALIAN CONSERVATION SOCIETY (ACF) SHOP Sydney arm of the Aust-ralian Conservation Foundation and everything for sale reflects this heritage. Writing papers, cards, soaps, and wooden toys – all made from recycled material. T-Shirts, soft toys and puppets – all Australian-made, 33 George Street.

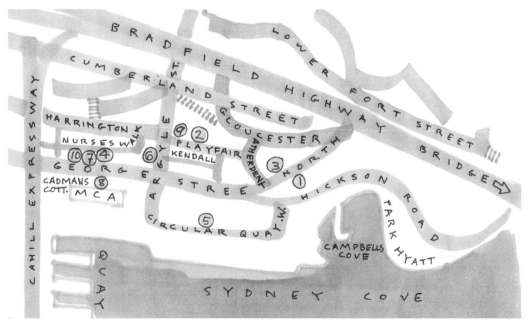

4 **KAMINSKI GALLERIES** Hand-woven tapestries collected by Gabriella Olsen. Local artists use Australian and New Zealand sheeps' wool, both kilim and Gobelin method. Gabriella has a unique buy-back offer – full credit anytime (even years later) if you trade in on a tapestry of equal value or more, 21 Nurses' Walk, The Rocks.

5 **NATURALLY AUSTRALIAN FURN-ITURE** Australian timbers are unique in grain, structure, colour, texture, bark. Jarrah, blackwood, Australian red cedar (quite different from US and middle-eastern kinds), blue gum, spotted gum, Huon pine, Southern Sassafras, Myrtle – all are used in the extraordinary and highly original furniture you'll find in this huge open warehouse behind the Overseas Passenger Terminal. You'll never see more beautiful or original furniture than here, 43, Circular Quay West, The Rocks.

6 **LA RENAISSANCE PATISSERIE,** with its courtyard cafe, is a patisserie recommended for a good French breakfast. 47 Argyle Street.

7 **BAKER'S OVEN** A constant procession of locals pass through the fragrant portals. Bread, pies and meat have been baked behind Bill Kriketos' shop since the colony's earliest days, when the local housewives brought the family dinner and bread along for communal cooking at bargain prices, 121 George Street. Through the back door is Bakehouse Place.

8 **THE MUSEUM OF CONTEM-PORARY ART (MCA) SHOP** A great place for imaginative jewellery, postcards, an interesting variety of books, ceramics and off-beat gifts – like the little brooch on our cover and on the last page of this chapter.

9 **THE ARGYLE DEPARTMENT STORES** Watch this space. We will review this, among other things, in our **Events Update** service.

10 **THE ROCKS STRIP** Ken Done managed to capture the sheer joy of Sydney in that original T-shirt, (12 were made to promote an exhibition of his paintings at the Holdsworth Galleries) and for the last decade he has gone on to spread that fresh, zesty Sydney sense of fun all over the world through his designs and paintings. Like most prophets in their own land, Done is taken for granted in Sydney. Artists aren't supposed to be rich and successful – Ken Done is both. You can still get the original T-shirt at **Done Art and Design,** 123 George Street, The Rocks and at the **Ken Done Gallery,** 1-5 Hickson Road, you can see his pictures (and Ken in person sometimes). Or, if you can't afford the original (not Ken, the pictures), you can get some of his charming posters which so well depict happy, hedonistic Sydney. Sometimes things and people rise above the "tourist" categorisation, and we think Ken Done is one of them.

REGIONAL SHOPPING CENTRES

Or the dreaded 'shopping malls'. As in most cities in the world, these spending circuses abound in all areas of Sydney. We see two main reasons for patronising them. The first is **$ Target,** a chain of pragmatic stores, selling all the clothing and homeware basics, formed in the Marks and Sparks mould, and **$ Woolworths** fresh food stores, which seem to have proved that bulk buying and high turnover can result in a vast variety of fresh fruits, vegies, meat and fish. The parking's fine.

Enough said about shopping malls.

$ MARKETS

Sydney has many excellent markets - some are annual and usually tied to specific ethnic national days (see Events Calendar at the end of Chapter 10). There are also many regular weekend markets – here is a selection of the best of them. Our favourite is the Balmain Market.

Balmain Market, St. John's Church, corner Darling Street and Curtis Road (Saturday); **Bondi Beach Markets** at Bondi Beach Public School Campbell Parade, Bondi (Sunday); **Glebe Markets,** Glebe Point Road, Glebe Public School, opposite Russell's at 53 (Saturday); **Newtown Markets,** Burland Hall, 220 King Street, Newtown (weekend); **North Sydney Noodle Market** Friday nights during summer; Sunday lunchtime winter, in the park between the Council Chambers and Stanton Library in Miller Street, North Sydney; **Paddington Bazaar** 395 Oxford Street, Paddington (Saturday); **Paddy's Markets,** Haymarket (weekend); **The Rocks Markets** (weekend).

SUBURBAN STRIPS

We have picked our favourite shops in a few good areas for particular types of shopping around Sydney from the tradition to the "off-the-wall". Keep in mind that the more avant garde a place or product is, the more chance there is of it moving, changing, or even going out of business. The UnTourist Co's **Events Update** service can keep you informed on any of these changes.

$$ to $$$ STYLE STRIP
Military Road Mosman

The whole of the Military Road strip from Neutral Bay through Mosman is flecked with good shopping. Serious "Style Strip" however, starts at Spit Junction and winds down to about The Avenue. Within this strip you will find some of the best shops for clothes and accessories in Sydney. However, to list all of them here would be overkill. By picking out only a few means we probably won't cover the particular reader's taste. Regardless, we have chosen 12 – *Zu, Bissett, Carla Zampatti, Vreelands, Liz Davenport, Marcs Menswear* and *Bespoke Millinery*. In a nice old building, in a perfect environment for its style of clothing and homewares – *Country Road*; for those who aren't thin as rakes – *Maggie T*; for children – *Bonza Brats, Kidstuff* and for household accessories, *Accoutrement*.

Above: Country Road
Left: Bonza Brats Top Left: Accoutrement

$$ SERENDIPITY ROAD
Glebe Point Road, Glebe

It is one of Sydney's most stimulating shopping strips – filled with surprises, as many of the shop names suggest. Here are a few of the stand-out places but these are by no means the only good things to buy on Glebe Point Road. In fact, in terms of value for shoe leather, Glebe Road has more to offer in a contained area than most places in Sydney and all with the minimum of tat.

Ah Ah! Dodo 25 Glebe Road. Great name – sells Australian decorative wearable art, hand-blown glass, designer jewellery and silver. **Badde Manors** claims the best coffee in Glebe. The best vegetarian food. The best Hungarian cakes. The best atmosphere – and humble to boot! 37 Glebe Point Road. (At nearby 58 Cowper Street, **Friend in Hand Pub**). **Gleebooks** is at 49 and 191 Glebe Point Road – arguably the most stimulating bookstore in the city. At No 49, current lists plus rare local and imported titles – a booklover's dream; at 191 – second-hand and children's books. **Russell's,** the largest natural food store in the southern hemisphere, has a number of branches, but its heart is in the Glebe Point Road store at 53.

Half A Cow – providers, in their words of "cultural effluent" – started as a bookshop and has branched out in every direction that took their fancy – T-shirts, CDs, posters and books. Open every day, 85 Glebe Point Point Road. **Glass Artists Gallery,** representing over 80 Australian glass artists, 70 Glebe Point Road. **Just Desserts,** is what it says, 114 Glebe Point Road. **Darling Mills** at 134 Glebe Point Road is a consistent winner in *The Sydney Morning Herald* Good Food Guide. **Demeter** bakery uses only finest quality bio-dynamic and organic ingredients and produces "gourmet" breads, pies, pastries. Mill flour on the premises, 65 Derwent Street. **Valhalla Cinema** – one of Sydney's traditional art-house cinemas. Open every night, 166 Glebe Point Road. Not far away, **Oddbins Wines** - Bill Ireland's great booze shop in Camperdown, see page 151.

$$$$ ANTIQUE ALLEY
Queen Street, Woollahra

This is sold gold suburbia - said to be the richest street in Australia. Queen Street is not a very long street, yet it has 27 antique shops. Our savvy locals with an eye for antiques have picked out 14 of their favourites. What they like to do best is to window-shop on a summer's evening. Starting from the Oxford Street end:

I Charles Hewitt – for antique prints, frames and decoration furniture, 20 Queen Street; **2 Anne Schofield Antiques** – beautiful jewellery and objects d'art, 36 Queen Street; **3 Ros Palmer Antiques** – a high point is to get an invitation to a Ros Palmer opening, 42-44 Queen Street; **4 Copeland & De Soos** – specialising in late 19th and 20th century decorative arts and design, 66 Queen Street; **5 Peter Lane Gallery and Au Lion des Neiges** – ancient cultural objects from Tibet, 76 Queen Street; **6 Richard J Wiche Antiques** – specialising in gilt mirrors and decorative antiques, 80 Queen Street; **7 Art of Wine and Food** – old French glass, curious corkscrews, decanters, rare old bottles, 92 Queen Street; **8 W F Bradshaw** – clocks, furniture and early keyboard instruments, 96 Queen Street; **9 André & Cécile Fink Antiques** – French antiques from the Renaissance to the Empire period, 102 Queen Street; **10 Martyn Cook** – 18th and early 19th century English furniture and fine arts, 104 Queen Street; **11 Michael A Greene Antiques** – porcelain, glass, silver, jewellery, pens and watches; **12 Janet Niven Antiques** – 18th and 19th century pottery, jewellery, miniatures and samples, 118 Queen Street; **13 G L Auchinachie & Son** – 17th, 18th and 19th century English and European furniture, ceramics and metals, 43 Queen Street; **14 Tim McCormick Antique Books**, 53 Queen Street; **15 Appley Hoare Antiques** – 18th and 19th century European and country antiques. And, by the way, Queen Street has a great pub and some terrific cafes.

Map labels:
HAROLD PARK PUB — WIGRAM — HEREFORD — VALHALLA CINEMA — ODDBINS WINES — MARRAKECH CLOTHES — BRIDGE ROAD — DEMETER BREADS — DARLING MILLS — ST. JOHNS ROAD — GLEEBOOKS KIDS + SECOND HAND BOOKS — DERWENT — JUST DESSERTS — MITCHELL — GLASS ARTISTS GALLERY — HALF A COW — RUSSELLS NATURAL SUPER MARKET — GLEEBOOKS — GLEBE MARKETS — ESSENTIAL ENERGIES — FRANCIS ST — BADDE MANORS — FRIEND IN HAND PUB — AH AH! DODO — PARRAMATTA ROAD — BROADWAY — OXFORD ST. — CHARLES HEWITT — G L. AUCHINACHIE AND SON — ANNE SCHOFIELD — TIM McCORMICK — APPLEY HOARE — ROS PALMER — COPELAND + DE SOOS — PETER LANE AU LION DES NEIGES — RICHARD WICHE — ART OF WINE + FOOD — W.F. BRADSHAW — ANDRÉ + CÉCILE — MARTYN COOK — MICHAEL GREEN — MOORE STREET — JANET NIVEN — SUE CARLTON'S QUEEN STREET FARE. — OCEAN STREET

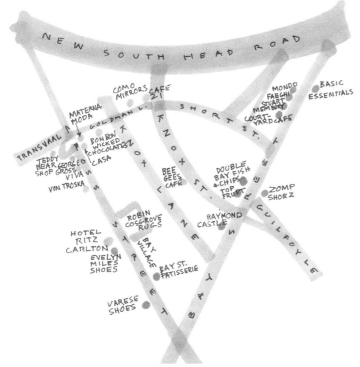

The map labels (as handwritten on the map):

NEW SOUTH HEAD ROAD

COMO MIRRORS · CAFE 21 · MONDO · FAECHI · STUART MEMBERY · BASIC ESSENTIALS · MATERNA MODA · GOLDMAN L. · SHORT ST. · COURTYARD CAFE · TRANSVAAL · BON BON WICKED CHOCOLATES · CASA · TEDDY BEAR SHOP · GEORGE GROSS · VIVA · VON TROSKA · BEE GEES CAFE · DOUBLE BAY FISH & CHIPS · TOP FRUIT · ZOMP SHOEZ · ROBIN COSGROVE RUGS · RAYMOND CASTLE · HOTEL RITZ CARLTON · EVELYN MILES SHOES · BAY VILLAGE · BAY ST. PATISSERIE · GUILFOYLE · VARESE SHOES · KNOX ST. · CROSS STREET · BAY STREET

Bon Bon

Raymond Castles

Transvaal Street

$$$ BAY BAY STYLE
Double Bay Village

"Bay Bay" or "The Bay" are colloquial descriptions for Double Bay. It really is tops in stylish, expensive and beautiful everything and it still has an appealing whiff of Europe in the air. Our Double Bay insider, Ruth Fischer, says the village has more hairdressers per square inch than anywhere else in Australia. We would say the same about its shoe shops and cafes.

We have picked out some special places to shop and a few eateries to allow you to take a break from spending all that money. If you have really overdone it, get some fish and chips from Double Bay Seafoods and sit in Steyne Park which overlooks the Double Bay Beach.

Bay St Patisserie

Steyne Park, Double Bay

$$ PINK PRECINCT
Oxford Street, Darlinghurst

Oxford Street strip starts near Crown Street Darlinghurst, crossing and then running through the high camp beats of Taylor Square, then becoming quietly eccentric as it nears Paddington before turning quite folksy and useful before Paddington runs out at Queen Street.

At 82, now sadly gone, was **Remo** the eclectic general store where Remo Giuffre sold only the best of everything, be it a wooden clothes peg or a hand-crafted silver watch. But fear not, the store has been taken over by another Sydney great, **Gowings** (see more about them on page 125). Just before you get there is the **Cash Palace Emporium** at 42 Oxford Street for gorgeous wedding frocks.) Across the road and a few doors up from the intersection of Oxford and

Crown, at 259 Crown Street is **Wheels & Doll Baby**, outfitters to the stars. Denim, leather and latex – as long as it's tight. 1970s psychedelia, silver glitter stilettos, gold sequined boob-tubes, sequin covered flares – as long as it sparkles it's in the **Zoo Emporium,** 332 Crown Street. At 96 Oxford Street is the one stop cowboy shop the **Pandarra Trading Co.** There are a few well-known watering holes around here too. But, be warned – according to Elisabeth Wynhausen in her *Pink Precinct* article in the *Australian Magazine* (August, 1995) a straight couple kissing in the bar of the **Oxford Hotel** (corner Bourke and Oxford Streets) was asked to desist so as not to distress the regular gay patrons. The **Albury Hotel** on the corner of Barcom and Oxford Streets is well enough known abroad to be listed in "Spartacus" the worldwide Gay Directory.

Zoo Emporium

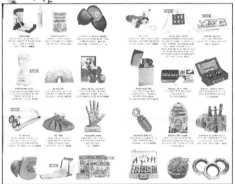

REMO catalogue

$$ CAMP ROW
City Centre

This is the area where all the off-roaders get their stuff. No-one knows quite why they have clustered in this part of town, but cluster they have.

The **Wilderness Society** has two entries in Camp Row. The office is in James Lane (1) while the shop is at (7) 92 Liverpool Street. This is a great place to pick up unusual, environmentally friendly things from clothing to books.

(2) **Paddy Pallin,** 507 Kent Street (3) **Kathmandu** is down in the Town Hall Arcade, for regular camping equipment. (4) **Mountain**

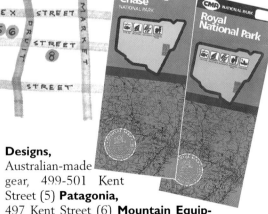

Designs, Australian-made gear, 499-501 Kent Street (5) **Patagonia,** 497 Kent Street (6) **Mountain Equipment,** 491 Kent Street (8) **Youth Hostels of Australia Membership** and Travel Centre, 422 Kent Street.

TREND STREET $$ to $$$

Where Oxford Street becomes Paddington is around **Sweet Art** which bakes works of art in the guise of cakes – 96 Oxford Street. At 180 Oxford Street is **Hot Tuna** – Australia's hottest surf-turned fashion label. Opera diva Jennifer McGregor who lives in the area, likes **Bracewell** at 264 Oxford Street – young trendy labels from Europe, Australia and Sainty of New Zealand. Another McGregor recommendation is Bill the butcher, or officially **Wilson's Meats,** 348 Oxford Street, which has both a greengrocer and a baked-on-the premises bakery. Derek Scott 336 Oxford Street – wonderful sheets; **Sid Brandon** for chic used furniture, 408 Oxford Street. Sanctum for Byron Bay based New Age beauty products. Essential oils fill the store with soothing aromas, 448 Oxford Street. **Paddington Pears** at 434 Oxford Street - designer fruit and vegies. **Dinosaur Designs** for beads, bangles and stuff, 339 Oxford Street – and so it goes. For those who are born to shop,

with a taste for the unusual, Oxford Street Paddington makes a dangerous walk.

By the time you reach the heart of Oxford Street, Paddington you'll feel like a good coffee. Try the **Sloane Rangers Cafe** at 312 Oxford Street or **New Editions** bookshop and tea rooms at 328. Between Elizabeth and George is **Hot Gossip** the deli and cafe with excellent coffee, special breads, cakes and super tempting morsels, 438 Oxford Street.

At the top of Oxford Street in the grounds of the local church is one of the best markets in Sydney. **The Paddington Bazaar** with its 250 stalls featuring old wares, paintings, original new and trendy vintage clothing, music and toys. This is a market which has managed to avoid the commercial exploitation which erodes so many similar places. The locals eat there, sing there, shop there and just strut around in the atmosphere. Open every Saturday, 10am till about 4pm, 395 Oxford Street.

$ ZAP STREET – King Street, Newtown

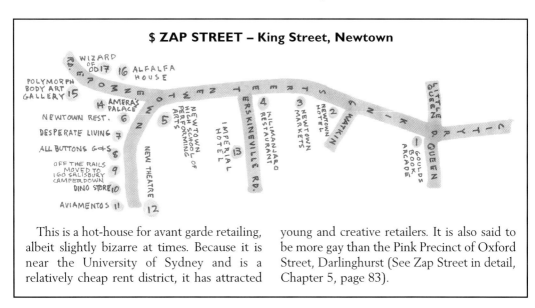

This is a hot-house for avant garde retailing, albeit slightly bizarre at times. Because it is near the University of Sydney and is a relatively cheap rent district, it has attracted young and creative retailers. It is also said to be more gay than the Pink Precinct of Oxford Street, Darlinghurst (See Zap Street in detail, Chapter 5, page 83).

UNTOURIST READING LIST

In *UnTourist Sydney* we have tried to give you a really good overall look at Sydney, but there are some specialist areas and/or day-to-day information requirements which you may still need. Here is a selection of publications you should find useful.

The Sydney Morning Herald

Sydney Morning Herald – published daily, except Sunday. A fine daily newspaper and required reading for Sydneysiders. It has an informed *Arts* section; *Good Living* gives you all the latest places to eat and the *Entertainment Guide* and *Metro* sections cover all the happenings in Sydney; **The Bulletin** weekly news magazine is also a long and fine Sydney tradition; **The Good Food Guide,** Edited by Sydney Morning Herald's foodies Jill Dupleix and Terry Durack gives you a comprehensive coverage of all the best eating houses all over the Sydney areas as well as towns and cities as far away as Canberra; **SBS Eating Guide** to Sydney by Maeve O'Meara and Joanna Savill (Text Publishing Company). A critical guide to ethnic eating in Sydney. Put out by those who should know – staff of SBS, the wonderful television station which started as a multicultural channel and now provides, in our opinion, the best television viewing in Sydney; Kangaroo Press publishes some fine specialist books on Sydney: **Sydney Bushwalks** by Neil Paton; **Sydney Walks** by Margaret White and **Sydney by Ferry & Foot,** written and illustrated by John Gunter, will give you extra insights into Sydney. As

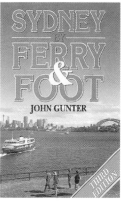

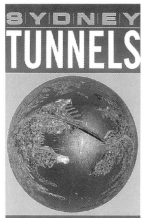

will the fascinating **Sydney Tunnels** by Brian and Barbara Kennedy and **Uncovering Sydney** by Graham Spindler. To learn something of the flora and fauna of the Sydney Region, **WILDthings** introduced by Burnum Burnum (Geoff Sainty & Associates).

Two celebrated writers Jan Morris and Ruth Park have written about Sydney – **Sydney** (Viking) and **A Companion Guide to Sydney** (Collins) respectively. If you can find a copy of **Sydney** by local journalist Gavin Souter, it is well worth the effort, as is *Ferries of Sydney,* by Graeme Andrews (Oxford University Press).

Shops not to be missed

More individual Sydney shops we consider exceptional in their various categories.

FOOD

Abla's Pastry Palace of Middle Eastern pastries, 425 New Canterbury Road, Dulwich Hill; **AC Butchery** Italian gourmet meat game shop, 174 Marion Street Leichhardt; **Antico's** Considered Sydney's best fruit and vegetable shop, Northbridge Plaza, Northbridge; **Arena's L'Antipasto Deli** 908 Military Road, Mosman; **Athena Cake Shop** 412 Illawarra Road.

Bar Italia Best gelati in town,169 Norton Street, Leichhardt; **Belaroma Coffee** A great range of roasted-on-the premises coffee, plus things to make it with 457 Penshurst Street, Roseville; **Cyril's Delicatessan** For 40 years - a Sydney tradition, 183 Hay Street, Haymarket; **Darya Deli** is Iranian and full of the most wonderful Middle Eastern specialties. Open every day, 331 Penshurst Street, Willoughby; **Dulwich Hill Roaster** where Maurice Hazim sells the freshest and the best beans and nuts. Corner Pigott Street and New Canterbury Road; **Il Gianfornaio** turn out a wondrous assortment of breads. Closed Sundays, 414 Victoria Avenue, Chatswood; **La Banette** 28 Avalon Parade, Avalon makes the best petits fours outside Paris; **Lucky Tom's** Treasure-trove of traditional Italian wedding trinkets. Open Mon-Sat, 379 Parramatta Road, Leichhardt; **Paesanella Cheese Factory** Locally made fresh Italian cheeses. Open Sun-Fri in the mornings to the public. 37 Gerald Street, Marrickville; **Penny's Butcher** Gourmet meats and poultry 880 Military Road, Mosman; **Sydney Fish Markets** Absolutely the best place in Sydney to buy fresh fish and shellfish, Pyrmont; **Tokyo Mart** serves the areas Japanese community with all the traditional foods 27 Northbridge Plaza, Northbridge; **Victoire** Great range of French breads – from fugasse to brioche. 85 Darling Street, Balmain; **Wrights** Gourmet meats and poultry, 32 Clovelly Road, Randwick.

CLOTHES

Moore and More Charming, flowing, white things a specialty 134 Blues Point Road, McMahon's Poin **Morrissy Edmonton** Great traditional women's gear. Strand Arcade, 412-414 George Street, Sydney **Maggie Shepherd** Wonderful jackets that sparkle and shimmer. Strand Arcade, 412-414 George Street, Sydney **Vintage Clothing** Second-hand dresses which present as new. 147, Castlereagh Street, Sydney

JEWELLERY

Rox Gems and Jewellery Just stand outside the window and dream a little. Strand Arcade, 412-414 George Street Sydney. **Markers Mark** Beatifully crafted Australian jewellery and precious objects d'art to wear. Chifley Plaza, 2 Chifley Square, Sydney.

IN HOUSE

Currently, some of the best value in oriental and Russian rugs is in Sydney.

Mr Brassman Great varity of kilim rugs, 71 Spit Road, Mosman. **Nomadic Rug Traders** Dealers in antique rugs of the highest quality. 125 Harris Street, Pyrmont. **Persian Carpet Gallery** Fine selection of Russian and other oriental rugs. 352 Kent Street

MIXED THINGS

Australian Geographic retail outlets spread around Sydney, sell environmentally friendly gifts and camping equipment. Main store, 34 Centrepoint, Pitt Street, Sydney. **Linen and Lace of Balmain,** 213 Darling Street, Balmain. **Punch Gallery** Wonderful rag dolls, pottery and fine tabby house cat that sits in the window. 209 Darling Street Balmain.

$ BARGAINS

Here is a list of individual bargain shops and a few areas renowned for their bargains.

Bexley Wholesalers Bargain priced top-name items from Pierre Cardin watch to cutlery; from small electrical goods to luggage. But not the kitchen sink. Open every day. 36 Sarsfield Crescent, Bexley North. **Birkenhead Shopping Centre** has had a spotty history but seems to have settled down now into factory seconds – mainly clothing, but also furniture. Open every day. Birkenhead Point, Drummoyne. **Burlington Centre** for everything you need for Chinese cooking - foodstuffs, pots and plates included. Thomas Street, Ultimo (Chinatown) and 285 Penshurst Street, Willoughby. **Hylands Shoe City** Forget going to New York for your Rockports – you can get them for the same price at Hylands. All big brand names in casual and sports shoes. Open every day. Corner Victoria Road and Darling Street, Rozelle. **St. Vincent De Paul** These Roman Catholic charity shops with their lovely old volunteer ladies, operate all over Sydney. Mainly clothing. You find the best bargains in the richest suburbs where they can afford to give away a better class of discards. **Tempe Tip** Here's a real Sydney institution, and that's what it's always been called, but the Tempe Tip isn't your run-of-the-mill garbage tip. It's actually the Salvation Army Red Shield Industries, and no visitor to Sydney should miss it. It's where you can find wonderful bargains in clothing, furniture, dishes, and just about anything else. Open 9.30am-3.00 pm Mon-Fri, 8.30-3 on Sat, closed Sun. **Tin Shed** For nationalistic junk from a railway station noticeboard to a pottery flying duck. Also home to the great Chester's Cafe. 148 Beattie Street, Balmain.

Here are a few areas for bargain shopping.

CABRAMATTA

For detail, see Chapter 4, West.

LEICHHARDT

OKB Warehouse

This is Sydney's only factory outlet for the much admired Orrefors and Kosta Boda glassware. You will find many of their main lines available. Thurs 9.30am-6pm; Sat 11am-4pm, Shop 4A, 1 Lords Rd, Leichhardt.

Sydney Bags

You can save up to 30% on the latest fashion styles and up to 70% on clearance items, and new stock is arriving every day, 168 Redfern Road, Redfern. Open every day. Shop 1a Lords Road Leichhardt.

Nike Factory Outlet

They also stock a huge range of aerobic, cycling, and work-out gear, sweatbands, sports bags and socks. Open daily, 576-580 Parramatta Road, Leichhardt.

SCHMUTTER TOWN

SURRY HILLS

There are actually bus tours which bring people to this area for special bargain shopping. Doesn't sound like a typical UnTourist way to travel but you have to admit, it's different. Here are some of the best "finds":

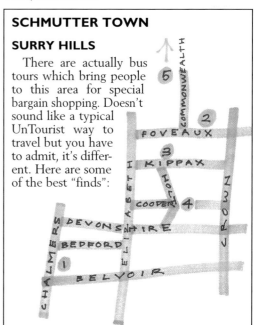

1 The Bead Company Czechoslovakian crystal beads to African finds, this one-stop bead shop has them all. They hold classes in beading as well. Weekdays and 10-4 on Saturdays, 184 Chalmers Street, Surry Hills.

2 Selected Design Bargain garments for day and evening wear. Shop 2, 17-51 Foveaux Street.

3 City Limits Knitwear Selected group of Australian-made knitted skirts, pants, cardis and sweaters at rock bottom prices. Open to the public at weekends only, 26-44 Kippax Street, Surry Hills.

4 K D's Lingerie Delicious lingerie at discount prices make K.D's well worth a visit. Stocking seconds and samples from all over the world. Specialise in the perfect fit at the right price. 9-5 weekdays and 9-3 on Saturdays and Sundays. Corner of Cooper and Holt Street, Surry Hills.

5 Fabric Fantasy Quite well-known designers tend to lurk around these rolls of Ungaro prints and Valentino wools. It's a fabric lover's dream. It's not just the big names either – Fabric Fantasy has a large range of fabrics pre-cut material and imported buttons. 9-5 weekdays and 9-4 on Saturdays, 101 Commonwealth Street, Surry Hills.

Memoirs of Sydney
(Tourists call them souvenirs)

THE SYDNEY ENSIGN

Adopted by the Harbourmaster of the Port of Sydney in 1988, it commemorates the Old Port of Sydney flag of the 1830. Measuring 60 x 30 cms, $30. Available also in larger sizes from Australiana Flags, 2/175 Sailors Bay Road, Northbridge.

HARBOUR BRIDGE BROOCH

This art deco brooch is available in various colour schemes, $12.95 at the Museum of Contemporary Art Store, 140 George Street North, The Rocks.

ORIGINAL KEN DONE T-SHIRT

Now part of Sydney folklore, $32.50. You can get it at Done Art and Design, 123 George Street, The Rocks.

SYDNEY SKY GUIDE

Watch the Southern Cross pop up in this great Southern Skies Pocket Guide. Available for $6.95 from the Observatory on Observatory Hill, the Powerhouse Museum, 500 Harris Street or The Mint, Macquarie Street.

FOOTY SWEATERS

All the local Sydney teams like St George, Canterbury, Easts, Cronulla. You may not play the game, but you may as well look as though you do. The big boofy blokes go to Gowings for theirs. Gowings Bros, Corner Market and George Streets. $75.95.

MUSEUM SHOPS

Some of the most interesting bits and pieces as mementoes can be found at the shops in the museums and galleries. You will find all the full names, addresses and telephone numbers in the Directory at the back of the book.

> **MUSEUM OF SYDNEY**
> **THE POWERHOUSE**
> **THE MINT•THE BARRACKS**
> AUSTRALIAN MUSEUM
> MUSEUM OF CONTEMPORARY ART
> **OBSERVATORY**
> **STATE LIBRARY**
> *AQUARIUM•MARITIME*
> **ART GALLERY**

SYDNEY SWEATSHIRT

From the eclectic general store, where it is all too easy to spend too much, comes a whole bunch of great ideas. Things are well made from pure stuff. Sweatshirt, $65. The design also comes in T-shirts with long $50 or short $40 sleeves. (Note: Remo, at 82 Oxford Street, is now closed down, replaced by a new Gowings).

BOOKS ABOUT SYDNEY

The Bathers Pavilion Cookbook, the authentic taste of Sydney by Victoria Alexander, $34.95; Burnum Burnum's *WILD-things of Sydney*, a charming book about Sydney's flora and fauna, $14.95; and, dare we suggest, as a gift for friends, *UnTourist Sydney*, $29.95.

Note: prices subject to change.

The Ingredient as Hero

9 EAT AND DRINK

INCLUDES: The new Modern Australian Cuisine, what it is and where to enjoy the best of it. Places to eat that are a little different, our favourites, the best of every nation in Sydney – no matter what type of food you want to eat, you will find it here.

Modern Australian Cuisine - the Gastronomic Gestalt

First came the English meat and potatoes period, then the French wine sauce period – that took care of the first 200 years of vittles in the white settlement in Sydney. It brings us to the time when we were introduced, in the early '80s to the versatile and highly decorative Nouvelle Cuisine, or Corsage Cuisine to be worn or eaten.

Corsage Cuisine

Even though this style of presentation could hardly be described as "a square meal under your belt", its great contribution lay in educating Australians – particularly Sydney-siders, to the "ingredient as the hero" (rather than the traditional recipe as it had been forever). In the '80s, when so many of the great kitchen gardens of Europe were considered a bit suss, either because of pollution or Chernobyl fall-out, the clean, green rim countries like New Zealand and Australia with their clean, green ingredients were looking pretty attractive. The export of food stuffs from these countries almost doubled during the decade – the moment of glory had arrived. Enter the "ingredient as hero" period and modern Australian cuisine.

We are what we eat. A city's affluence, climate, topography and heritage is reflected in its food styles. Take, for example, multi-culturalism.

If, in a city of mixed nationalities, individual groups continue to maintain pockets having their own food styles, no matter how enjoyable the variety or how authentic this "ghetto" food is – if this is the only result of the mix of cultures, then you can be sure that true assimilation has not taken place.

If, on the other hand, food foibles merge, and from that combination of the different influences a new and different style emerge – if this new "whole" is better than the sum of the parts, then a gastronomic gestalt is formed.

Surely this is a sign that true multiculturalism is happening. The New Australian cuisine cannot be tracked to any one nation's influence. Yes, one can identify Thai, Italian, Japanese, Greek, French – even the often denigrated English meat and potatoes have their place. But at the heart of this culinary style is the access to fresh ingredients, put together resourcefully, and presented with a large dollop of good old Aussie lack of pretension.

It is true, however, that, due to the well-developed competitive spirit that exists among the many young, hip Sydney chefs you will at times be presented with an over-enthusiastic offering such as :

Scorched Balmain Bug tails on a Bed of Aniseed Couscous with Crêmed Petit Pois and Botany Bay Greens

or

Wood smoked, milk fed, lamb fillets encased in a choux of bread crusts served in a pool of fig and parsnip pesto.

– things of this nature. But these are early days. Bon appetit!

Researching

🦆 🦆 SYDNEY'S BEST MODERN AUSTRALIAN CUISINE

The following is a list of those restaurants generally considered to be the best at cooking and serving Modern Australian Cuisine. We have chosen ones which are relatively well-established, as Sydney restaurants have a mercurial quality about them and tend to change their names or addresses as often as their table napkins. It is therefore wise to check first rather than just turn up.

Let's not split hairs, all these restaurants are in two duck territory – some a little more, some a little less....

A GRAND OPERA FEAST

The more famous the building, the worse the food. That was until the new Sydney Opera House restaurants opened. Now the food is as special as the setting. There are three major restaurants: the **(1) Bennelong ($$$$),** a celebration of Australian Modern Cuisine; **(2) Concourse ($$),** a first-class bistro style eatery; **(3) Harbour ($$),** which we rate as one of the two best fish restaurants in Sydney. (Inside on the box office level right at the entrance to the concert and opera hall, there is the fine little cafeteria-style **Mozart** cafe). All are licensed and, as well as having discerning wine lists, they serve wine by the glass. None is in the cheap eats category – in fact the Bennelong is one of the most expensive restaurants in Sydney, but the value is there.

What makes all these restaurants so special is the ambience. The **Bennelong** in its "mini Opera House" or "kennel" as the more irreverent Sydneysiders have dubbed it, looks out over its domain with a certain proprietorial air. The **Harbour** is right on the northern tip of the building and is very much an indoor/outdoor environment, as is the **Concourse.** Even the Mozart has a behind-the-scenes atmosphere and is usually patronised by those who are grabbing a quick bite before the curtain goes up.

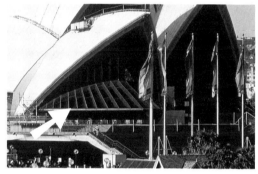

Above: Sitting outside the new Concourse Restaurant
Top right: The great new Bennelong Restaurant
Bottom right: The Harbour, one of Sydney's best fish restaurants in an unbeatable location

IN AND AROUND THE ROCKS

(4) SYDNEY COVE
OYSTER BAR $$ C
On the walkway to the Opera House
TEL: 9247 2937   Licensed•Credit Cards
   This is the place to set you off in the right
mood before an Opera House performance with
a glass champagne and a plate of Sydney rock
oysters. Best of all is to take a table out-of-doors
and watch the rush-hour evening traffic bustle
by on the water.

(5) BILSON'S $$$$ C
Modern Australian
Overseas Terminal, The Rocks
Tel: 9251 5600   Licensed•Credit Cards
   In the running with the Opera House
restaurants, Unkai and Forty One for the title of
heavyweight owner of the best view of Sydney
Harbour. Started in the late '80s by one of
Australia's greatest contributors to the art of fine
dining, this restaurant travelled down a
somewhat rocky road after Tony Bilson left.
Now, however, it has regained the track under
the intelligent guidance of Guillaume Brahimi,
ex The Pond and trained by Paris' Joel
Robuchon. You'll die and go to heaven on
tasting his basil-infused tuna; if that doesn't get
you - the mashed potatoes that are equal parts
spuds and butter surely will. Lunch Mon-Fri;
dinner Mon-Sat,

(6) GALILEO $$$$ C
Modern Australian
Observatory Hotel 89- 113 Kent Street, The Rocks
Tel: 92562222   Licensed•Credit Cards
   Representative of a fine dining room, with
culinary emphasis on the best of Australian
produce shining through a Italio-Aussie guise.
This and the Orient Casfe are both restaurants
run by the fine hand of executive chef Anthony
Musarra, ex Kings Cross' Mesclun, who has
brought inner-city swish to grand hotel dining.
Lunch Mon-Fri; dinner Mon-Sat.

(7) ORIENT CAFE $$ C
Modern Australian
Observatory Hotel, 89-113 Kent Street, The Rocks.
Tel: 9256 2222   Licensed•Credit Cards
   The Orient Cafe speaks with a bit of an Asian
accent, serving up a bit of brasserie-style East
meets West now classic fare. As with the Galileo,
it is run by the fine hand of executive chef
Anthony Musarra, ex Kings Cross' Mesclun.

(8) PALISADE RESTAURANT $$ C
Modern Australian
Palisade Hotel, 35 Bettington Street, Millers Point
Tel: 9251 7225   Licensed•Credit Cards
   Situated in a classic old pub (indeed, the
rooms, while somewhat spartan, offer fab views
of the Harbour), this dining room was taken

over and reworked in mid '95 by another of
Sydney's most influential chefs, Annie
Parmentier, of the upper North Shore's well-
known Clareville Kiosk. Featuring what can by
now practically be deemed traditional food,
with its emphasis on the finest of local produce
tarted up in an amalgam of Mediterranean and
Asian styles, you'll dine here secure in the
knowledge that you're eating real Australian
fare, 1990s' version. In winter a fireplace around
which to have pre-dinner drinks and there's a
residential part for an overnight stay, if you
want. There's one of the great views of the
harbour and city from the hotel's "widow's
walk". Ask if you can go-see. Lunch Mon-Fri;
dinner Mon-Sat; lunch Sunday.

(9) KABLE'S $$$$ C
Modern Australian
Regent Hotel, 199 George Street, Sydney
Tel: 9255 0226   Licensed•Credit Cards
   Opened more than a decade ago by executive
chef Serge Dansereau, Kable's made its mark
early on, setting a standard that almost all new
Modern Australian cuisine proponents have
tried to emulate. Dansereau himself has done
more for leading Sydney's food scene out of the
Dark Ages of the '70s than anyone else, by
encouraging growers and manufacturers to
seduce the dining public with food items never
before available in this country. While the menu
in the main changes almost daily, some classics
remain and are well worth sampling for the
innovative tweak given them by the kitchen
Lunch Mon-Fri; dinner Tues-Sat.

(10) MCA CAFE $$ C
Modern Australian
Museum of Contemporary Art
140 George Street, The Rocks
Tel: 9241 4253   Licensed•Credit Cards
   The simple, clean-lined style of the museum
spills over into this cafe/restaurant where the
best seating on a fine day is under umbrellas on
the terrace overlooking the Quay. The menu is
mostly Mediterranean and lends itself to
choosing two entrees instead of a main dish if
that's your preference. It is popular with
business people in the area, so you should book
ahead if possible - otherwise waiting your turn
from a queue is bearable. Mon-Fri 11am-5pm;
Sat-Sun 9am-5pm.

(11) THE TREASURY $$$$ C
Modern Australian
Hotel Inter-Continental,
117 Macquarie Street, Sydney
Tel: 9240 1270   Licensed•Credit Cards
   Eating off the menu can be done for as low as
the first-quoted price, without wine, but for
sheer ecstasy, spend the extra and indulge in

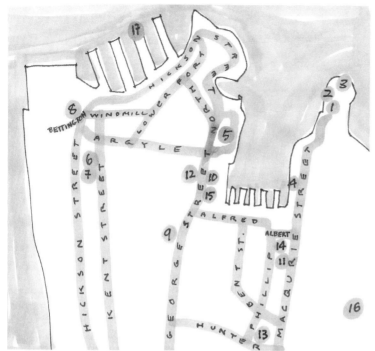

the Hotel Inter.Continental, and then up the tower to the 41st level, this restaurant with its drop-dead views north, east and south over the city, has got to be experienced to be believed. Managed by chef Dietmar Sawyere, the kitchen turns out food as glam and exciting as the surrounds. Certainly one of the best dining rooms in town... but relaxed and amusing at the same time. Try to steal a look out the mens'room windows even if you're of the other gender. Lunch Mon-Fri; dinner Mon-Sat.

(14) MERRONY'S $$$ C
Modern Australian
2 Albert Street, Sydney
Tel: 9247 9323   Licensed•Credit Cards
Paul Merrony is another of the Oz cuisine brat pack, but in this eponymously titled, centrally located venue, he's come of age, as has the style of food he's been so instrumental in discovering and developing. Diners can sense the classic French rudiments of the food but go mad over the cool '90s spin that Merrony's alchemy puts on it. Open late, it's situated just up Macquarie Street from the Opera House for a truly grand finale on a night out. Lunch Mon-Fri; dinner Mon-Sat.

(15) SAILOR'S THAI $$$ C
Thai
106 George Street, The Rocks
Tel: 9251 2466   Licensed•Credit Cards
Sailor's Thai is the latest venture by David Thompson who for years has single-handedly and determinedly enlightened Sydney diners about the joys of Southeast Asian cuisine at his Darley Street Thai (28-30 Bayswater Road, Kings Cross, Tel 9358 6530). Here, he loosens up in The Canteen, serving upteen noodle dishes that, like Jacob's coat, appear in a hundred amazing colours - soups, salads, stir-fried, desserts. Downstairs is a classy cutting-edge room serving a full range of primarily classic Thai dishes. Close to the MCA in case you need a chilli fix after viewing the hot art Noodle Bar open daily 12-8. Restaurant, Lunch Mon-Fri; dinner Mon-Sat.

eight food and wine pairings selected and compiled in a degustation menu by arguably one of Sydney's greatest chefs, Tony Bilson. After leaving Bilson's and cooking around town for a few years, Bilson has again confirmed his exciting prowess with his masterly and memorable menu. If you want to know you've sampled the best of end-of-the-century Australian cuisine, book in at The Treasury. Lunch Mon-Sat; dinner daily from 5.30 pm.

(12) ROCKPOOL $$$$ C
Modern Australian
107 George Street, Sydney
Tel: 9252 1888   Licensed•Credit Cards
Rockpool (and the MCA Cafe across the street) are owned and operated by the wunderkind of Oz tucker, Neil Perry, these two restaurants can be spoken of together because they show in detail the vast spectrum that Modern Australian Cuisine encompasses, from the casual, breezy "fast-food" of the East and the Mediterranean like noodle and focaccia dishes, to their more refined siblings such as tea-smoked poultry with refined dressings. If you haven't eaten Perry's food, you haven't eaten Australian. Lunch Mon-Fri; dinner Mon-Sat.

(13) FORTY ONE $$$$ C
Modern Australian
Level 41, Chiffley Tower, 2 Chifley Square, Sydney
Tel: 9221 2500   Licensed•Credit Cards
Just up the road from the Opera House and

(16) BOTANIC GARDENS RESTAURANT $$ C

Modern Australian
The Royal Botanic Gardens
Art Gallery Road, Sydney
Tel: 9241 2419   Licensed•Credit Cards

Hidden in one of the prettiest parts of the Royal Botanic Gardens - Sue Burrows' charming restaurant. The high ceilings, the large, round, glass-walled verandahs give the impression of being suspended in a large pigeon-loft over the fig trees at the bend in the creek, where the ducks and swans appear to be most vocal and active. Here you can enjoy modern Australian cuisine with a Greek bias in a delightful environment. You can enter from Art Gallery Road and ask at the Gardens enquiry office, or approach from the back of the Conservatorium and walk through the gardens. Lunch daily.

Charles Blackman's sketch of his friend Sue Burrows at work

(17) WHARF $$ C

Modern Australian
Pier 4, Hickson Road, Walsh Bay
Tel: 9250 1761   Licensed•Credit Cards

Dining at the Wharf adds such a worthwhile dimension to an evening at the theatre that it should almost be a mandatory addition to your ticket. Simple but tasty food, with fresh salads and seafood predominant and prompt service to get you to the theatre on time - unless you get side-tracked by the intoxication of the surroundings, not to mention wine. Once a working wharf, the Pier is a magnificent timber structure still favoured by hobby fishermen at any time of day. Do book ahead. Lunch and dinner Mon-Sat, supper Mon-Sat.

SPECIAL EXPERIENCES

The following places have been selected on the basis of the special experience they offer, whether it is because you can arrive by boat or maybe the environment is special to Sydney – whatever. Some are cheap, some are expensive, some are in town, some are out of town – but they all have something special about them as well as very good food.

THE FISH MARKETS $ C

It's not that the restaurants and cafes are so special here at the Fish Markets – they aren't. In fact we recommend that you buy your seafood and have it cooked for you on the spot by the Manettas who own Peter's fish retailing at the markets. Then you might like to seat yourself at the tables outside, near the wharf where the fishing boats are moored. You can pick up your choice of wine or beer there also. As we have mentioned in a previous chapter, your only problem will be the seagulls - they're a pushy bunch, but they accept bribes.

BAC LIEU $ W

Vietnamese and Chinese
302 Illawarra Road, Marrickville
Tel: 9558 5788   BYO
We were led here by a Hong Kong musician who prides himself on discovering the best and cheapest Asian restaurants in Sydney. The Bac Lieu is in the best tradition of this kind of restaurant - all the family helps out. Thankfully the menu is also in English and you can simply be guided by the descriptions. But don't miss out on Bun Chao Tom prawn sugar cane with vermicelli. Open Mon-Sat, 9am-9.30pm.

BATHERS PAVILION $$$ N

Modern Australian
4 The Esplanade, Bondi, Balmoral
Tel: 9968 1133   Licensed•Credit Cards

A meal here is more than just about food: it's one of the great Sydney experiences. Located in what years ago was built as a bathers' changing room and done up in a fashion that could be termed Grecian-island-meets-San-Tropez,

Victoria Alexander's restaurant sits slam on the Balmoral Beach esplanade where all the world strolls by as you dine. Beyond, the view leads you out through the Heads to the Pacific, and sitting here you'll feel like you wouldn't change places for anything in the world. Oh, yes... the food's exemplary, too, morning, noon and night. Breakfast weekends and public holidays. Lunch and dinner daily.

CHINESE NOODLE RESTAURANT $ C

Northern Chinese
LG7, 8 Quay Street, Haymarket
Tel: 9281 9051   BYO Credit Cards

A tiny restaurant with food and atmosphere that might have been spirited form Peking yesterday. When he has finished making his noodles Xiao Tang Qin will entertain you by playing Chinese and Western music on his er-he, the two-string Chinese instrument. The best way to get there is from Thomas Street (left-hand side heading toward Hay Street). About halfway down, you pass the Burlington Supermarket (excellent for every kind of Chinese food imaginable); then comes the Prince Gallery, an arcade of shops where the restaurant can be found to the left of the escalator, on the ground floor.

CHURCH POINT TOP ROOM $$ N

General
McCarrs Creek Road, , Church Point 2105
Tel: 9979 9670   BYO Credit Cards

On top of the small supermarket which serves the residents of Scotland Island and McCarrs Creek, this small cafe is worth a visit, particularly for breakfast on Saturday and Sunday. If the weather's fine and not windy, ask for a table on the balcony to enjoy a delightful view of the western foreshores of Pittwater and the local traffic of commuters, ferries and other small craft. Mon-Fri 1 lam-4pm; Sat-Sun 8-1 lam; Fri and Sat 6-12pm.

CICADA $$$ E

Modern Australian
29 Challis Avenue, Potts Point
Tel: 9358 1255   Licensed•Credit Cards

Sydney is lucky enough to be home a pair of siblings who have both been instrumental in the creation of its singular, spectacular cuisine. The one in charge here is brother Peter Doyle, and the food he produces confirms that his grasp of marketforces is as sure as ever; he downsized and altered this venue from an almost traditionally French room long-known as Le Trianon to its current hip, elegant-bistro

incarnation with great success.

COTTAGE POINT INN $$ N

See chapter 10, page 163.

EDNA'S TABLE $$$ C

Modern Australian
Lobby Level, MLC Centre, Martin Place, Sydney
Tel: 9231 1400   Licensed•Credit Cards

Edna's Table could only be in Sydney - it is a bit "over-the-top", but in the nicest, friendliest way, demonstrating something of the innate come-in-and-enjoy-yourself character of Sydneysiders. The decor is based on vigorous Aboriginal motifs; the food borrows from Koori tradition (the owners have Aboriginal ancestry) with bush-tucker concepts like paper-bark cooking wraps and native pepper berries and ground bush tomatoes. Jennice is always thrilled to explain to customers the cultural traditions of the food if they are interested. Lunch Mon-Fri; dinner Mon-Sat.

JONAH'S $$$ N

New Australian
69 Bynya Road, Palm Beach
Tel: 9974 5599   Licensed•Credit Cards

The best way to enjoy all Jonah's has to offer is to have dinner there and stay the night, choosing one of the rooms overlooking the ocean, and watch the sun come up. Then, at breakfast, you can enjoy the spectacular view in cinemascope, wonderful in perfect weather, stunning in a storm. Mediterranean decor, Jonah's has plenty of style across the board, – food with some interesting middle-eastern touches. Lunch and dinner daily; breakfast Sat-Sun 8-10am.

POWERHOUSE GARDEN RESTAURANT $$ C

Australian Cuisine
500 Harris Street, Ultimo
Tel: 9217 0559   Licensed•Credit Cards

Variety, imaginative environments, surprise – all hallmarks of the sure touch of the Powerhouse Museum, now extended to the cafe/restaurant painted by Ken Done in abundant, joyful designs up walls and across ceilings. An excellent place to adjourn to revive for further viewing of the exhibits. Vegetables and salads are tops. There is a special, practical children's menu - fish and chips, ravioli etc. Scones and a choice of biscuit, cakes and slices. 10am- 11 am light snacks, lunch served from 11am-3.30pm.

RAVESI'S ON BONDI BEACH $$ E

Modern Australian
Corner Campbell Parade and
Hall Street Bondi Beach

Tel: 9365 4422   Licensed•Credit Cards

Bondi has managed to keep its unpretentious heritage while adding some excellent restaurants, cafes and other food outlets to its welcome. We've chosen Ravesi's because it embodies some of the best of this contemporary Bondi. Lots of salads, seafood and a general Asian influence. There's a bar and Sunday brunch is the really busy time. Lunch and dinner daily. Breakfast from 7.30am.

RITZ-CARLTON
LOBBY LOUNGE $$ **E**

General

The Ritz-Carlton Double Bay,
33 Cross Street, Double Bay 2028

Tel: 9262 2023   Licensed•Credit Cards

Excellent buffet lunch here - very popular with the locals who are often well known about-town identities. To eat here is to experience how the Eastern Suburbs likes to take lunch while meeting up with friends to gossip or catch up on the news. Daily and brunch Sunday.

TETSUYA'S $$$$ **W**

Modern Australian

729 Darling Street, Rozelle

Tel: 9555 1017   Licensed•Credit Cards

Another shrine at which to worship Modern Australian cuisines's wonders, as well as another restaurant that's bloody hard to get a booking in – people have been known to will a reservation at Tet's to their children. Try by any means possible to get a table there, for lunch (it's a little expensive) or dinner to partake of his exquisite degustation of six courses of Franco-Nippon supernal innovation. Lunch Wed-Sat; Dinner Tues-Sat.

THE PIER $$$$ **E**

Modern Australian

595 New South Head Road, Rose Bay

Tel: 9327 6561   Licensed•Credit Cards

Greg Doyle, one of the tearaway twosome of brothers who had great impact in the shaping of Modern Australian cuisine, lit here in the heart

of other-Doyle-cooking-family territory some years back after moving around the greater metropolitan area in a number of different ventures, and here he's stayed. Who wouldn't? The Pier is sited out over the water, in a long, yellow-brick-road of a restaurant having the lights of Sydney scattered out like mica at its end. The food sparkles here, too, in a menu that focuses on seafood dishes shining superlatively in their sensitive treatment. Lunch and dinner daily.

TIN SHED/CHESTER'S CAFE $ **W**

Modern Australian

148 Beattie Street, Balmain 2041

Tel: 9555 2185   BYO

With its total lack of pretension and anarchic disregard for convention, the Tin Shed epitomises Balmain. The food is imaginative, fresh and tasty – from natural muesli or home-made baked beans on toast to vitello tomato and rocket and roasted peppers and tahini chicken salad etc. It started out as a junk yard where locals came to browse and chat and eventually a coffee shop emerged. It now manages each role

admirably, and without compromise to the other. Customers range from singletted builders to mobile phone yuppies. VERY casual. A must for a real Balmain experience. Open daily 8am-4pm.

WOCKPOOL $$$ **E**

Modern Asian

155 Victoria Street, Potts Point

Tel: 9368 1771   Licensed•Credit Cards

Until recently called Rocket, Wockpool is an awkward pun of a name relating the Rockpool (its sister restaurant) to the new Asian influence on its formerly Mediterranean menu. No matter - vigour and directness reign in its Thai and Chinese influenced dishes and the popular Oyster Bar lives on here. When you book, ask to be seated to the front of the restaurant for a spectcular view of the city skyline. Lunch Mon-Fri; dinner Mon-Sat 6.30pm-11pm.

EAT YOUR WAY AROUND
ETHNIC SYDNEY (See map over page)

AUBURN At Auburn railway station you'll look up to see the twin spires of the Turkish mosque as this is the heart of Sydney's Turkish community. Only a little of Turkey's rich culinary tradition represented yet, but a good start.

BONDI Not really an ethnic description, but such an important influence it is worth a mention. In fact, the whole of Hall Street is worth a visit. Stark's Kosher deli is our favourite for its old-worldliness – not to mention the variety of the delicious goodies.

CABRAMATTA
"Vietnamatta" is the stereotype, rather than the real picture as the Vietnamese have some excellent shops and restaurants here. Cambodians and Chinese are the major property owners.

CAMPSIE One of the most popular tourist stops for Korean visitors is, would you believe, Campsie. One of the main reasons is that the price of beef in Australia is so much cheaper than back home. Good restaurants and shops.

DOUBLE BAY It will be a sad day when the elegant, elderly middle-European women who came as immigrants during World War II are no longer with us. They considerably enhance the strong European stylishness of Double Bay village.

FAIRFIELD Chilean, Uruguayans and Agentinians are the major South American nationalities living in Sydney. Fairfield is where you will find both restaurants and food stores. At La Paula is a wonderful bakery and you'll get fine coffee too. Laotian food is best found here or Cabramatta. Very healthy style – rather like Thai.

HAYMARKET Before Australians became more sophisticated in their food tastes, the traditional Aussie family meal out was Chinese. There are still few towns in Australia without a Chinese restaurant. Haymarket is, of course, where you get the best.

LEICHHARDT Since Italian immigration began in earnest in the 1950s, Leichhardt has been thought of as Italian. Norton Street has many excellent cafes. Norton Street Market is tops and the wonderful AC Butchery has free-range poultry, game and loads of character.

MARRICKVILLE The Greeks settled here well before the Vietnamese and they are still the major presence with delicatessens, restaurants, tavernas. The Corinthian for Greek family atmosphere; the Bac Lieu for the authentic feel of Vietnam.

NORTHBRIDGE
When the Japanese began to settle in the Northbridge area, a general food store to meet their needs soon arrived. Tokyo Mart is tops – with every kind of Japanese delicacy for the homesick and the culinary curious.

PENDLE HILL From the unassuming corner store, Sam's Maltese Foods, you'll get everything from Kinnie (like the Italian chinotto) to a range of Maltese biscuits. Pendle Ham and Bacon Curers breed their own pigs – fresh as fresh can be.

PETERSHAM Portuguese charcoal chicken shops are now ubiquitous throughout Sydney. Little Portugal is at the intersection of New Canterbury Road and Stanmore Road. Restaurants and mouth-watering cake-shops and, if you're lucky, strains of fados as you pass by.

RANDWICK The large numbers of Indonesian students at the University of New South Wales has encouraged the emergence of a number of inexpensive and good restaurants offering Javanese to Pedang – (southwest Sumatran) food.

WILLOUGHBY/CHATSWOOD Intense preparation is the hallmark of Iranian food. What makes those meats and sweet stews so succulent? By marinating raw meat in onion juice. Many Iranians in Sydney are of Armenian origin, so food generally has an Iranian-Armenian heritage.

🦅 🦅 GOURMET SPECIALS

JAPANESE – Unkai Dining Room and Sushi Bar: Considered by locals to have the freshest and widest varieties of sushi and sashimi in town, you can also try other authentic Japanese foods not often found outside the country. ANA Hotel, Cumberland Street, The Rocks, Tel 9250 6123.

THAI – Darley Street Thai A serene and embracing atmosphere comes from magic created by simple and confidently coloured decor. Seafood delicacies; combinations of herbs; special spices et al. 28-30 Bayswater Road, Kings Cross, Tel 9358 6530.

CHINESE – The Golden Century, (Cantonese seafood) 393-399 Sussex Street Sydney Tel 9212 3901

ITALIAN – Buon Ricordo, 108 Boundary Street, Paddington Tel 9360 6729

INDIAN – Indian Empire 5 Walker Street, North Sydney Tel 9923 2909

EAT YOUR WAY ROUND
ETHNIC SYDNEY

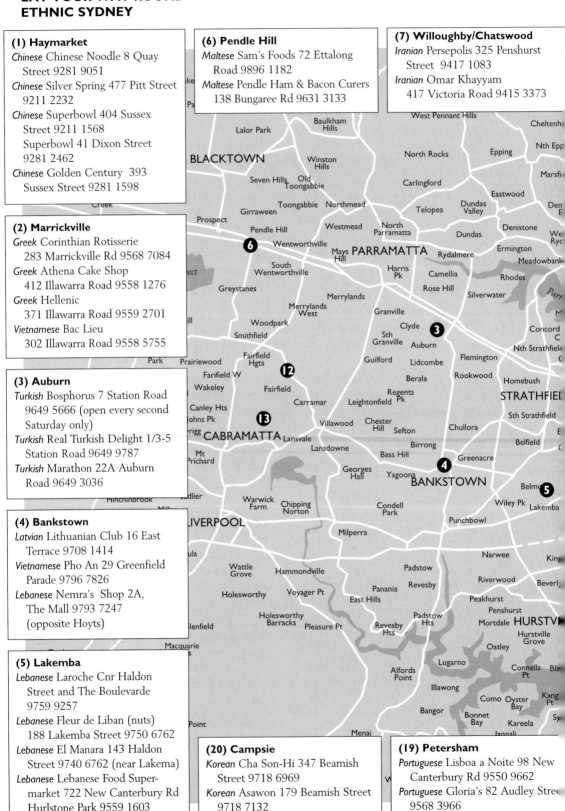

(1) Haymarket
Chinese Chinese Noodle 8 Quay Street 9281 9051
Chinese Silver Spring 477 Pitt Street 9211 2232
Chinese Superbowl 404 Sussex Street 9211 1568
Superbowl 41 Dixon Street 9281 2462
Chinese Golden Century 393 Sussex Street 9281 1598

(2) Marrickville
Greek Corinthian Rotisserie 283 Marrickville Rd 9568 7084
Greek Athena Cake Shop 412 Illawarra Road 9558 1276
Greek Hellenic 371 Illawarra Road 9559 2701
Vietnamese Bac Lieu 302 Illawarra Road 9558 5755

(3) Auburn
Turkish Bosphorus 7 Station Road 9649 5666 (open every second Saturday only)
Turkish Real Turkish Delight 1/3-5 Station Road 9649 9787
Turkish Marathon 22A Auburn Road 9649 3036

(4) Bankstown
Latvian Lithuanian Club 16 East Terrace 9708 1414
Vietnamese Pho An 29 Greenfield Parade 9796 7826
Lebanese Nemra's Shop 2A, The Mall 9793 7247 (opposite Hoyts)

(5) Lakemba
Lebanese Laroche Cnr Haldon Street and The Boulevarde 9759 9257
Lebanese Fleur de Liban (nuts) 188 Lakemba Street 9750 6762
Lebanese El Manara 143 Haldon Street 9740 6762 (near Lakema)
Lebanese Lebanese Food Supermarket 722 New Canterbury Rd Hurlstone Park 9559 1603

(6) Pendle Hill
Maltese Sam's Foods 72 Ettalong Road 9896 1182
Maltese Pendle Ham & Bacon Curers 138 Bungaree Rd 9631 3133

(7) Willoughby/Chatswood
Iranian Persepolis 325 Penshurst Street 9417 1083
Iranian Omar Khayyam 417 Victoria Road 9415 3373

(20) Campsie
Korean Cha Son-Hi 347 Beamish Street 9718 6969
Korean Asawon 179 Beamish Street 9718 7132

(19) Petersham
Portuguese Lisboa a Noite 98 New Canterbury Rd 9550 9662
Portuguese Gloria's 82 Audley Stree 9568 3966

(8) Randwick

Malaysian Taste of Malaysia
142 Avoca Street 9399 3309

Randwick Oriental (groceries)
61-63 Belmore Road 9398 2192

(9) Double Bay

Hungarian Twenty-One 21 Knox
Street 9327 2616

Dee Bees 27 Knox Street
9327 6695

(10) Northbridge

Japanese Tokyo Mart Shop
27 Northbridge Plaza, Sailors Bay
Rd 9958 6860

(11) Leichhardt

Italian Frattini 122 Marion Street
9569 2997

Italian Norton Street Market 55
Norton Street 9568 2158

Italian AC Butchery (gourmet
poultry) 174 Marion Street
9569 8686

Italian Bar Italia (gelati) 169 Norton
Street 9560 9981

(12) Fairfield

Laotian Song Fang Khong 7 Anzac
Avenue 9728 4552

South American Martinez Bros
33 Spencer Street 9724 5509

South American La Paula 9 Barbara
Street 9726 2379

(13) Cabramatta

Cambodian Camira 50 Park Road
9728 1052

Vietnamese Pho 54 254 Park Road
9726 1992

Vietnamese Tahnh Binh 56 John
Street 9727 9729

(14) Newtown

African Kilimanjaro 280 King Street
9557 4565

(15) Dulwich Hill

Lebanese Dulwich Hill Roaster
407 New Canterbury Road
9569 6674

Lebanese Abla's Pastry 425 New
Canterbury Road 9560 5088

(16) Kingsford

Indonesian Sarinah 325 Anzac
Parade 9663 1761

Indonesian Favourite 481 Anzac
Parade 9349 5438

Indonesian Ratu Sari 476 Anzac
Parade 9663 4072

(18) Rockdale

Macedonian Macedonian Hot Bread
34 Walz Street 9567 6659

Macedonian Makedonska Prodavnica
Kings Court, King St 9567 1627

(17) Bondi

Jewish Savion 1/38 Wairoa Avenue
9130 6357

Jewish Stark's Kosher Deli 95 Hall
Street 9130 3872

© The UnTourist Co 1995

149

CAFES/COFFEE HOUSES

Bar Baba Haven of Leichhardt's coffee aficionados, 31 Norton Street, Leichhardt.

Bar Coluzzi One of the most famous cafes in Sydney. Open every day from 5.30am, 322 Victoria Street.

Bar Italia Has great coffee and snacks and makes the best gelati in town, 169 Norton Street, Leichhardt.

Bookoccino Bookshop provides great coffee and cakes with the latest New York and LA Times, 37a Old Barrenjoey Road, Avalon.

Box The skinniest coffee bar ever. Home to the ultra-chic coffee crowd. Open from 7.30am, 28A Bayswater Road, Kings Cross.

Cafe Badde Manors Quirky and fey, great coffee and cakes, 37 Glebe Point Road, Glebe.

Cafe Gioia Younger Italians meet here to drink coffee and cruise. Open every day, 126A Norton Street, Leichhardt.

Cafes You'll find them in most museums, the Art Gallery, the State Library and they are invariably excellent.

Carmel's By The Sea Carmel serves good basic tucker – fabulous setting, Boathouse, Governor Phillip Park, Palm Beach.

Centennial Park Cafe Corner Grand and Parkes Drive, Centennial Park.

Chelsea Coffee House The local lorikeets fly freely around the tables, 48 Old Barrenjoey Road, Avalon.

Chester's Cafe At the Tin Shed junkyard – top Balmain haunt, 148 Beattie Street.

Church Point Top Room Above the general store at Church Point wharf – overlooks Pittwater, McCarrs Creek Road.

Courtyard Since Double Bay discovered pavement extensions to cafes, the place has never been better. This is only one of several, 37 Bay Street.

Daily Grind Great little coffee house adored by the locals, 29 Belgrave Street, Manly.

Deans Cafe Read a book, play chess and enjoy gourmet goodies well into the wee hours of the morning. From around 5pm-5am, 5 Kellet Street, Kings Cross.

Deckside At The Quays marina Great setting, menu for lunch and dinner too, 1086 Pittwater Road, Church Point.

Bathers Pavilion

Hawthorn Cottage Cafe, 707 Military Road, Mosman

Ibiza Popular with the young locals – huge log fire in winter, 47 Old Barrenjoey Road, Avalon.

Il Gianfornaio The best cappuccino on the northside, 414 Victoria Avenue, Chatswood.

La Renaissance Café-Patisserie Café-au-lait, hot chocolate, croissants and brioche. Open every day, 47 Argyle Street, The Rocks.

Le Crêpe Café A mecca for ad types, models, celebs and the self-appointed living legends of Bondi. From 7am, 2 Lamrock Avenue, Bondi.

Le Petit Crème Coffee is great, as is the breakfast-time atmosphere. Mon-Fri, 7am-4pm, Sat-Sun 8am-6pm, 118 Darlinghurst Road, Darlinghurst.

New Editions Bookshop and tea rooms. Papers and magazines to read too, 328 Oxford Street, Paddington.

Picnic Cafe Tucked in the corner of the village, a favourite with the locals, 3 Military Road, Watson's Bay.

Roma A tradition with Sydney coffee and pastry enthusiasts for years, Parker Street, Cnr Hay, Haymarket.

Rugantino's Formerly the local funeral parlour, 13 Norton Street, Leichhardt.

Sydney Dance Cafe Newest and best hip harbourside place in town. Great coffee, meals to the beat of rehearsals. Easy parking, 7.30am - 8.30pm daily (weekends - call to check, 9241 5021). Pier 4 Hickson Rd The Rocks.

Sloane Rangers Cafe Great snacks, lovely courtyard, 312 Oxford Street, Paddington.

Town Hall Cafe Wood-lined, old-fashioned, clubby, nice. Go in the main entrance, up the stairs and turn left.

Twenty-One A visit to this cafe puts you in

touch with the fine middle-European cafe tradition of Double Bay, 21 Knox Street.

BREAKFAST

Ancora Cafe Weekends from 9.30am, 1112 Barrenjoey Road, Palm Beach.

Babylon Sisters Sat-Sun 8am, 266 Darling Street, Balmain.

Bathers Pavilion Weekends and public holidays from 9am, 4 The Esplanade, Balmoral.

Biboteca Sat-Sun from 8am, 252 Campbell Parade, North Bondi.

bills Mon-Sat from 7.30am, 433 Liverpool Street, Darlinghurst.

Brazil Daily 8am, 46 North Steyne, Manly.

Cafe Crown Daily 7am, 355 Crown Street, Surry Hills.

Caffe Agostini Daily 8am, 118 Queen Street, Woollahra.

Coonanbarra Cafe Sun 9.30am, 64 Coonabarra Road, Wahroonga.

Deans Cafe Daily 5am, 5 Kellet Street, Kings Cross.

Ditto Sat-Sun 8.30am, 296 Victoria Road, Darlinghurst.

Fez Cafe Mon-Sat 7am; Sun 8am, 247 Victoria Street, Darlinghurst.

Jonah's Sat-Sun 8am, 69 Bynya Road, Palm Beach.

L'otel Daily 7am, 114 Darlinghurst Road, Darlinghurst.

La Passion Du Fruit Mon-Sat 8am, 633 Bourke Street, Surry Hills.

Lavender Blue Cafe Sat-Sun 8am, 165 Blues Point Road, McMahon's Point.

Le Kiosk Sun 9am, Shelly Beach, Manly.

Mesclun Daily 6.30am, 33 Bayswater Road, Kings Cross.

Ravesi's Daily 7.30am, Cnr Campbell Parade and Hall Street, Bondi.

Ritz-Carlton Noted for its Sunday brunches, 33 Cross Street Double Bay.

Sydney Fish Markets Breakfast Tour Information Tel 9660 1611.

Thomas Street Tues-Sun 8am, 2 Thomas Street, McMahons Point.

Village Green Cafe, 3 Mandalong Road, Mosman

Watermark 8am, 2a The Esplanade, Balmoral Beach.

BEST FISH AND CHIPS

From *Doyle's Fish Cookbook* by Alice Doyle (Angus & Robertson).

After all my years of battering fish, Tim, our youngest son, has just told me: "Mum, I think I have worked out the best batter of all." "What is it, Tim?"

Tim's Batter (It takes time to make the perfect batter, but you know the old saying: "If it's worth doing, it's worth doing well.")

340 ml (small can) light beer
2 egg yolks
1 soupspoon olive oil
pinch salt and pepper
1275g (2 cups) best-quality plain flour

Mix all ingredients together, adding flour last. Using a hand-held beater or whisk, beat until smooth. (If you like a fluffier batter, the beaten egg whites can be folded in last thing.)

Coat fish lightly in plain flour, and dip into batter. Fish pieces should not be too large, and don't overload your deep-frying with cooking oil.

Fry fish at not less than 185° to 190°C (about 375°F) for five to ten minues according to thickness of fish.

("Yes, delicious, madam. You may now go to the top of the class and ring for a top chef's job.")

Lakeside Fish Markets

Consumer friendly – they'll cook anything in the shop from the window – eg whole bream or filleted. Fish not pre-cooked. All cooked fresh. Made to order for budget, taste. Platters for picnics. Outstanding Food Supplier Award. Finalist in the "overall Consumer Choice Award". Open 7 days 9am-5pm. Ask for Phil and Ralph, 1489 Pittwater Road, Narrabeen, Tel 9913 8318

Seafood at the Beach

Fish market and cooked fish and seafood. Select your fish. Fresh high quality. Low cholesterol cooking oils for health conscious. Salads available. Special steaming oven for steamed fish and seafood. Choices – steamed, fried or barbecued. Huge variety – eg Cajun blue eyed cutlets or perch with avocado and chilli salsa. Situated opposite park and beach. Cook to order anything, anyway, ring your order. Prepare picnics ahead of time for large parties. Ask for John. Open 7 days, 10am-8pm. 12A the Strand, Dee Why Beach, Tel 9971 9666

Bondi Surf Seafood

128 Campbell Parade, Bondi 9130 4554

Cronulla Fish & Chips

Cnr Laycock and Cronulla Streets.

Doyles

At the Fish Markets and Watsons Bay

Kirribilli Seafoods

By Appointment to Kirribilli and Admiralty Houses – so to speak. Prime Ministers and Governors General and have been known to slip out for the odd serving of fish and chips. 12 Fitzroy Street, Kirribilli Tel 9929 4680

Ocean Foods Cafe

40 The Corso, Manly, Tel 9977 8347. Seating available, fresh salads. Choose your fish fresh for frying.

Seaforth Sea Foods

557 Sydney Road, Seaforth, Tel 9948 7876

Brett's Seafood

536 Sydney Road, Seaforth, Tel 9907 0766

OUR CRITICS' CREDENTIALS

Julie Moy – beautiful person, proud mother and horse owner; **Pauline Sheldrake** – environmentalist, Associate Diploma Park Management, Certificate of Horticulture, permaculture consultancy and both fish and chipaholics.

WINES

Bill Ireland of Oddbins Pty Ltd is acknowledged as a man who knows his wine and has an excellent palate. We asked him to prepare this piece for us.

The visitor to Australia is presented with a huge choice of local wines. Grapes are grown in every state and the climates of our wine regions are the most varied in the world. On the one hand we have warm climates similar to the central valleys of California, and just a few hundred kilometres away, grapes are grown in a region which is as cool as Champagne. Our wine regions have in common their clean,

unpolluted environments and the high levels of skill and training of Aust-ralian wine-makers. Our wine industry is the most tehnologically advanced in the world, producing well-made, appealing wines over a wide range of styles. Local wines are renowned for their generous, clean fruit flavours.

The state of New South Wales has several grape-growing regions:

The Riverina – 700km southwest of Sydney is a warm, dry region, famous for producing large volumes of inexpensive wines. In fact, 20% of Australia's wine comes from the Riverina. Its dry whites offer marvellous value for money, and its Botrytis dessert wines are world-renowned.

The Hunter – two hours' drive north of Sydney, is one of the country's oldest and most charming wine producing regions. Because of its proximity to Sydney, it is a favourite attraction and it caters well for the visitor who may consider a one or two day visit to the Hunter wineries.

Mudgee – a further two hours' drive from the Hunter. A visit can easily be fitted in with a trip to the Hunter, returning via the Blue Mountains.

Because of its high altitude, Mudgee's climate is cooler than the Hunter, and the wines in general are more delicate.

Cowra – 300km west of Sydney, is a promising new area where good quality whites, especially Chardonnay, are being produced with good commercial yields. Nearby Young is a renowned fruit growing area. The cool climate is producing some excellent whites and reds.

Mount Pleasant Elizabeth

Semillon grapes grown in the lower Hunter. Bottle aged and released to market when ready to drink. A most reliable dry white in the Graves style.

Tulloch Hector of Glen Elgin

Shiraz from the Hunter Valley in a rich, full-flavoured Rhone-style.

Lindemans Hunter River Semillon

The Hunter is famous for its Semillon. This crisp, dry white is delicious with some of Australia's famous seafood.

Rosemount Estate Chardonnay

A famous wine from the Upper Hunter. Midway between Chablis and White Burgundy in style. Smooth fruit and discrete oak.

Richmond Grove Cowra Verdelho

A full-on dry white, made from the grape of Madeira. The flav-our is best described as fruit salad. A distinctive, well-made wine.

Rothbury Cowra Chardonnay

Crisp and dry, show casing the Chard-onnay grape, with light application of oak. A really fine accompaniment to our marvellous seafood.

McWilliams Barwang Shiraz

A fine, full-bodied Shiraz (Hermitage) with enormous depth of fruit. This is the style of red which makes Aust-ralian wines so appealing. Just the wine to wash down a big juicy steak.

Rosetto Semillon

Clean, crisp dry white from Griffith in the Riverina region. True to the fruit and trem-endous value.

Wilton Estate Chardonnay

Riverina Chardonnay with the full wood treatment. A wine with complexity at a bar-gain price.

De Bortoli Noble One

Botrytis Semillon from the Riverina. This is a dessert wine which holds its own with the great 'stickies' of the world. Abundant sweet fruit, huge botrytis, every sip a mouthful of smooth, rich flavour.

Premium Lager

Sydney's only boutique brewery makes a gem of a beer. American Dr Chuck Hahn has worked for Coors, and for New Zealand's Steinlager prior to setting up his own operation. The beer is a gem – a full flavoured highly hopped lager with a very clean finish.

Oddbins Pty Ltd, 140 Parramatta Road, Camperdown.

WATERING HOLES

Tilbury Hotel One of the best entertainment venues in town. The style could be described broadly as cabaret but regardless of your musical tastes or standards, the Tilbury will deliver a great evening, corner of Nicholson and Forbes Street, Tel 9358 1295.

Watsons Bay Hotel with its excellent fish and salad bar is a great way to enjoy the village of Watsons Bay around the waterfront and the pier, Tel 9337 4299.

Albury Hotel Post Mardi Gras the festivities live strong at the Albury. Enjoy a free show witnessing a 6-foot diamante-laden man impersonating Marilyn Monroe. Live shows every night make the Albury a great meeting point. All shows are free, open till very, very late! Oxford Street, Paddington, Tel 9361 6555.

Beach Road Hotel, the Pavilion Pool Hall. This is the only place to shoot pool and drink your favourite drop if you want to keep your cool credibility while in Bondi. A game here will set you back a few dollars. Open from 10am till about 1am, every day, Beach Road, Bondi, Tel 9130 7247.

Green Park Hotel Any night of the week you'll find the locals heading for their watering hole, the Green Park Hotel. It's a great place to meet friendly folk and play a fast game of pool, 360 Victoria Street Darlinghurst, Tel 9380 5311.

Kings Cross Hotel, positioned at the top of the Cross, has a spectacular view of Sydney from the roof. Known only to a few, it's a great place to meet and drink with fellow travellers from all over the world. This bar's bonus is that it is open 24 hours, 7 days. 248 Victoria Street, Kings Cross, Tel 9358 3377.

l'Otel is the preferred place to eat, drink and get merry with the Darlinghurst crowd. L'otel (bar, restaurant and hotel) sure does pack them in. It's where any famous model/mega star worth their salt will stay. Serving 7am-12pm every day of the week, 114 Darlinghurst Road. Darl-inghurst, Tel 9360 6868.

Bondi Icebergs A Bondi landmark since 1929, a visit will confirm why the Bondi Icebergs still packs them in. Enjoy a cool one by the bar overlooking the Pacific blue, Notts Avenue, Bondi Beach, Tel 9130 3120.

Sugar Reef is as sweet as it sounds and home to a very cool collection of party-goers. Sugar Reef's added advantage is its huge choice of cocktails shaken under their Caribbean inspired 'hut'. Don't get eager, nothing hots up here till after midnight. Ends very, very late, 20 Kellet Street, Kings Cross, Tel 9357 7250.

Fortune of War Hotel For pub drinkers and eaters who like a flutter, there is a backroom full of TV screens, and the odds are telephoned in from the TAB. Upstairs for real Australian pub food (damper on weekends), 137 George Street. Tel 9247 2714.

Renaissance Hotel You can see a flotilla of blue-suited business executives from the Sydney Stock Exchange and office workers exercise that inalienable Sydneysiders' right – to stand outside and drink draught beer.

Hero of Waterloo Built in 1845, still with its detention centres down below, 81 Lower Fort Street, Tel 9252 4553.

Lord Nelson The oldest pub in Sydney and brews its own beer, has a bistro, 19 Kent Street, Millers Point, Tel 9251 4044.

Palisade Hotel Popular as a location for films and television drama series, recently refurbished, set in a key position in one of the best preserved parts of The Rocks, 35 Bettington Street, Tel 9247 2272.

Paragon Hotel 100 years old and done up in Art Nouveau style, is dedicated to the provision of ice-cold drinks and all the latest in gambling for the discerning punter. A great place for a relaxing afternoon if you've plenty of serious change in your pocket, 1 Loftus Street (just off the Circular Quay area), Tel 9241 3522.

CBD Hotel On the lower floor is a bar which, on Friday evenings, spills out onto the pavement with the young and upwardly mobile in mating mode, corner King and York Streets, Tel 9299 8292.

Newtown Hotel One of the major factors behind the revit-alisation of Newtown is the growing presence of the gay and lesbian community. If you feel like a spot of drag call into the Newtown hotel for a sparkling night of sequins and song. Tues Wed Thurs Drag Show 10.15pm, Sunday 8.30pm, 174 King Street, Tel 9557 1329.

Imperial Hotel This is the pub where memorable scenes from drag flick, *Priscilla, Queen of the Desert*, was filmed. Call in and sing-along with the Abba Show and reminisce about your favourite parts in the movie. Abba Show Thurs Sun 11.30pm and 12.30am, 33 Erskineville Road, Erskineville (runs off King Street), Tel 9519 9899.

The **Leichhardt Hotel** cleverly combines a florist shop, art gallery and working space for painters, print-makers, photographers and sculptors. Predominantly a lesbian hotel, it's closed on the eve of the Gay Mardi Gras, but you can witness the fabulous leather-clad Dykes on Bikes roar off for their night of nights, corner Balmain Road and Short Street, Tel 9569 1217.

Harold Park Hotel became famous as a venue for Australian writers to give readings from their works. The hotel still has strong literary associations, but no more sessions open to the public. However, these days you can participate in *Politics in the Park* each Friday night. A political issue of the day is discussed, often with well known politicians leading the debate, 115 Wigram Road, Tel 9692 0564.

Dry Dock Hotel (nee Dock Inn), built in 1867, is the oldest continuously operating hotel in the area. Its success was no doubt due to the fact that it was the watering hole for Mort's Dock, which was where the main ship-building action was in the mid-1800s. In recent years, it was the first to have entertainment, then the first to open a beer garden. Today it has one of the best pub restaurants in the area, corner of Cameron and College Streets, Tel 9555 1306.

Sir William Wallace Named for a 13th century patriot and built in 1879, this is prob-

ably the only hotel in Balmain still in its original state, 11 Cameron Street, Tel 9555 8570.

The Cat and the Fiddle More histrionic than historic – a great entertainment venue. Like the Tilbury in Woolloomooloo, it concentrates on the unusual and the unusually talented. *Opera in the Pub*, with stars of the Australian Opera belting out Verdi and Puccini at the bar is a memorable program. Call for details, 456 Darling Street, Tel 9810 7931.

London Hotel (1870) (nee Golden Eagle/Circular Saw) does a great trade on Saturdays as it is across the road from the popular Balmain markets . The London, among other distinctions, has the benefit of being the "local" for the UnTourist Co, 234 Darling Street, Tel 9555 1377.

Riverview Hotel (built 1880), has fallen foul of renovation and looks a bit ersatz. It is still referred to as "Dawn Fraser's pub", even though Dawn sold it many years ago. Any time, any day, you'll find the journalists, the shipwrights and the old Tiger supporters holding up the bar at the Riverview. Good food and regular trad jazz, 29 Birchgrove Road, Tel 9810 1151.

Newport Arms Hotel is *the* pub for people who live on the Peninsula. Has a pleasant beer garden, overlooking Pittwater and has regular, plentiful smorgasbord fare, Kalynia Street, Newport, Tel 9997 4900.

Don't just hang around
– do something.

10 THINGS TO DO

INCLUDES: *The sort of things that make the savvy locals glad they live in Sydney – ranging from a quick and cheap few hours to fill in when the weather's "crook", as they say in the vernacular, to a couple of days of sheer heaven and hang the expense. We've restricted this chapter to collections of things, or special experiences rather than one-offs like "go see the Opera House". You'll find plenty of these in the area and specialty chapters.*

Rain, Hail or Shine

In any weather, for any age, any interest, any purse (empty or full), Sydney has plenty of things to do. Here are a few more ideas.

WHEN THE WEATHER'S CROOK

In this context, "crook" means wet and thundery weather. On the other hand "scorchers", meaning extremely hot weather, are not considered crook because the sun is shining. That kind of Sydney weather simply provides a good excuse to cool off in the sea or by the water somewhere.

"Pissing down with rain, but still afloat – snug in my Drizabone coat." (From the beaut Gowings catalogue)

• **Take a ride on a Manly Ferry** When the sea is really rolling and the sky is rumbling , we suggest you grasp the opportunity to take a ride to Manly on one of the older ferries. There are more thrills a minute in crossing the Heads in these conditions than a ride on the Big Dipper at Luna Park. This was former Prime Minister Paul Keating's favourite "things to do" when he was a boy.

If you find the trip all too much and you don't fancy a return voyage, you could have a comforting fish lunch at Armstrongs on Manly Wharf and take a bus back via the Spit Bridge and Mosman, always worthwhile in any weather.

Alternatively, you could simply roll up in bed with a good book (see suggestions, Chapter 8).

• **Visit the Powerhouse Museum** Visiting any museum, the Art Gallery or the State Library is a great thing to do on a wet day, but the Powerhouse offers, in our view, the greatest range of things to do to occupy several hours. You can design your own historic gown or tea pot on touch-screen computers; try shearing a sheep; test your body's electricity or brew your own beer on computer. Visitors also get to explore the world of cinema in the 1930s, or see what changes in style Australia has experienced over 300 years. Exhibitions are many and varied.

Maybe you should have stayed home with a good book. From the deck of the South Steyne *circa 1940, now on view in Darling Harbour*

Powerhouse. Call for more information.

WALKS/RUNS

Whether it is so you can get to know an area more intimately, or whether it's because you want to take in fresh air and the scenery, walking is a great way to see Sydney and there are walks to suit everybody – in the city, in the suburbs and in the surrounding national parks which form part of the 20% of the Sydney region which is still

• **Go to the movies** The main cinema centre is in George Street, just down from the Town Hall. Sydney also has many art-house cinemas – the Dendy in Martin Place and George Street; the Valhalla in Glebe; the Mandarin in Elizabeth Street; Walker Street Cinema in North Sydney; Academy Twin, Paddington. (See the daily newspapers for films and screening times.) There are specialty film showings at the Metcalf Auditorium at the State Library of NSW on Fridays and Sundays and also regularly at the undeveloped. *Throughout the book we have described a number of walks – eg in Chapter 1 there is a map with detail about Wharf Parks and Harbour Beaches; in Chapter 6 we suggest a walk down King Street Newtown to introduce you to an exotic variety of shops and in Chapter 4 we tell you who to call on for historical Balmain walks. And here are a few more, all favourites of Sydney insiders.*

• **Bondi to Bronte** *Insider Hamish Campbell thinks this walk gives a great feeling for the Sydney beach lifestyle.*

Best to start at North Bondi and walk the length of Bondi Beach along the promenade, past the Pavilion until you get to the southern end of the beach and Notts Avenue, with Bondi Baths on your left. Continue up Notts Avenue and you will emerge onto a track taking you along the cliff edge which takes you to Tamarama Beach. If you are walking on a hot day, the wafting scent of coconut oil will probably reach you before the sight of gorgeous (mostly male) bodies tanning on the beach.

After crossing Tamarama Beach (or Glamourama as it is also known locally) continue walking by the waterfront until you get to Bronte Beach. Across Bronte Park is the famous **Bronte House,** though it is only open to the public for six days a year. Described as 'stylistically confused', Bronte House was built in 1845 and is of Gothic-Italianate design with turrets reminiscent of a medieval French chateau. For information about open days, call Waverley Council, Tel 9369 8000.

• **Circular Quay/The Rocks** *Anne Deveson, author, journalist, lives near the water in Balmain and this is the place where she likes to take visitors to Sydney.*

"I have one of those houses with real estate 'harbour glimpses' – which means you have to hang out of the bathroom window, standing on the lavatory seat, or sit on my front doorstep to see anything resembling water. But the harbour is only a hundred yards away, and on a sunny Sunday morning my treat is to read the newspapers on my front doorstep with the

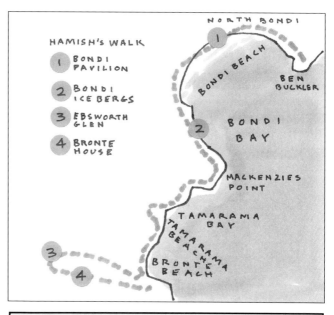

HAMISH'S WALK

1 BONDI PAVILION

2 BONDI ICEBERGS

3 EBSWORTH GLEN

4 BRONTE HOUSE

NORTH BONDI — BONDI BEACH — BEN BUCKLER — BONDI BAY — MACKENZIES POINT — TAMARAMA BAY — TAMARAMA BEACH — BRONTE BEACH

whole expanse of the harbour stretched out before me, ferries, yachts and tug boats, canoes and cargo boats and sometimes even the odd liner nosing its way under the Harbour Bridge. If you don't have a harbour doorstep, then nearly every ferry stop has its own small harbour park, with some of the best views in the world. Free.

"Then I like to catch the ferry to **(1) Circular Quay,** preferably in the company of visitors, so that I can show them the delights of the Sunday morning buskers, all ages and talents, playing Mozart or Country and Western, didgeridoos and harmonicas. There are the fire-eaters and the jugglers, magicians and stilt-walkers, while people fish or stroll, or sit in the open air cafes, drinking coffee or aperitifs. Sometimes I walk along the eastern side of Sydney Cove – over the **(2)** brass plaques dedicated to famous Australian writers – as far as the Opera House at the very tip of Bennelong Point, once known as **(3) Cattle Point.** Other times I take the other side of Sydney Cove and head towards the Rocks, via the

159

(4) Museum of Contemporary Art which is always interesting (and also has excellent coffee).

"The Rocks is now frankly touristy but if you're lucky there may be an excellent outdoor concert (last time I heard French and English madrigals). In the Rocks my goal is the 1848 **(5) Garrison Church,** the soldiers' church where the redcoats marched up for communion every Sunday morning. I delight in the beautiful Georgian houses of Lower Fort Street, and finish up in the **(6) Palisade Hotel** (Bettington

By the Quay *by Sydney foreshores painter David McBride*

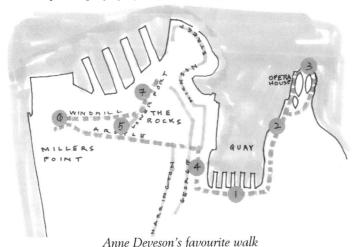

Anne Deveson's favourite walk

Street) which must have one of the best views in Sydney, or else the **(7) Hero of Waterloo** (81 Lower Fort Street), built in 1845, still with its detention centres down below. Last time I visited, when I was thinking about living in Fort Street, locals offered me Frank, a grizzled old man: 'He'll watch over you love' – and – 'a real nice rest home, right on the spot when your days are done'. Allow two to three hours for this

excursion – longer if you take up the rest home offer."

• **Inner City** *Jessica Anderson, author, often does this walk when she is at work in the State Library.*

"I devised this walk as a break from research in the **State Library** in Macquarie Street, and always intend it to be Green, Triangular, and Thirty Minutes Long.

"You leave the Library from the columned porch of the old wing, and make the first side of the triangle by walking across the grassy **Domain** towards the similar porch of the **Art Gallery**.

"Opposite the Gallery, you turn harbour-wards and begin on the base of the triangle by crossing the overpass of the Cahill Expressway. This admittedly broaches the concept of Green, but quickly opens it again by bringing you to the Woolloomooloo Gates of the **Botanical Gardens**.

"And it is here, just after I go in, and am passing the beautiful dark swamp mahogany trees, that my Triangular intention is most likely to break down. What I should do is broaden the base of the triangle, and then complete it by making for the Morshead Foun-tain Gate opposite the Library, but the Gardens are enticing, and it is easy to wander by herb beds and greenhouses, duck ponds and palm groves.

"But, though the walk is no longer Triangular, it is still predominantly Green, and hasn't taken more than an hour. It is when the interiors of Library and Gallery also entice that the whole concept dissolves. But there are compensations; you could call them Cultural. The Library also has a gallery, and both Library and Art Gallery offer good coffee and light food.

"And there is, perhaps, time for a quick walk through the Gardens, in the dusk, just before they close the gates."

CRONULLA

1

PORT HACKING

2

BUNDEENA

3

SCARBOROUGH STREET

MARLEY BCH 4

5 GARIE BEACH

6 NORTH ERA BEACH

8 GARRAWARRA

7 SOUTH ERA BEACH

• **Bay Run** *Editorial Director, Suzanne Baker, used to do this run regularly.*

The Bay Run is 8km and takes a well-marked route around Iron Cove, touching on the suburbs of Drummoyne, Five Dock, Haberfield, Leichhardt and Lilyfield and the lovely grounds of Rozelle Hospital. A good starting point is at the Drummoyne Baths and Rowing Club, to the left of the western end of the Iron Cove Bridge. There's plenty of parking round here, or in nearby Birkenhead Point Shopping Centre car park. At regular intervals throughout this well-marked run, there are recommend-ations for supplementary exercises so that by the end of the run, all muscles and joints will have had a good workout. And, as a bonus, you'll get a pleasant view of some inner harbour foreshores.

• **Rozelle Hospital Grounds** *Insider Linda Browne says this is one of Sydney's great "secret" walks.*

"Officially on the border of Leichhardt and Rozelle, this is one of Sydney's best kept secrets. The 64 hectares hiding behind high stone fences include landscaped parklands, formal gardens, a miniature rain forest and an oriental garden. The sweeping harbour foreshores and small sandy coves are dotted with Moreton Bay fig and casuarina trees. Take a look at some of the old sandstone buildings, namely the Kirkbride Quadrangle. Built in the late 1800s it is perhaps the largest complex of colonial sandstone buildings in Australia. Wander through at dusk, the eerie towers and quadrangles look spectacular against a Sydney sunset. On the corner of Church and Glover Street, Leichhardt. Enter at the main gates."

• **Royal National Park** *Before he became Premier of NSW, Bob Carr had been a Minister for the Environment. He is a keen walker and each year, in spring or autumn, this is his favourite bush walk.*

"It takes you from **Bundeena** in the north to **Garrawarra** in the south. A short distance from Cronulla railway station there is a ferry wharf [the Cronulla Marina]. Here you catch the regular ferry from Port Hacking to Bundeena, the suburb on the edge of the park. Ask for directions to Scarborough Street. At the end of this street, you'll find the track that takes you into the Royal and across heathland to the coast.

"Descend onto **Marley Beach**, climb to the cliff line at its southern end and continue to Wattamolla, where there is shade and water and you can eat lunch. Then resume walking along the cliff line to **Garie Beach** and to North and South Era beaches before turning westward and steeply upwards towards **Garrawarra** car park. This is a marvellous walk offering opportunities to swim. It gives you sweeping ocean views. You observe wildflowers at the right time of year. In the right season, you might spot a passing whale. It's a tough but manageable 13km walk, tough because you'll know you've done a hard slog by the end of it. And you will have to arrange to be met by a car at Garra-warra." (METRO, *Sydney Morning Herald*, October 1994.)

• **South Head** *Although insider Margaret Pearce lives on the North Side, this walk is her favourite Sydney experience.*

"A visit to South Head is Sydney in its essences – our closeness to the ocean, the drama of our coastline, and some of the surprising intimacies and variety of the harbour most visitors never get to know about. All this can be done by relatively easy walking and, after you've done that, there are some great places to eat and other things to do if you want to explore further.

"To begin this magic adventure, you can drive there by car or bus, or go on a ferry which stops at Watson's Bay (check your ferry schedule on 13 15 00 for times – River Cats have now joined

Historic Vaucluse House

[Map with labels: SOUTH HEAD, numbered locations 1-10, WATSONS BAY, ROSE BAY, VAUCLUSE, OLD SOUTH HEAD ROAD]

popular beach and fine views across the Harbour. At the end of Camp Cove beach, you'll find a wooden staircase which joins a bush path to **(5) Lady Bay Beach** (also called **Lady Jane** by the locals). If you've forgotten your swimming gear, all's well – you can strip down to your birthday suit and enjoy a dip at this specially designated nudists' beach.

"From here, the path continues to **(6) Hornby Lighthouse** set in a wild, starkly beautiful area sloping to the water. On a calm day you can get to the very edge – where Sydney Harbour meets the Tasman Sea. There is rarely anyone here.

"On your return, you can walk the length of Camp Cove to Laing's Point, find Pacific Street, then **(7) Marine Parade** where **Doyles** fish restaurant dominates the scene. Eat here or, for a lot less money, enjoy fish and chips with a beer next door at Doyle's pub, or at the Fisherman's Wharf take-away on Watson's Bay pier.

"In the vicinity are the following places which are worth seeing – **(8) Parsley Bay**, where you can walk across the suspension bridge, and historic **(9) Vaucluse House** where you can picnic in the lovely grounds. A little further around is **(10) Nielsen Park** which has a shark-netted beach and fine kiosk – my recommendations are a lentil burger, great coffee and fresh fruit juice – about $10 all up."

the run). If you are approaching **Watson's Bay** along Old South Head Road, you pass **(1) Macquarie Lighthouse**, the **(2) Signal Station,** and just as you head down the hill toward the Bay is one of Sydney's breathtaking views across to North Head and Manly.

"At the end of the road, you will find a car park and it's easy to find your way to **(3) The Gap** walk – it's a bit of a climb but worth it for the view and the sound of the ocean crashing on the rocks below.

"To get to South Head you walk along Cliff Street, past the original fishermen's cottages, which takes you to **(4) Camp Cove** with its

Cottage Point Inn, Cowan Waters

GREAT DAY TRIPS

🐦 🐦 • **Cottage Point** *This is a great favourite of German UnTourist, Jane von Sponeck Krumnow. There are three ways to get there, but our choice for variety and value is one which includes the ferry ride:*

1 To get to Palm Beach Wharf to catch the ferry, the journey by car from the city centre takes about an hour through Frenchs Forest and past the northern beaches on Barrenjoey Road. On the Pittwater side of Palm Beach, park in the carpark opposite Barrenjoey House, then catch the ferry across Pittwater and up into the heart of Ku-ring-gai Chase. Lunch is at **Cottage Point Inn** restaurant which offers Australian cuisine with an emphasis on seafood. This trip operates year-round, though in the winter it

Jane von Sponeck Krumnow

may not be available on Mondays or on some Saturdays. To make a booking, call Peter or Mark Verrills of Palm Beach Ferries, Tel 9918 2747 or Cottage Point Inn, Tel 9456 1008. A bonus is Mark Verrills' amusing and informative commentary on the local scene.

2 Take a seaplane from Rose Bay and land in front of Cottage Point Inn restaurant. This is a fabulous flight, flying low along the northern beaches then over the Ku-ring-gai Chase to Cottage Point Inn. There is an all-inclusive deal with lunch – for detail and arrangements, call Cottage Point Inn, Tel 9456 1008 or Sydney Harbour Seaplanes 1800 803 558. To turn this into a real indulgence and to give you a greater

experience of the Pittwater area, why not stay overnight at Jonahs at Whale Beach, in a room overlooking the ocean and have another fine meal that night? It's a short taxi ride from the seaplane base at Palm Beach to Jonahs, which Jonahs would be happy to organise for you. Or you might prefer to stay at the great bed-and-breakfast Darwinia and get Gabrielle and Harl to show you around. See details on both places to stay, Chapter 7.

3 You can also travel by car from Sydney (about 45 mins) direct to the Cottage Point Inn. Call the restaurant for directions, Tel 9546 1008.

• **Palm Beach Experience** *Kit Moore is a Pittwater local and has devised this trip to introduce people to the best of her beloved home territory.*

Palm Beach is home to the fairy penguin, goanna, sea eagle, dolphin and whist-ling kite – and a holiday retreat for the rich and famous. Just one hour's drive north of the city and you

Sunsail in Newport offers bareboat and skippered charters.

Francis Firebrace, Aboriginal story-teller

are in one of Australia's most beautiful spots. You can take a guided tour which leaves Sydney at 9am. At 10am there's morning tea at Palm Beach, right on the water's edge looking across Pittwater to the national park.

Next is a guided walk on the heritage track to Barrenjoey Headland and lighthouse and time with an Aboriginal storyteller. Then there is a choice of activities, from a scenic flight to sailboarding, fishing, kayak, snorkelling scuba-diving or golf. A barbecue lunch is followed by a one-hour ferry trip on Pittwater, then back to Sydney. Bookings 9974 1096. Enquiries, Kit Moore 018 602 986.

• **Out of the City** *Rosemary and Tony Rich, who organise home-stays in Sydney and farm-stays out of it, have devised the following day trips out of the city to help visitors to experience some "real" outer Sydney environments.*

♦ "A visit to the beautiful gardens at Mt Wilson off the Bell's Line of Road on the way to the **Blue Mountains,** followed by lunch at the Victoria and Albert at Mt Victoria.

♦ "Head down the Hume Highway to **Berrima** to see a fine example of a truly authentic Australian village of a previous era. Have lunch at either the Surveyor-General Inn, the oldest continuously licensed inn in Australia still trading within its original walls, or the beautiful and elegant White Horse Inn with a history spanning 150 years.

♦ "A cruise up the Hawkesbury River with the **Riverboat Postman.** Have lunch while he delivers the mail and other items to the people living along the river banks. Take a train to Hawkesbury River Station, then catch the ferry which leaves Mon-Fri 9.30am and returns 1.15pm. Enquiries, 9387 6681."

NOTE: City Rail offers a special tour which takes in this trip. It departs weekdays and includes train from Central Station and cruise on the Last Riverboat Postman, duration seven hours.

♦ "Take a picnic to **West Head** in the Ku-ring-gai Chase National Park with its magnificent views over Pittwater and with the Aboriginal rock carvings on The Basin Track within easy reach. At **Akuna Bay** at Coal and Candle Creek there are a variety of water crafts for hire, ranging from rowing boats to cabin cruisers."

If you have a couple of days to spare and want to experience authentic Australian country life out of Sydney, get in touch with Rosemary and Tony, Tel 9387 6681 or Fax 9387 8121.

• **Blue Mountains** The Blue Mountains is 100 kms west of the city and is a popular place for a day trip or a weekend break. Sydneysiders are particularly fond of the mountains in the winter because it is cold enough (sometimes there's snow) to justify large, open log fires. If you have time to stay overnight, try the delightful two-storey **Rose Lindsay Cottage** on part of the original Norman Lindsay Estate at 113 Chapman Parade, Faulconbridge. Just across the road is the **Norman Lindsay Gallery** with its wonderful house, art collection, gardens and bushwalks designed by the famous painter/cartoonist himself. Open six days a week (not Tuesday) from 11am-5pm, Norman Lindsay Crescent, Faulconbridge. You'll have a very enjoyable dinner (Australian Cuisine) at the Conservation Hut, Valley of the Waters Centre, Fletcher Street, Wentworth Falls. They also serve breakfast. Open every day.

BICYCLING

• **Around the Harbour** *Australian culture and heritage conservation guru, Leo Schofield, an enthusiastic cyclist, describes this ride around the harbour as the finest in the world.*

"It's a bit of a push, but for anyone wanting a unique combination of fresh air, some healthy exercise, a crash course in the topography of Sydney and some of the least hackneyed but most spectacular views of this great harbour city, this track is the go.

See Sydney by bicycle and ferry with World Beyond

"Best to schedule it for early Sunday morning when the traffic is light. You start in the city. Any place, so long as you head for The Rocks. Pass under the Argyle Cut and head up Observatory Hill. A set of steps leads to the cycleway of the Sydney Harbour Bridge and as you pedal across you'll enjoy sweeping views westward of the Parramatta River and the heartland of maritime Sydney.

"Once across, it's a quick walk downstairs and a long meandering cycle that takes you around Neutral Bay to Mosman Bay with umpteen charming views en route. Uphill then to Bradleys Head Road, where a dedicated cycleway leads to the Zoo. Veer left for an exhilarating downhill run that leads to Bradleys Head where there's a tap for refilling water bottles, a loo and a lookout from whence you'll get the quintessential heart-stopping view of the Harbour.

"A little further downhill is the wharf where the Zoo ferries put in. One of these will take you back to town (bikes welcome on board), or, if you've any puff left, catch the one to Watson's

Bay or Rose Bay and put in a few more kilometres.

"Either way, it's the finest city ride in the world."

NOTE: Centennial Park and Manly are favourite places for bicycling and are good places for bicycle hire. In Sydney, bicycles are prohibited at both Darling Harbour and Martin Place and it's compulsory for cyclists to wear a helmet at all times.

Centennial Park Cycles Children's bikes, accessories, weekend, weekly and monthly rates are also available. 50 Clovelly Road, Randwick, Tel 9398 5027/8138

Australian Cycle Co 28 Clovelly Road, Randwick, Tel 9399 3475

Woolys Wheels 82 Oxford Street, Paddington, for mountain and hybrid bikes, Tel 9331 2671

InLine Action Shop 2, 93-95 North Steyne, Tel 9976 3831

Manly Cycle Centre Racers and Mountain bikes available. 36 Pittwater Road, Tel 9977 1189

Inner City Cycles 31 Glebe Point Road, Tel 9660 6605

NOTE: You can cycle Sydney in the company of others with **World Beyond** which combines ferries, bicycles and history to show you around the harbour and across it. *The Harbour Shoreline* is a medium ride of 35 kms which departs every Sunday and the *Governor's Trail* is an easy ride of 25 kms which departs on Saturdays – the cycling starts at Watsons Bay and concludes at an historic sandstone pub in The Rocks. All excursions start from Campbell's Cove, Tel 9555 9653.

CHILDREN'S INTERESTS

• **Museums** All Sydney museums have imaginative presentations for children, but the Powerhouse probably has the best because of its emphasis on interactive components. Their KIDS (acronym for Kids' Interactive Discovery Spaces) UNITS are designed for children under eight and they are based on individual themes, eg music, the home, engineering, film and TV.

During school holidays there's always an array of demonstrations and events for children. Call for more information. Powerhouse Museum, 500 Harris Street, Ultimo, Tel 9217 0111.

MORE CHILDREN'S INTERESTS

• **Tried and transported** In the days of transportation up to 1848, around 30,000 male convicts passed through the Hyde Park Barracks. Now the Barracks, partly in association with the Police and Justice Museum, recreates opportunities for you to find out what it is like to be sentenced; to sail aboard a square-rigger; to live on bare rations; to be treated – well – just like a criminal.

It is possible to stay overnight, just like the convicts did, in a hammock at the Barracks. A wonderful experience for young people. Public programs are usually scheduled at the beginning of the year, on special days like Australia Day and on school holidays on a Friday night. Enquiries, Tel 9223 8922.

• **Nutcote** For younger children Nutcote, the home of children's author May Gibbs is a charmer. May Gibbs' classic Snugglepot and Cuddlepie is about two incorrigible little characters who wear eucalypt gumnuts on their heads – and other bushland characters who have thrilled Australian children for generations. Nutcote is the house where May Gibbs lived, worked and found inspiration for her stories. Open Wed-Sun 11am-3pm. For more information, call the Nutcote Trust, Tel 9953 4453.

• **Dinosaurs** Kristin Robson and George Washingmachine wanted to set up a toy store with a difference. For a start, it's not just for kids and, secondly, it's in a cave. Wander into a prehistoric time-warp and you'll find great classics like Twister, and a Barrel Of Mon-keys as well as a model dinosaur. There's not a battery-operated gismo or violent toy in sight. **Dino Store** hosts kids' parties, complete with pith helmets and explorers kits. The mini-archaeologists embark on an expedition through the rear of the shop which has been transformed into a pre-historic jungle. Here they will dig up dinosaur bones and learn lots about these ancient creatures and their environment whilst munching on volcano cake. 453 King Street, Newtown, Tel 9557 4637.

ODDMENTS

• **Dancing Lessons** Sydney's top dance company, the Sydney Dance Company, holds classes for under $20 for most dance styles. Just give them a call and they'll give you the times and options. Pier 4, Hickson Road, Walsh Bay, Tel 9867 9721. Or maybe you'd prefer belly

By Carly from Haberfield Public School

dancing lessons? Once you've stepped into this Aladdin's cave of glittering costumes, vivid beads and sequins you'll be raring to swing your hips and sign up for your first class. Women-only classes are held most evenings. Amera's Palace, 12A Enmore Road, Newtown, Tel 9519 4793.

• **Who am I?** Anyone looking for their Australian antecedents can check it out at the Society of Australian Genealogists.

Non-members of the Society can do research there for a daily research fee of a few dollars and also enjoy the beauty of the building itself. "Richmond Villa" was built by colonial architect Mortimer Lewis in 1849 as a private residence. It was then on a site fronting the Domain behind Parliament House. It has had many occupants: it was headquarters for the parliamentary librarian until 1900 and a book storage depot until 1922. The Country Party occupied it from 1922 to 1975. That year it was dismantled to make room for additions to Parliament House, and re-erected stone by stone on the present site. Open from 10.30am-4pm Tues, Wed, Thur and Sat at 120 Kent Street (Australasian Collection). The Society also has an overseas collection and book shop at Rumsey Hall, 24 Kent Street. For both: Tel 9247 3953.

• **High tea and graciousness** High tea, in the finest English tradition, is served at The Hughenden between 1pm and 4pm on Sundays. If you'd also like to check out one of Sydney's smartest streets, its history and its fine antique shops, we suggest having high tea first at the Hughenden, and then take advice from the helpful and knowledgeable staff about how to seek out all the interesting bits of beautiful, tree-lined Queen Street (see also Antique Alley, Chapter 8). There are also some excellent art galleries and restaurants in the vicinity. The Hughenden itself has been converted from a grand Victorian mansion and stables. Hughenden, 14 Queen Street, Woollahra, Tel 9363 4863.

• **University of Sydney** The University of Sydney is Australia's oldest and it has some fine buildings and collections. There are frequent buses from the City, grounds open to foot visitors, limited car-parking for a fee.

Built on rising ground to the south of the town, Australia's first University, with its main quadrangle in the neo-Gothic style, now hosts over 30,000 students on numerous scattered campuses. Parramatta Road, near Glebe.

Under the Gothic clock-tower you can find the Chancellor's Committee souvenir shop and information centre, right next to a cast-iron pump which was once the University's only water supply. Here, between 10am-3pm on weekdays, volunteers will direct you and give you a free map-guide. To see the main campus, you can make a booking on Tel 9351 4002.

If you prefer to wander unescorted, there are two special points of interest, for archaeology aficionados and biology buffs, and your visits won't cost you more than a small donation.

Sandstone Gargoyles – Sydney University

The Nicholson Museum. This small, well-lit and well-presented display of artefacts brought back by generations of University archaeologists from their digs, is presided over by Rob Thornley, who knows and loves the collection well. Notable items include the Jericho Head, one of only nine skulls ever found on sites around that ancient battleground of Joshua; the coffin case of Egyptian dignitary Pediashiket, and a sculpture thought to be of Horemheb, Tutankhamun's general, later himself a pharaoh. Several fine craters and amphorae, including one by the painter Antimenes, are the pride of an extensive ceramic collection; Roman sculptures, glass and fragments of wall frescoes are all well documented and handsomely displayed. On sale, a volume on the collection for $225, lavishly illustrated and meticulously compiled under the direction of the University's distinguished Chair of Archaeology, Professor Cambitoglou. On the south side of the main quadrangle and open 10am-4pm weekdays.

The Macleay Museum is a delightfully cluttered display of biological materials and presents less than one percent of the large collections of the Macleay family – (Alexander, entomologist (1767-1848); William Sharp, naturalist (1792-1865); William John, ethnographer (1820-1891). The Victorian notion of fireproofing is exemplified in a vast cast-iron staircase and roof arches, and the museum, over 100 years old, includes many specimens of rare or extinct birds and marsupials, including one of the Tasmanian Tiger (*Thylacinus cynocephalus*), the last known individual of which species died in captivity in 1936. Gosper Lane, University of Sydney (opposite the Post Office). For opening hours, best check on 9692 2274.

Other unique and fascinating material includes Australia's finest collection of foreign insects, some collected on the voyages of Captain Cook, Charles Darwin and Sir Stamford Raffles (the founder of Singapore); one of the best collections in Australia of artefacts from Irian Jaya; and some of the oldest bark paintings in the world.

There is also a brilliant collection of photographs of NSW pioneering times, dating from the 1850s to the 1950s, and if you want yet more insects, there are 700,000 of them kept in air-conditioned rooms in a separate building. For a frisson of sheer horror, don't call Hammer films, just get a close-up view of *Titanus giganteus*, the world's largest beetle, measuring 160mm. Staff, on the other hand, are friendly and well-informed.

As you leave, turn right into Science Road to enjoy various snacks and drinks in the Sydney University Union's Holme building. Or, if you are in a studious mood, turn left, walk under the Botany War Memorial arch to the Front Lawn, and cross it to the Fisher Library, which has more books than any library in the Southern Hemisphere. Down on the second floor you will find a small but choice collection of rare books and manuscripts which the Curators will be glad to show you. Opening hours vary according to the University calendar, so check before you go on 9692 3711. For your other special academic interests, check the Sydney telephone directory.

• **Korean Bath House** Aches and pains? Walked too far yesterday? Looking for total peace and quiet without checking another itinerary or map? Known only to lucky locals, the Hotel Capital's authentic Korean Bath House provides pampering from $20. Open daily from 10am-10pm. Hotel Capital, 111 Darlinghurst Road, Kings Cross, Tel 9358 2755.

• **Body Piercing** If you'd like to participate in a spot of body-piercing this is the place to go. Polymorph is thriving with the latest demand for pierced navels, eyebrows, noses, nipples and other more interesting and, dare we say, more painful places. The shop also operates as a gallery featuring exhibitions with an emphasis on body art. They also stock the largest range of body jewellery in Sydney, ranging from the ornate to the industrial. Polymorph caters for all tastes. Wed-Sat 12-8pm, Sun 12-6pm, Polymorph Body Art Gallery, 82 Enmore Road, Newtown, Tel 9519 8923.

• **City Gym** Feel like a workout at 3 in the morning? City Gym goes all day and all night, every day and every night! The only place to enjoy an instructed class or private workout, no matter what the time. A very effective jet-lag cure. Casual visit is inexpensive, 107 Crown Street, Darlinghurst, Tel 9360 6247.

• **RSL Clubs** It is amazing to a Sydneysider to find that visitors, whether they be from interstate or overseas, are fascinated by our registered clubs.

To be sure, a visit to one is a good way to find out about how quite a few locals spend large slabs of leisure time. The clubs are locally popular because they are inexpensive, friendly, safe and relaxing and they offer good services because of the income provided by the poker machines which form the heart of each club. If you want to meet a local, put a few coins through a poker machine yourself because chatting to your next door neighbour is usually part of the ritual. The clubs generally offer good quality, inexpensive meals, entertainment, and often a range of recreational facilities. All you need to do for entry is to check with the club and take your driver's licence or photo ID showing you live more than five kilometres from the club.

AFTER DARK

• **Sydney Observatory** *It's logical that the Sydney Observatory should be open most nights for telescopic views of the stars and planets of the Southern Skies.*

Great hands-on astronomy, so visitors can view their favourite constellations and discover ones they didn't know about (even see pictures of the Big Bang). Fascinating videos of the skies are shown continuously so you can rest your feet while being entertained and informed. Bookings necessary for night visits and they include guided tours of the building, films and videos. Open every night except Wednesday. Entry fee. Watson Road, Observatory Hill, The Rocks. Monday to Friday for information and bookings, Tel 9217 0485.

• **Hotels/Clubs** For an experience which taps you in to the sophistication and creativity of two of Sydney's most stylish lifestyle entrepreneurs, try the *Hotel CBD*, a collection of "stages" for meeting, eating, drinking, playing and being, right in the middle of the city. Created by stars of the Sydney fashion retail scene, John and Merivale Hemmes, the CBD melange is in the historic National Bank building. On the lower floor, a bar which, on Friday evenings, spills out onto the pavement with the young and upwardly mobile in mating mode. On the first floor, a restaurant; on the floor above, a pool and games bar; on the floor above that, a Club – if you've an insider friend who's a member, it's a great place to meet, or if you're going to the restaurant, club manager and fine jazz and blues singer Brooke Tabberer, might invite you in if it's not too busy. Corner King and York Streets. Restaurant, Tel 9299 8911; Bar, Tel 9299 8292.

Post-Mardi Gras the festivities live on at the

Sydney Observatory

Albury Hotel. Enjoy a free show witnessing a six foot diamante-covered man impersonating Marilyn Monroe. 2-6 Oxford Street, Paddington, Tel 9361 6555.

Spending time at the *Pavilion Hall Hotel* makes you feel like you're on the set of a cigarette commercial. Laid-back types play pool with a vengeance at this unexpected haunt. This is the place to shoot some pool and drink your favourite drop if you want to keep your cool credibility while in Bondi. A game here will set you back a few dollars. Open from 10am till about 1am, every day. Beach Road Hotel, First Floor, 71 Beach Road, Bondi, Tel 9130 7247.

If you love the nightlife you'll want to boogie at *DCMs* . This is the place for those who like lycra, leather and lather. Sydney's best DJs will have you on the floor all night long. Ever wanted to dance on a floor filled with foam? DCM was the first venue to ever host a Foam Party, so call ahead and check when they are next planning to pump up the suds. 33 Oxford Street, Darlinghurst, Tel 9267 7380.

Once a popular venue for Australian writers to give readings from their works, the *Harold Park Hotel* still has strong literary associations,

but no more sessions open to the public. However, these days you can participate in *Politics in the Park* each Friday night. A political issue of the day is discussed, often with well-known politicians leading the debate, 115 Wigram Road.

The pub where memorable scenes from drag flick, "Priscilla, Queen of the Desert" was filmed – the *Imperial Hotel.* Call in and sing-along with the Abba Show and reminisce about your favourite parts in the movie. Abba Show Thurs 12.30am and 1.30am, Sun 11.30pm and 12.30am, 35 Erskineville Road, Erskineville (runs off King Street).

RIDES

Like most big cities, Sydney has a metropolitan transport system which caters extremely well for tourists, and savvy UnTourists know when to use well-organised infrastructures to help them to get to know a place really well. We've already nominated Sydney Ferries as one of the best things about Sydney. Here we have singled out for special mention some water-borne trips by three privately run companies which we think you'll enjoy. And it's hard to go past the Explorer buses for value and convenience in helping you to get a good overview of Sydney.

BY VINTAGE FERRY

• **The Lane Cove River** gives access to a national park and passes through some lovely suburbs. A trip on *MV Reliance* is a treat. *Reliance* was built in 1919 and was the original mail boat for the Hawkesbury River, north of Sydney Harbour off Broken Bay. She has been lovingly restored by shipwright/ seaman/ teacher/ owner Captain Bill Moseley. The trip goes up the river to the Lane Cove National Park and, after lunch, takes passengers to see the native animals of the Kukundi Wildlife Shelter. Captain Moseley believes in indulging both body and soul. The menu for lunch is filled with delicious titbits, like gourmet sausages, marinated chicken wings, pasta salads and fresh bread rolls. There is a cash bar to slake the thirst. *Reliance* leaves from the Harbourside Jetty at Darling Harbour every Saturday and Sunday at 11am, returning at 2.45pm. Tel 9566 2067 or 018 252 933.

• **Sydney Harbour Islands** At the turn of the century, the islands of Sydney Harbour were popular for day outings. Now you can rediscover them by going on a cruise on one of *Banks*

Marine's lovely vintage ferries. There are a variety of options involving a visit to one or more of the following islands: Shark, Clarke, Rodd, Spectacle and Fort Denison. You can take your own picnic, or make a choice from the delicious catering options offered by the company, ranging from barbecues, picnic hampers and the traditional Billy Tea and lamingtons. Recommended as a unique harbour experience. Island Events, Tel 9555 1222.

BY SQUARE-RIGGER

A faithful replica of Captain Bligh's 18th Century vessel, the *Bounty* offers a range of cruises from a short sail with refreshments, to an evening dinner sail with three-course buffet. Departs daily from Campbells Cove where 200 years ago similar ships unloaded cargo and convicts for the colony.
For bookings, Tel 9247 1789.

The Bounty, *as seen from the deck of the America's Cup challenger,* Kookaburra II

BY BUS

• *Sydney Explorer* can be boarded at bus stops with Red Explorer signs. This bright red bus operates a circular route every 15 minutes, from 9.30am to 7pm, seven days a week, excepting Christmas day. Visitors can get off at any stop, browse for as long as they like and then board the next available bus to travel to another point of interest. Tickets can be bought on board.

1 Sydney Cove – Circular Quay, harbour cruises, ferries to Taronga Park Zoo, Darling Harbour, Manly

2 Sydney Opera House – opera and drama theatres, restaurants, guided tours

3 Royal Botanic Gardens – harbour views, exotic plants, Conservatorium of Music

4 State Library – Old Mint, Hyde Park Barracks, museums, churches, Supreme Court

5 Mrs Macquarie's Chair – superb views from harbourside

6 Art Gallery of NSW – Australian and overseas collections, bookshop, tours, the Domain Park

7 Hard Rock Cafe – a favourite with the young

8 Kings Cross – a cosmopolitan atmosphere, lively night life

9 Macleay Street – El Alamein Fountain, Victorian terraced houses, Fitzroy Gardens

10 Elizabeth Bay House (entrance fee) – elegant colonial house, gardens, open 9am-5pm

11 Potts Point – stately homes and bohemian lifestyles

12 Woolloomooloo Bay – Harry's Cafe de Wheels, pavement dining, naval docks

13 The Australian Museum (entrance fee) – natural history museum, Hyde Park, War Memorial

14 Central Railway Station – interstate and suburban train terminal

15 Chinatown – Dixon Street, Chinese restaurants, specialty shops, Entertainment Centre, Monorail

16 Powerhouse Museum (entrance fee) – interactive exhibits, open 10am-5pm

17 Australian National Maritime Museum (entrance fee) – maritime history, open 10am-5pm

18 Darling Harbour – Festival marketplace, food, shopping, the Convention Centre

19 The Chinese Garden (entrance fee) – Chinese bicentennial gift to Sydney

20 Sydney Aquarium (entrance fee) – family concessions available

21 Harbour Bridge, Milsons Point – cross the "coathanger" for views of harbour and skyline

22 Wynyard Park –York Street, shopping, suburban trains and walk through to stop 24

23 Queen Victoria Building – near Sydney Tower, Strand Arcade, Town Hall, St Andrew's

24 Wynyard Station – close to GPO, Martin Place, MLC Building, shopping, banks

25 The Rocks – Museum of Contemporary Art (entrance fee) open 11am-7pm, shopping

26 The Rocks Visitors' Centre – Cadman's Cottage, The Earth Exchange, open 10am-5pm

NOTE: For visitors who would like to do the Bondi & Bay Explorer trip as well, there's a ticket that covers travel on the Bondi & Bay Explorer one day and on the Sydney Explorer the next.

• **Bondi & Bay Explorer** can be boarded at the Blue Explorer signs at bus stops. Operating in a similar way to The Sydney Explorer, the blue Bondi & Bay Explorer has a 35 kilometre "beach and bay" circuit with twenty different stops. It's the same system – get on or off at any of the destinations and browse for as long as you want, then rejoin another service. Tickets are available on board. The Bondi & Bay Explorer operates seven days a week between 9am-6pm.

1 Sydney Cove – Circular Quay, harbour cruises, ferries to Taronga Park Zoo, Darling Harbour, Manly

2 Kings Cross – art deco buildings, cafes, bistros, shops, restaurants and night life

3 Top of the Cross – Studebaker's Disco, Darlinghurst, St Michael's Anglican Church, Jewish Museum

4 Rushcutters Bay – Cruising Yacht Club, marina, harbourside parks

5 Double Bay – fashionable boutiques, cafes, restaurants, delicatessens, gift shops, galleries, book shops, the Ritz Carlton Hotel

6 Rose Bay ferry wharf – scenic flights, waterfront restaurants, the Royal Sydney and Woollahra Golf Clubs, peak hour ferry service to Circular Quay

7 Rose Bay Convent – Heartbreak Hill

8 Vaucluse Bay – Vaucluse House, Neilsen Park, Greycliffe House, bush walks

9 Watsons Bay – *HMAS Watson* Naval Base, The Gap, anchor of the shipwrecked Dunbar, seafood restaurants, cliff walk to South Head

10 The Gap Park – panoramic views, walks to St Peter's Anglican Church and Macquarie Lighthouse

11 Bondi Beach – surf, sun and sea, the Bondi Baths, the Pavilion, restaurants, cafes and shops

12 Bronte Beach – barbecue facilities, spectacular views, surf and sun

13 Clovelly Beach – rock pool

14 Coogee Beach – Coogee Bay Hotel, shopping and scenic views, heritage Wylie's Baths

15 Royal Randwick Racecourse – Sydney's premier race course – all welcome on race days

16 The SCG – Sydney Cricket Ground and football stadium, Sportspace Museum

17 Paddington – Paddington markets (weekends), shops, art galleries, restaurants, pubs, quaint terrace houses

18 Oxford Street – shops, cafes, exotic boutiques, Edwardian facades. Nearby – Hyde Park South, Anzac War Memorial, Captain Cook statues, the Australian Museum, Sydney Grammar School

19 Hyde Park – the Archibald Fountain, Sandringham Memorial Gardens

20 Martin Place – the Cenotaph, GPO, Barrack Street, MLC Centre, Pitt Street Mall, NSW Travel Centre

NOTE: For visitors who would like to do the Sydney Explorer trip as well, a few more dollars buys a Sydney Explorer ticket for one day and one for the Bondi & Bay Explorer the next.

CALENDAR OF ANNUAL EVENTS

This calendar of events does not include sporting and arts events. For these, see conclusion of the relevant chapters.

JANUARY

Event	Location	Phone
Australia Day (various events)	City (C)	9247 2130
Australia Day celebrations	Darling Harbour (C)	9286 0100
Australia Day celebrations	Parramatta (W)	9635 8299
Australia Day concert	City (C)	(005) 551 995
Baulkham Hills Shire Australia Day Festival	Baulkham Hills (W)	9843 0555
Blessing of the Waters at Yarra Bay (Greek tradition)	La Perouse (S)	9698 5066
Chinese New Year	Haymarket (C)	9267 3166
Ferrython	City (C)	9265 0444
Flags Afloat	Darling Harbour (C)	9247 2130
Outdoor Festival, The Rocks	City (C)	9265 0444
Oz Day 10 K (wheelchair event)	City (C)	9809 5260
Survival Concert	La Perouse (S)	9281 2144
Sydney Festival (various events)	City (C)	9265 0444
Tall Ship Race	City (C)	9247 2130

FEBRUARY

Event	Location	Phone
Australian Perspective (each even year)	City (C)	9225 1744
Holland Festival	Fairfield (W)	9609 6765
Penrith Show	Penrith (W)	(047) 21 2375
South American Festival	Bondi Beach (E)	9130 3325
Sydney Gay and Lesbian Mardi Gras – various events	Darlinghurst (E)	9557 4332
Sydney Pet and Animal Expo	Paddington (E)	9876 4600
Sydney World Trade Fair	Darling Harbour (C)	9241 5555
Victoria Barracks Open Day	Paddington (E)	9339 3000
Yalunga Festival	La Perouse (S)	9311 3379

MARCH

Event	Location	Phone
Castle Hill Show	Castle Hill (W)	9634 2632
Clean Up Australia	City (C)	9552 2255
Gay and Lesbian Mardi Gras – performing arts program	City (C)	9557 4332
Gay and Lesbian Mardi Gras – parade and party	City (C)	9557 4332
GPS Head of the River	Penrith (W)	9630 0201

Event	Location	Phone
Camellias in the Garden	Granville (W)	9692 8366
International Golf Show	Darling Harbour (C)	9344 0811
Model Military Hobbies Exhibition	Parramatta (W)	9477 6696
National Aboriginal and Torres Strait Islander Week	Parramatta (W)	9689 9333
NSW Doll Collectors Fair	Liverpool (W)	9634 2564
Paddington Festival of Arts and Heritage	Paddington (E)	9252 1817
Sakura Bonsai Exhibition	Epping (N)	9450 2455
Sydney International Boat Show	Darling Harbour (C)	9438 2077

AUGUST

Event	Location	Phone
Australian International Home Show	Darling Harbour (C)	9282 5000
Camden Antique Fair	Camden (S)	(046) 57 1329
Courier Festival of Foods	Randwick (E)	9353 0941
Japan Festival	City (C)	954 0111
University of Western Sydney Campus (Hawkesbury) Open Day	Richmond (W)	(045) 78 2725

SEPTEMBER

Event	Location	Phone
19th Century games for kids	Parramatta (W)	9635 9488
Australian International Music Show	Darling Harbour (C)	9525 6755
Belgenny Farm Open Weekend	Camden (S)	(046) 293 333
Camden Park Open Weekend	Camden (S)	(046) 55 8466
Cowpastures Bush Music Festival	Camden (S)	9876 6667
Festival of the Winds (kites)	Bondi Beach (E)	9130 3325
Government House Open Day	City (C)	9931 5221
Great Garden Show	North Rocks (W)	9871 1233
Orange Blossom Festival	Castle Hill (W)	9651 4510
Sleaze Ball	Moore Park (E)	9557 4332
South Pacific Ballroom Dancing and Theatre Dance Championships	Homebush (W)	9439 4855
Spring Festival	City (C)	9231 8111
Taste in Hyde Park	City (C)	9265 9593
Variety Club Bash	Bondi (E)	9555 1799
Wisteria Day	Vaucluse (E)	9388 7922
Wisteria Garden Festival	Parramatta (W)	9840 3000

OCTOBER

Event	Location	Phone
Australian International Motor Show	Darling Harbour (C)	9361 0537
Blessing of the Fleet	Darling Harbour (C)	9286 0100
City To Turf	Parramatta (W)	9383 3899
	City (C)	9320 6181

Event	Location	Phone
Royal Easter Show	Moore Park (E)	9331 9111
Senior Citizens at Elizabeth Farm	Granville (W)	9635 9488
Senior Citizens Week at the Archives	Kingswood (S)	9673 1788
Seniors Week	City (C)	9360 1139
St. Patrick's Day Parade	City (C)	9211 3410
Walk Against Want	Darling Harbour (C)	9264 1399

APRIL

Event	Location	Phone
Anzac Day (25th)	City (C)	9299 2671
Army Engineer Museum Open Day	Moorebank (W)	9600 4975
Australian Museum Open Day	City (C)	9320 6181
Caged Bird Society of Nepean District	Penrith (W)	(047) 33 3062
Dragon Boat Races Festival	Darling Harbour (C)	9356 2850
Heritage Week	City (C)	9258 0164
Heritage Week	Parramatta (W)	9630 3703
Law Week	City (C)	9220 0287
Sydney Garden Festival	Darling Harbour (C)	9436 3266

MAY

Event	Location	Phone
Australian Museum Open Day	City (C)	9320 6181
Festival of Body, Health and Harmony	Moore Park (E)	9846 2377
Miniature Fair and Dolls House Exhibition	North Rocks (W)	9872 2623
Mother's Day Soiree	Parramatta (W)	9635 9488
Norton Street Festival	Leichhardt (W)	9367 9286
Preserve Your Precious Past	City (C)	9230 1566
Randwick Antique Fair	Randwick (E)	9399 0820

JUNE

Event	Location	Phone
Australian Women's Weekly Needlework and Craft Fair	Darling Harbour (C)	9977 0888
Manly Food and Wine Festival	Manly (N)	9977 1088
Environment and Hands-on Exhibition	Penrith (W)	(047) 31 3000
Home Computer Show	Darling Harbour (C)	03 867 4500
Sydney Quilt Festival	Darling Harbour (C)	9529 8638

JULY

Event	Location	Phone
Aboriginal Week	City (C)	9211 3555
Artists of Hill End	City(C)	9225 1744
Australian Book Fair	Darling Harbour (C)	9977 0888

Event	Location	Phone
Granny Smith Festival	Ryde (W)	9809 5847
Hambledon Cottage Open Day	Parramatta(W)	9635 6924
Home Ideas Expo	Penrith (W)	(049) 29 7685
Navy Week	City (C)	9266 2095
Penrith City Festival	Penrith (W)	(047) 39 8733
Puppeteers Picnic	City (C)	9755 2586
Sydney Antique Arms Fair	Moore Park (E)	9810 6645
Sydney Stamp Show	City (C)	9267 6116
Wooden Boat Festival	Darling Harbour (C)	9810 7805

NOVEMBER

Event	Location	Phone
Australian Craft Show	Moore Park (E)	9566 4820
Christmas Parade and Christmas Lighting Ceremony	City (C)	9265 9007
Festival for Mind, Body, Spirit	Darling Harbour (C)	9552 6833
Foundation Day Celebrations	Parramatta (W)	9689 9333
Glebe Street Artisan and Food Fair	Glebe (W)	9552 1546
Kings Cross Carnival	Kings Cross (E)	9871 1233
Mexican Festival	City (C)	9362 4270
Persian Cultural Festival	City (C)	9823 4371
Porcelain Exhibition and Expo	Parramatta (W)	(047) 74 8305
School Spectacular	Haymarket (C)	9266 4800
Scottish Week	City (C)	9232 2473
Teddy Bears' Picnic	Darling Harbour (C)	9692 6365

DECEMBER

Event	Location	Phone
Carolfest, Sydney University	Glebe (W)	9310 1731
Carols by Candlelight, Elizabeth Farm	Granville (W)	9635 9488
Carols by the Nepean River	Penrith (W)	(047) 32 7672
Carols in the Domain	City (C)	9319 7874
Carols in the Park	Castle Hill (W)	9634 2412
Christmas at the Town Hall	City (C)	9265 9554
Darling Harbour Christmas Pageant	Darling Harbour (C)	9286 0100
Light Fantastic Festival	Darling Harbour (C)	9286 0100
New Year's Eve	Darling Harbour (C)	9286 0129
New Year's Eve Skyshow	Darling Harbour (C)	9955 1800
Old Government House Carols in the Courtyard	Parramatta (W)	9635 8149
Premier's Christmas Concert for Senior Citizens	Haymarket (C)	9367 6831
St George and 2WS Christmas Carols	Parramatta (W)	9671 2411

The 25th Sun Herald City to Surf Run, August 13, 1995. This is when 43,481 perfectly sane men, women and children ran from William Street in the city on to Bondi Beach. They do it every year about this time. Why? We asked Bryce Courtenay, Australia's best-selling author who has done it 18 times and lived to write again.

Most unlike the articulate Bryce, he couldn't quite give us the answer.

11 SPORTS

INCLUDES: The three indigenous Sydney sports – surfing, sailing and 'footy'. Surfing – an expert's run-down on the quirks of the surfing beaches; 18-footer sailing – how to see the best of it – and a run-down on Rugby League. We also cover cricket, golf, tennis, bowls, fishing, horse-riding, horse and harness racing; plus a calendar of Sydney's year-round sporting events.

Playing the Game

Two of the things Australians excel at are sport and war. They apply the same rules to both – a sense of fair play, resourcefulness and an abundance of enthusiasm. "Right Sport?"

In Sydney, sport is certainly more than a leisure activity – it is an integral part of the lifestyle. Participating, watching, reading about it or just talking about it. Sport is big.

The sports consuming most passion and enthusiasm in Sydney are Rugby League, surfing and sailing – so they will be playing centre court in this chapter.

SAILING

THE "SKIM DISHES" OF SYDNEY HARBOUR

The Eighteens, as they are known, have been considered the world's fastest single-hull boats since their invention in 1895. Originally they were heavy wood-planked boats with vast sail areas only kept upright by crews of up to 14 men, and in light winds. Some crew were discarded overboard at the turning marks.

Modern Eighteens are space-age flying machines with small keeled hulls, complex sails of exotic material and now just three athletes suspended on trapezes outboard on aluminium outriggers. These miracle machines can actually run faster than the wind.

Commerce crept into the races in the 1930s when the Eighteens were joined by ferry-loads of spectators, hell-bent on having a wager. They were then joined by bookmakers to call the odds. It all got a bit heavy for the government of the day which, prodded by opponents of gambling, made police raids on the ferries. One bookmaker was known to have leapt overboard to avoid arrest. Many punters thought, uncharitably, that he was trying to avoid paying out on his bets. He became known as "Dick the Diver".

Nothing much has changed since that time and the club ferries turn on a great afternoon on Sydney Harbour filled with family, punters and friends all in dogged pursuit of those harbour flying machines.

The modern Eighteens, with names like Xerox, Prudential, Ella Bache, Old El Paso, Mitsubishi Electric and 2UE can be seen racing on Sydney Harbour every Saturday and Sunday afternoon during the sailing season (mid-September to Easter). The spectator ferries of the **Sydney Flying Squadron** and the **Australian 18 Footers** leave at convenient pick-up points around the harbour and both welcome visitors. Spectators are returned to their destination at the end of the two to three-hour trip. The ferries have a bar and serve substantial finger-food. Call the clubs to make a booking – you'll find both of their numbers in our Directory in the yellow pages at the back of the book.

SYDNEY TO HOBART YACHT RACE

One of the world's most spectacular starts to any sporting event in the world happens in Sydney Harbour on Boxing Day each year. Hundreds of thousands line the foreshores and expert helmsmanship and nerves of steel are required as spectator-fleet boats try to jockey for positions without interfering with the race participants.

Racing for a week – depending on weather conditions – the yachts often face treacherous

From A Century of Sydney's Flying Sailors *by Margaret Molloy*

weather even before they get to the notorious Bass Straight. Out of a recent race of 100 starters, only 50 finished.

The Sydney to Hobart Yacht Race started in 1945 when Royal Navy Captain John Illing-worth persuaded a group of Sydney yachtsmen to turn a 630 miles cruise to Hobart into a race. *Rani*, Illing-worth's 35' cutter won, sailing to Hobart in just under seven days. The 50th anniversary of the race in 1994 saw nearly 400 yachts start – the largest field ever to compete in an ocean race.

FOR VISITORS

You can sail on Syd-ney Harbour and you will find the inform-ation listed under "Boats Hire" and "Boat Charter Services" in the A-K section of the Sydney Telephone Directory's Yellow Pages. Keep in mind it can get pretty hectic out there on the summer week-ends. We have a Danger Map in Chapter 1 for your guidance.

Eastsail at Rushcutter Bay has a fleet of fifteen *Cavalier*, *Robertson* and *Beneteau* yachts. There are sailing courses for beginners through to experienced sailors; yacht charter and twi-light racing. Instructors are fully qualified with the Australian Yachting Federation, d'Albora Marina, New Beach Road, Rushcutters Bay.

THE SURF

Former Prime Minister, the late Sir Robert Menzies, nominated Surf Life Saving as the main activity which he considered uniquely Australian and Sydney historically lays claim to being the birthplace of this great Aust-ralian tradition.

SAFE SURFING

You have nothing to fear surfing on Sydney beaches, providing you follow this good advice from Surf Life Saving Australia.

1   Note any signs indicating the presence of blue-bottles, stingers, rips or strong currents.

2   Look for the areas marked "craft users". Avoid them.

3   Do not swim alone. Save worry – swim with a friend.

4   If in difficulty, do not panic but float and signal for help by raising one arm straight in the air (do not wave or friendly observers may just wave back).

5   Select a beach where qualified surf lifesavers patrol. Lifesavers are recognised by their red and yellow caps, yellow T-shirt and red shorts. Cute.

Cute.

Since the early 1900s surfing in Australia has been watched over by the Surf Life Saving Association, which originated from Manly Beach. Since that time, more than 350,000 rescues have been carried out by surf lifesavers. Interestingly enough, the first recorded rescue was of the famous Australian aviator Charles Kingsford Smith who was rescued on Bondi Beach in 1907.

Surf Life Saving Australia organises surf carnivals at many of Sydney's beaches throughout the summer. Competition venues change each year – for more information con-tact Surf Life Saving Australia, 128 The Grand Parade, Brighton-Le-Sands, or refer to the entertainment pages of the *Sydney Morning Herald*. Also, check pages 184, 185.

Sun-bleached hair, baked brown bodies, surfboards and the smell of take-away food signal the surf culture of the Sydney beaches. Surfing aficionados who favour the northern beaches say there is nothing better – devo-tees of Maroubra and Cronulla would, of course, strongly disagree. But no matter where the surf is rolling, there'll be riders or body-surfers.

Andrew Kidman guides the serious surfer and board rider through the Sydney beaches. South-erners (those who surf on beaches south of the Harbour) may detect more than a slight bias towards the northern beaches in Andrew's writing, they would be right. Since he was old enough to swim, Andrew has surfed them all regularly.

SURFING SYDNEY

Palm Beach A long beach and usually uncrowded. The southern end is called "Kiddies Corner". A small wave, perfect for beginners and long boarders. The northern end is fickle but sometimes when the breaks are in position a left called "The Joey" will barrel to the beach in big north-east swells. Rare.

Bilgola Rarely good. Though on occasions in the wintertime if the sand is in place and the swell is deep from the south a left will peel from the northern corner to the beach. Generally uncrowded.

Newport Home to Australia's most famous surfer, Tom Carroll. At the southern end is "Newport Reef" – works on a solid south swell, but rare. "The Peak" breaks all year round, working best in a medium south swell. "The Peak" offers a sharp, pitching take-off over the reef followed by left and right walls that crack off to the beach.

Mona Vale Much like North Narrabeen, working on similar swells and facing in a similar direction. Unfortunately, Mona Vale hasn't the lagoon to feed sand onto the banks. But when the breaks are in place a hollow left will drive its way down the beach. The Basin also offers a short break for bodyboarders and a rare right-hander that breaks down the rocks on a big south swell.

North Narrabeen Probably the most consistent and famous wave of the northern beaches. The low lagoon that runs out into the break at Narrabeen at low tide feeds a constant flow of sand in the break causing a triangle bank for the waves to peel left and right on. Breaks best on north-east swells with long tubes on the

Whale Beach South "Whaley" offers right-hand barrels when the swell is big from the south-east. "The Wedge", which breaks in the northern corner is one of the best drops on the northern beaches when the swell fires in from the north-east. A consistent summer location, though heavily localised.

Avalon Breaks on a variety of swells and at a variety of locations along the beach. "LA", a reef setup, barrels best in a north-east swell. A long pitching barrel – heavily localised and for experienced surfers only. South Avalon breaks best in the wintertime on south swells. A right-hander can peel from the back of the rocks to the beach. North Avalon offers a small right-hand suck-up near shore and out the back deep, long, fast barrels when the swell is anywhere from the south-east to the north-east, depending on the banks.

Bungan A very uncrowded wave. In big south swells a right-hand barrel peels off the southern end called "Rock Pools". It's a fickle wave and relies heavily on the tides. The beach break works best in peaky south swells and north-east wind swells on an incoming tide. Generally picks up a lot of swell.

Warriewood Another protected location. Breaks best in the wintertime when the solid south swells wrap around the headland. If the breaks are in place a right-hander will peel off to the middle of the beach. At the northern end and sometimes a barrelling peak is offered on north-east swells.

Narrabeen When the banks are in place and the swell is from the south, left-handers can peel off for a couple of hundred metres. But, sadly, for most of the year it's a closeout. In summertime when the north-east wind swells sweep down the beach and the tide is low some

Collaroy The most protected location on the northern beaches. A soft rolling wave, perfect for beginners. The surf schools are usually held at this break.

Dee Why Its best feature is "The Point" – a ledging right-hand reef break that comes out of deep water and throws into a long wedging tube. Heavily localised and for experienced surfers only. It breaks best in a deep south/south-east swell and sometimes in the winter on the north-east wind swells if the tide is right. The middle of the beach also has its fair share of peaks, depending on the banks and swell direction.

Harbord A small beach that works well in the summertime but tends to close out in the winter. A right hand rip bowl often forms in the southern corner and is good on small south swells and medium north-easters.

North Steyne It's more open to various swell conditions. It breaks best on big south swells with offshore winds. Often producing long left-hand tube rides. In the summertime it also picks up the north-east wind swells, offering punchy little peaks.

Manly The south end of Manly is usually smaller and more protected than the rest of the beach. Good for beginners. It breaks best in a large south swell and south-west winds.

Cronulla, Wanda, Elouera In the winter these three beaches provide rideable wave of reasonable size when the southern swells come through. During summer the waves are generally small.

large outer reef called 'The Bombie' breaks left and right in big south swells and is a perfect testing ground for experienced big wave riders. A handful of smaller reefs weave their way north around the point and break on various sized south swells. A right hander also breaks at the entrance of the lagoon when the sandbanks are in place.

Curl Curl A long beach broken up by various sandbanks. In the southern corner during the winter time the south swells pound onto the outside banks sometime forming large tubes. The northern corner tends to be protected and is good for beginners.

Queenscliff Famous for its short breaks. Lefts and rights close down out the back reforming as they approach the shore. Queenscliff picks up the north-east swells well but is battered by the larger south swells in the wintertime.

Bronte, Clovelly, Coogee Good for the "Clubbies".

Bondi, Maroubra These two beaches are the only two other beaches which provide rideable waves, which only peak when they are favoured by a north-easterly swell. Usually these conditions occur during the summer.

Boards and wetsuits are on hire from different outlets at the various beaches, and the average cost for 3 hours is around $20 (includes board and suit). For more information on suppliers consult the Sydney Telephone Directory Yellow Pages under "Surfing Equipment."

FOOTY

There are four different football games played in Sydney.

Aussie Rules, based on Gaelic football, is fast and exciting. Originating in Victoria, it climaxes each season with the AFL grand final. This form of football is virtually unknown outside Australia. **Rugby Union,** "the game that is played in heaven" according to its fans, was considered the gentleman's amateur game but has recently joined the ranks of the professional teams. **Soccer** has become increasingly popular with the increase in European immigration to Sydney. Finally, the indigenous football game of Sydney – the big game with the gladiatorial image is **Rugby League.**

Rugby League is one of the hardest and toughest football games in the world. Each region in Sydney has its team of professional players and its fanatical followers. Regular games are held at local suburban club grounds on Friday, Saturday and Sunday through the winter season, with special events such as the State of Origin or International – New Zealand (Kiwis) vs Australia (Kangaroos) being held on any day of the week.

The Rugby League season runs from April to September and climaxes with the grand final competition for the J Guiltman Sheild at the end of September, held at the at the Sydney Football Stadium, Moore Park.

Rugby League in Sydney started with eleven suburban teams, followed passionately by their local supporters. With the formation of the new Super League many of the smaller local Sydney clubs have changed, merged or been dissolved and no-one is quite sure how this will affect fan behaviour in the future.

The Rugby League's headquarters has an excellent information service giving general updates, including City verses Country news, State of Origin and for test dates, for venues and bulletins.

From top: Sydney Football Stadium, Sydney Cricket Ground and the Showground (soon to become part of the 20th Century Fox studio complex)

CRICKET

The first Australian cricket team to tour abroad were Aborigines and they set out from Sydney. Sporting theatrical names like Bullocky, Twopenny and Mosquito, they cut quite a swathe through the conservative British MCC in 1868 by winning a respectable number of games and drawing even more. They were captained by the entrepreneurial English cricketer Charles Lawrence who seven years earlier had been brought out to Australia as part of the first touring British team. He remained in Australia and, no doubt, saw an opportunity in managing this talented and colourful team as they toured the English cricket grounds, spicing up the entertainment by giving boomerang-throwing exhibitions in between innings.

One of the most important pieces of "dirt" in the world, for cricket fans, is the hallowed grounds of the Sydney Cricket Ground. The SCG, with a capacity of 45,000, has hosted major cricket matches since 1878. Home to such legendary players as Don Bradman, Victor Trumper and Bill O'Reilly, the SCG has seen many of cricket's greatest performances. The SCG is used for international matches from November to January and interstate games from October to April.

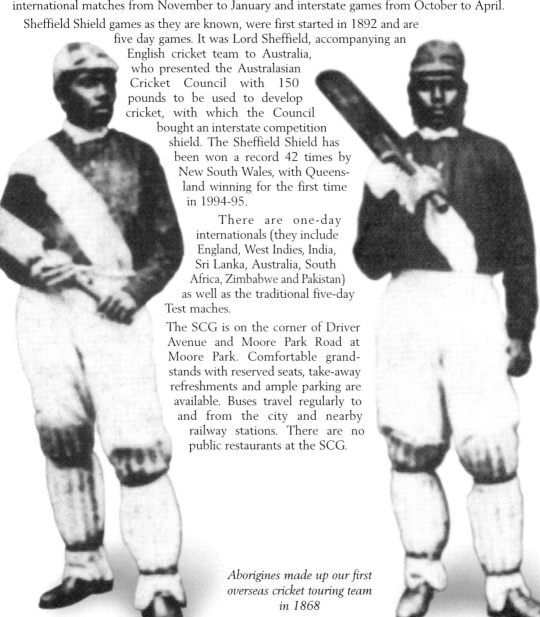

Sheffield Shield games as they are known, were first started in 1892 and are five day games. It was Lord Sheffield, accompanying an English cricket team to Australia, who presented the Australasian Cricket Council with 150 pounds to be used to develop cricket, with which the Council bought an interstate competition shield. The Sheffield Shield has been won a record 42 times by New South Wales, with Queensland winning for the first time in 1994-95.

There are one-day internationals (they include England, West Indies, India, Sri Lanka, Australia, South Africa, Zimbabwe and Pakistan) as well as the traditional five-day Test maches.

The SCG is on the corner of Driver Avenue and Moore Park Road at Moore Park. Comfortable grandstands with reserved seats, take-away refreshments and ample parking are available. Buses travel regularly to and from the city and nearby railway stations. There are no public restaurants at the SCG.

Aborigines made up our first overseas cricket touring team in 1868

SPORTSPACE

This is sort of a sporting museum with a difference. Sporting legends come to life as you play a part in some of the greatest moments in sport. When matches are not in progress at the SCG and the adjacent Sydney Football Stadium, there are behind-the-scenes guided tours available. A tour includes the dressing rooms, run-down tunnel, cricket museum, original 1886 Members Stand and coverage of over 100 years of history. The one-and-a-half hour tours depart at 10am, 1pm and 3pm, Mon-Sat. For more information call Sportspace Tours on Tel 9380 0383.

HORSES

A bunch of horses, necks outstretched, nostrils flaring, ears laid back, flat out as they vie for position over the last half furlong before the post, with jockeys in brilliant colours perched high on their withers. It is quite a sight to see, and the racing season in Sydney is all year round. The major racecourses are: Randwick, Rosehill, Warwick Farm and Canterbury.

At all courses, horses, trainers, jockeys and stable-hands are busy from daylight – horses are doing fast-work or half-pace conditioning, or the youngsters are having barrier practice. It is possible for a visitor to Sydney to see early morning trackwork, but only after getting permission from course management. The horses are valuable and skittish and the trainers are zealous about their charges and protective of the work their horses are doing.

At each of the clubs, breakfast and/or a toddy to go with your early morning coffee are available. Call for permission to attend early morning work at the courses: Randwick, Tel 9663 8400; Rosehill, Tel 9682 1000.

On race days, the courses are open to any paying guest and there are usually special buses and trains from the city to the course.

Harness Racing Trotters and square gaiters, the high-stepping harness horses race less frequently than their galloping cousins but normally there is a six- or seven-race program from Harold Park Raceway or Bankstown at least once a week. For details of these race meetings, call Bankstown Harness and Racing Club, Tel 9708 4111 and Harold Park Raceway, Tel 9660 3688.

But if you are not only interested in racing, but like to ride....

RIDING

A favourite venue for riding in central Sydney is Centennial Park. Several riding schools have

Training at dawn

permanent homes at a pavilion in the Showground at Moore Park.

Rides generally leave on the hour and are over approximately five km. Lessons are available, and all schools have helmets (some have boots) available for their riders. Contact numbers for Centennial Park Riding are listed in the Sydney Telephone Directory Yellow Pages under "Horse Riding". Other Sydney venues, also listed, are at Terrey Hills, Ryde and Randwick.

QUEEN OF THE TURF

"I didn't fight for my licence for two years to be a puppet, Dad. By all means advise me, I'm open to all suggestions from you, but I have to train the horses."

"Dad" is the legendary T.J.Smith, Australia's most famous horse-trainer and father of Gai Waterhouse who had to take on the all-powerful Australian Jockey Club for over two years before she finally got her licence to train. Now she is the undisputed "Queen of the Turf" – not because she was the first woman trainer, but because she is simply the best.

Here's how Les Carylon described Gai on Derby Day at Randwick: "'Come on, come on,' she (Gai Waterhouse) shouts, making a windmill motion with her handbag, her face alive with joy. The crowd bubbles and cheers. It is one of those rare moments when a sport rises above its cliches and, for just an instant, seems special. It has heroes and it has heart; the insiders and the crowd are one. Gai made it happen." *Sun-Herald, 2/7/95.*

Between 5-6.30am at the end of Bowral Street, Randwick, trackwork begins and Gai has been up since 4.30am. Gai's love of the turf, of the horses and the whole environment of the sport comes through clearly and drive her through the day.

Now you can come and see what it's all about. Call Denise Martin of Star Thoroughbreds' on her pager number 9962 5835 and a pick up at your hotel can be arranged. After the training session, you can have a tour of the stables. If you'd like to go to a race day, the same pick-up arrangements can apply and there's lunch included. By the way, the early-bird racing fraternity has two favourite coffee houses which are only a few minutes from the racetrack (at this time of day, there's no traffic about – in normal hours it's about 30 minutes away). The coffee houses are Tropicana and Bar Coluzzi, both in Darlinghurst Road, Darlinghurst. Gai highly recommends the macciato and cappuccino in both places.

CALENDAR OF THE MAIN ANNUAL SPORTING EVENTS IN AND AROUND SYDNEY

For those readers who are followers of water-skiing, motorbike and car racing – for environmental reasons, these events are not covered in this calendar.

JANUARY

Event	Location	Phone
Australian Open Beach Volleyball	Manly Beach (N)	9319 5255
Grand Prix Sailing (18-Footers)	Milsons Point (N)	9332 2177
NSW Beach Volleyball Series	Manly (N)	9763 0166
NSW Multiple Events and 10km Walks	Olympic Centre Homebush (W)	9552 1244
NSW Open Tennis	White City (E)	9331 4144
NSW v Victoria – cricket	Moore Park (E)	9360 6601
Surf Carnival at North Bondi	Bondi Beach (E)	9311 3298
Surf Carnival	Manly Beach (N)	9938 2041
Australian Open Pro-Beach Volleyball Tournament	Manly (N)	9957 1240

FEBRUARY

Event	Location	Phone
Surf Rescue Challenge	Manly Beach (N)	9663 4298
Bridge to Bridge Swim	Penrith (W)	9132 7671
Challenge – golf	Terrey Hills Golf Club (N)	9450 0155
Swim Classic	Bondi Beach (E)	9365 5386
International Rugby League World Events	Moore Park (E)	9266 4800
Manly Ocean Classic – swimming	Manly Beach (N)	9976 1566
NSW Track and Field Championships	Olympic Centre Homebush (W)	9552 1244

MARCH

Event	Location	Phone
Rugby League Matches, Rounds 12-14	Moore Park (E)	9232 7566
State Novice Championship – gymnastics	Olympic Centre Homebush (W)	9763 0177

JULY

Event	Location	Phone
NSW Country Championship Final – Australian Rules football	Moore Park (E)	9552 6055
Premier State Quarterhorse Championship	Nelson	9654 9057
Rugby League Matches, Rounds 15 -18	Moore Park (E)	9232 7566
Rugby Union Bledislo Cup Australia vs New Zealand	Moore Park (E)	9715 9991
Troutfest Fishing Competition	Penrith (W)	9176 1357

AUGUST

Event	Location	Phone
City to Surf Fun Run	Sydney City (C)	9282 6616
Rugby League Matches, Rounds 19-22	Moore Park (E)	9232 7566
Rugby Union Semi-Final and Grand Final Matches	Concord (W)	9747 2400
Sydney Marathon 5km walk	Olympic Centre Homebush (W)	9325 6777
Sydney Marathon 10km run	Five Dock (W)	9325 6777
Sydney Marathon 42kms run	Sydney suburbs	9325 6777
Sydney Turf Club's Spring Carnival – racing	Rose Hill (W)	9799 8000

SEPTEMBER

Event	Location	Phone
AJC Spring Racing Carnival	Randwick (E)	9663 8400
Australian Rules Football Matches	Moore Park (E)	9266 4800
Cycle Sydney	Sydney City (C)	9283 5200

Event	Location	Phone
Cobbitty Polo Tournament	Cobbitty (W)	9552 1620
Cleanwater Wavemasters – surfing	Manly Beach (N)	9979 8227
Golden Slipper Festival – racing	Rose Hill (W)	9799 8000
GPS Head of the River Regatta – rowing	Penrith (W)	9630 0201
Liverpool Cup – racing	Warwick Farm (W)	9602 6199
NSW Veterans Track and Field Championships	Olympic Centre Homebush (W)	9579 5492
NSW v South Australia – cricket	Moore Park (E)	9360 6601
Rugby League Matches, Rounds 1-4	Moore Park (E)	9232 7566
Sydney Grand Prix Track and Field Meet	Olympic Centre Homebush (W)	9552 1244

APRIL

Event	Location	Phone
AJC Autumn Racing Carnival	Randwick (E)	9663 8400
League Netball	Olympic Centre Homebush (W)	9266 4800
National Wheelchair Games	Sydney suburbs	9489 3861
Polo International Day	Warwick Farm (W)	9552 1260
Rugby League Matches, Rounds 5-8	Moore Park (E)	9232 7566

MAY

Event	Location	Phone
Half Marathon	Sydney City (C)	9282 3606
Rugby League Matches, Rounds 9-11	Moore Park (E)	9232 7566
State of Origin – interstate rugby league	Moore Park (E)	9232 7566

JUNE

Event	Location	Phone
Countess of Dudley Cup – polo	Warwick Farm (W)	9552 1260

Event	Location	Phone
International Lawn Bowls	Blacktown (W)	9283 4555
Rugby League Semi and Grand Final NSW Premiership	Moore Park (E)	9232 7566
Tattersalls Day Race Meeting	Randwick (E)	9663 8400

OCTOBER

Event	Location	Phone
Australian Indoor Tennis Championships	Haymarket (C)	9266 4800
World Cup (Soccer)	Penrith (W)	9248 1949
Interstate one-day cricket games	Moore Park (E)	9261 5155
Pacific Power Commonwealth Bank Cycle Classic	Sydney City (C)	9540 1699
Sheffield Shield – cricket	Moore Park (E)	9261 5155
Sydney Badminton Grand Prix	Olympic Centre Homebush(W)	9819 4300
Sydney Turf Club's Silver Slipper Race Meeting	Rose Hill (W)	9799 8000
The Australian PGA Golf Championship	NSW Golf Club (S)	9661 4455

NOVEMBER

Event	Location	Phone
Test Cricket Series	Moore Park (E)	9266 4800
Greg Norman's Holden Classic	The Lakes Golf Club (S)	9669 1311
Melbourne Cup Day – Sydney race meeting	Randwick (E)	9663 8425
Sydney to the 'Gong Bicycle Ride	Moore Park (E)	9287 2929

DECEMBER

Event	Location	Phone
World Cricket Series	Moore Park (E)	9261 5155
Sydney to Hobart Yacht Race	Sydney Harbour	9363 9731
Triathalon	Penrith (W)	9135 2544
Ironman and Ironwoman	Manly Beach (N)	9261 1777

TENNIS

Wally Masur playing at White City Court, Rushcutters Bay, Sydney. Masur has been a member of the Australian Davis Cup team for many years. He is now part of the training team developing younger, stronger players to reclaim the top form Australia once had when it regularly fought for Davis Cup honours with the United States.

Court hire and private coaching are available for visiting participants at numerous venues throughout Sydney. Most courts are open for daily and evening use and courts are listed in the Sydney Telephone Directory Yellow Pages under "Tennis Courts for Hire".

BOWLS

Bowls were first played by the "sporting gentlemen" of Sydney in 1845. "Sporting ladies" started bowling in 1925, forming their own association in 1929. Following are details of some centrally located clubs. Visitors are welcome, but call beforehand as they all tend to play on different days.

Mosman Bowling Club 15 Belmont Road, Mosman. Established 1902, heritage listed, famous for scones at after-noon tea. Tel 969 4211/5198.

North Sydney Bowling Club Ridge Street, North Sydney. One of the oldest clubs in Sydney, established in 1888, has stunning views of Sydney Harbour. Tel 9202 8896.

Warringah Bowling Club Bradleys Head Road, Mosman. Two abbreviated morning games are held twice a week for older men, referred to fondly by the club as games for "the old and the bold". Free tuition. Tel 969 4313.

Kirribilli RSL Bowling Club 11-23 Harbour View Crescent, Milsons Point. Tel 0055 2245

For more information on bowling clubs, facilities, competitions etc, contact the Royal New South Wales Bowling Association, 309 Pitt Street, Sydney.

FISHING

Sydney produces good fishing all year round. You can hire a boat or fish from shore. Experienced charter skippers can almost guarantee to put you onto good fish.

March and April tend to be the most productive months, and blue water anglers can expect to catch marlin, yellowtail kingfish, mahi mahi and big sharks.

However, there is also good reef fishing which will allow you to tackle mulloway, snapper, flathead and morwong, to name a few of the more common species.

Sydney's beaches produce bream, whiting, tailer and the occasional mulloway and beautiful rock platforms abound with bream and luderick and sometimes kingfish and tuna.

In May the winds drop off and anglers can fish the warm offshore currents more comfortably. In winter the harbour and other estuaries will produce trevally, bream, leatherjackets and those monsters of the deep – hairtail which can be around two metres long – watch those razor-sharp teeth.

West of Sydney are Lakes Lyall and Oberon where trout fishing is allowed year round. You can fish there with fly, lure or bait, as flocks of cockatoos wheel overhead and kangaroos watch from Australia's unique bushland.

Best of all, Sydney's anglers are a pretty friendly bunch, so don't be afraid to ask. Most fishing tackle shops will soon point you in the right direction. Please remember there are rules about angling and you should check these out with the local fisheries department. Enquiries, NSW Fisheries, Tel 9566 7807.

GOLF

Major courses in Sydney are:

The Australian Bannerman Crescent, Rosebery. It has reciprocal arrangements with international and interstate clubs. Course description: sand belt and is a great test of golf. Tel 9663 2273.

Royal Sydney Kent Road, Rose Bay, has reciprocal arrangements with interstate and international clubs. Players must be introduced and partnered by a member. Top facilities are of the highest order. Course description: level walking, excellent course, good test of golf. Tel 9661 4455.

The Lakes King Street, Eastlakes, has reciprocal arrangements with overseas and interstate clubs. Visitors, Monday and Thursday only. Strict dress regulations. Bookings essential.

Course description: not for beginners; plenty of water graves for wayward shorts. Tel 9669 1311.

New South Wales Golf Club Henry Road, La Perouse, has restricted times available. Strict dress regulations. Bookings essential. Course description: ranked in the world's top 100; butted against the sea; blind shots; swirling terrain; tricky greens; magnificent fairways. Seabreeze can play havoc – exciting and challenging. Tel 9661 4455.

Bonnie Doon Golf Club Banks Avenue, Pagewood, is one of Sydney's more prominent private golf clubs. Only eight kilometres from the city. Overseas and interstate visitors Mon, Tues, Thurs and Fri afternoons. Bookings essential. Course description: well maintained; undulating sandhill; influenced by prevailing winds – stern test for all level of play. Tel 9349 2101.

Public Courses At least 80 courses within the limits of Sydney with approximately half of them open to the visitors. Many others accept players with golfing handicaps. All courses are listed in the Sydney Telephone Directory Yellow Pages under "Clubs" or "Golf Courses, Public".

The days when Les Darcy and Dave Sands drew huge crowds to the big fights at Sydney's old Rushcutters Bay Stadium have gone. Possibly this is as much a consequence of our easy access to combative entertainment in other forms, as it is to society's gentrification. When in the '80s, the crowds were drawn to see Black and Blue, *they came to see the Sydney Dance Company turn boxing into an art form. And so, from our Sports chapter to Art and Shows* • • •

The Opera House, centrepiece of the performing arts in Sydney, is itself the subject of a new opera – The Eighth Wonder, *by Australian composer and lyricist team, Alan John and Dennis Watkins. This is designer Brian Thomson's sketch for the opera's Act II.*

12 ARTS AND SHOWS

INCLUDES: *The Opera House as cultural catalyst; music – from classical to a cappella and jazz; opera from "grand" to pub; new ideas and challenges from the city's West; theatre from classical to cutting-edge; dance, cinema, and the blaze of crossover talents; the art galleries, the writers, and where to find out where it's all happening.*

From Famine to Feast in Forty Years

Sydney is a city filled to the brim with experience-seekers. They embrace displays, spectacles, celebrations and parades with extraordinary enthusiasm. You see this thrill-seeking in their commitment to sport, gambling, or a combination of both. You see it in the speed with which they adopt new products and ideas (and discard them just as quickly). It is possibly this, rather than the existence of any intellectual pretensions, which explains why the arts and entertainment section of the *Sydney Morning Herald* has nearly as many entries as the *New York Times*.. And why Sydney hosts four ballet troupes, 12 orchestras, 15 resident chamber music groups, 80 cinemas, 30 musical societies, 29 repertory companies, six choral societies and one of the very few full-time opera companies in the world – all serving only around three and a half million people.

In the '50s, Australian artists and others left their country in droves for "the mother country" England, Europe and America. Now they are coming back – and one hears talk in arts circles about America being too "derivative" or Europe being "used up" and about Sydney being "hot". Rather than the mecca being "over there", there are confident comparisons being made.

Australian Elijah Moshinsky, one of the world's top opera directors and a major contributor to the Australian Opera, was quoted by the *Australian* newspaper recently as having "almost given up working in Europe because the opera scene was such a mess". Moshinsky, who is also a highly regarded film, television and theatre director, commented that: *"the shift to modernism (particularly in Germany), with its playful references to the past and focus on style over meaning, [have] swept all other styles of opera away in the past decade."* American Samiel Dixon, an arts administrator recently wooed to Sydney by the ABC. *"....there isn't the rigidity of thinking [in Australia] about what is music or what isn't music."*

In the dreaded '50s, Sydney was considered a cultural wasteland, not just by the rest of the world but by Australians. It seemed that whatever was happening was happening in Melbourne. or "overseas". The painting and sculpting Nolans and Boyds; the film makers, writers and arts intellectuals like Phillip Adams, Barry Humphries, David Williamson, Fred Schepsi and Bruce Beresford – they were all doing it in Melbourne which was then considered to be both the artistic and financial capital of Australia. Yet it was in the 50's, on May 17, that the New South Wales Parliament took the pivotal decision to build, at great expense, an Opera House for Sydney. This curious decision was not taken because of public pressure – the Sydney tax-payer at the time had little or no interest in opera. Nor was it for visionary or philanthropic reasons – there wasn't much of that around at the time. No, it was more for competitive reasons.

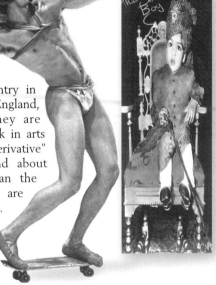

Kim Walker, with wings and skateboard, makes an unassuming entrance in Daphnis and Chloe in New York City.

"Stolen Boy" design concept by Catherine Martin for Benjamin Britten's A Midsummer Night's Dream.

Melbourne had its economic, political and cultural nose in front in rivalry stakes between the two cities. It had been announced that it had won the Olympic bid and old Joe Cahill, the then NSW Premier, was not to be overshadowed. Sydney needed an international icon and hang the expense.

The building of the Opera House was eventually paid for by a State Government-run public lottery. So had it not been for Sydney's competitive spirit and love of gambling, the Opera House may not have eventuated – a sobering thought.

It took 14 years to complete and it was a painful birth. In 1973 the opening of this now internationally acclaimed cultural icon became a turning point in the cultural growth of the city. It happened at a time when Gough Whitlam, a great patron of the arts, had become Australia's

Prime Minister. This further enhanced the confident artistic mood of the time all over Australia. However, it was the Sydney Opera House that seemed to give Sydney performers and patrons alike the confidence and permission to emerge, to become a part of the world of the arts.

Now the artistic traffic has become a two-way street. It is just as common for artists to be based in Sydney and tour Europe, Asia and America, as it is for Australians to permanently leave the country as they did in the '50s. Sydney is now exporting its culture very successfully. The Australian Opera's Baz Luhrmann's production of *A Midsummer Night's Dream* was the high point of the Edinburgh Festival in 1995. During their first New York tour, The Sydney Dance Company's Kim Walker's entrance on a skateboard in *Daphnis and Chloe* brought even the blase New York audiences to their feet. The much travelled Australian Chamber Orchestra received acclaims at the BBC Proms at the Albert Hall in London. It got standing ovations in Europe with Australian guitarist John Williams as soloist and made its North American debut at Carnegie Hall in 1993 where it now regularly appears. The Sydney Symphony Orchestra received critical acclaim in London in 1994....and so it goes on. Welcome cultural exports from what was a cultural wasteland only 40 years ago.

Is Sydney now the cultural capital of Australia? Probably – by sheer weight of enthusiastic numbers. In this chapter we will hope to give you some insight into the cultural life in Sydney, the people and the stories behind the great feast that awaits you – from dance to cabaret, from galleries to pub gigs. Grand and small, in town and out of town – enjoy the show.

> **For telephone numbers and addresses, see the yellow pages Directory at the back**

GIGS

CABARET

Although Sydney people tend to identify Robyn Archer with cabaret, her range of talents extends further – in acting, directing, writing and as an arts festival director. Judi Conelli is another cabaret-based performer who has developed into one of Sydney's great entertainers. Her wonderful portrayal of Katisha in *The Mikado* with the Australian Opera, illustrates the amazing range of her voice and breadth of her talent. A number of Sydney's leading opera singers, like Jennifer McGregor and Suzanne Johnson, started in cabaret. The new cabaret, like so many other forms of music, is crossing over into different areas. The best can be heard at places like the **Tilbury** (see Chapter 3).

JAZZ

Modern jazz got serious in Sydney when wind guru Don Burrows was appointed to the staff of the Conservatorium of Music. There are regular modern jazz concerts at the Conservatorium and the people there are probably the best starting point for you to discover the who, when and where of the Sydney contemporary jazz scene. As to trad jazz, the groundwork was laid by people like Dick Hughes, Abe Monsborough, Ken Flannery and the great Graham Jackson. It is still alive and well in Sydney, with regular gigs in the Basement in the city, and many of the pubs around town. Check *Metro* in the *Sydney Morning Herald* for details. The **Sydney Jazz Club** meets every month on beautiful little Berrys Island for a barbeque and some thumping good music. It's a great day. Call for details.

The big established Sydney names to look for in modern, trad and crossover jazz are Bill Morrison, Judy Bailey and Dale Barlow - but check out the *SMH Metro* for the younger comers.

BUSH AND A CAPPELLA

These forms of music work very much on a network basis. In other words, you have to suss about to get the information. Call the **A cappella Association.** Watch out for any concerts by The Song Company – if you like a capella, you'll love this group. Pubs like the **Tilbury** in Woolloomooloo and the **Cat and the Fiddle** in Balmain are worth watching.

There are two Bush Dances a month run by the **Bush Music Club** – the first Saturday in every month at the Beecroft Community Centre in Beecroft and the third Saturday in each month at the Glebe High School on the corner of Taylor and Pyrmont Streets, Glebe. For information about bush music, call the Bush Music Club.

BANDS

Apart from the regular big rock concerts, most bands from rock to reggae perform at the pubs around town. There are two specialist papers *On the Street* and *Beat*, which are free, and you pick them up at coffee shops and other hip places. Sometimes even from newsagents.

OPERA

Unlike the other Australian national arts company, the Australian Ballet which is based in Melbourne, the Australian Opera is based in Sydney. It is one of the largest ensemble opera companies in the world today and certainly one of the most admired. It employs a permanent artistic, technical and administration workforce of 285 people – almost all Australian. Based in Sydney, with the Sydney Opera House as its home venue, it tours Melbourne and at least one capital city each year. In 1995 that touring program included an invitation to the Edinburgh Festival where the ecstatic reception for Baz Lurhmann's production of *A Midsummer Night's Dream* further enhanced its growing reputation as one of the most innovative, yet consistent, performance companies in the world today.

There are a couple of reasons why the Australian Opera is the darling of the Sydney Arts scene. The first is that Sydney people genuinely seem to love opera, whether it is Opera in the Park or opera in the pub. This is reflected in the high ratio of ticket sales to subsidy – one of the highest in the world, much higher than La Scala or Covent Garden, and particularly impressive for a company which (unlike most opera companies in the world) performs nearly all year-round to a small population. The second reason is that the AO is very good by anybody's standards. Its yin/yang partnership of Moffatt Oxenbould, the Artistic Director and Donald McDonald, General Manager, has attracted the most outstanding talent in all branches of Australia's creative world to direct, sing and conduct: Graeme Murphy from dance; Neil Armfield from the theatre; movie-maker and creative all-rounder Baz Lurhmann; celebrated author David Malouf; cabaret singer Judi Conelli and educator Richard Gill. In addition, AO has trained up a team of exceptional young Australians both behind as well as in front of the scenery, people who are now "over there", enhancing the proscenia of the major opera companies of the world.

OZ OPERA

Oxenbould's new baby, Oz Opera, is an exciting chamber opera concept utilising interesting venues such as the Domaine Chandon "Green Point" Vineyard at Coldstream in Victoria, and performing both contemporary and historic works. Oz Opera is designed to reflect the beginnings of opera with Handel and Monteverdi, as well as creating a medium for new works and providing Australia with a smaller, more practical touring company.

The UnTourist Co's **Events Update** service can supply the details of all Australian Opera and Oz Opera programs well in advance – see the yellow pages at the back of this book.

The "boys"– Verdi's *Rigoletto*, director *Elijah Moshinsky*.

Simone Young, conductor. You read about her as "brilliant" and "outstanding"– accolades from London, Munich, Vienna, Paris, New York. Then, on her return to Australia, you hear her conduct Aida *in the Australian Opera's winter season in the the Opera House. The opening bars – you know this young woman from Manly is a knockout.*

GRASS ROOTS AND COMERS

Community culture, according to Professor Donald Horne, former chairman of the Australia Council, is being given important creative stimulus from the western suburbs of Sydney. He saw Sydney's West as a catalyst for confronting older Australian stereotypes, given the reality that one in five people have been born in non-English speaking countries and around two out of five households speak a language other than English.

The Casula Powerhouse in Casula, near Liverpool, offers a wide range of exhibition, performance and rehearsal resources, infra-structure and programs as well as an ongoing program of arts projects and programs of activities within the community.

Q Theatre It began life as a lunch-time theatre performing near Circular Quay. Now firmly established in the West in Penrith, the company now has two theatres and regularly presents a season of plays. Corner of Belmore Street and Railway Street, Penrith.

Theatre of the Deaf has developed a unique visual style making the productions accessible to all. It is the only theatre of its kind in Australia and specialises in performances for young people. The Performance Space, 199 Cleveland Street, Redfern.

Performance Space Centre for the research and development of the contemporary arts. Includes: exhibition programs – curating performance art, installation and conceptual art; gallery exhibitions; off-site projects and collaboration; conference/festival events (eg Oceania 96 - in collaboration with Casula Powerhouse and Bondi Pavilion - a celebration of art and performance by peoples of the Pacific).

Then there's: **Death Defying Theatre; Open City Inc; REM Theatre for Young People; Sidetrack Performance Group** and no doubt more to come.

MUSICA VIVA

Started 50 years ago by viola player and inventor Richard Goldner on the profits of his invention called the Triplex Fastener, Music Viva has grown to become the world's largest entrepreneur of chamber music and is one of the most successful and innovative arts organisations in the world. It manages extensive education and touring programs across the country and its artists are as distinguished as they are diverse. For Sydney concert inform-ation, see the UnTourist Co's form for its **Events Update** service (see yellow pages at the back of this book).

Synergy This exciting percussion group is part of the Musica Viva stable and gives regular concerts at the Opera House and other venues around Sydney. A memorable partnership was created with Synergy and the Sydney Dance Company in the Graeme Murphy ballet *Synergy with Synergy*.

SYDNEY SYMPHONY ORCHESTRA

"We have heard of the kangaroo – but an Orchestra!" So a Viennese taxi driver remarked to a member of the Sydney Symphony Orch-estra's entourage during their 1974 European tour. That we might have a lively arts scene seemed unlikely. In fact, it took a while to build.

The Sydney Symphony did not attract a Chief Conductor until 1946 when the Orchestra expanded to full symphonic size. It was Eugene Goossens who persuaded a new State government to set the land aside in 1954 for what was to become the site for the Sydney Opera House. By 1973 the Orchestra had several Chief Conductors and its first Sydney Opera House concerts were conducted by Willem van Otterloo, the Dutch conductor.

The first Australian to become the Sydney Symphony's Chief Conductor was Sir Charles Mackerras, who was appointed in 1982, followed by Stuart Challender who took over the Orchestra's artistic leadership in 1987 at the age of 40 and died tragically in 1994. In 1992, marking the Australian Broadcasting Corp-oration's 60th anniversary, Dutch conductor Edo da Waart made his debut with the Sydney Symphony conducting Ross Edwards' *Maniyas*. (Young Australian violinist, Dene Olding, was the soloist) and Mahler's *5th Symphony*.

The Sydney Symphony is now Australia's largest and busiest orchestra, and performs more than 150 concerts a year to an audience of more than 400,000. Performances are given through-out the year in Australia's best concert venues. The Orchestra's home is the magnif-icent Concert Hall of the Sydney Opera House – some concerts are also given in the Victorian splendour of the Sydney Town Hall. In January each year the Sydney Symphony's free outdoor *Symphony Under the Stars* concert attracts an audience of more than 80,000. Many thousands more across Australia hear and see the Sydney Symphony's performances regularly on ABC Classic FM and ABC/TV. For concert information, see the UnTourist Co's **Events Update** (yellow pages at back of this book). For full details of the Orchestra's performance call the Sydney Symphony box office or write to Sydney Symphony Bookings, GPO Box 4338, Sydney, NSW 2001.

Resident conductor, Edo da Waart, rehearsing with the Sydney Symphony Orchestra.

The Australian Chamber Orchestra, under the direction of Richard Tognetti, play follow-the-leader.

AUSTRALIAN CHAMBER ORCHESTRA

"One of the world's finest small orchestras" Washington Post, 1993.

In 1975, John Painter, founder of the ACO had a dream to form a small string orchestra operating part-time, working in much the same way as a string quartet. Now, under the auspices of Musica Viva, it operates full-time, comprising some of Australia's finest musicans, travelling nationally and globally and working in collaboration with an array of top soloists.

GALLERIES

If you want to check out galleries, you can't do much better than be guided by *Metro* in the Friday edition of the *Sydney Morning Herald..* Where else could you find out there was a giant egg yolk floating in a Centennial Park pond – part of a recent installation art series by artists associated with the Sydney College of the Arts and the Performance Space? At last count, *Metro* had 99 galleries listed, all with useful descriptions and some of the better-known regional galleries. And *Metro* is particularly helpful to newcomers to Sydney by highlighting which are the major galleries.

Our favourite major gallery happens to be the **Museum of Contemporary Art.** Of the smaller galleries, our pick is: *Annandale*, 140 Trafalgar Street, Annandale; *Australian*, 15 Roylton Street, Paddington; *Beatty*, 6 Kings Lane, Darlinghurst; *Coventry*, 56 Sutherland Street, Paddington; *Craftspace*, 88 George Street. The Rocks; *Ken Done Gallery*, 1 Hickson Road, The Rocks; *Legge*, 183 Regent Street, Redfern; *Mori*, 168 Day Street, City; *Michael Nagy*, 159 Victoria Street, Potts Point; *Olsen Carr*, 72A Windsor Street, Paddington; *Ray Hughes*, 270 Devonshire Street, Surry Hills; *Robin Gibson*, 278 Liverpool Street, Darlinghurst; *Utopia*, 50 Parramatta Road, Stanmore; *Watters*, 109 Riley Street, East Sydney.

ABORIGINAL ART

The increasing popularity of Aboriginal art has recently brought to light the traditional practice of a painting being worked on by a group, rather than always being the total work of the individual to whom the painting is formally attributed. This by no means indicates that the painting is necessarily "inauthentic" as communal collaboration is perfectly legitimate from the Aboriginal point of view. However, it is a cultural framework which runs so strongly against the Western definition of authenticity that buyers are often very confused.

This traditional practice is further complicated by the increasing number of cases of Aboriginal art fraud. To find your way through to what is an "authentic" Aboriginal painting, be sure you buy from a reputable dealer. Christopher Hodges from Utopia Art (50 Parramatta Road, Stanmore) represents the work of Australia's most famous Aboriginal painter, Emily Kngwarreye and it was he who recently alerted public galleries and the Australian Commercial Gallery Directors Association to a number of "fake" Emilys reaching the market. "Fake" in this context is paintings which are presented as hers without her input.

NOTE: There are fine collections of Aboriginal art at both the **Art Gallery of NSW** and the **MCA.** Even if they are not on show on the day of your visit, ask the curator and chances are you will be able to view them.

Graeme Murphy takes a bow.

from the University of Tasmania and in Philosophy from Queensland University. In May 1995 at 40 something, he returned to the stage to give Sydney "a high kick in the groin", as described by leading arts critic from the *Bulletin*, Brian Hoad, to star in his funny celebration of sex, *Fornicon*.

DANCE

The Sydney Dance Company is the leading dance company in Sydney and from its creative portals have come some wonder-ful dancers such as Paul Mercurio, who danced his way through Baz Lurhmann's joyful film *Strictly Ballroom*. The source of training for most of Sydney's great dancers and choreographers, be they in

No Sydneysider who loves music and the theatre could be unaware of Graeme Murphy. He has achieved National Treasure status in this city and throughout Australia, not only as an innovative. dancer, choreographer and director of both opera and ballet, but as a gentle and generous person.

Graeme was born in Melbourne and spent his younger formative years in Tasmania. It was after stints with The Australian Ballet, Sadlers Wells Royal Ballet in London and Les Ballets Felix Blaska, Grenoble France, that he took up the position in Sydney of Artistic Director of what is now called the Sydney Dance Company. It was in this environment that his most outstanding works have been developed. With virtuoso dancer Janet Vernon, his marvellous artistic partner, who he describes as *"...the backbone of my inspiration. She forces me to put my little bits of soul into dance pieces"*, he has created works for the Australian Ballet and has toured the Sydney Dance Company in Asia, the UK, Europe and the US on many occasions.

Graeme has brought his unique imagination to opera, directing four operas – Richard Strauss' *Salome*, Puccini's *Turandot*, Brian Howard's *Metamorphosis* and the massive two part production of Berlioz' *Les Troyens* – all for the Australian Opera.

He has been awarded the medal of Australia (AM) and in 1987 he was named Australian of the Year. He holds an honorary degree in Letters

traditional ballet or modern dance, has been The Australian Ballet. This expensive role as practical educator is the lot which falls on national arts companies such as the Australian Ballet and the Australian Opera and is rarely fully appreciated or reflected in terms of financial subsidy.

The Australian Ballet, a classical company, is based in Melbourne and tours to the major cities in Australia as often as finances will permit.

Paul Mercurio in Edging – *prior to dancing the fandango in the movie,* Strictly Ballroom.

Legs On The Wall *Beth Kayes and Brian Keogh. By combining circus, acrobatic skills and story-telling, the company illuminates contemporary experience with the use of physical narrative. They have performed in the desert, off freeway overpasses, at arts festivals. Although their primary interest is in making full-length, in-theatre work, they can tailor their work to any environment, any occasion. 24/142 Addison Road, Marrickville .*

THE MOVIES

The second golden age of Australian cinema started in the '70s (the first was in the silent era) and the majority of films were created or entrepreneured from Sydney. Among them: Patricia Lovell's *Picnic at Hanging Rock*, Gillian Armstrong's *My Brilliant Career* and George Miller's *Mad Max*. By the 1980s, Lovell and Peter Weir's *Gallipoli*, then Paul Hogan's *Crocodile Dundee*. The '90s brought Baz Luhrmann's *Strictly Ballroom*, Jane Campion's *The Piano* and soon after, *Priscilla, Queen of the Desert* and then George Miller's *Babe* and Baz Luhrmann's *Romeo and Juliet*. Just keep watching that screen – there's more to come. Perhaps the greatest effect that the recent establishment of the 20th Century Fox studio at Sydney's Showground will have on local film-making is that our home-grown talent will be able to work more in their own town.

From Priscilla, Queen of the Desert

THEATRE

SYDNEY THEATRE COMPANY AT THE WHARF

"As an actor, a more perfect performing arts complex is impossible to imagine. To be able to take a break from the rigours of rehearsals and choose between a light snack to replenish, or a hearty dinner at the end of the day in the Wharf Restaurant; to be able to wander into the workshop, and see your set under construction.... to be able to rehearse on your set and perform a season of a play in a world class theatre – all under the one roof, is truly, truly a marvel." Thus spake Ruth Cracknell, undisputed queen of Sydney Theatre and inaugural patron of the Sydney Theatre Company's performing space at the Walsh Bay Wharf which gives as much pleasure to the performers as it does to the patrons. The Sydney Theatre Company performs works from a classic repertoire, including Australian Plays by leading playwrights like David Williamson. The Company also performs in the drama theatre at the Opera House.

COMPANY B AT THE BELVOIR THEATRE

In 1984 Chris Westward made more phone calls in one night than she is ever likely to make again. Her "baby", the Belvoir Theatre, which she had been nurturing as director for six years, had lost its government funding. In that long, hard night, Chris summoned up a list of new patrons that read like a Who's Who in the arts: *Robyn Archer, Neil Armfield, Gillian Armstrong, Peter Carey, Ruth Cracknell, Judy Davis, Mel Gibson, Max Gillies, David Williamson, Dorothy Hewitt, Nicole Kidman, Sam Neal, Dame Joan Sutherland, and the estate of the late Patrick White.*

With their help, Chris saved the theatre, and then moved on to a post as artistic director of the Adelaide Arts Festival. She left the Belvoir in good hands. **Company B** which is based at the Belvoir, is a new star of Sydney theatre and is now under the innovative direction of Neil Armfield whose talents are divided between the Australian Opera and Company B.

"One of the problems of Australian theatre" said Armfield, *"is that we are trying to address the lack of inspiring traditions on our stages; that productions are made for consumption and disposal, and this 'quick turn around' syndrome means that roots never really take, and that nothing lasting ever grows. Great plays, performances and productions disappear from*

Jacqueline McKenzie as Ophelia *in* Hamlet

memory because the actors are hired for three months then disperse: what is being discovered is constantly being lost. We want to revive such productions and keep them alive. That is how traditions will form."

With this as the basis of the Belvoir philosophy, it means that delighted audiences have the opportunity to see again, for example, the inspiring *Hamlet* which was the turning point for both the company and its audience. American actor Steve Martin has been thought of as a B grade funny man. However, his talent as a playwright changed that preconception forever at the world premiere of his witty, beautifully crafted play *"Picasso at the Lapin Agile"* which took place at the Belvoir in 1995. It is now part of their permanent repertoire.

THE GRIFFIN AT THE STABLES.

"This tiny theatre which began life as the Nimrod, and is now home to the GriffinTheatre Company, has a special place in the affections of Sydney theatre-goers and in the history of the development of professional theatre in the City" Leo Schofield, culture guru and bicycle enthusiast (see Chapter 10) *Sydney Morning Herald* August 14, 1993.

The Griffin Theatre Company has more than filled the gap that existed for a serious "new product development" company in Sydney. The company has consistently nurtured and promoted new Australian works and many successful Australian plays have been first performed at their charming little 120 years old theatre in Kings Cross.

The Griffin is now accepted as a hothouse for the best of the new Aust-ralian plays and players. Because the works are fresh and challenging, the company is luring top young actors away from the more traditional playhouses, as well as from film and television. Its artistic manifesto under the direction of Ros Horin is to present top quality productions of new Australian writing which are unashamedly at the cutting edge – breaking new ground in form as well as content. Ros Horin, who took over as artistic director in 1992, has a reputation for making great things happen.

Moment Musical

Ravel's Bolero

PUBLICATIONS

There are many specialist arts and show magazines in most newsagents, and the *Sydney Morning Herald* and its Friday *Metro* lift-out are essential reading. There are, however, some other publications and information sources that we believe deserve special attention:

• **Oz Arts** It is more than a magazine – it is more a quarterly glossy, full-colour book which covers all forms of arts and innovative culture in Australia. It is produced in Sydney by Dr Carolyn Skinner and will introduce you to the best. Available at most newsagents for around $14.

• **ArtsWest** It is a more modest publication but is stacked with information about the new grass-roots art scene in the West of Sydney. ArtsWest is a subscription magazine under the enthusiastic and knowledgable editorship of Katherine Knight – her phone, fax and address are in our Directory.

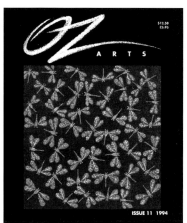

• **Sydney Review** A free magazine which you will often find at newsagents and at museums you may be visiting.

• **24 Hours** is published by the Australian Broadcasting Corp-oration and gives you all radio program details, plus good insider stuff on the arts generally. You can pick it up at newsagents or the ABC shops. Even if you don't have a radio, it's worth getting for Don Fish's drawings.

• **UnTourist Events Update** How often have you arrived in a city for short visit and found out too late that a great performance is on but totally booked out? The UnTourist Co can supply you with advance program details (and booking information) for most of the arts and shows in Sydney at the time of your visit. This way you can avoid disappointment by booking ahead. *See yellow pages at the back of this book for how to get your Events Update.*

ARTS EVENTS CALENDAR

JANUARY

Event	Location	Phone
Midsummer Night's Dream	Royal Botanic Gardens (C)	9968 3442
Mostly Mozart	Opera House (C)	9250 7777
Opera In The Park	Sydney City (C)	9265 0444
Shakespeare by the Sea	Balmoral (N)	9557 3065
Steward of Christendom	Chippendale (C)	9266 4828
Summer Nights with the Sydney Symphony Orchestra	Sydney City (C)	9264 9466
Sydney Festival	Sydney City (C)	9265 0444
Sydney Writers' Festival	Sydney City (C)	9230 1605
Symphony Under The Stars	Sydney City (C)	9265 0444

FEBRUARY

Event	Location	Phone
Great Performers Series	Opera House (C)	9264 9466
Moet & Chandon Art Prize	Sydney City (C)	9255 1744
Sydney Symphony Orchestra	Sydney Town Hall (C)	9265 9189

MARCH

Event	Location	Phone
20th Century Orchestra	Sydney City (C)	9266 4800
Great Classics Series	Opera House (C)	9250 7777
Philips Master Series	Opera House (C)	9264 9466
Philips Mozart Master Series	Opera House (C)	9333 1615

APRIL

Event	Location	Phone
Archibald, Wynne & Sulman Exhibition	Sydney City (C)	9225 1800
Great Classics Series	Opera House (C)	9250 7777

Event	Location	Phone
Sydney International Piano Competition	Sydney City (C)	9230 1234
Winter Coffee Concerts	Opera House (C)	9250 7406

AUGUST

Event	Location	Phone
Great Classics Series	Opera House (C)	9250 7777
Meet the Music Series	Opera House (C)	9250 7777
Musica Viva	Sydney Town Hall (C)	9250 7777
Otello	Opera House (C)	9250 7777
Philips Master Series	Opera House (C)	9264 9466
Philips Mozart Master Series	Opera House (C)	9250 7777
Piano Series	Sydney City (C)	9264 9466
Sydney Rock Eisteddfod	Haymarket (C)	9266 4800
Tea and Sympathy Series	Opera House (C)	9250 7777
World Symposium of Choral Music and World Choirs Festival	Sydney City (C)	9363 9499

SEPTEMBER

Event	Location	Phone
Aust. Chamber Orchestra	Opera House (C)	9250 7777
Australia Ensemble	Kensington (S)	9285 4871
City Festival of Arts	Fairfield (W)	9725 5546
Cowpastures Bush Music Fest	Camden (W)	9876 6667
Ensemble Theatre Performances	Milsons Point (N)	9929 0644
Great Performers Orchestra Series	Opera House (C)	9264 9466
Manly Jazz Festival	Manly (N)	9905 4070
Meet the Music Series	Opera House (C)	9250 7777
Musica Viva performances	Opera House (C)	9250 7777

Event	Venue	Phone
Philips Mozart Master Series	Opera House (C)	9333 1615
Piano Series	Sydney City (C)	9264 9466

MAY

Event	Venue	Phone
20th Century Orchestra	Sydney City (C)	9266 4800
Australian B & W artists	Sydney City (C)	9230 1566
Meet the Music Series	Opera House (C)	9250 7777
Philips Master Series	Opera House (C)	9264 9466
Piano Series	Sydney City (C)	9264 9466

JUNE

Event	Venue	Phone
Great Classics Series	Opera House (C)	9250 7777
Great Performers Series	Opera House (C)	9264 9466
International Music Festival	Sydney City (C)	9310 2125
Meet the Music Series	Opera House (C)	9250 7777
Philips Master Series	Opera House (C)	9264 9466
Philips Mozart Master Series	Opera House (C)	9250 7777
Sydney Film Festival	Sydney City (C)	9660 3844

JULY

Event	Venue	Phone
Aboriginal Week	Sydney City (C)	9211 3555
Australian Book Fair	Darling Harbour (C)	9977 0888
Biennale (even years)	Sydney City (C)	9368 1411
Great Classics Series	Opera House (C)	9250 7777
Great Performers Series	Opera House (C)	9264 9466
Philips Master Series	Opera House (C)	9264 9466
Philips Mozart Master Series	Opera House (C)	9250 7777
Stuart Challender Trust	Opera House (C)	9350 7777

Event	Venue	Phone
Puppeteers' Picnic	The Rocks (C)	9755 2586
St. Stephen's Monday Music	City (C)	9221 1688
Sydney Philharmonia Choirs	Opera House (C)	9251 2024
Young Artists	The Rocks (C)	9252 4033

OCTOBER

Event	Venue	Phone
20th Century Orchestra	Sydney City (C)	9266 4800
Great Classics Series	Opera House (C)	9250 7777
Musica Viva	Seymour Centre (C)	9250 7888
Philips Master Series	Opera House (C)	9264 9466
Philips Mozart Master Series	Opera House (C)	9333 1615

NOVEMBER

Event	Venue	Phone
Annual Gala Benefit Concert	Opera House (C)	9250 7777
Great Classics Series	Opera House (C)	9250 7777
Great Performers Series	Opera House (C)	9264 9466
Jazz	Vaucluse House (E)	9692 8366
Philips Master Series	Opera House (C)	9264 9466
Philips Mozart Master Series	Opera House (C)	9333 1615
Piano Series	Sydney City (C)	9264 9466

DECEMBER

Event	Venue	Phone
Australian Watercolour Institute's Exhibition	Sydney City (C)	9258 0172
Carols in the Park	Castle Hill (W)	9634 2412
Christmas at the Opera House	Opera House (C)	9250 7777
Messiah	Opera House (C)	9266 4800
New Year's Eve Gala	Opera House (C)	9250 7777

13 GETTING AROUND

INCLUDES: *How the transport system around sprawling Sydney works: the water taxis, the ferries, big and little, the different ways to get around, whether by bicycle, motor bike, by foot. Information on buses trains, cars, parking, shuttle services. With emphasis on how to use the harbour highway to best advantage*

Loco No. 1 *doesn't get around much anymore, but in 1863 she hauled NSW's first train from Sydney to Parramatta. The journey and the original steam train are perfectly displayed at the* Powerhouse Museum *(see chapter 2).*

Giving the Destination Heart

Like meditation, the journey can be the goal – or as travel writer Paul Theroux recognised early on in his writings:

"The way you choose to travel can transform the place you're going to." "It is the journey" he said, "that gives the destination heart."

Public transport generally doesn't work quite as well in an extremely large, sprawling, undulating city like Sydney as it does in a more tightly packed urban environment such as New York or London.

Sydneysiders appear to be totally committed to the use and personal independence of the motor car with all its accruing facilities – good roads, city parking, etc – but there is also a constant clamour for improved public transport. In other words, as its Lord Mayor has stated: "Sydney hasn't made up its mind whether it wants to be a car city like Los Angeles or a public transport city like London." Right now they are having difficulties with both, and getting around Sydney can be a trap for the unwary – hence our advice:

Go by water if you can. Take a ferry or a water taxi or beg, borrow or hire a boat – but see as much of Sydney as possible from the water

Sydney is a water city. Over 80% of its suburbs have access to water. To get the best out of Sydney, therefore, use water whenever you can. Obviously this can't be done for the shop-hop to here and there, but when you have the time and you are planning a Sydney experience, don't let traffic jams, the difficulty of getting a cab, or having to drive around for half an hour trying to park your car spoil what could be a great day.

We suggest you plan your day with the foibles of Sydney transport in mind and, if you can organise it, go by water where you have a choice of ferries, water taxis or hiring your own boat and doing a bit of water exploring yourself.

Despite all this, Sydney has a fairly good public transport system comprised of trains, buses and ferries. In fact, we think the public ferry service is the best in the world.

Some old-timers mourn the passing of the trams, which are still operating in Melbourne and are part of its folklore. The old saying "he shot through like a Bondi tram", no longer applies to Sydney, alas.

FERRIES

The harbour ferries, Rivercats and Jetcats depart **Circular Quay,** located city centre in Sydney Cove, between The Rocks and the Opera House. **The Sydney Ferries Information Centre** is opposite **Jetty 4** at Circular Quay. For all information about the State Transit Sydney Ferry Services, call the Public Transport Information Line 6am-10pm daily, Tel 13 15 00.

Circular Quay is the heart of the harbour and has been home to the ferries since 1861. It also houses a train station and allows visitors easy access to interconnecting travel on all forms of public transport. Ferry services cover most of Sydney Harbour in an easterly direction and call at 28 destinations. **Jetty 2** is located on the eastern side of Circular Quay (the Opera House) with **Jetty 6** on the western side (The Rocks). Principal services operate between 6am and 11.30pm and depart as follows:

Jetty 2   **Jet Cat** to Manly (Departs every 30 minutes – takes 15 minutes)
Ferry to Taronga Park Zoo (Departs every half-hour – takes 12 minutes)

Jetty 3   **Ferry** to Manly (Departs every 30 minutes – takes 30 minutes)

Jetty 4   **Ferry** to Mosman via Cremorne Point, Musgrave Street Mosman and old Cremorne (Departs every 30 minutes Mon-Sat, hourly on Sun . The journey takes 18 minutes)
Ferry to Neutral Bay via Kirribilli (Departs every 30 minutes Mon to

Sat, every two hours Sun – takes 15 minutes)
Ferry to Rose Bay (Departs 7.15am-9.35am and 1.30pm-7.05pm weekday peak hours only – takes 20 minutes)
Ferry to Watsons Bay via Taronga Park Zoo (Departs 9.25am, 10.55am, 12.55pm, 2.30pm, 4pm and 5.30pm Sat, Sun and public holidays – takes 35 minutes)

Jetty 5 **Ferry** to Meadowbank via McMahons Point, Milsons Point, Drummoyne, Gladesville, Chiswick and Abbotsford (Departs every 50 minutes – takes 45 minutes)
Ferry to Darling Harbour via Luna Park (Departs every 30 minutes – takes 25 minutes)
Ferry to Balmain (Departs every 30 minutes Mon to Sat, every two hours Sun – takes 10 minutes)
Ferry to Hunters Hill via (Luna Park after 6.30pm) Birchgrove, Greenwich and Cockatoo Island (Departs hourly Mon to Sat, every two hours Sun – takes 15 minutes)
River Cat to Parramatta via McMahons Point, Drummoyne, Gladesville, Abbotsford, Meadowbank and Rydalmere (Departs nine times Mon-Fri, 11 times Sat, 15 times Sun – takes 60 minutes)

A private ferry service, **Hegarty's Ferries** (Tel 9206 1167) also operates from Circular Quay as follows:

Jetty 6 **Ferry** to Kirribilli via Luna Park, Lavender Bay, McMahons Point (Departs at irregular intervals every day – takes 10-25 minutes depending on the service)

State Transit tickets are not valid on privately operated ferries. Fares for Hegarty's Ferries are payable at Jetty 6. Tokens can be bought from Circular Quay. Between-wharf transfers are payable on board.

Most harbour cruises depart from Jetty 6

Payment for ferries is made at Circular Quay (on departure or arrival) or on board, if necessary. The State Transit Authority offers special travel passes for families and individuals, covering return ferry travel from Circular Quay and admission to attractions. Jetcats and Rivercats are slightly more expensive than ferries. Tickets are presented to automatic turnstiles at the entry to the jetty at Circular Quay and Manly.

A SydneyPass is also available, giving access to the Airport Express Bus, the Sydney Explorer Bus, the Bondi & Bay Explorer, the three sightseeing cruises operated by the State Transit Authority, and unlimited travel on all Sydney buses and harbour ferries. (Most ferry services have a connecting bus service.) A Sydney Pass is available for three, five or seven days of consecutive travel and can be bought at Sydney Airport, Circular Quay, the Queen Victoria Building, some travel agents and the New South Wales Travel Centre, open weekdays, 9am-5pm, 19 Castlereagh Street, Tel 9231 4444.

LOST PROPERTY

Property lost on Sydney ferries is kept at Jetty 5, Circular Quay, Tel 9256 4656.

INFOLINE – TTY

Telephone typewriter directory service for the deaf or people with impaired speech, Tel 1800 637 500.

BUSES

For all information about the Urban Transit Sydney Bus Services, call the Public Transport Information Line, daily from 6am-10pm, Tel 13 15 00.

Sydney has an extensive network of blue and white buses connecting all the inner suburbs with the city centre. Although slow compared with trains, especially in rush hour, there are some areas of Sydney where buses are the main form of connecting public transport – for example, Bondi Beach in the east and Palm Beach in the north.

Terminals for the buses are at **Wynyard Park** on York Street, **Town Hall** on George Street,

Central Railway Station and **Circular Quay,** where they connect with the trains and ferries. Most buses going north leave from York and Wynyard and those going south, west and east depart from Circular Quay and Town Hall. The fares are measured in sections and charged according to the number of sections to be travelled. Tickets are bought from the driver. A child's fare applies to those who are 15 years of age and under. Children are free of charge if under 4 years of age.

For route information see the front of the A-K Sydney Telephone Directory or pick up a free transit guide and timetables from State Transit sales outlets at Loftus Street, Circular Quay, Carrington Street, Wynyard or the Queen Victoria Building in the city, or at the Bondi Junction Interchange, Manly Wharf or any State Transit Depot.

SPECIAL BUS SERVICES

Urban Transit runs regular red and blue bus services to key stops in the city and suburbs – see Chapter 10.

THE AIRPORT EXPRESS BUS SYDNEY – ROUTES 300 AND 350

A fast and comfortable Urban Transit Authority service provides an uncomplicated link with the city for visitors arriving at, or leaving from, Mascot airport. The yellow and green airport express bus runs daily, every ten minutes, to and from the city and takes fifteen to thirty minutes, depending on the pick-up and set-down location.

Route 300 is from the airport to Circular Quay and return and Route 350 transports passengers from the airport to Kings Cross and return. The buses run between both the international and domestic terminals at Mascot. There is a return ticket valid for two months available. The service operates from 5.30am-9.30pm from the city, from 4.50am-9.50pm from Kings Cross and from 5.55am from the airport. No bookings are required and passengers can embark at any of the departure points along the route. Just look for the Airport Express sign and buy a ticket on board.

Following are pick-up and set-down points for the Airport Express:

ROUTE 300 AND 350:

  International Terminal (2 stops)
  Qantas Jet Base – Sydney Airport
  Domestic Terminal (2 stops)
  Tenth Street
  Qantas Centre

ROUTE 300

Set-down stops:
  Central Railway Station
  Chinatown
  Town Hall Station
  Queen Victoria Building
  Corner George and King Streets
  Wynyard Station
  Bridge Street
  Macquarie Place

Pick-up and set-down stops:
  Inter-Continental
  Circular Quay
  The Rocks
  Harbour Rocks
  The Regent

Pick-up stops:
  George Street opposite Grosvenor Street
  Corner George and Hunter Streets, Wynyard
  Strand Arcade
  Hilton Hotel
  Sydney Electricity, Town Hall
  World Square
  Corner George and Goulburn Streets
  Haymarket

ROUTE 350

Set-down stops:
  Central Railway Station
  Corner Elizabeth and Goulburn Streets
  Hyde Park
  Park Ridge Apartments on Oxford Street
  Greyhound/Pioneer Terminal
  Supreme Court, Taylor Square
  St. Vincent's Hospital
  Corner Darlinghurst and William Streets

Pick-up and set-down stops:
  Kings Cross Railway
  Victoria Street Backpackers
  Challis Avenue
  Macleay Avenue
  Greenknowe Avenue
  Manhattan Hotel
  Roslyn Gardens
  Elizabeth Bay
  Sebel Town House Hotel
  Seventeen Elizabeth Bay Road
  Madison's Hotel
  Bayswater Road

Pick-up stops:
  Top of the Cross
  Corner Victoria and Liverpool Streets
  Taylor Square
  Corner Oxford and Riley Streets

Corner Oxford and Brisbane Streets
The Southern Cross
CB and Westend Hotels

After 9pm the Airport Express becomes a combined City and Kings Cross service. Certain stops are not used after this time and passengers wishing to take the Airport Express should check pick-up locations.

PRIVATE AIRPORT BUS SERVICE

A private bus service operates between Kings Cross, the City, Glebe and Darling Harbour. Bookings to the airport are essential (three hours notice is required), with the first bus available from 5.30am and the last at 8pm. Pick-ups are *only* available *from* a motel, hotel or hostel in these areas. The same service operates from the airport, from 6am, departing every twenty or thirty minutes until the arrival of the last flight at night. The driver will drop visitors in any of the areas listed above, at *any* location, including a motel, hotel or hostel. A small flat fee is charged. Reservations and further enquiries, Tel 9667 3221/0663.

LOST PROPERTY

Property mislaid on bus services will be kept at the depot from which the bus operates. For contact numbers of lost property office see the listing "Sydney Buses" in the L-Z section of the Sydney White Pages.

INFOLINE – TTY

Telephone typewriter directory service for the deaf or people with impaired speech, Tel 1800 637 500.

TRAINS

The rail system has been largely set up to give an efficient, fast and frequent service to Sydney's commuters, connecting the suburbs to the city. The rail service in Sydney is known as CityRail. For all information about CityRail, call 6am-10pm daily, Tel 13 15 00.

From the north, trains cross the Harbour Bridge and come into Central Station via Circular Quay. However, certain areas of the north (Manly to Palm Beach) are not serviced by the railway. The eastern train service comes into Martin Place linking Kings Cross and Bondi Junction. Note – Bondi and its beaches are not connected to any rail service; however, there is a direct rail service to Cronulla Beach.

In the south there is a line linking Sutherland and Cronulla. In the west the lines go to Parramatta, Liverpool and Bankstown. Most suburban trains stop at Central Station. Circular Quay is a terminal for connecting buses or ferries.

The most useful line for getting around in the centre of Sydney is the City Circle which joins up the city. This stops at Central Station, Town Hall on George Street, Wynyard on York Street, Circular Quay, St James, the northern end of Hyde Park and the Australian Museum at the southern end. This line offers a quick way of travelling around the city. A ticket must be bought prior to travel and single and return and pensioner tickets are available for the day of issue only. Tickets are valid to and from the stations requested, and can be bought right through to the final destination, even if changing trains or lines. Tickets are not, however, valid for travel further than the destination printed on the ticket. Weekly and longer-term tickets, bought in advance, are also available and offer a range of concessions.

Off-peak return tickets are excellent value, with fares that are only slightly more expensive than a one-way ticket. When travelling off-peak, journeys must start after 9am, Mon-Fri or take place at the weekends.

CITYHOPPER

A CityHopper provides the quickest and most economical way of travelling in Sydney. Journeys must be started after 9am on weekdays or take place at the weekend or on public holidays. An unlimited travel ticket on the city circle line, the line over the Harbour Bridge to North Sydney and the line to Kings Cross is available on a CityHopper.

EASY ACCESS

CityRail is providing a network of 33 Easy Access stations featuring lifts, ramps, help points, hearing loops, continuous handrails, additional lighting and special signage.

Many stations are accessible to passengers in wheelchairs. Passengers are advised to telephone their departure station in advance as staff assistance can be arranged. Free rail, bus and ferry travel are available to visually impaired persons and their Seeing Eye or Hearing Dog. For further information, Tel 9224 4615. An Easy Access brochure, listing all facilities and stations, is available from CityRail and State Transit outlets.

LOST PROPERTY

Property mislaid on train services will be sent to the lost property office at Central Station. It generally takes about four days for items to reach the office. For further information, Tel 9219 4397/4757.

INFOLINE – TTY

Telephone typewriter directory service for the deaf or people with impaired speech, Tel 1800 637 500.

THE MONORAIL

Sydney's link between Darling Harbour and the city centre. Trains run from early morning to late at night (Sun 8pm) every three to four minutes over a 3.6 kilometre circuit that takes twelve minutes and has six stops. Two stations are located at Darling Harbour – the Harbourside Market Place for shopping, Convention Square for the Convention Centre and the Sydney Exhibition Centre. Another station is located at Haymarket, conveniently near the Sydney Entertainment Centre and the Powerhouse Museum. Travelling further on, you come to World Square, Park Plaza, for city trains and bus passengers, City Centre and then back to Darling Harbour.

Entry is by token, bought from machines, or an "All Day Pass" on sale at any Monorail Station, which is valid for one day, between 9am-7pm, allowing visitors to hop on and off as many times as they wish. Operating hours (subject to change): WINTER Mon-Wed 7am-9pm; Thurs-Sat 7am-Midnight; SUMMER Mon-Sat 7am-Midnight; Sun 8am-9pm. For more information, Tel 9552 2288.

TRAVEL DEALS

For all information about Urban Transit and State Transit travel passes, call between 6am-10pm, Tel 13 15 00.

The State Transit Authority and Urban Transit Authority offer the following travel passes, all of which can be bought at State Transit Sales Outlets, some newsagents and travel agents.

TRAVELTEN – valid for ten trips on Sydney buses. There are five different adult and concession categories: blue, red, green, orange and purple. You buy the colour according to the distance you wish to travel. **Blue** TravelTen is the pass you need if you only intend travelling a short distance. **Red** will allow you to travel 3-9 sections, **green** 10-15 sections, **orange** 16-21 sections and **purple** 22-27 sections. There are no time limits on TravelTen and it offers savings for both adults and children, and on student concession fares.

FERRYTEN – ten adult or concession trips on the ferries. Separate FerryTens are available for the JetCat, Manly Ferry, Inner Harbour services and Parramatta RiverCat. You save 40% and there is no expiry date for travel – just go at your leisure.

SYDNEYPASS – gives access to the Airport Express Bus, the Sydney Explorer Bus, the Bondi & Bay Explorer, the three sightseeing cruises operated by the State Transit Authority, and unlimited travel on all Sydney buses and harbour ferries. Most ferry services have a connecting bus service. A SydneyPass is available for three, five or seven days of consecutive travel and can be bought at Sydney Airport, Circular Quay, the Queen Victoria Building, some travel agents and the New South Wales Travel Centre open weekdays 9am-5pm, 19 Castlereagh Street, Tel 9231 4444.

NOTE: the return portion to the airport on the Airport Express Bus on a SydneyPass is available for *two* months.

TRAVELPASS – a weekly, quarterly or yearly ticket that allows you unlimited travel on the buses, ferries and trains. Buy the colour according to the distance and form of travel. **Red, green, yellow, pink, brown** or **purple** passes are for the buses ferries and trains. **Blue, orange** or **Pittwater** passes are for buses and ferries and a **two zone** TravelPass is for bus travel in two adjacent city zones or between the northern beaches and Pittwater.

A useful tip for a seven day TravelPass is to start your travel after 3pm on the first day. It will then be valid until midnight seven days later. If travel is started before 3pm the seven day TravelPass will expire at midnight six days later.

CONCESSION TRAVELPASS – available for seven days to any adult or full-time student with the appropriate concession card. These include Disabled Persons ID Card, Pensioner (NSW/Vic) Concession Card, School Pupil Railways of Australia ID Card, Seniors Card (NSW), Student NSW ID Card, Student Railways of Australia ID Card (NSW) and War Widow Concession Card (NSW/Vic). School children under 16 years of age are also entitled to the Concession TravelPass.

CITYHOPPER – provides the quickest and most economical way of travelling around Sydney. Journeys must be started after 9am on weekdays or take place at the weekend or on public holidays. All day travel offered on a CityHopper is cheap and includes the six stations around the city, the Harbour Bridge to

North Sydney and Kings Cross.

OFF-PEAK TRAVEL – saves up to 45% of the normal fare if you travel after 9am or at the weekends or on public holidays. Off-peak travel covers all areas of CityRail's network, which stretches over 300 kilometres to the north, and includes the south coast and the Blue Mountains in the west.

LUNAPASS – the all-in-one ticket that includes a return ferry trip to Luna Park plus bonus points to Luna Park's famous rides.

ZOOPASS – includes return ferry and bus, and Zoo admission, from Circular Quay.

AQUARIUM PASS – a combined return ferry and entry to Sydney Aquarium.

OCEANPASS – of particular interest to families, giving return ferry travel to Manly and entry into Oceanworld.

SYDNEY EXPLORER – running every twenty minutes, the Sydney Explorer links 26 points of interest. The journey lasts about one and three quarter hours. Visitors can hop off and explore any of the destinations and then rejoin the next available service.

BONDI & BAY EXPLORER – operating every thirty minutes, has twenty stops around Sydney Harbour and the eastern bayside suburbs. Like the Sydney Explorer, visitors can get on and off at any of the destinations and then catch the next available service.

TWIN TWO-DAY EXPLORER TICKET – valid for two consecutive days, travel on the Sydney Explorer one day and the Bondi & Bay Explorer the next.

HARBOUR CRUISE - the ticket offering the option of two day-time cruises – the River Cruise in the morning and the Harbour Cruise in the afternoon – or one evening cruise, to experience the harbour by night.

BUSTRIPPER – an all-day bus ticket that allows you to travel as far as you wish on as many buses as you like for a day. It's a great ticket for shopping or just going where you want. The BusTripper is not available for travel on the Sydney Explorer, Bondi & Bay Explorer, Airport Express or with private bus companies

DAYPASS – an all-day ticket allowing travel as far as you like on both bus and ferry services. This is the pass that can take you all round Sydney. The DayPass must be pre-bought and is valid from start of travel.

CHILDREN'S FARES – under the age of four children travel free of charge on all public transport. Children 15 years and under travel for 50% of the adult fare.

Other travel passes issued by private companies are:

ALL DAY PASS – valid for one day, between 9am-7pm, the All Day Monorail Pass allows visitors to travel above the traffic between Darling Harbour and the city, hopping on and off as many times as they wish. Available from any Monorail Station. For more information, Tel 9552 2288.

PRIVILEGES CARD – admission to museums for two adults for the price of one, savings of up to 50% at a range of popular restaurants; savings on tours; harbour cruises and car rental and low cost entry to leading city cinemas; city parking; film processing; bike hire and balloon flights. On sale at NSW Travel Centre, 19 Castlereagh Street, Sydney, Tel 9231 4444.

THE ROCKS TICKET – includes admission to three attractions, a walking tour, a meal and a cruise around Sydney Harbour. The ticket can be used consecutively or on separate occasions. On sale at The Rocks Visitors Centre, 106 George Street, The Rocks, Tel 9255 1700.

LOST PROPERTY

Property mislaid on bus services will be kept at the depot from which the bus operates. For contact numbers of lost property office see the listing "Sydney Buses" in the L-Z section of the Sydney White Pages.

For property lost on Sydney Ferries, Tel 9256 4656.

For property lost on CityRail, Tel 9219 4397/4757.

INFOLINE – TTY

Telephone typewriter directory for the deaf or people with impaired speech, Tel 1800 637 500.

TAXIS

Sydney has an excellent network of taxis which can be booked, found at a rank, or waved down in the street. Like most cities, a difficult time to get hold of a taxi is when it's raining and during peak hours. There is also the Sydney 3pm horror time – when the drivers all change their shifts at the same time. Ridiculous, but true!

All taxis are metered and fares are reasonably priced. An hour's journey from Palm Beach to the airport would cost approximately $50-60 and the fifteen minute journey from the city to the airport about $15, depending on the time of day and weather conditions. Taxi drivers for the most part are friendly and honest, and their nationalities reflect a cosmopolitan society.

Taxis are licensed to carry four people at any one time. A surcharge for excess baggage, telephone bookings and Harbour Bridge or Tunnel tolls can be charged at the discretion of the company.

There are many ranks throughout Sydney as well as ranks located outside, or near, major hotels, railway stations and bus terminals. Most taxis are air-conditioned and many are non-smoking although a passenger can often "light up", on request.

Payment by change or small notes is appreciated by a driver, with some of the companies accepting credit cards. Tipping is also appreciated, but not mandatory. No abuse will be hurled if a visitor considers a tip inappropriate, but rounding the payment to the nearest dollar is probably the thing to do.

Wheelchair accessible taxis for the disabled are available, Tel 9339 0200.

WATER TAXIS

Although more expensive than the normal taxi, this is a speedy and exhilarating way to travel from one point to another across the harbour.

An example of prices for four people from Circular Quay to Watsons Bay is around $50, to Darling Harbour about $40 and Kirribilli around $35. Major credit cards are generally accepted on board and personalised services are offered to suit individual needs.

Water taxis operate 24 hours a day and can be the ideal method of getting to, or from, one of the many harbourside restaurants. Ask in advance what the fare will be.

DRIVING

As in most big cities, driving can be frustrating, nerve racking and confusing, particularly during peak hour traffic in central Sydney, which should be avoided at all cost. Sydneysiders are intolerant on the road, and even they find it easy to get lost in the challenging and irregular inner city road layout which stems from colonial days.

Main access to the city centre from the north is via the Harbour Bridge or the Harbour Tunnel. When using the Bridge or Tunnel, travelling either north or south, motorists should take care in the selection of their lane, as changing lanes can be dangerous, and sometimes impossible. The choice of a wrong lane can result in visitors arriving a long way from their intended destination.

There is a toll fee of $2 for both the Harbour Bridge and the Tunnel, paid by southbound motorists. Each lane provides automatic and manual toll booths. The automatic booths accept 10, 20, and 50 cent pieces, $1 and $2 coins (you just throw them in a basket). No change is given at the automatic booths, so the correct change is essential.

Two main roads service the north, via the Harbour Bridge and Tunnel – the Pacific Highway (1) to Hornsby and the Pittwater Road (14) to Manly, the northern beaches and Palm Beach. To the south there is the Anzac Parade (70) to La Perouse, South Darling Street (64) to the airport and the Princes Highway (1) to Sutherland. The principal roads in the east are New South Head Road (70) to Watsons Bay and Oxford Street joining the Bondi Road to Bondi. In the west the main exits are, to the north west, the Parramatta Road (44) which joins the Great Western Highway and to the south west, the Hume Highway (31).

The NRMA (National Roads & Motorists Association) has an invaluable road service assisting its members in every kind of emergency. It is highly recommended for motoring visitors staying any length of time to become an NRMA member. The cost is very reasonable and it's well worth it, knowing an NRMA saint will save you. The NRMA has reciprocal arrangements with other interstate associations and with some parallel organisations overseas. The NRMA can be contacted for further information on Tel 13 21 32, for a road service call on Tel 13 11 11, for emergency help and expert advice on Tel 13 29 00, or at their head office, 151 Clarence Street, Sydney, Tel 9260 9222.

The minimum age for an Australian to drive in New South Wales is 17. A new driver is a given a probationary licence for a year, (represented by a "P" sign on the back and front of their vehicle) before graduating to a fully fledged licence. Overseas visitors can drive in New South Wales on their domestic licence for six months, but will need to take a test for a NSW licence should they stay longer.

Driving is on the left-hand side of the road. Speed limits in most areas of Sydney are 60km/h (the speed permitted in a built-up zone) unless otherwise indicated (on a freeway or faster road), where speed can increase up to 110km/h. Seat belts must be worn at all times in the front and back of cars and babies must be transported in approved safety carriers. The driver is responsible for all passengers and their safety. Most garages are self-service, although willing help is generally on hand, should it be required.

A word of warning: the laws in New South Wales are extremely strict regarding drink driving and all roads in Sydney are well monitored by the police, with random breath tests carried out. The alcohol limit is 0.05%. If in doubt, please don't risk it; go by public transport or call a taxi.

CAR RENTALS

Sydney is well represented by all the major rental companies, as well as a number of smaller operators. The major companies have offices located at the airport and throughout Sydney with their city offices centred on or around William Street. Prices are difficult to quote as they fluctuate according to the time of year, the car and the specials being offered.

There is often a minimum age for drivers of 21, but, depending on the company and the car, this can vary from 21 up to 25 years of age. Some restrictions may also apply to drivers over the age of 60. Insurances vary from company to company. Exact coverage should be checked. Never assume that coverage is automatic or included in the price.

Rentals for all occasions and requirements,

from Chauffeur Driven Limousines, Mini Buses, Utes to Animal Vehicles, Caravans and "Wrecks and Ruffies" are available. If you require one of these out of the ordinary services, or for that matter prefer a smaller car rental operator, good advice is to consult the Yellow Pages of the Sydney Telephone Directory.

PARKING

Parking in the city can be both difficult and costly as most streets have time zones and parking is controlled by metres. Fines can be heavy if you overstay your welcome. Sydney is nevertheless well equipped by Wilson Parking, which has parking stations located throughout the city and its congested suburbs.

A special "Earlybird Parking" is available at most of their carparks, offering discounts to vehicles entering between 7am-9.30am and exiting between 3pm-7pm. Rates vary between for the day. Credit card payment is welcome at many of the carparks and nearly all stations are open to casual visitors. Other services of interest include weekend and night parking. There are, of course, other companies operating in Sydney, and motorists looking for parking should watch out for the P signs which indicate the nearest station.

SEA PLANES

For the ultimate view, a spectacular way to discover Sydney is by seaplane.

South Pacific Seaplanes for charter, Tel 9544 0077 and Sydney Harbour Seaplanes, Tel 9918 7472 operating from Rose Bay, have scenic flights, return restaurant flights or return flights with restaurant and an overnight stay.

CRUISES

State Transit Harbour Cruises, Tel 13 15 00

History Cruise departs daily 10am from Circular Quay (Jetty 4) to Fort Denison, Shark and Clark Islands, the Lane Cove River, Cockatoo, Spectacle and Goat Islands and Darling Harbour. Time two and a half hours. (Commentary included – refreshments available.).

Sights Cruise departs daily 1pm weekdays, 1.30pm weekends and public holidays from Circular Quay (Jetty 4) to Middle Harbour and Watsons Bay. Time two and a half hours. (Commentary included – refreshments available.).

Lights Cruise departs Mon to Sat 8pm from Circular Quay (Jetty 4) to the Opera House, Harbour Bridge, Garden Island, Fort

Denison and Darling Harbour. Time one and a half hours.

The "Reliance" Riverboat and Wildlife Cruise

The original mail boat for the Hawkesbury River. Departs Sat and Sun 11am from Harbourside Jetty, Darling Harbour to the Lane Cove River. Time three and three quarter hours. (Includes Aussie barbecue, visit to native animals at the Kukundi wildlife shelter and an informative commentary.) Tel 9566 2067 or 018 252 933.

Island Events

Personalised ferry trip to Shark, Clark, Rodd and Spectacle Island. Departs by arrangement. Time and itinerary by arrangement for any event or occasion. (Includes a visit to one or more of the islands, optional BYO or full barbecue/ sausage sizzle/ sandwich lunch/ billy tea/ lamingtons.) Recommended as a unique island experience.Tel 9555 1222.

"Kookaburra" Speed Boat

Scenic Sydney Harbour tours in a triple cockpit mahogany speed boat, for up to seven passengers. Departs by arrangement. Time and itinerary by arrangement. (Can include restaurant transfers, pick-up/drop-off at any waterfront destination.) Tel 018 415 02 or 9552 6300.

BICYCLE HIRE

Like many major cities, the busy traffic can make bike riding hazardous. Popular venues for this pursuit tend, therefore, to be away from the city centre. Centennial Park is a favourite, where there are several companies which hire bikes.

At *Centennial Park Cycles*, 50 Clovelly Road, Randwick, Tel 9398 5027/9398 8138, individuals can rent Mountain bikes and Racers, children's bikes and accessories. Weekend, weekly, monthly and hourly rates are available. A deposit is required for all cycle hire.

Other companies in the area include the *Australian Cycle Co*, 28 Clovelly Road, Randwick, Tel 9399 3475, and *Woolys Wheels*, 82 Oxford Street, Paddington, Tel 9331 2671 who rent Mountain and Hybrid bikes. A holding deposit is required (credit cards are accepted).

In the suburbs, it's common to see cycling enthusiasts enjoying a great day out. At Manly – a great spot for cyclists – *InLine Action*, Shop 2, 93-95 North Steyne, Tel 9976 3831 and the Manly Cycle Centre, 36 Pittwater Road,

Tel 9977 1189 have competitive rates and are open every day.

In Glebe, new mountain bikes of all sizes can be hired from *Inner City Cycles*, 31 Glebe Point Road, Glebe, Tel 9660 6605.

Note that in Sydney bikes are prohibited at both Darling Harbour and Martin Place and it's compulsory for cyclists to wear helmets at all times.

BY FOOT

Although it's a big city, Sydney has the advantage that many of its attractions are located in close proximity. An excellent way to explore, therefore, is by foot.

There are some excellent walking guides available – *Sydney by Ferry & Foot* by John Gunter, *Sydney Walks* by Margaret White, *Uncovering Sydney* by Graham Spindler, *Sydney Wildflower Bushwalk* by Jane Mundy and *Walks in The Sydney Harbour National Park* by Neil Paton. (See Chapter 1 for some of the walks around the Harbour.) They are very descriptive, bringing Sydney to life and within the reach of everyone. We also recommend a pamphlet, *Walkabout with Sydney Ferries*, published by the State Transit Authority.

The NSW National Parks and Wildlife Service run guided walks. Their walks take place in the National Parks between the Hawkesbury River and the city and range from the medium/ difficult (steep and energetic) to easy (downhill, leisurely stroll, snack stops). Tel 9457 9853.

The bushwalking clubs of New South Wales provide a service for members of the public wanting to go bushwalking with a bushwalking club. Some clubs specifically cater for the short-term visitor to Australia. A recorded message gives information on how to get the list of NSW clubs, Tel 9548 1228.

There are not too many "dos and don'ts" attached to walking, but please remember that hat, the protective sunscreen and a bottle of water, at least a litre per person on hot days.

In the National Parks and on walkways, keep to the tracks to minimise soil erosion, remember that all fauna, flora, Aboriginal sites and rock formations are protected, and that fires are only allowed in barbecues at designated picnic areas. Vehicles, motorbikes and horses are not permitted on tracks, and dogs are not allowed on the beach or in National Parks. Please also remember to "do the right thing" and take your rubbish with you, at the end of the day.

14 THINGS TO KNOW

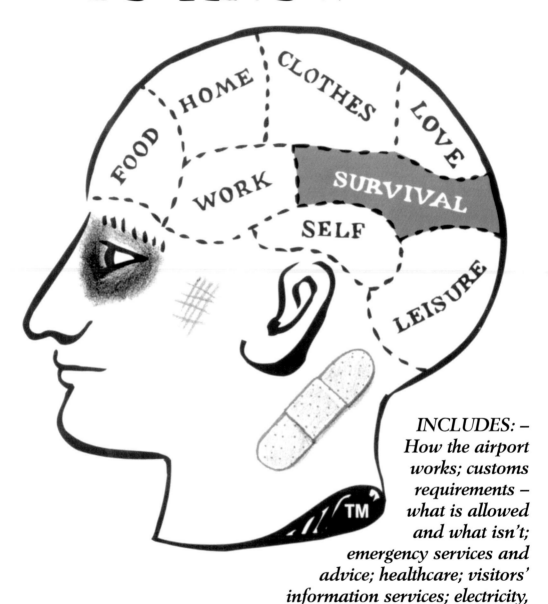

FOOD HOME CLOTHES LOVE WORK SURVIVAL SELF LEISURE

TM

INCLUDES: –
How the airport
works; customs
requirements –
what is allowed
and what isn't;
emergency services and
advice; healthcare; visitors'
information services; electricity,
weights and measures, mail,
money and the media; school
and public holidays;
telephones; time zones; tipping;
consulates; visas and finally,
Sydney weather.

This head with a few abrasions added, is the
trademark of the wonderful eclectic general sotre
REMO (see Chapters 3 and 8)

Everything You Didn't Know You Needed

It is always the little things that seem to upset your plans when you are travelling; so, for those readers who are unfamiliar with Sydney, or indeed Australia, we have listed a few basic "things to know" in order to help solve the problems that inevitably arise when you are out of your own environment.

INFORMATION SERVICES

C **The New South Wales Travel Centre** open weekdays 9am-5pm, 19 Castlereagh Street, Tel 9231 4444.

The Rocks Visitors Centre 106 George Street, Tel 9255 1700.

Information Centre Observation Deck Sydney Tower, Tel 9229 7430.

Travellers Information Service Sydney Coach Terminal or Eddy Avenue, Central Station enquiries and bookings for bus services and accommodation, Tel 9281 9366.

The Sydney Information Booth Martin Place enquiries and bookings, Tel 9235 2424.

Sydney Info Sydney City Library, Floor 3, 456 Kent Street, Tel 9265 9007.

NRMA Travel 151 Clarence Street, Sydney Tel 13 11 22.

American Express Travel Service 345 George Street, Sydney Tel 9262 3666.

Thomas Cook Travel 175 Pitt Street, Sydney, Tel 9229 6611.

N **Manly Visitors Information Bureau** open daily 10am-4pm, Ocean Beach, South Steyne, Tel 9977 1088.

Hills District Tourist Information Centre Castle Hill Park, Old Northern Road, Tel 9651 4510.

W **Parramatta Visitors Centre** open weekdays 10am-4pm, Sat 9am-1pm, Sun 10.30am-3pm, corner Market and Church Street, Tel 9630 3703.

Macarthur Country Information Centre corner Hume Highway and Congressional Drive, Liverpool, Tel 9821 2311.

S **Travellers' Information** open daily 5am-11pm, International Terminal, Sydney Airport, Tel 9669 5111.

USEFUL ADDRESSES

For visa extensions Department of Immigration and Ethnic Affairs, 88 Cumberland Street, The Rocks, Tel 9258 4555.

NOTE: Most embassies are located in Canberra. Addresses and telephone numbers can be found in the A-K section of the Telstra yellow pages under the heading "Consulates and Legations".

Motoring enquiries National Roads and Motorists Association (NRMA) 151 Clarence Street, Sydney, Tel 9260 9222/13 21 32.

Services for the disabled The Disability Information and Referral Centre, Tel 9369 3594.

National Parks and Wildlife National Parks Information Centre, Cadmans Cottage, 110 George Street, Sydney, Tel 9247 8861.

The Australian Conservation Foundation 33 George Street, Sydney, Tel 9247 4285.

SYDNEY AIRPORT

For Reservations and Enquiries :
Qantas – Tel 13 13 13 or 13 12 23
Ansett – Tel 13 13 00 or 13 15 15

Sydney's Airport, Kingsford-Smith, commonly known as Mascot, is eight kilometres south of the city centre. Serviced by both international and domestic terminals, its principal carriers include Ansett Australia (domestic) and Qantas (international and domestic), as well as many of the major overseas airlines.

Qantas flights leave from both terminals, with flights QF 001 to QF 399 departing from the international terminal, and flights QF 400 and over, leaving from the domestic terminal. All Ansett flights depart from the domestic terminal, together with other Australian internal carriers.

Passengers twelve years of age and over, departing from Australia to an overseas destination, pay a departure tax of $27. The departure tax can be paid at the airport or, prior to departure, at any post office in Australia. All international flights should be reconfirmed with the airline 72 hours before departure.

Passengers arriving at the international terminal exit at ground level, with check-in and departures for outgoing passengers on the first floor.

Check-in at the domestic terminal for

outgoing passengers is on ground level, with most departures and arrivals on the first floor.

Overseas passengers should check in at least two hours, and domestic passengers one hour, before to departure.

Trolleys are available at both terminals and can be hired for $2, refundable on return of the trolley. Currency exchange facilities are open from 5.30am-11.30pm. Thomas Cook is located on both the upper and ground floor levels of the international terminal Tel 9317 2100. There is an information service for travellers in the international terminal on the ground floor, open 5am-11pm Tel 9669 5111. The airport, and flights within Australia, are smoke-free.

The Urban Transit Authority provides an Airport Express Bus (routes 300 and 350), an easy link with the city for visitors arriving at, or leaving from, Mascot airport. The yellow and green airport express bus runs every 10 minutes to and from the centre of Sydney and takes fifteen to thirty minutes, depending on the pick-up and set-down location.

Route 300 is from the airport to Circular Quay and return, and Route 350 transports passengers from the airport to Kings Cross and return. The buses run between both the inter-national and domestic terminals. A return ticket costs around $8 and is valid for two months. Tickets can be purchased on board the bus.

Alternatively there is a private bus service operating between Kings Cross, The City, Glebe and Darling Harbour. Bookings to the airport are essential (three hours' notice is required), with the first bus available from 5.30am and the last at 8pm. Pick-ups are only available from a motel, hotel or hostel in these areas.

The same service operates from the airport from 6am, departing every twenty or thirty minutes until the arrival of the last flight at night. The driver will drop visitors in any of the areas listed above, at any location, including a motel, hotel or hostel for a small flat fee. For reservations and further enquiries telephone 9667 3221/0663.

There are taxi ranks at both terminals and the fifteen minute journey to or from the city is about $15, depending on the time of day and weather conditions.

CUSTOMS

Customs authorities have strict laws on the import of weapons and firearms. Also, animals, animal, vegetable or plant matter and food are subject to quarantine. All food, including herbs, sweets and any items bought, or carried, while in transit, must be declared on arrival in Australia.

There are severe penalties for illegal drugs, and importation of products from endangered species is prohibited. All ingoing and outgoing passengers will be subject to x-ray security checks.

There is a $400 duty-free goods allowance for non-residents aged 18 years of age and over, as well as the usual 200 cigarettes, 250 grams of cigars or tobacco and one litre of alcohol.

Visas are required for most overseas visitors for entry into Australia. Visas are generally valid for a six month period, with a maximum one year stay. A processing fee is payable by citizens of some countries wishing to stay longer than three months.

VISAS

All overseas visitors, excepting New Zealanders, require a visa and passport to enter Australia. New Zealanders need a passport only. Tourist visas, as a rule, are valid for 6-12 months maximum, and can be obtained through the nearest Australian authority (embassies, consul-ates, high commissions etc) in the home country.

Visa application forms are generally available through travel agencies or from the Australian Authority. On applying for a visa, a passport, photos and proof of a return ticket will be required, as well as proof of sufficient funds to support the visitor for the duration of their stay.

There may well be a processing fee, depending on the country, for visitors intending to stay longer than three months. A fee is also incurred for visas that are extended after arrival in Australia. All visa applications should be made well in advance, and at least four weeks in advance if applying by mail.

Extensions of visas are made through the Department of Immigration and Ethnic Affairs, 88 Cumberland Street, The Rocks, Tel 9258 4555. Extensions should be applied for at least a month prior to the visa's expiry

Working visas are available for young people between the ages of 18-26 from the United Kingdom, Ireland, Holland, Canada and Japan. (Occasionally, a visitor from these countries will still be considered young at the age of thirty and, in an exceptional circumstance, can apply for a working visa.)

A working visa should be applied for in the home country. Successful applicants are entitled to stay twelve months and to take up some casual employment while they are here. The idea of a working visa is to give young people the opportunity to visit Australia. The philosophy of this visa, therefore, is holiday oriented, and casual work is generally restricted to three months.

The CES (Commonwealth Employment Service) assists with job placements. Overseas visitors will be required to present their work permit. The central CES office is located at 105 Pitt Street, Sydney, and has a CES Temp Line for casual office positions, Tel 9320 2600.

For other casual employment in Sydney the CES has a City Casuals office at 10 Quay Street, Sydney, Tel 9201 1166, open from 6.30am-12pm, Mon-Fri. Jobs offered by City Casuals are generally of the labouring kind, and can involve both physical and heavy work. It is advisable to apply for a position before 10am, as most vacancies are filled by this time.

Left Luggage Luggage facilities are available at Central Station, Town Hall and Wynyard stations. Luggage can be left there for 24 hours for a small sum. There are also facilities near the Travellers Information Service office, outside Central Station, close to the Eddy Avenue bus terminal.

Business Hours General hours of trading for businesses and retail outlets are from 8.30am/9am-5pm/5.30pm Mon-Fri. Most shops in Sydney are open on a Saturday morning – some all day – with larger department stores and a number of shopping malls and arcades open on a Sunday. Late night shopping in the city centre is on a Thursday night, with stores staying open until 9pm. During school holidays and in the summer months, many shops in coastal suburbs are open every day, although trading hours vary.

Many large supermarkets open seven days a week until midnight during the week and between 7-10pm at the weekends, depending on the area and the supermarket. Some supermarkets are open 24 hours.

Banks operate from 9.30am-4pm Mon-Thurs, and close at 5pm on a Friday. Some inner city banks trade on a Saturday morning. Australia Post is open from 9am-5pm Mon-Fri and all banks, post offices and government offices are shut on public holidays. Liquor shops are closed on Good Friday and Christmas Day. Chemists open for emergencies at set times outside normal trading hours. Details of chemists and their hours of opening can be found through the local newspaper or by consulting a local doctor or chemist.

MONEY AND BANKS

Operating on the decimal system, the Australian currency unit is the dollar, with 100 cents to the dollar.

One and two cent pieces have been phased out during the last few years and coins are now only minted in denominations of 5 cents, 10 cents, 20 cents, 50 cents (silver coins), one dollar and two dollars ("gold" coins). Bank notes are in denominations of $5, $10, $20, $50 and $100. Recent printing has produced a plastic note which, although hard to fold, is less difficult to destroy. Prices in shops marked with odd cents can still be seen. On payment the bill will be rounded to the nearest five cents.

Leading banks are the Commonwealth, Westpac, National and ANZ. They all have many branches throughout Sydney. Banks operate from 9.30am-4pm Mon-Thurs, closing at 5pm on Friday. Some inner city banks also trade on Saturday morning. Banks are shut on all public holidays as well as bank holidays. (In Australia, the individual states' bank and public holidays are not always the same.) Bank accounts can be opened by an overseas visitor for six weeks from their date of arrival in Australia. A passport will be required as identification.

Many visitors find the most practical method of organising their finance is with travellers cheques (foreign currency travellers cheques will incur a fee on exchange) or with an American Express, a Visa or Mastercard account, widely accepted throughout Sydney.

Most banks have an ATM (Automatic Teller Machine). Thomas Cook has exchange facilities at the airport in the international terminal, open from 6am-11pm daily. Visitors using EFTPOS (Electronic Funds Transfer at Point of Sale) will find that most service stations, supermarkets and other convenient stores are linked to the system.

Useful addresses for the money market are: **Thomas Cook,** 175 Pitt Street, Sydney, Tel 9229 6611. Thomas Cook also has branches in the Queen Victoria Building, Kings Cross and the airport.

American Express, 92 Pitt Street, Sydney, Tel 9239 0666. Emergencies Tel 886 0666. After hours Tel 9886 0688.

TELEPHONES

Local calls from a private phone cost 25c. Local calls from public phones cost 40c. The cost for local calls, from both public and private phones, is for an unlimited length of time. Most public phones accept phone cards (on sale at newsagencies, pharmacies and other retail outlets). Phone cards cost $5, $10, $20 or $50. Coins accepted by public phones are 10c, 20c, 50c, and $1 coins. Long distance calls (STD-Subscriber Truck Dialling) and international calls (IDD-International Direct Dialling) can be made from most public phones. Prices are listed at the end of the A-K section of the telephone directory.

Rates for STD calls drop significantly out of peak hours (8am-6pm Mon-Sat). The economy rate is from 6pm-8am Sat-Mon and from 10pm-8am every night. The night rate is from 6pm-10pm. Mon-Fri. Rates for IDD calls, depending on the country, are cheaper on a Sunday, and can be found at the end of the A-K section of the telephone directory.

Useful telephone numbers are:

For Directory Assistance:
013	Sydney area
0175	Other areas in Australia
0103	Overseas

For an operator connected service in Australia:
011	From a private phone
0176	From a public phone
11333	With a Telstra Telecard

For an operator connected service overseas:
0101	From a private phone
0107	From a public phone
11332	With a Telstra Telecard

For a wake-up and reminder call:
0173

For an overseas call:
0011   International access code (followed by the country code, the area code and the local number).

Area and country codes:
Can be found at the end of the A-K section of the telephone directory.

Free Calls:
Calls are toll free on numbers commencing by:1800
31 (cost of a local call)

Optus:
Dial 1456 before the number to use Optus from a private phone.

The Telstra phone centre, located at 130 Pitt Street, Sydney, Tel 9233 1177 has 48 public telephones and is open 8.30am-10pm Mon-Fri, 10am-7pm weekends and public holidays.

MAIL

Australia Post has offices located throughout the city centre and the suburbs of Sydney. All offices and services are listed in the A-K section of the telephone directory under the heading "Australia Post". The standard rate within Australia is 45c for letters and 40c for cards. Books of ten stamps or boxes of 100, as well individual stamps, can be purchased from the post office. Some newsagencies also sell 45c stamps.

All postcodes in New South Wales (NSW) and the Australian Capital Territory (ACT) commence with 2, Victoria (Vic) 3, Queensland (Qld) 4, South Australia (SA) 5, Western Australia (WA) 6, Tasmania (Tas) 7 and the Northern Territory (NT) 08. Postcodes are listed at the back of the A-K section of the telephone directory and it is advisable to use them on correspondence, to avoid delays.

Overseas mail is expensive, with prices ranging from 70c/75c for a letter to New Zealand to $1.20 for European mail. The maximum weight for a standard airmail letter is 20 grams. National faxes sent from the post office will generally cost about $4 per page, while international faxes can cost up to $12 for the first page and $6 for every other page.

Australia Post has recently changed its image and most outlets now sell a range of retail lines, including cards for all occasions, writing paper, gifts wraps etc. Open Mon-Fri 9am-5pm

There are numerous courier services in

Sydney offering local, domestic and overseas deliveries. The best advice, should you need a rapid delivery, is to consult the A-K section of the Sydney Telephone Directory's yellow pages under the heading "Courier".

MEDIA

The most important daily newspaper in Sydney, *The Sydney Morning Herald*, is also considered to be one of the world's best newspapers. Printed six days a week (Sunday excluded) it comes with supplements that include business, money, real estate, the arts, entertainment, employment and a mass of classifieds.

Other widely read national newspapers are Rupert Murdoch's *Australian* which has an informative weekend edition, and the seriously business orientated *Financial Review*, commonly referred to as the *Fin Review*.

Sydney has its share of interesting weekly and monthly publications covering the Australian way of life, national and international news and politics. International newspapers and magazines are readily available in central Sydney. Newspapers are not published on Good Friday and Christmas Day.

Sydney has five television channels and numerous radio stations. The national television and radio network is the ABC (Australian Broadcasting Corporation), frequently referred to as "Aunty" (sister to the BBC). The ABC, on Channel 2, is advertising-free.

Our favourite channel is SBS (Special Broadcasting Service) which is devoted to multi-cultural programs. Foreign films, in their original language, are regularly shown on the SBS network and they have excellent overseas news, arts and music programs. Some areas of Sydney have difficulty in receiving the SBS station.

The other networks are Channel 7, Channel 9 and Channel 10, all commercially operated and all offering popular entertainment.

Peak time viewing for the news on all channels is between 6pm and 7.30pm and at 10.30pm. Television programs are advertised daily in the national newspapers.

A host of radio stations are operated on both AM and FM and allow the listener a large number of programs ranging from talkback shows to alternative music.

THERE ARE THREE TIME ZONES IN AUSTRALIA :

Eastern Standard Time ten hours in advance of Greenwich Mean Time. States operating in this time zone are New South Wales, Queensland, Victoria and Tasmania.

Central Australian Time nine and a half hours in advance of Greenwich Mean Time. The Northern Territory and South Australia operate in this time zone.

Western Standard Time eight hours in advance of Greenwich Mean Time. Western Standard Time is used exclusively by Western Australia.

New South Wales operates on Daylight Saving during the summer months – one hour ahead of Eastern Standard Time, with clocks currently going forward by one hour from the last Sunday in October until the first Sunday in March.

During winter, at 6pm in the evening in Sydney, it will be :
6pm in Brisbane, Melbourne and Hobart
5.30pm in Darwin and Adelaide
4pm in Perth
Overseas, at 6pm the times will be :
12am in Los Angeles
3am in New York
8am in London
9am in Paris
4pm in Hong Kong
8pm in Auckland

ELECTRICITY

Voltage is 220-240AC, plugs are three pin, except for lighter appliances which carry two pins. Adaptors for overseas appliances can be found at most hardware stores. Some of the more expensive hotels, however, have these available for their clients.

WEIGHTS AND MEASURES

Australia has been on the metric system since the early 1970s. As in other converted countries, older people still tend to converse in feet and inches, pounds and ounces and miles instead of kilometres.

Needless to say, under the metric system, milk and petrol are sold by litres, potatoes by grams and kilos, distance is measured by centimetres, metres and kilometres, speed limits are in kilometres per hour and weather temperatures are in Centigrade not Fahrenheit.

If you are confused, following is a brief conversion table :

1 metre = 3.28 feet
1 kilometre = 0.62 miles (think two to a mile)

1 kilo = 2.20 pounds (think two to a pound)
1 litre = 1.8 pints (UK – think two)
25° Centigrade = 77° Fahrenheit.

TIPPING

Restaurants and hotels do not add service charges and tipping is voluntary rather than mandatory – a refreshing change after travelling elsewhere in the world.

In the more up-market restaurants tipping is an accepted practice and 10%-12% is the right tip for good service. Most small restaurants or cafes have a box or plate for their staff for left-over change, always gratefully received, but not expected.

As a general rule, taxis do not expect a tip. Nevertheless, the thing to do is to round the fare up to the nearest dollar, and if the journey's been a long one, and the fare is say $27, round it up to $30.

In hotels the staff don't expect a tip, but if your bags are heavy or numerous, a few dollars to the porter is welcome.

Tipping is at your discretion. If the service is good and the people friendly, then an extra dollar to show your appreciation will never go astray.

SCHOOL AND PUBLIC HOLIDAYS

Peak holiday periods in New South Wales are the public school holidays.

The school year in New South Wales is divided into four terms and, although holiday dates vary each year, they are approximately as follows:

Summer – begins one week before Christmas and ends at the end of January/first week of February.

Autumn – dictated by Easter – generally starts the Thursday before Easter and ends the following Monday week.

Winter – First two weeks of July.

Spring – Last week of September and first week of October.

Private schools generally break up at least one week before the public schools and two weeks before, in the summer.

Following are public holidays celebrated in New South Wales (some dates vary due to the calendar year) :

January 1	New Year's Day
January 26	Australia Day
March/April (variable)	Good Friday
March/April (variable)	Easter Monday
April 25	Anzac Day
June (variable)	Queen's Birthday
October (variable)	Labour Day
December 25	Christmas Day
December 26	Boxing Day

It should be noted that Australia's most famous horse race, the Melbourne Cup is run each year, in Melbourne, on the first Tuesday in November. Although this is not officially a public holiday, the public on the east coast of Australia have unofficially made it one. It is not uncommon therefore, on the afternoon of the race, to find businesses closed down. This unofficial holiday is one of national celebration!

Also to be noted, is that bank holidays in New South Wales are not always the same as public holidays (one such holiday occurs for banks in August each year) and if public holidays, such as New Year's Day, fall at the weekend the holiday will be celebrated on the Monday, extending the weekend into a long one.

WEATHER

Sydney has a climate that lends itself to living in "the great outdoors". In winter there are often clear blue skies, with summer boasting long hot lingering days. Autumn is delightful, as is the spring, though in spring there's much more chance of rain.

Hottest months are December, January and February, these being equivalent to July, August and September in Europe and the States. Summer officially begins on December 1st and ends on the last day of February, with winter commencing on June 1st and ending August 31st.

Night temperatures in the winter rarely fall below 10°C, while the average daytime temperature is about 17°C.

In the summer temperatures average around 25°C but can soar to a stifling 40°C with high humidity that makes living oppressive. The only solution – a dip in the deep blue sea. Often Christmas is considered the hottest time of year. Perhaps it's the food, or perhaps it's in the mind; in any event, turkey isn't the only thing that roasts.

When it rains, it rains! Torrential storms are not uncommon between October and March. Average monthly rainfall is between 75 -130mm.

It has been said of the weather in Sydney that all four seasons can be experienced in any one day. Many people are caught – sweltering in a sweater as skies clear and the sun comes out – freezing in a T-shirt as the wind gets up – or soaked to the skin as the heavens open and the clouds burst.

A good tip is to be prepared. Even on the best

of days, come rain or come shine, you may well find that an umbrella, light jacket and dark glasses are useful, or that they save the day.

HEALTH

Vaccinations are not required for entry into Australia, unless an infected country has been visited within 14 days before arrival. Medical care and hygiene standards in Australia are first class.

The cost of a visit to a doctor is approximately $30. Health insurance is available from private health funds. There is generally a waiting period, after registering, before claims can be made. From time to time, specials are on offer, when the waiting period is waived. Major health funds are HCF Tel 9290 0311, MBF Tel 1800 801 901 and Medibank Private Tel 13 23 31.

The United Kingdom, New Zealand, Italy, Malta, Holland and Sweden have reciprocal health arrangements in Australia. Visitors from these countries can register with Medicare at their nearest Medicare office. For all Medicare enquiries Tel 9794 2701.

For an emergency health problem, contact the casualty section at the nearest public hospital.

The contraceptive pill is available on prescription only, so a visit to a doctor is required. Doctors are listed in the Yellow Pages under the heading "Medical Practitioners".

Visitors should be aware that AIDS exists in Sydney, as it does in many of the major cities throughout the world. Appropriate precautions should be taken. Condoms are available from chemists, newsagencies, supermarkets, other convenience stores and some public toilets. There is a 24-hour AIDS information line.

TAKING CARE

Sydney is not a dangerous city – the Aust-ralians are both friendly and honest. However, as in all major cities, common sense should prevail.

Cars should be locked and luggage not left unattended. Theft should be reported to the police as soon as possible and the bank notified if credit cards or cheques are stolen. Most banks have a 24-hour lost or stolen property number listed under "Banks" in the A-K section of the Yellow Pages.

Australians enjoy celebrating and on occasions, such as New Years Eve, are known to be high-spirited. Certain areas, The Rocks and Kings Cross for example, should perhaps be avoided at these times. Many areas in Sydney are

now, however, alcohol free zones – the con-sequence of previous over-zealous celebrations.

Many beaches around Sydney have designated swimming areas, marked by flags. As the surf can be extremely strong and the undertow treacherous, it is strongly recommended that appointed areas be used. These beaches are also patrolled by lifesavers, so help is always at hand.

Remember that Australians suffer from a high incidence of skin cancer. The sun's intensity is strong and ultra-violet rays are dangerous. Hats should be worn at all times during the summer months, as well as a strong protective cream. Make sure that children are not left uncovered on the beach; an extra T-shirt is indispensable for swimming, as their shoulders quickly get sunburnt.

Shark attacks are infrequent, but it is advisable to remember they exist. Many Sydney beaches are netted as a deterrent, and in peak season planes patrol the more popular beaches. Life savers also keep a sharp eye out for that dreaded fin. Needless to say, if a shark alarm is raised (a loud siren or bell), the water should be vacated immediately.

There are some poisonous marine animals which include, among others, the blue-ringed octopus, stonefish, bullrout and stingray. The best advice is not to touch anything you are unsure about.

Very occasionally, a beach will be closed by the authorities because of an invasion of jelly fish. It is a good idea, in any case to stay out of their way. In particular, avoid bluebottles as they can be extremely unpleasant.

Other potential "animal" dangers are spiders, snakes and ticks.

The two most disagreeable spiders are the redback and funnel-web. The redback, so named because it has a red back, lurks under pots and ledges etc. Its bite is not lethal, but should be taken seriously.

The funnel-web, found principally in the north of Sydney, is an ugly brute, not to be messed around with. It digs holes in the ground, where it lives. Children should be stopped from poking their fingers into holes they see in the garden or in the bush, as a potentially dangerous predator could be concealed there. If bitten by a funnel-web, immediate help must be called, as a bite from this beast can be fatal.

All snakes in Australia are protected. In Sydney, snakes are obviously found in National

Parks or bushland only. Some snakes are deadly, although few are aggressive, and they're generally happy to move on their way when people approach. (Snakes can't hear; they feel vibrations.) Obvious precautions should be taken – don't put your hands in holes, don't pick up logs without turning them over, and wear long trousers, thick socks and heavy-soled shoes when walking through dense grass.

If bitten by either a snake or spider, help should be called immediately. Never move the victim, bandage the affected limb as tightly as possible and immobilise the limb to avoid the venom entering the blood system. Any information on the type of spider or snake is useful, as hospitals carry antivenene.

Ticks affect both humans and animals and should be watched for when visiting leafy areas or bushwalking. The tick can be dangerous if left in the skin, as its toxin can cause paralysis and, in rare circumstances, death. The presence of a tick in the skin is indicated by an itchy lump. The tick should be bathed with methylated spirits or kerosene and tweezers used to remove it intact.

A constant danger for Sydney is bushfires. This was never more apparent than in 1994, when Sydney suffered the most widespread bushfires in its history. Scars from this devastation can still be seen, in spite of the regrowth of much of its vegetation.

From October 1st (the start of summer), through to March 1st (the beginning of autumn) certain types of fires may not be lit without a permit, obtainable from the local fire officer.

During a total fire ban no fires at all may be lit, including barbecues. Penalties for dis-regarding fire bans can be severe and include heavy fines and jail sentences.

As Sydney is surrounded by eucalyptus forests, fire prevention should be a matter of common sense during the hot months. It should go without saying, never throw cigarette butts out of car windows – remember, it is better to be safe than sorry.

EMERGENCY SERVICES

POLICE OR AMBULANCE : TEL 000

Police Switchboard 151-241 Goulburn Street, Surry Hills, Tel 9281 0000.

City Police Stations 192 Day Street, Sydney, Tel 9265 6499, corner George and Argyle Street, The Rocks, Tel 9265 6366.

Crime Stopper Hotline 24 hours, Tel 9384 6467 or toll-free 1800 025 122.

Ambulance Bookings 93 Quay Street, Sydney, Tel 13 12 33.

Doctors addresses and telephone numbers can be found in the L-Z section of Telstra's yellow pages under the heading "Medical Practitioners".

HOSPITALS

Sydney Hospital, Medical Emergency, Tel 9228 2111.

Royal North Shore Hospital (general) open 24 hours, Pacific Highway, St. Leonards, Tel 9438 7111.

St. Vincent's Hospital (general) open 24 hours, Victoria and Burton Streets, Darlinghurst, Tel 9339 1111.

Camperdown Children's Hospital (paediatric) open 24 hours, Pyrmont Bridge Road, Camperdown, Tel 9519 0466.

Dentists addresses and telephone numbers can be found in the A-K section of Telstra's yellow pages under the heading "Dentists". The Dental Emergency Information Service (referral service after hours), Tel 9962 6557.

AIDS Information 24 hour information line, Tel 9332 4000.

Prescriptions Emergency Prescription Service (will advise the nearest chemist) open 24 hours, Tel 9235 0333.

Electricity Sydney area, Tel 13 13 88.

Vehicle Breakdown NRMA, enquiries, Tel 13 21 32, emergency road service, Tel 13 11 11.

PHOTOGRAPHIC CREDITS

Page 12 Jack Mundey's Rocks arrest © John Fairfax & Sons

Page 12 Burnum Burnum, courtesy Angela Finnigan

Page 13 Sir Joseph Banks, © Image Library, State Library of NSW

Page 17 Lorikeet, © Geoff Sainty

Page 18-19 © News Limited

Page 29 Mosman Chamber of Commerce

Page 34-35 Courtesy and © Naval Photographic Unit

Page 36 © Image Library, State Library of NSW

Page 39 © MCA

Page 40-41 © Sydney Cove Authority

Page 44 © Powerhouse Museum

Page 50 Courtesy, Capitol Theatre

Page 54 © National Maritime Museum

Page 55 Antipodes © Australian National Maritime Museum Movie Poster © Greater Union Group

Page 56-57 Bondi in Winter by Benjamen Huie

Page 62 Float © Gay and Lesbian Mardi Gras Ltd

Page 62 Clover Moore MPs – Courtesy and © Jamie Dunbar

Page 64 Courtesy and © Centennial Park Trust

Page 65/66 Courtesy and © National Maritime Museum

Page 70-1 Haberfield Public School by Benjamen Huie

Page 78 Courtesy, Balmain Association

Page 90-1 Courtesy of Josef Lebovic Gallery © Annand family (also on book cover)

Page 95 © Taronga Zoo

Page 96 Courtesy, Brian Dermott, South Steyne

Page 96 © National Maritime Museum

Page 80-1 © National Library, Canberra

Page 100 Courtesy Kit Moore (Palm Beach Experience)

Page 101 Courtesy Kit Moore (Palm Beach Experience)

Page 120-121 Courtesy Australiana Flags (see Directory)

Pages 102-3 © Hyde Park Barracks FOC

Page 129 Courtesy Mosman Chamber of Commerce, photographer Michael Thompson

Page 131 Courtesy Double Bay Chamber of Commerce

Page 138-9 *The Ingredient as Hero* by Benjamen Huie

Page 140 Courtesy Royal Tasmanian Salmon

Page 141 Courtesy Dennis Wolanski Library

Page 156 Courtesy British Film Institute

Page 158 Courtesy Brian Dermott, South Steyne

Page 176 From *A Century of Sydney's Flying Sailors*, by Margaret Molloy

Page 177 Courtesy Surf Life Saving Australia

Page 180 Courtesy, Sportspace

Page 181 © Image Library, State Library of NSW

Page 182 Courtesy Australian Jockey Club

Page 186 Courtesy NSW Tennis Association

Page 186-7 © John Fairfax & Sons

Page 199-200 Courtesy Powerhouse Museum

Page 210-211 Courtesy REMO General Store

INDEX

Name

Address

Phone

Name

Address

Phone

Name

Address

Phone

Name

Address

Phone

Name

Address

Phone

Name

Address

Phone

Name

Address

Phone

Name

Address

Phone

Name

Address

Phone

Name

Address

Phone

Name

Address

Phone

Name

Address

Phone

Name

Address

Phone

Name

Address

Phone

Name

Address

Phone

Name

Address

Phone

Name

Address

Phone

Name

Address

Phone

Name

Address

Phone

Name

Address

Phone

Name

Address

Phone

Name

Address

Phone

Name

Address

Phone

Name

Address

Phone

Name

Address

Phone

Name

Address

Phone

Name

Address

Phone

Name

Address

Phone

Name

Address

Phone

Name

Address

Phone

Name

Address

Phone

Name

Address

Phone

Name

Address

Phone

Name

Address

Phone

Name

Address

Phone

Name

Address

Phone

Name

Address

Phone

Name

Address

Phone

Name

Address

Phone

Name

Address

Phone

Name

Address

Phone

Name

Address

Phone

Name

Address

Phone

Name

Address

Phone

Name

Address

Phone

Name

Address

Phone

Name

Address

Phone

Name

Address

Phone

Name

Address

Phone

Name

Address

Phone

Name

Address

Phone

Name

Address

Phone

Name

Address

Phone

Name

Address

Phone

Name

Address

Phone

Name

Address

Phone

Name

Address

Phone

Name

Address

Phone

Name

Address

Phone

Name

Address

Phone

Name

Address

Phone

Name

Address

Phone

DIRECTORY

A cappella Association Tel 9519 5083

Aboat Taxis Tel 9555 1155

Aboriginal Arts and Tribal Art Centre, 117 George Street, The Rocks 2000 Tel 9247 9625 Fax 9247 4391

AC Butchery, 174 Marion Street, Leichhardt Tel 9569 8686

Alfalfa House, 113 Enmore Road Enmore 2042 Tel 9519 3374

All Buttons Great and Small ,419a King Street Newtown 2042 Tel 9550 1782

Amera's Palace, 12A Enmore Road Newtown 2043 Tel 9519 4793

Apia Club, 38-42 Frazer Street, Leichhardt 2040 Tel 9810 0187

Armstrongs, Manly Wharf, Tel 9976 3835

ArtsWest PO Box 1424 Parramatta 2124 Tel 9831 1441/Fax 9831 1439

Athena Cake Shop, 412 Illawarra Road, Marrickville Tel 9558 1276

Audley Visitors Centre, Royal National Park Tel 9542 0648

Australian Golf Club, Bannerman Crescent, Rosebery 2018 Tel 9663 2273

Australian Museum, corner College and William Street 2000 Tel 9320 6000

Australian 18-footers, Double Bay 2028 Tel 9363 2995

Australiana Flags, 2/175 Sailors Bay Road, Northbridge, 2063 Tel 9958 3246

Aviamentos - Ribbons & Braids, 457 King Street Newtown 2042 Tel 9550 3774

Bac Lieu, 302 Illawarra Road, Marrickville 2204 Tel 9558 5755

Balmain Association, Tel & Fax 9818 4954

Balmain Pub Crawl with Kath Hamey, Tel & Fax 9818 4954

Banjo Patterson Cottage restaurant, end Punt Road, Gladesville 2440 Tel 9816 3611

Banks Marine, 81 Grove Street, Balmain 2041 Tel 9555 1222

Bar Baba 31 Norton Street, Leichhardt 2040 Tel 9564 2044

Bar Italia, 169 Norton Street, Tel 9560 9981

Barnaby's Riverside, 66 Phillip Street, Parramatta 2150 Tel 9633 3777

Barrenjoey Boathouse Palm Beach 2108 Tel 9974 4229

Basement, The, 29 Reiby Place, Sydney Tel 9251 2797

Bathers Pavilion, 4 The Esplanade Balmoral Beach 2088 Tel 9968 1133

Beachside Brasserie, 20 Gerrala Street, Cronulla 2230 Tel 9527 4222

Bennelong Restaurant, Sydney Opera House 2000 Tel 9250 7578

bill's, 433 Liverpool Street, Darlinghurst 2010 Tel 9360 9631

Bilsons Restaurant, Circular Quay Terminal Building Tel 9251 5600

Bistro Moncur, 116 Queen Street, Woollahra 2025 Tel 9363 2782

Black Panther, 1260 Princes Highway, Engadine 2233 Tel 9520 8888

Boatshed Cafe , La Perouse 2036 Tel 9661 9315

Bondi Surf Club, Queen Elizabeth Drive Bondi 2036 Tel 9300 9279

Bonnie Doon Golf Club, Banks Avenue, Pagewood 2035 Tel 9349 2101

Botanic Gardens Restaurant, Royal Botanic Gardens 2000 Tel 9241 2419

Boulders at the Rocks, 143 George Street, The Rocks 2000 Tel 9241 1447

Bounty Cruises 29 George Street, The Rocks 2000 Tel 9247 1789

Bower The, 7/9 Marine Parade, Shelly Beach 2261 Tel 9977 5451

Burlington Centre, 258 Penshurst Street Willoughby 2068 Tel 9417 2588

Burnum Burnum's WILDthings book Tel 9332 2661

Bush Music Club Tel 9631 9533/ 015 212136

Cafe for Obscure Avalon Painters, 1 MacMillan Court, Avalon Parade 2107 Tel 9918 9963

Cafe Gioia 126A Norton Street, Leichhardt, Tel 9564 6245

Camira, 50 Park Road, Cabramatta, 2166 Tel 9728 1052

Capitol Theatre, Campbell Street, near George 2000 Tel 9320 9122

Car rentals
    Avis Tel 9902 9292
    Budget Tel 13 27 27
    Hertz Tel 9360 6621
    Thrifty Tel 9380 5399

Casula Powerhouse Tel 9824 1121

Cat and the Fiddle, 456 Darling Street, Balmain 2041 Tel 9810 7931

Catalina, Lyne Park, Rose Bay 2029 Tel 9371 0555

Centennial Park and Moore Park Trust, Tel 9331 5056

Centennial Park Cafe, Cnr Grand and Parkes Drive Tel 9360 3355

Chesters Cafe 148 Beattie Street Balmain 2041 Tel 9555 2185

Chinese Noodle Restaurant, LG7, 8 Quay Street, Haymarket 2000 Tel 9281 9051

Church Point Top Room, McCarrs Creek Road, Church Point 2105 Tel 9979 9670

Cicada, 29 Challis Avenue, Potts Point 2011 Tel 9358 1255

City Rail - information on public transport Tel 13 15 00

Concourse Restaurant, Sydney Opera House 2000 Tel 9250 7300

Conservation Hut, Fletcher Street, Wentworth Falls 2782 Tel 9157 3827

Conservatorium of Music, Macquarie Street, Sydney 2000 Tel 9230 1222

Corinthian Rotisserie, 283 Marrickville Road, Marrickville Tel 9568 7084

Cottage Point Inn, 2 Anderson Place, Cottage Point Tel 9456 1011

Courtney's Brasserie, 2 Horwood Plaza, Parramatta 2150 Tel 9635 3288

Cronulla Marina 2230 Tel 9523 6919

Cronulla National Park Ferry Cruises, Tonkin Street Wharf Tel 9523 2990

Danny's Seafood, La Perouse 2036 Tel 9311 4116

Darley Street Thai, 28-30 Bayswater Road, Kings Cross 2011 Tel 9358 6530

Darling Mills, 134 Glebe Point Road, Glebe 2037 Tel 9660 5666

Darya Deli, 331 Penshurst Street Willoughby 2068 Tel 9417 2035

David McBride, 8 Crown Street, Henley 2111 Tel 9817 3869

Death Defying Theatre Tel 9698 3344

Desperate Living, 415a King Street Newtown 2042 Tel 9516 5898

Dino Store, 453 King Street Newtown 2042 Tel 9557 4637

Disability information
Telephone typewriter directory service for the deaf or people with impaired speech Tel 1800 637 500

Discovery Centre, Kurnell 2231 Tel 9668 9111

Done Art and Design, 123 George Street, The Rocks 2000 Tel 9251 6099

Doyles Wharf Restaurant, 11 Marine Parade Watson's Bay 2030 Tel 9337 1572

Dry Dock Hotel, 90 College Street Balmain 2041 Tel 9555 1306

Dulwich Hill Coffee Roaster, 407 New Canterbury Road Dulwich Hill 2203 Tel 9569 6674

Eastsail, d'Albora Marina, New Beach Road, Rushcutter Bay 2011 Tel 9327 1166

El Greco, 362 Canterbury Road Dulwich Hill 2203 Tel 9569 1511

Experiment Farm Cottage, 9 Ruse Stereet, Parramatta 2150 Tel 9635 5655

Fish Market, Sydney, Pyrmont 2009 Tel 9660 1611

Fishface, 132 Darlinghurst Road, Darlinghurst 2010 Tel 9332 4803

Flagship Charters, Tel 018 415 022

Fort Denison Information Tel 9555 9844/9901

Garden Island Information Tel 9181 3308

Garden Island Naval Museum Tel 9359 9111

Geoff Sainty & Associates, Box 1219 Potts Point 2011 Tel 9332 2661

Golden Century, 393-399 Sussex Street, Haymarket 2000 Tel 9281 1598

Gonsalves, Palm Beach 2108 Tel 9974 4409

Gould's Book Arcade, 32 King Street Newtown 2042 Tel 9519 8947

Govindas, 112 Darlinghurst Road, Darlinghurst 2010 Tel 9380 5162

Gowings Bros, Cnr Market and George Streets Tel 9264 6321

Great Synagogue, 166 Castlereagh Street 2000 Tel 9267 2477

Green Park Hotel, 360 Victoria Street, Darlinghurst 2010 Tel 9380 5311

Griffin (at the Stables Theatre) 10 Nimrod Street, Kings Cross 2011 Tel 9332 1052

Haberfield Rowing Club, Dobroyd Parade, Haberfield 2045 Tel 9797 9523

Hai Ha Fabrics, 45 John Street, Cabramatta 2166 Tel 9728 3581

Hakoah Club, 61 Hall Street Bondi 2036 Tel 9130 3344

Halvorsen Boats, PO Box 2, Turramurra, 2074 Tel 9457 9011

Hamey, Kath Tel or Fax 9818 4954

Hamey, Kath, Balmain Association, Tel & Fax 9818 4954

Harbour Islands, Banks Marine Tel 9555 1222

Harbour Restaurant, Sydney Opera House 2000 Tel 9250 7191

Harbour Shuttles Tel 9810 5010

Harold Park Hotel, 115 Wigram Street, Glebe 2037 Tel 9692 0564

Hegarty's Ferries Tel 9206 1167

Historic Houses Trust of NSW, 61 Darghan Street, Glebe 2037 Tel 692 8366

Hong Kong Children's Fashions, 2/68 John Street, Cabramatta 2166 Tel 9724 6191

Hong Kong Wedding House, 24-32 Hughes Street, Cabramatta 2166 Tel 9726 1668

Hotel CBD corner King and York Streets 2000 Restaurant, Tel 9299 8911 Bar, Tel 9299 8292

Hyde Park Barracks, Macquarie Sreet (next to Mint) 2000 Tel 9223 8922 Cafe bookings Tel 9223 1155

I Canottieri, 81 Parriwi Road Mosman 2088 Tel 9960 3229

Il Gianfornaio, 414 Victoria Avenue Chatswood 2067 Tel 9413 4833

Imperial Hotel, 33 Erskineville Road, Erskineville 2043 Tel 9519 9899.

Imperial Peking Harbourside, 15 Circular Quay West, The Rocks 2000 Tel 9247 7073

Indian Affair, 79 Macquarie Street, Parramatta 2150 Tel 9635 9476

Jonah's, 69 Bynya Road Plam Beach 2108 Tel 9974 5599

Justice and Police Museum, Corner Phillip and Albert Streets 2000 Tel 9252 1144

Kareela Golf Club, Bates Drive, Kareela 2232 Tel 9521 5555

Ken Done Gallery, 1-5 Hickson Road, The Rocks 2000 Tel 9247 2740

Kiliminjaro Restaurant, 280 King Street Newtown 2042 Tel 9557 4565

Kingsway, Cronulla Beach 2230 Tel 9527 3l00.

Kirribilli RSL Bowling Club, 11-23 Harbour View Cresc. Milsons Point 2060 Tel 9955 2245

Kit Moore Tel 9974 1096

Kookaburra speedboat Tel 018 415 022

Korean Bath House, 111 Darlinghurst Road, Kings Cross 2011 Tel 9358 2755

l'Otel, 114 Darlinghurst Road, Darlinghurst 2010 Tel 9360 6868

La Palma, 1108 Barrenjoey Road, Palm Beach 2108 Tel 9974 0011

La Paula, 9 Barbara Street, Fairfield 2165 Tel 9726 2379

Lakes Golf Club King Street, Eastlakes 2018 Tel 9669 1311

Laperouse Museum 2036 Tel 9311 3379; 9311 2765

Le Kiosk, end of Bower Street, Shelly Beach 2261 Tel 9977 4122

Legs On The Wall 24/142 Addison Road, Marrickville 2204 Tel 9560 1025

Leichhardt Council, Wetherill Street, Leichhardt 2040 Tel 9367 9222

Leichhardt Hotel, Corner Balmain Road and Short Street, Leichhardt 2040 Tel 9569 1217

Leichhardt Park Aquatic Centre, Mary Street, Leichhardt 2040 Tel 9555 8344

London Hotel, 234 Darling Street Balmain 2041 Tel 9555 1377

Lord Nelson Brewery Hotel, 19 Kent Street, Millers Point 2000 Tel 9251 4044

Lucky Toms, 379 Parramatta Road, Leichhardt 2040
Tel 9560 0439

Luna Park, Milsons Point 2061 Tel 9922 6644

Lydham Hall Tel 9567 4259

Manly Visitors Information Bureau, North Steyne 2095
Tel 9977 0078

Mariners Cove Restaurant, Gunnamatta Bay, Cronulla
2230 Tel 9527 4798

MCA, 140 George Street, The Rocks 2000
Tel 9241 5892
McBride, David 8 Crown Street, Henley 2111
Tel 9817 3869

McKillop Place, 7 Mount Street North Sydney 2060
Tel 9954 9688

Mezzaluna , 123 Victoria Street,Potts Point 2011
Tel 9357 1988

Mint Museum, Queen Square, Macquarie Street,
Sydney 2000 Tel 9217 0111

Mosman Bowling Club 15 Belmont Road, Mosman
2088 Tel 9969 4211

Mosman Council 2088 Tel 9960 0900

Mosman Rowing Club, Mosman Bay 2088
Tel 9953 7966

Mother Chu's Vegetarian Restaurant, 367 Pitt Street
2000 Tel 9283 2828

Museum of Contemporary Art (MCA), 140 George
Street, The Rocks 2000 Tel 9241 5892
Cafe, Tel 9241 4253 Store, Tel 9241 5865

Museum of Sydney, Corner Phillip and Bridge Streets
2000 Tel 9251 5988

Musica Viva Tel 9698 1711

MV Reliance Harbourside Jetty, Darling Harbour 2000
Tel 9566 2067 or (018) 252 933.

National Boat Hire, Ku-ring-gai National Park
Tel 9457 9011

National Maritime Museum, Darling Harbour, 2000
Tel 9552 7777
Recorded information Tel 0055 62002

National Park Hire, Ku-ring-gai National Park
Tel 9457 9011

National Trust, Watson Road, Observatory Hill 2000
Tel 9258 0123

Naval Repository and Museum, Spectacle Island
Tel 9181 2110

New South Wales Golf Club Henry Road, La Perouse
2036 Tel 9661 4455

New Theatre, 542 King Street Newtown 2042
Tel 9519 3403

Newton's Restaurant, 403 King Street Newtown 2042
Tel 9519 8211

Newtown High School of Performing Arts High School,
opposite 381 King Street Newtown 2042
Tel 9519 1544

Newtown Hotel, 174 King Street Newtown 2042
Tel 9557 1329

Norman Lindsay Gallery, Norman Lindsay Crescent,
Faulonbridge 2776 Tel (047) 511 067.

North Sydney Bowling Club Ridge Street, North
Sydney 2060 Tel 9202 8896

Novotel, The Grand Parade and Princess Street,
Brighton-le-Sands 2216 Tel 9597 7111

NSW Art Gallery, Art Gallery Road, Domain 2000
Tel 9225 1700

NSW Cricket Association 51 Druitt Street Sydney 2000
Tel 9261 5155

NSW State Archives, 2 Globe Street, The Rocks 2000
Tel 9237 0254

NSW Travel Centre, weekdays, 9am-5pm,
19 Castlereagh Street Tel 132 077

Nutcote Trust PO Box 577 Neutral Bay 2089
Tel 9953 4453

Observatory Watson's Road, Observatory Hill,
The Rocks 2000 Tel 9217 0485

Oddbins Pty Ltd, PO Box 105 Camperdown 2050
Tel 9550 3177

Off The Rails, 60 Salisbury Road, Camperdown
Tel 9550 5355

Old Government House, Parramatta 2150
Tel 9635 8149

Olympic Information Centre, Darling Harbour 2000
Tel 9267 0116

Omar Khayyams, 417 Victoria Ave Chatswood 2067
Tel 9415 3373

Omnivore, 333 Darling Street, Balmain 2041
Tel 9810 1393

Open City Inc Tel 9332 4549

Pacific Herbal Clinic, 37 Ultimo Road, Haymarket 2000
Tel 9281 7922

Paesanella Cheese Factory, 27 Gerald Street,
Marrickville 2204Tel 9519 6181

Palisade Hotel, 35 Bettington Street, Millers Point 2000
Tel 9247 2272

Palisade Restaurant, 35 Bettington Street, Millers Point
Tel 9251 7225

Palm Beach Experience, Tel 015 602 786

Paragon Cafe, corner Loftus Street and
Circular Quay 2000 Tel 9241, 3888

Parks and Wildlife Service (South Metropolitan District)
Tel 9542 0666

Parramatta Information Centre, Cnr Church and Market
Streets, 2150 Tel 9630 3703

Pendle Ham and Bacon Curers, 38 Bungaree Road,
Pendle Hill 2145 Tel 9631 3133

Performance Space 199 Cleveland Street, Redfern
2016 Tel 9698 7235

Pho 54 Shop 2/54 Park Road, Freedom Plaza,
Cabramatta 2166 Tel 9726 1992

Pier, 594 New South Head Road, Rose Bay 2029
Tel 9237 6561

Pink Water Taxi (Pittwater area), Tel 08 238 190

Pittwater Water Taxi, Tel 018 408 831

Polymorph Body Art Gallery, 82 Enmore Road
Newtown 2043 Tel 9519 8923

Portuguese Community Club,100 Marrickville Road,
Petersham 2049 Tel 9550 6344

Powerhouse Museum, 500 Harris Street Ultimo 2007
Tel 9217 0111

Public Transport Information Line 6am-10pm daily
Tel 13 15 00.

Q Theatre Tel 047 21 5735

Quarantine Beach, Bookings Tel 9977 6522

Quarantine Station, Tel 9977 6522

Raffan & Kelaher Auctioneers, 42 John Street,
Leichhardt 2040 Tel 9552 1899

Randwick Racecourse Tel 9663 8400

Ravesi's on Bondi, Cnr Campbell Pde and Hall Street
2036 Tel 9345 442

Reliance Harbourside Jetty, Darling Harbour 2000
Tel 9566 2067 or 018 252 933.

Riverboat Cruises, Sans Souci Wharf 2219
Tel 9583 1199

Riverside Theatre Complex, Cnr Church and Market
Streets, Parramatta 2150 Tel 9683 6166

Riverview Hotel, 29 Birchgrove Road, Balmain 2041
Tel 9819 1151

Rockpool, 107 George Street, The Rocks 2000
Tel 9252 1888

Rocks Visitors Centre, 106 George Street,
The Rocks, 2000 Tel 9255 1788

Rodd Island, Banks Marine Tel 9555 1222

Rooty Hill Resort, Sherbrooke Street, Rooty Hill 2766
Tel 9625 5500

Rose Lindsay Cottage, 113 Chapman Parade, Faulconbridge 2776 Tel (047) 514 273

Royal New South Wales Bowling Association, 309 Pitt Street, Sydney 2000 Tel 9267 7155

Royal Prince Alfred Yacht Club, Newport 2106 Tel 9979 7117

Royal Sydney Golf Club Kent Road, Rose Bay 2029 Tel 9661 4455

Rugantino's, 13 Norton Street, Leichhardt 2040 Tel. 9569 7117

Rugby League of NSW,165 Phillip Street, Sydney 2000 Tel 9232 75 66

Russell's, 53 Glebe Point Road, Glebe 2037 Tel 9552 4055

S H Ervin Gallery, Watson Road, Observatory Hill 2000 Tel 9258 0173

Sam's Maltese Foods, 72 Ettalong Road, Pendle Hill 2145 Tel 9896 1182

Savion, 38 Wairoa Road, Bondi 2036 Tel 91306357

Shores, Parriwi Road at Spit Bridge 2088 Tel 9960 3391

Sidetrack Peformance Group Tel 9560 1255

Silver Beach Motel and Caravan Park, Silver Beach, Kurnell 2231 Tel 9668 82l5

Silver Spring, 477 Pitt Street, Sydney 2000 Tel 9211 2232

Society of Australian Geneologists, 120 Kent Street, The Rocks 2000 Tel 9247 3953

South Pacific Seaplanes, Cronulla Marina Cronulla 2230 Tel 9544 0077

Spectacle Island Tel 9181 3308 /9359 2551

Spitlers, a'Albora Marina, Spit Road, Mosman 2088 Tel 9969 8538

Sportspace Tours, Sydney football Stadium, Tel 9380 0383

St. James Church, King Street, Sydney 2000 Tel 9232 3022

St. Johns Anglican Church, Darlinghurst Road, Darlinghurst 2010 Tel 360 6844

Stables Theatre, 10 Nimrod Street, Kings Cross 2011 Tel 9361 3817

Stapleton's Restaurant, 782 Princes Highway, Sutherland 2232 Tel 9521 8747

Star Thoroughbreds, 2 Birtley Place, Elizabeth Bay 2011 Tel 9358 5930

Stark's Delicatessan, 95 Hall Street, Bondi 2026 Tel 9130 3872

State Library of NSW Macquarie Street, top of Hunter Street, Sydney 2000 Tel 9230 1414

State Parliament House, Macquarie Street, Sydney 2000 Gallery bookings, Tel 9230 2111.

State Transit (6am-10pm) Tel 13 15 00

Sunsail, PO Box 163, Newport 2106 Tel 9979 7117

Superbowl, 41 Dixon Street, Haymarket 2000 Tel 9281 2462

Surf Life Saving Australia, 128 The Grand Parade, Brighton-Le-Sands 2216 Tel 9597 5588

Sydney Aquarium, Aquarium Pier 2000 Tel 9262 2300

Sydney By Sail, Darling Harbour 2000 Tel 9907 0004

Sydney Cricket Ground, Tel 9360 6601

Sydney Dance Company, Pier 4, Hickson Road, Millers Point 2000 Tel 9221 4811

Sydney Fish Market, Pyrmont 2009 Tel 9660 1611

Sydney Flying Squadron, 76 McDougall Street, Milsons Point 2061 Tel 9955 8350

Sydney Football Stadium, Moore Park Tel 9360 6601.

Sydney Harbour National Park Information Tel 9977 6522

Sydney Harbour Seaplanes Tel 1800 803 558

Sydney Holocaust Museum, 398 Cleveland Street, Surry Hills 9318 2855

Sydney Jazz Club Tel 9452 5831

Sydney Jewish Museum, 148 Darlinghurst Road, Darlinghurst 2010 Tel 9360 7999

Sydney Rowing Club, Abbotsford wharf 2046 Tel 9712 1199

Sydney Symphony Bookings, GPO Box 4338, Sydney 2001 Tel 9264 9466

Sydney Theatre Company, Pier 4, Hickson Road, Millers Point 2000 Tel 9250 1700

Sydney Tramway Museum, Tel 9542 3646

Tahnh Binh, 56 John Street, Cabramatta 2166 Tel 9727 9729

Taronga Zoo, Bradleys Head Road Mosman 2088 Tel 9969 2777

Taxis
  Legion Tel 9289 9000
  Premier Radio Cabs Tel 13 10 17
  RSL Tel 9581 1111

Taxis Afloat Tel 9955 3222

Taxis Combined Tel 9332 8888

Tempe Tip, 7 Bellevue Street St Peters 2044 Tel 9519 1477

Theatre of The Deaf, 6/245 Chalmers Street, Redfern 2016 Tel 9310 1255

Tilbury Hotel, Nicholson and Forbes Street, Woolloomooloo 2011 Tel 9368 1295

Tokyo Mart 27 Northbridge Plaza, Northbridge, 2063 Tel 9958 6860

Valhalla Cinema, 166 Glebe Point Road, Glebe 2037 Tel 9660 8050

Vaucluse House Tea Rooms, Wentworth Avenue, Vaucluse 2030 9388 8188

Warringah Bowling Club Bradleys Head Road, Mosman 2088 Tel 9969 4313

Water Taxis
  Taxis Afloat Tel 9955 3222
  Harbour Shuttles Tel 9810 5010

Watermark 2a The Esplanade Balmoral Beach 2088 Tel 9968 3433

Waterways Access Line 131 256 or 9563 8555

Waverley Council Tel 9369 8000

Wayside Chapel, Hughes Street, Kings Cross 2011 Tel 9358 6577

Wharf Restaurant, Pier 4, Hickson Road, Millers Point 2000 Tel 9250 1761

Wharf, The Pier 4, Hickson Road, Walsh Bay Tel 9250 1761

Willoughby Council 2068 Tel 9777 1000

Wizard of Od, 115 Enmore Road Enmore 2042 Tel 9557 2418

Wockpool, 155 Victoria Street, Potts Point 2011 Tel 9368 1771

Wollondilly Heritage Centre, c/o Sth Highlands Visitors Centre Tel (048) 712 888

World Beyond, Campbell's Cove 2000 Tel 9555 9653

Youth Hostels of Australia 422 Kent Street Tel 92641 1111

Zigolini's, 2 Short Street, Double Bay 2028 Tel 9328 7614

Zoo Taronga, Bradleys Head Road Mosman 2088 Tel 9969 2777

About our Events Update Service

USUALLY THE BETTER
THE EVENT, THE LESS
CHANCE YOU HAVE
OF GETTING IN AT
THE LAST MINUTE

AS OUR EDITORIAL DIRECTOR FOUND OUT WHILE ON A VISIT TO ST PETERSBURG, RUSSIA

She sat in her hotel room fuming while across the road from the hotel, her very favourite cellist, Rostapovitch, was playing in an historic concert. She missed out because, without knowing it was on, she couldn't book in advance. That's why we designed Events Update to help avoid this kind of disappointment.

EVENTS

The UnTourist Co's Events Update allows you to find out all the best things that are on during your visit. Not just the broad events (as described in the Events Calendars in this book), but the detail of exactly what, when, how and who (See SPECIAL NOTE below). This avoids the disappointment of missing out on something you would love to see during your stay.

UPDATE

In addition to the events information, you will also receive any updates which may be relevant to your trip and things which have come up since the publication of the guide book.

YOU ALSO GET

Variations and/or additions to:

- Places to Stay
- Eating and Drinking
- Things to Buy
- Things to Do
- Things to Know
- Getting Around
- Sports
- Arts and Shows
- Plus any errata

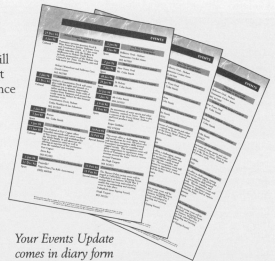

Your Events Update comes in diary form

SPECIAL NOTE: We also give you the contact information so you can book ahead, direct with the organisation concerned. The UnTourist Co takes no commission or booking fee. You pay us for the service of providing you with the information.

Have you seen our special UnTourist Guide to Tasmania?

HERE IS WHAT REVIEWERS HAVE SAID ABOUT IT:

"What a relief it is to see something both innovative and useful", David McNicholl, Bulletin, March '95.

"It —is jammed with information about local accommodation, experiences and sights off the well-worn track." Australian, March '95

"'Tasmania for the UnTourist' – is for those who wish to soak up the environment rather than impose themselves upon it", Gourmet Traveller, April '95.

"Full marks to 'Tasmania for the UnTourist' – if you are headed for Tasmania, stow this in your luggage." Adelaide Advertiser, March '95.

"Anyone who has been brushed aside or ignored when asking the travel agent about places off the beaten track will love the UnTourist Co", Australian Country Looks, June '95.

"It's travellers like me who shudder at being labelled a 'tourist' that 'UnTourist Tasmania' is aimed", News-Mail, March '95.

"Anyone – who comes out in hives if they are herded into a tourist bus should take a look at 'Tasmania for the UnTourist'. The UnTourist Co has plans for a number of other guides for the freedom loving. Watch this space", Sun-Herald, April '95

UNTOURIST QUEENSLAND –

will guide you around the sunshine state, picking out all the best bits and leaving the rest for the tourists. It will be on sale in 1996.

UNTOURIST MELBOURNE –

will uncover the best places in Melbourne to stay and all the city's secret joys that never get onto the tourist brochures. On sale, 1996.

UNTOURIST SYDNEY –

The first discerning in-depth guide to one of the great resort cities of the world. On sale now.

TASMANIA FOR THE UNTOURIST

You can buy Tasmania for the UnTourist it at all good book stores, or you can order it from the UnTourist Co direct.

It's actually more than a book – it's a package of information – 155 pages packed with the best things to do, see, eat buy and the best places to stay. It is ring-bound and comes in a full colour folder which also contains a sturdy, full-colour travel map of Tasmania – the best we could find, plus a wilderness facilities guide and map.

Tasmania for the UnTourist (with travel map)
I 4 D A Y M O N E Y B A C K G U A R A N T E E

Name _____

Address _____

_____

City _____ State _____

Country_____ Area Code _____

COST OF BOOK
(ENTER WHICHEVER APPLICABLE)

		Quantity	Total
Within Australia	$29.95 x		$
Other countries ($29.95 + delivery charge of $10)	$39.95 x		$

FINAL TOTAL AMOUNT FROM ABOVE BOX $

METHOD OF PAYMENT

☐ Mastercard ☐ Bankcard ☐ Visa ☐ Cheque (Australia only) ☐ Money Order

☐ ☐ ☐ ☐ ☐ ☐ ☐ ☐ ☐ ☐ ☐ ☐ ☐ ☐ ☐ ☐

EXPIRY DATE: /

_____

Signature:

_____

SEND COMPLETED FORM TO:
UnTourist Co PO Box 209 Balmain NSW 2041 Australia

OR CALL OR FAX US :
Tel: 61 2 9974 1326 • Fax 61 2 9974 1396
Free call from within Australia: 1 800 066 818
e-mail: untouris@acay.com.au INTERNET: http://www.acay.com.au/~untourist
If ordering by telephone, please have this form in front of you for reference.

UNTOURIST ORDER FORM

Events Update

Includes events during the time of your visit and updated general information.
NOTE: Turn to page 241 for detail of what you get.

Name _____

Address _____

City _____ State _____ Country _____ Area Code _____

DESTINATION & ARRIVAL/DEPARTURE DATES (FILL IN WHICHEVER APPLIES)

TASMANIA   From _____ To _____

SYDNEY   From _____ To _____

I WOULD LIKE MY EVENTS UPDATE DELIVERED (TICK ONE)

Immediately ☐

Hold until a few weeks before I am due to leave to include the latest
information. (A ten day allowance should be made for delivery). ☐

	PRICE	ORDER
SYDNEY	$15	_____
TASMANIA	$15	_____

DELIVERY CHARGE

Within Australia (by mail)	$3.00	_____
Faxed within Australia	$6.00	_____
Outside Australia (by mail)	$6.00	_____
Faxed outside Australia	$12.00	_____

ADD DELIVERY CHARGE+ [   ]

TOTAL: $ [   ]

METHOD OF PAYMENT

☐ Mastercard ☐ Bankcard ☐ Visa ☐ Cheque (Australia only) ☐ Money Order

[ ][ ][ ][ ][ ][ ][ ][ ][ ][ ][ ][ ][ ][ ][ ][ ]

EXPIRY DATE: _____ / _____

Signature: _____

SEND COMPLETED FORM TO:

UnTourist Co PO Box 209 Balmain NSW 2041 Australia

OR CALL OR FAX US :

Tel: 61 2 9974 1326 • Fax 61 2 9974 1396

free call from within Australia: 1 800 066 818   e-mail: untouris@acay.com.au

INTERNET: http://www.acay.com.au/~untourist

Please have this form in front of you for reference. (Prices valid to 31/12/97)